THE QUEST FOR JUSTICE ON THE JOB

To Carolyn, the fairest of them all

THE QUEST FOR JUSTICE ON THE JOB

ESSAYS AND EXPERIMENTS

JERALD GREENBERG

SAGE Publications
International Educational and Professional Publisher
Thousand Oaks   London   New Delhi

For information address:

SAGE Publications, Inc.
2455 Teller Road
Thousand Oaks, California 91320
E-mail: order@sagepub.com

SAGE Publications Ltd.
6 Bonhill Street
London EC2A 4PU
United Kingdom

SAGE Publications India Pvt. Ltd.
M-32 Market
Greater Kailash I
New Delhi 110 048 India

Printed in the United States of America

Library of Congress Cataloging-in-Publication Data

Greenberg, Jerald.
   The quest for justice on the job: Essays and experiments / Jerald
Greenberg.
      p. cm.
   Includes bibliographical references and indexes.
   ISBN 0-8039-5967-2 (cloth: alk. paper). — ISBN 0-8039-5968-0
(pbk.: alk. paper)
   1. Employee rights. 2. Supervision of employee. 3. Personnel
management. I. Title.
HD6971.8.G74 1995
658.3—dc20   95-35744

This book was printed on acid-free paper.

96 97 98 99 10 9 8 7 6 5 4 3 2 1
Sage Production Editor: Diana E. Axelsen

Contents

Preface

Few concepts are as fundamental to human social interaction as justice. Whether it is a court decision, the outcome of a sporting event, the assignment of household chores, or just about any other type of social exchange, matters of fairness are bound to arise. And these issues have captured the attention of social scientists hungry to grasp this important facet of human nature and social life.

In recent years, scholars interested in justice have turned their attention to a previously neglected setting: the organization. At the same time, scientists interested in organizations have discovered the importance of a "new" (to them, at least) work-related attitude: perceived (in)justice. The combination of both these trends has been responsible for a rush of interest in what I have been calling *organizational justice*—people's perceptions of fairness in organizational settings. It is as if the intellectual floodgates opened up, and scientists flocked to feed in the now fertile plains. For those who were primarily interested in justice, organizations have proved to be a rich context in which to study several key issues. For those whose primary interest has been in social behavior in organizations, the concept of justice has provided considerable insight into matters of interest as well. Today, we stand poised at the intersection of these two movements—a point that has become a heavily traveled intellectual crossroads.

I have been in the fortunate professional position of being one of the first social scientists to focus on the rapprochement between justice and organizations as fields of study. But my journey to this spot was not on an express track. Long interested in both justice (as nurtured by my mentor, Gerald S. Leventhal) and organizations (a product of my training in industrial-organizational psychology), it took me 10 years to consider the possibility of combining them by looking at matters of justice as they pertain to organizations. When I began this work in the early 1980s, there was simply no precedent for going beyond the only established approach to fairness in organizations—Adams's theory of inequity. Based on Homans's concept of distributive justice, equity theory generated a great deal of research in the 1960s. Several damning critiques cited problems of validity and limitations in tests of equity theory's basic tenets, however, threatening to put it on the scientific endangered list. Although studies of equity theory per se had passed their prime in the 1970s, scientific criticism could not extinguish the broader importance of justice in organizations.

During the mid-1970s, when disenchantment with equity theory was all the rage, Jerry Leventhal wrote several chapters attempting to answer the question "What should be done with equity theory?" The general conclusion was that although the distributive justice orientation was valuable, it was limited with respect to the range of issues it addressed. Equity theory needed to be supplemented by an approach that focused on *how* outcomes were determined, as well as *what* those outcomes were. Elaborating on this, he presented some rudiments of a procedural justice approach to social interaction. In so doing, Leventhal's contributions paralleled those of John Thibaut and Laurens Walker. This psychologist-attorney team conducted a series of studies in simulated legal settings that compared people's reactions to different conflict resolution techniques. In general, they examined people's reactions to conflicts resolved by a variety of different procedures. They found that the most strongly preferred procedures were those that gave disputants opportunities to control the processes used to settle their disputes. Little did Leventhal, Thibaut, and

Walker know that their work, grounded in sociolegal tradition, would later be so influential in guiding thinking about organizations.

In the early 1980s, after conducting research on distributive justice for a decade, I found myself rereading these works, recognizing that they had clear implications for the study of organizations. Ideas about procedural justice came to my awareness one day as I found myself discussing an organizational problem with several employees of a large company. Two things about this conversation impressed me. First, matters of perceived injustice consistently came up in one form or another—some, with great passion. Second, none of these concerns ever took forms that could be explained by equity theory. The whole issue of balancing outcome/input ratios never arose in the minds of the disgruntled employees—although they were extremely concerned about the injustices they experienced. At this point, I realized that Leventhal was right—the equity heuristic was rather limited in addressing the broad range of injustices that occurred in the workplace. The procedural issues that both he and Thibaut and Walker identified, however, were highly relevant.

To capture this point, I can recall a discussion I had with an office worker who was extremely upset because her supervisor failed to consult her work group about the schedule for covering the phones during the lunch hour. Although this may seem a trivial matter, it was important enough to the individual to cause her to complain that she had been treated "very unfairly." What did equity theory have to say about that? Not too much, I thought. But from the perspective of procedural justice, the situation made a great deal of sense. Failing to give the employees a voice in the decision concerning the office staffing caused them to believe that the situation was handled unfairly—a clear violation of procedural justice.

This incident led me to wonder what other work-related contexts could be identified in which issues of procedural justice arise in organizations. I posed this question to Rob Folger, one of my contemporaries (and a former student of John Thibaut), who shared my background in studying justice in social contexts. Because both of us were intrigued by the idea that procedural justice could be applied to understanding behavior in organizational settings, we gave the matter much thought and collaborated on two chapters representing the first attempts to extend procedural justice concepts to the workplace. Although these early chapters now seem rather naive (a sure sign of progress, I suppose), they did much to solidify my own interest in organizational justice, propelling me down a path marked by dozens of subsequent empirical and conceptual studies, many of which appear in this book. My objective in reprinting these works as an anthology is not so much to chronicle my own professional history as to provide an overview of the field from the perspective of one of its proponents. This should not only help orient readers who desire a summary of the field's contributions but also guide those who believe that the time has come to critically assess its current status.

The chapters in this book represent 17 key markers along my journey through the world of organizational justice—both distributive and procedural. Some of the chapters are conceptual in nature, whereas others are empirical. The empirical studies rely on both laboratory and field techniques. Some chapters are heavily theoretical; others are more applied. This balance reflects not only the style of my academic career as a whole but also my firm belief that the study of justice in organizations demands a diversity of approaches to be valuable both conceptually and practically. By presenting these works together in a single book, it is my hope that the reader will come to appreciate the importance and scope of the topic of organizational justice—a whole that is greater than the sum of its individual parts. And who do I envision as the reader of this book? This work should be of interest to scholars in a variety of social sciences, especially those most closely related to management (e.g., organizational behavior, human resources management, industrial-organizational psychology, social psychology, occupational sociology, and public policy management) and legal studies (e.g., employment law and criminology).

To organize the material, I have divided the book into six parts, each reflecting a basic theme. The first part consists of three chapters intended to orient the reader by distinguishing between various approaches to organizational justice, describing the field's background and current status, and highlighting the major trends of today. Each of the remaining parts consists of chapters focusing on different sets of focal issues that are critical to the study of organizational justice. Part II, for example, examines the basic issue of fairness as an impression management tool. The central questions are these: Do people care about looking fair, and does appearing to be fair matter in organizations? Part III turns to fairness in performance appraisals. These four chapters examine the elements of fair performance evaluations, the procedural and distributive aspects of fair performance appraisals, and a specific technique for attaining fair performance appraisals. The three chapters in the fourth part of the book represent my current research focus—people's reactions to various ways of presenting threatening information. This conceptual issue is applied to two topical organizational problems: employee theft and acceptance of smoking bans. Part V examines matters of justice as they apply to monetary rewards, the issue of pay fairness so widely studied by human resources scholars today. Finally, Part VI extends this work by examining the less frequently studied nonmonetary aspects of pay. In particular, the chapters in this section focus on two types of rewards—those associated with the design of the workplace and job titles.

To help the reader use each chapter individually, I have kept the original set of references used at the end of each chapter. I trust that the reader will find the price paid with respect to redundancy to be made up for by convenience. In addition to using reference cites in standard form, I indicate citations referring to chapters appearing in this book by showing their chapter number in brackets, like this: [n].

In conclusion, I gratefully acknowledge the numerous colleagues who have helped me through the years in conceptualizing, conducting, and reporting the work presented here. In particular, I wish to recognize the help of Bob Bies, Joel Brockner, Rob Folger, Allan Lind, and Tom Tyler, whose own contributions have been most inspiring. I also wish to acknowledge several generous research grants from the Ohio State University and the National Science Foundation that have made it possible for me to do the work reported in this book. Last, I wish to acknowledge the family of the late Irving Abramowitz, whose generous endowment to the Ohio State University supported my work in recent years.

Jerald Greenberg

PART I

Background
WHAT IS ORGANIZATIONAL JUSTICE?

THE first part of the book is designed to launch the analysis of organizational justice. It presents three chapters that orient the reader to the work that follows later in this book.

I originally wrote the article appearing as Chapter 1 in 1986 as a way of introducing various justice concepts to the world of management scholars. It was my reaction to the not uncommon, misleading practice of citing equity theory whenever referring to any form of fairness in organizations. Recognizing that many of the points made in the literature were relevant but frequently misattributed, I thought it would be useful to organize the variety of justice theories that existed in a way that not only distinguished between them logically but also highlighted their importance to the study of organizations. In this article, I introduced the term *organizational justice,* referring to the various theories as organizational justice theories. Properly, I realized that the theories were general conceptualizations that were applied to organizations, rather than theories specifically intended to explain behavior in organizations per se. Still, recognizing the heuristic value of a catchy phrase, I found the appeal of

1

referring to them collectively as organizational justice theories to be too great to ignore. Hence, Chapter 1 outlines a taxonomy of organizational justice theories.

By late 1989, when I wrote the article in Chapter 2, the field of organizational justice had grown to the point at which some critical self-assessment was in order. In this chapter, I summarize the state of knowledge to that point, review some of the major research directions being pursued, and speculate about what the future might hold. Looking back at such an article years later is always a risky practice. Nevertheless, readers will still find the chapter to be a useful account of where the field currently stands. (For those wishing more, I offer further insights into the state of the field and its future directions in the Epilogue.)

In one notable recent trend, researchers and theorists have expanded on conceptualizations of procedural and distributive justice by turning attention to the interpersonal aspects of justice, the perceived fairness of the way people are treated by others. With this work came some confusion as to whether this approach, referred to as *interactional justice,* was itself really a unique form of justice or simply a variant of the already established procedural or distributive forms. In Chapter 3, I take a stance on this issue, which I believe not only sheds light on the conceptual matter but also independently argues strongly for the value of interpersonal aspects of justice. I chose to present this discussion in this introductory section of the book because issues concerning the interpersonal aspects of justice appear in several places throughout this book.

—
1
—

A Taxonomy of Organizational Justice Theories

Stimulated by conceptualizations of justice in organizations by such theorists as Homans (1961), Adams (1965), and Walster, Berscheid, and Walster (1973), organizational researchers devoted considerable attention in the 1960s and 1970s to testing propositions about the distribution of payment and other work-related rewards derived from equity theory (for reviews, see Campbell & Pritchard, 1976; Greenberg, 1982). Although reviews and critiques of equity theory once dominated the pages of organizational journals (e.g., Goodman & Friedman, 1971; Pritchard, 1969;

AUTHOR'S NOTE: This chapter was originally published in the *Academy of Management Review,* Vol. 12, No. 1, 1987, pp. 9-22, under the title "A Taxonomy of Organizational Justice Theories." Copyright © 1987 by the Academy of Management. Reprinted by permission.

Weick, 1966), more recently it has been the subject of far less attention (Reis, 1986). It would be a mistake, however, to view this trend as an indication that organizational scientists are less interested in matters of justice and fairness in organizations than they used to be. Indeed, concerns about fairness have been expressed in such organizational domains as conflict resolution (Aram & Salipante, 1981), personnel selection (Arvey, 1979), labor disputes (Walton & McKersie, 1965), and wage negotiation (Mahoney, 1975), to name just a few. Although research inspired by equity theory has slowed down greatly, a variety of different approaches to justice have emerged that are at least as useful in explaining behavior in a broader assortment of organizational contexts. Because of a proliferation of such newer approaches and because these may be less familiar to organizational scientists, this chapter will categorize various conceptualizations of justice around a taxonomic scheme. This taxonomy not only will offer a parsimonious way of organizing these various conceptualizations but also in so doing will highlight their interrelationships and their importance to the study of organizations.

DIMENSIONS OF THE TAXONOMY

I derived this taxonomy by combining two conceptually independent dimensions: a reactive-proactive dimension and a process-content dimension. It is not assumed that these are the only organizing dimensions that may be identified. Indeed, it is possible that different taxonomic schemes may be proposed that are based on completely different conceptual dimensions. The dimensions identified in this taxonomy, however, appear to be useful for organizing a wide range of conceptualizations of interest in the field of organizational behavior.

Reactive-Proactive Dimension

The *reactive-proactive* dimension was suggested by a distinction made by Van Avermaet, McClintock, and Moskowitz (1978). I used it to organize the equity theory literature (Greenberg, 1982). The distinction is between seeking to redress injustice and striving to attain justice.

A *reactive* theory of justice focuses on people's attempts either to escape from or to avoid perceived unfair states. Such theories examine reactions to injustices. By contrast, *proactive* theories focus on behaviors designed to promote justice. They examine behaviors attempting to create just states.

TABLE 1.1 Taxonomy of Organizational Justice Theories With Corresponding Predominant Exemplars

Reactive-Proactive Dimension	Content-Process Dimension	
	Content	*Process*
Reactive	*Reactive Content* Equity theory (Adams, 1965)	*Reactive Process* Procedural justice theory (Thibaut & Walker, 1975)
Proactive	*Proactive Content* Justice judgment theory (Leventhal, 1976b, 1980)	*Proactive Process* Allocation preference theory (Leventhal, Karuza, & Fry, 1980)

Process-Content Dimension

The *process-content* dimension was inspired by legal research distinguishing between the way verdicts are derived and what those verdicts are (Walker, Lind, & Thibaut, 1979). Mahoney (1983) made a similar distinction by differentiating between the processes by which wages are determined and the outcome of those processes. As such, one may distinguish between approaches to justice that focus on the ends achieved and approaches that focus on the means used to acquire those ends.

A *process* approach to justice focuses on how various outcomes (in organizations, pay and recognition are good examples) are determined. Such orientations concentrate on the fairness of the procedures used to make organizational decisions and to implement those decisions. In contrast, *content* approaches are concerned with the fairness of the resulting distribution of outcomes. These perspectives address the relative fairness of the outcomes received by various organizational units (typically either individuals or groups).

IDENTIFYING THEORIES
WITHIN THE TAXONOMY

It is assumed that the reactive-proactive dimension and the process-content dimension are independent of each other, thereby yielding four distinct classes of justice conceptualizations when the two dimensions are combined. Table 1.1 organizes these approaches and identifies a primary exemplar of each.

Two points must be made regarding the theories in this taxonomy. First, no attempt has been made to be exhaustive. Instead, the theories identified and described are either ones that are well established or promising ones within psychology or sociology, fields within which the study of justice in organizations traditionally has been rooted. Limiting the examples does not imply that other theories would not fit in. Rather, in view of the clarifying function of this chapter, excluding them is more reflective of a judgment regarding the limitations of their demonstrated or potential value for organizational study.

Second, although some of the theories classified by this taxonomy have been widely applied to organizational contexts, none were formulated with organizations in mind as their exclusive focus. Even Adams's (1965) popular theory of inequity, originally tested in work settings, has been described as a general theory of social behavior (Walster et al., 1973). Other theories presented here originated within the legal milieu (e.g., Thibaut & Walker, 1975). Nonetheless, because the theories have been or are now used to explain organizational behavior, I refer to them collectively as theories of organizational justice.

Reactive Content Theories

Reactive content theories are conceptual approaches to justice that focus on how individuals respond to unfair treatment. Organizational scientists are probably most familiar with this class of justice theory because most popular conceptualizations of justice in organizations fall within this category. Included among these theories are Homans's (1961) theory of *distributive justice* and Adams's (1965) and Walster et al.'s (1973) versions of *equity theory* (see also Walster, Walster, & Berscheid, 1978). Despite several differences in the specifics of their formulation (see Cohen & Greenberg, 1982), these theories share an important common orientation in explicitly stating that people will respond to unfair relationships by displaying certain negative emotions, which they will be motivated to escape by acting to redress the experienced inequity. This aspect of the theories qualifies them as reactive content theories: They focus on how people react to unfair distributions of rewards and resources.

Conceptually rooted in the tradition of balance theories popular in the 1950s and 1960s (e.g., Festinger, 1957; Heider, 1958), these approaches to justice conceptualized "equitable" or "distributively just" relations as ones in which there was an equal balance between the ratio of a person's contributions and his or her outcomes. Unequal balances, such as those that existed whenever workers were either overpaid or underpaid relative to another person with equal contributions, were assumed to be unpleasant, which were theorized to prompt changes in job satisfaction and/or performance. In particular, Adams's (1965) theory of inequity, the approach that inspired most of the justice-related research in organizational settings, specified that overpaid workers would feel guilty and that under-paid workers would feel angry. These negative states were expected to motivate behavioral and/or attitudinal changes in the workers involved that altered, either behaviorally or perceptually, the relationship between their own and another's contributions and outcomes (cf. Greenberg, 1984). For example, workers perceiving an inequitable state may react behaviorally by altering their performance levels and/or cognitively by attempting to justify the outcomes received (Walster et al., 1978).

It was, no doubt, because the theoretical metrics were so explicitly suited to work-related exchanges that equity theory became so popularly applied to organizational research. Indeed, it was within simulated work settings that most of the research on equity theory was conducted (e.g., Lawler & O'Gara, 1967; Pritchard, Dunnette, & Jorgenson, 1972). In the prototypical test of equity theory, the experimenter manipulated inequity by leading worker-participants to believe that the basis for their payment was unfair—thereby creating either "underpayment inequity" or "over-payment inequity." For example, this may have included (a) leading partici-pants to believe that an error occurred that caused them to receive the same wage as their more qualified coworkers, thereby manipulating over-payment (e.g., Adams & Rosenbaum, 1962) or (b) allowing participants to discover through conversations with coworkers that they were equally qualified but unequally paid (e.g., Garland, 1973).

Typically, performance on some work task—popularly a proofreading task for which quantity and quality measures could be taken—constituted the dependent variable. According to equity theory, underpaid workers should be less productive and less satisfied than equitably paid workers, and overpaid workers should be more productive and less satisfied than equitably paid workers. In general, and across a wide variety of ex-perimental settings, support was found for these predictions (for a review, see Greenberg, 1982).

Several sociological theories that have developed in response to certain aspects of Adams's conceptualization, particularly the nature of social comparisons, also should be included within the category of reactive content theories. Among these is the *status value* version of equity theory proposed by Berger and his associates (Anderson, Berger, Zelditch, & Cohen, 1969; Berger, Zelditch, Anderson, & Cohen, 1972). According to this formulation, a person's feelings of inequity and reactions to inequity result not from comparisons made with a specific other person (referred to as a "local comparison") but from comparisons with a generalized other (referred to as a "referential comparison"), such as an occupational group. Extending this approach, Jasso's (1980) theory of distributive justice ignored the outside comparisons in justice evaluations altogether and defined justice as the comparisons people make between their actual share of goods and their beliefs about a "just share." Despite some important conceptual differences between these theories and the more familiar Adams's formulation, their similar focus on how people react to beliefs about the unfair distribution of outcomes (regardless of the comparative basis on which these judgments are formed) allows these theories to be clearly categorized as reactive content theories.

More closely related to traditional equity theory and the final reactive content theory of justice to be identified is the *theory of relative deprivation* (Crosby, 1976). Based on findings dating to World War II (Stouffer, Suchman, DeVinney, Star, & Williams, 1949) but also more recently examined in organizational contexts (Crosby, 1984; Martin, 1981), the relative deprivation orientation to justice is becoming increasingly more popular among organizational scientists. In its most general form, the relative deprivation approach asserts that certain reward distribution patterns will encourage people to make certain social comparisons, which will lead to feelings of deprivation and resentment, causing a variety of reactions ranging from depression to the outbreak of violent riots (Martin, 1981).

The term *relative deprivation*, first used by Stouffer et al. (1949), refers to the counterintuitive finding that black soldiers stationed in the South felt more satisfied with military life than black soldiers stationed in northern bases despite more favorable socioeconomic conditions in the North. These effects were attributed to the tendency for black soldiers in the South to feel more privileged than their civilian counterparts in the South, whereas black soldiers in the North felt relatively less privileged than their civilian counterparts in the North. Although most of the subsequent relative deprivation research focused on violent attempts to change political systems (Crosby, 1976), some efforts have focused on how aggrieved employees react to organizationally induced discontent (Martin, 1981). For example, large-scale survey studies by Crosby (1982, 1984) found that working women, especially those in high-prestige jobs, although they may be more advantaged than nonworking women, tend to be more aggrieved because they compare themselves with working men, relative to whom they are less advantaged. Research of this type is typical of that generated today by relative deprivation theory. Because it examines how people will respond to perceived unfair reward distributions, relative deprivation theory clearly can be identified as a reactive content theory.

Proactive Content Theories

In contrast to reactive content theories, which focus on how workers respond to fair and unfair outcome distributions, proactive content theories focus on how workers attempt to create fair outcome distributions. The major theoretical statements in this category have come from Leventhal (1976b, 1980), who in the late 1960s and early 1970s conducted a series of laboratory studies in which the basic pattern of independent and dependent variables found in traditional reactive accounts of justice was reversed. Leventhal and his associates typically manipulated concerns about justice (through appropriate instructional sets) to examine their effect on reward allocation decisions (for reviews, see Freedman & Montanari, 1980; Mikula, 1980).

Leventhal (1976a) contended that people sometimes proactively strive to create equitable distributions of reward—those in which the rewards received are proportional to the contributions made—because these will be the most beneficial to all concerned parties in the long run. Indeed, many studies (e.g., Greenberg & Leventhal, 1976; Leventhal & Michaels, 1969) have shown that allocators often divide resources equitably between recipients (for reviews, see Adams & Freedman, 1976; Freedman & Montanari, 1980). Additional research, however, has shown that allocators of rewards sometimes distribute those rewards in ways that violate the equity norm—such as by distributing rewards equally or in accordance with recipients' needs (Schwinger, 1980). Recognizing that such violations of the equity norm may be completely fair under appropriate circumstances, Leventhal (1976b, 1980) formulated his *justice judgment model.* This model proposed that individuals attempt to make fair allocation decisions by variously applying several possible allocation rules to the situations they confront. For example, in situations in which the importance of maintaining social harmony between group members is stressed, the perceived fair allocation practice calls for following the equality norm—dividing rewards equally regardless of possible differential contributions among recipients (Deutsch, 1975).

Although Leventhal's approach to reward allocation practices is instrumental in character, another proactive content theory of justice, Lerner's (1977; Lerner & Whitehead, 1980) *justice motive theory,* is decidedly more moralistic. Lerner (1982) argued that justice is the preeminent concern of human beings and that the quest for justice as a means to a profit-maximizing end (as Leventhal proposed) is a mythical illusion. Like Leventhal, however, Lerner recognized that allocation practices often go beyond the possibility of proportional equity. In fact, Lerner identified four principles that are commonly followed: (a) *competition*—allocations based on the outcome of performance, (b) *parity*—equal allocations, (c) *equity*—allocations based on relative contributions, and (d) *Marxian justice*—allocations based on needs.

Briefly, justice motive theory stipulates that the form of justice that will be followed in making allocation decisions will depend on the nature of the relations between the parties involved in conjunction with the focus of the parties on each other as individuals or as occupants of positions. For example, the theory predicts that an individual reacting to a close friend as an individual will emphasize that person's needs when making an allocation decision. Similarly in more distant relationships, people are expected to follow the parity norm when the other is recognized as an individual and the equity norm when reacting to the other as a role incumbent. Research relating various reward allocation practices to the nature of the relationship between people has been supportive of justice motive theory (e.g., Carles & Carver, 1979).

Despite some differences in underlying philosophies, both justice judgment theory and justice motive theory make similar predictions about how people will allocate rewards under various circumstances—predictions that largely have been supported by research (for a review, see Deutsch, 1985). Both of these approaches clearly qualify as proactive content theories of justice because they deal with how people seek to make decisions about the allocation of reward.

Reactive Process Theories

Although it appears that theories focusing on the fairness of the processes used to make decisions (process theories) do not differ appreciably from those theories focusing on the fairness of the resulting decisions (content theories), this is not the case because process theories stem from a different intellectual tradition—in particular, the law. In fact, legal scholars have commonly accepted that the procedures used to make judicial decisions will have a profound influence on the public's acceptance of them (Fuller, 1961).

At approximately the same time when proactive content theories were formalized and researched (the early 1970s), Thibaut and Walker (1975), a team of researchers at the University of North Carolina influenced by the tradition of research on legal procedures, undertook a series of investigations designed to compare reactions to various dispute resolution procedures. Their *theory of procedural justice* distinguished between three parties: two disputants (such as the litigants in a court case) and an intervening third party (such as a judge) and two stages of the dispute resolution process: the process stage, during which evidence is presented, and the decision stage, during which the evidence is used to resolve the dispute. The ability to control the selection and development of the evidence used to resolve the dispute is referred to as *process control*. The ability determine the outcome of the dispute itself is referred to as *decision control* (Thibaut & Walker, 1978).

The procedures used can vary regarding the degree of control the various parties have over each stage. In particular, procedures may be identified that give third parties control over both outcomes and procedures, *autocratic procedures;* decisions but not processes, *arbitration procedures;* processes but not decisions, *mediation procedures;* and neither processes nor procedures, *bargaining procedures.* Finally, *moot procedures* are those in which the disputants and third parties share control over outcomes and processes. (Sheppard, 1984, has proposed a more extensive system.)

Although reactions to all of these procedures were assessed, Thibaut and Walker were most interested in comparing autocratic and arbitration procedures because these most closely distinguished between the major legal systems. For example, the adversary system, used in American and British courts, gives judges control over the verdict but leaves the process (e.g., selection of attorneys and presentation of evidence) in the hands of the disputants themselves. The inquisitorial system, however, used in continental Europe, gives judges control over the collection and presentation of evidence as well as the verdicts. The theory is concerned with how people will react to each of these decision-making procedures, thereby qualifying as a reactive process theory. The theory predicts that both litigants and observing disinterested parties will be more satisfied with procedures giving them process control (e.g., the adversary system) than those that do not (e.g., the inquisitorial system). The verdicts resulting from procedures offering process control are hypothesized to be perceived as fairer and to be better accepted than those resulting from procedures denying process control. Many studies using a simulated legal decision-making methodology (e.g., Lind, Kurtz, Musante, Walker, & Thibaut, 1980; Walker et al., 1979) have supported this claim (for reviews, see Folger & Greenberg, 1985; Thibaut & Walker, 1975). Procedures giving disputants a voice in the decision-making process tend to enhance the acceptance of even unfavorable decisions (LaTour, 1978; Lind et al., 1980).

Other research has generalized the Thibaut and Walker findings to less formal settings. For example, Tyler and his associates found that reactions to encounters with police officers (Tyler & Folger, 1980), politicians, and teachers (Tyler & Caine, 1981) also are heavily influenced by the procedures that these authorities follow in treating their clients. Organizational researchers have actively attempted to extend and apply Thibaut and Walker's theory of procedural justice to a variety of organizational contexts, such as the resolution of labor disputes (Sheppard, 1984) and the appraisal of job performance (Greenberg, 1986a[6], 1986b[8]), among others (for reviews, see Folger & Greenberg, 1985; Greenberg & Folger, 1983; Greenberg & Tyler, 1987).

Proactive Process Theories

Of the theories identified in this taxonomy, probably the least well known fall into the proactive process category. The predominant theoretical position within this category is Leventhal, Karuza, and Fry's (1980) *allocation preference theory*. This is an outgrowth of Leventhal's (1976b, 1980) justice judgment model (described earlier) and is proposed as a general model of allocation behavior. Because the theory has been applied almost exclusively to procedural decisions rather than to distributive ones (e.g., Fry & Cheney, 1981; Fry & Leventhal, 1979), however, it has operated as a proactive process theory. Thus, in contrast to the emphasis on dispute resolution procedures typical of the reactive process theories, the proactive process orientation tends to focus on allocation procedures. This orientation seeks to determine what procedures people will use to achieve justice.

Allocation preference theory asserts that allocation procedures will be preferred to the extent that they help the allocator attain valued goals, including the attainment of justice. In particular, the theory proposes that people hold expectancies that certain procedures will be differentially instrumental in meeting their goals and that the procedure believed to be most likely to help attain one's goal will be the most preferred one. Eight procedures are identified that may help promote the attainment of justice. These include procedures that (a) allow opportunities to select the decision-making agent, (b) follow consistent rules, (c) are based on accurate information, (d) identify the structure of decision-making power, (e) employ safeguards against bias, (f) allow for appeals to be heard, (g) provide opportunities for changes to be made in procedures, and (h) are based on prevailing moral and ethical standards.

The limited research inspired by allocation preference theory offers general support for it. The studies have been of two types—those in which the participants respond to open-ended requests for examples of perceived fair or unfair procedures and those in which participants rate the importance of various allocation procedures manipulated in written scenarios. In one open-ended questionnaire study, Sheppard and Lewicki (1987) asked white-collar managers to identify unfair incidents across a variety of managerial roles. Among other principles, they found that participants identified consistency, bias suppression, correctability, and ethicality, all principles of procedural justice proposed by Leventhal et al. (1980).

Similarly, when I asked middle managers to identify determinants of perceived fair performance evaluations (Greenberg, 1986a[6]), I found procedural determinants consistent with Leventhal et al.'s (1980) theory, namely, (a) the soliciting of workers' input prior to evaluations and using it as the basis of evaluations, (b) the availability of two-way communication during appraisal interviews, (c) the opportunity to challenge and/or rebut the evaluation received, (d) the degree of the evaluator's familiarity with the ratee's work, and (e) the consistent application of evaluation standards.

In addition, in several role-playing investigations, Fry (with Cheney, 1981; with Leventhal, 1979) found that consistency was believed to be the most important procedural determinant of fairness across a variety of allocation settings. In a more extensive study, Barrett-Howard and Tyler (1986) confirmed that consistency was a powerful determinant of perceived fairness across a wide variety of situations and social relationships. The other procedural elements identified by Leventhal et al. (1980), however, were found to be perceived as differentially important as determinants of fairness in different types of social relationships.

IMPLICATIONS OF THE TAXONOMY

The present taxonomy serves several useful functions. Among these are its ability (a) to clarify conceptual interrelationships, (b) to track trends in organizational justice research, and (c) to identify needed areas of research and conceptual development.

Clarifying Conceptual Interrelationships

Given the proliferation of research and theory about organizational justice, the present taxonomy is a useful clarifier. By showing how the various theories are distinct and interrelated, the taxonomy provides a schema for conceptually organizing a growing body of work. One result of such a framework is reduced conceptual confusion.

An important beneficial effect of this clarifying role is that it encourages researchers to be cognizant of existing conceptualizations and to apply the most useful ones to their own work. In the absence of such a taxonomy, it is too easy for researchers to use terms and apply concepts in ways that fail to incorporate existing precedents, thereby potentially adding confusion to the literature.

To illustrate this point, consider the recent program of research on workplace justice by Dalton and Todor (1985a, 1985b). In several archival

TABLE 1.2 Representative Research Questions and Dependent Measures for Each
Type of Organizational Justice Theory

Type of Theory	Representative Question	Prototypical Dependent Measures
Reactive Content	How do workers react to inequitable payments?	Reactions to overpayment or underpayment inequity (reviewed by Greenberg, 1982)
Proactive Content	How do workers attempt to create fair payments?	Adherence to justice norms in reward allocations (reviewed by Freedman & Montanari, 1980)
Reactive Process	How do workers react to unfair policies or legal procedures?	Reactions to unfair payment methods or dispute resolution methods (reviewed by Folger & Greenberg, 1985)
Proactive Process	How do workers attempt to create fair policies or procedures?	Perceptions of procedural fairness (reviewed by Lind & Tyler, 1988)

studies, these researchers uncovered evidence that women were more preferentially treated than men in grievance resolution settings. These findings of objective differences in outcome distributions were then taken as evidence of differences in "workplace justice outcomes." Although it is conceivable that these findings reflect perceived unfair states, it is not possible to conclude from the Dalton and Todor data that subjective feelings of unfairness resulted from the objective outcomes identified. Because this was not their intent and because they make no such claim, the investigators cannot be faulted.

The point, however, is that they are using the term *justice* in a way that is not in keeping with a voluminous literature that emphasizes justice as a subjective state or quality. This is not to say that new, more objectively defined perspectives are without merit but simply to say that current researchers on organizational justice should be aware of previous conceptual advances, such as those identified through the present taxonomy.

Tracking Trends in
Organizational Justice Research

The present taxonomy identifies trends in the questions about justice posed in organizational research. Table 1.2 summarizes the representative questions asked by researchers developing the various types of theories and the corresponding dependent measures used.

Although some recent investigations have been inspired by equity theory (e.g., Greenberg & Ornstein, 1983[17]) and some conceptual clarifications (e.g., Cosier & Dalton, 1983), it is clear that interest in reactive content approaches has waned (Reis, 1986). Instead, the emphasis has been on more proactive and more process-oriented conceptualizations. In essence, then, two shifts are identified—a shift from reactive to proactive theories and a shift from content to process theories.

In reaction to the reactive approach of Adams's work in the 1960s (e.g., Adams & Rosenbaum, 1962), investigators such as Leventhal and Michaels (1969) and Messé (1971) pioneered a more proactive approach in the late 1960s and early 1970s. With this, there was a shift from asking how workers reacted to inequitable payments to asking how they attempted to create equitable payments. Proactive content research continues and is especially popular among European social scientists. For example, recent representative efforts have focused on issues such as (a) the distinctions allocators make between various types of contributions in making fair allocations (Törnblom & Jonsson, 1985), (b) the commitment to justice principles among different classes of people (Montada, Schmitt, & Dalbert, 1986), and (c) the reliance on considerations of need in the attainment of justice (Schwinger, 1986). With the continuation of such research, a better understanding appears to be developing of the ways workers behave in the interest of being fair.

When Thibaut and Walker (1975) began their research on procedural justice in the early 1970s, it was not a reaction against the shortcomings of reactive process theories; rather, it was inspired by an interest in the attributes of various dispute resolution techniques. Theorists such as Deutsch (1975) and Leventhal (1976a) first pointed out that procedural justice research may be viewed as an extension of equity theory research into the domain of allocation processes. Folger (1977) was among the first researchers whose work reflected a shift from how workers react to inequitable outcomes to how they react to unfair procedures. His work showed that giving workers the opportunity to have a voice in the decisions affecting them under some conditions enhanced their reactions to the outcome of those decisions (for a review, see Greenberg & Folger, 1983).

The question of how workers react to various organizational procedures is not only the newest one to interest organizational justice researchers but also one of the most actively researched areas today. (For a statement on the state of the science, see Greenberg & Tyler, 1987.) Indeed, the attention procedural justice has received in professional symposia (e.g., Folger, 1986b) and in special publications devoted to the topic (Greenberg & Tyler, 1987; Lind & Tyler, 1988) attests to the current high level of interest in applying proactive process orientations to the study of organizational justice. As more organizational researchers continue to develop a rapprochement between their interests and a process orientation to justice, there has been a shift away from legal-based questions regarding fair procedures to more organizationally based questions. The growing body of research and theory considering these questions promises to extend the knowledge of organizational justice.

For example, the present taxonomy proves to be useful in tracing the conceptual roots of two rapidly evolving and related lines of theory development in organizational justice. One of these, Folger's (1986a, 1987) *referent cognitions theory,* expands on relative deprivation theory and equity theory when explaining relative satisfaction with work outcomes. The theory extends the reactive content orientation of its predecessors by distinguishing between two types of reactions—those based on relative comparisons, leading to feelings of (dis)satisfaction, and those based on beliefs about what should have happened, leading to feelings of resentment and moral outrage. Resentment reactions are theorized to be based on the procedures used to bring about various outcomes, whereas satisfaction with those outcomes is based on beliefs about the relative outcome levels themselves. With regard to the present taxonomy, referent cognitions theory expands the concept of relative deprivation to a process prospective beyond its more traditional, content perspective.

Similarly, related research by Bies (1987; Bies & Moag, 1986) focuses on feelings of moral outrage. Bies asserts that justice perceptions are better explained by the social accounts given for them than by the appearance of an inequity based on comparisons of relative outcomes and inputs. Social accounts of events—including those that claim mitigating circumstances, invoke superordinate ideological goals, refer to likely future states, and offer apologies for current states—are offered as likely determinants of reactions to injustice. Bies also claims that social accounts can be used to explain reactions to outcome distribution procedures as well as the outcome distributions themselves. As such, Bies's conceptualization, like Folger's, provides a framework for integrating the process-based and the content-based reactions to injustice. In addition, Bies's work examines an important deficiency of reactive theories of organizational justice—namely, the conditions under which different reactions are likely to be exhibited.

The present taxonomy helps in recognizing the conceptual traditions from which new theoretical developments, such as those of Folger (1986a) and Bies (1987), were derived and, as such, facilitates appreciation for their integrative nature. In thinking of these developments as markers of justice theories, readers may view the taxonomy as a road map that helps chart the course of theoretical progress.

Identifying Needed Areas
of Research and Theory

By highlighting the relationships between the various types of organizational justice theories, the present taxonomy helps identify areas of theoretical and empirical deficiency. In particular, it helps spot research areas across categories in which parallel types of investigations have not been undertaken. Most notable are questions stemming from the proactive process orientation. In the abstract, this should not be surprising, given that the proactive process approach is the newest theoretical approach to organizational justice. Questions should be asked, however, about the type of research that needs to be conducted in this area relative to that which already has been done. As described earlier, in studies inspired by the proactive process, participants were asked either to generate and categorize lists of perceived fair-unfair job behaviors or to assess the importance of various theoretically derived procedural determinants of fairness manipulated in written scenarios. Both types of research essentially serve as validation studies of the research from which they were derived. Although these investigations are useful, they are not parallel to those found in the proactive content category because how participants make procedural decisions was not observed directly.

Although in proactive content studies the resource allocation decisions made by participants are observed under a variety of different conditions (see Freedman & Montanari, 1980), investigators interested in procedural issues have not as of yet conducted analogous studies. Indeed, a program of research designed to determine the conditions under which people make various procedural decisions would be useful to theory development in the proactive process area. Two types of investigations are warranted. First, laboratory studies could be conducted in which personal and situational factors are manipulated to see how they influence decisions about what procedures should be used. Second, a post hoc, policy-capturing investigation could be done in which investigators analyze the conditions under which various actual procedural decisions are made.

One area in which a contribution of the present taxonomy may be realized is pay satisfaction. In particular, Heneman (1985) identified "pay policies and administration" as a class of variables that need to be included in his model of pay satisfaction. Citing evidence (Dyer & Theriault, 1976; Weiner, 1980) showing that understanding *how* pay raises were determined added to the explained variance in pay satisfaction beyond pay level alone, Heneman (1985) concluded that "perceptions about how pay is administered do appear to have a bearing on people's pay satisfaction" (p. 132). In making this claim for a direction in which to extend theories of pay satisfaction beyond equity theory, Heneman recognized the distinction between content and process theories of organizational justice articulated here. Heneman's insight may have been realized earlier given the present taxonomy. Still, seeing how well the taxonomy fits Heneman's conceptualization provides encouragement for using it to derive further insight about pay satisfaction. Indeed, process theories of organizational justice may be used to suggest factors likely to enhance satisfaction with pay and the consequences of perceived unfair pay determination practices.

In addition, the present taxonomy provides a useful framework for appreciating the context within which several newly emerging areas of research are derived. For example, my research on performance appraisal (Greenberg, 1986b[8], 1987[9]) was inspired by attempts to apply research and theory on procedural justice to employee evaluation situations. Similarly, Sheppard's (1985) efforts at applying his model of organizational dispute resolution (1984) were inspired by a tradition of research applying procedural justice notions to legal disputes. Both these lines of research represent areas made salient by the present taxonomy.

CONCLUSION

In 1966, Weick referred to equity theory as "among the more useful middle-range theories of organizational behavior" (p. 439). In 1984, Miner classified equity theory among those in his list of "not so useful" theories of organizational behavior. Equity theory has fallen into disfavor partly because of its limited applicability and partly because of its internal validity as a theory (Furby, 1986). Perhaps also, researchers have grown weary of the restricted range of questions about organizational justice it addresses. Yet questions about justice still arise in many organizational milieus, among them contexts as diverse as pay plans (comparable worth) (Mahoney, 1983), grievance procedures, selection and placement practices, and evaluation policies (Folger & Greenberg, 1985; Greenberg & Folger, 1983). The questions raised about justice in these contexts are not ones that equity theory, or any of the other reactive content theories, are equipped to address. There are, however, other theories of organizational justice presented in this chapter that may be particularly well suited to such matters. To the extent that this taxonomy has brought them to the attention of organizational researchers, then it has paved the way for increased understanding to emerge—an understanding of various organizational phenomena and of justice itself.

REFERENCES

Adams, J. S. (1965). Inequity in social exchange. In L. Berkowitz (Ed.), *Advances in experimental social psychology* (Vol. 2, pp. 267-299). New York: Academic Press.

Adams, J. S., & Freedman, S. (1976). Equity theory revisited: Comments and annotated bibliography. In L. Berkowitz & E. Walster (Eds.), *Advances in experimental social psychology* (Vol. 9, pp. 43-90). New York: Academic Press.

Adams, J. S., & Rosenbaum, W. B. (1962). The relationship of worker productivity to cognitive dissonance about wage inequities. *Journal of Applied Psychology, 46,* 161-164.

Anderson, B., Berger, J., Zelditch, M., & Cohen, B. P. (1969). Reactions to inequity. *Acta Sociologica, 12,* 1-12.

Aram, J. D., & Salipante, P. F., Jr. (1981). An evaluation of organizational due process in the resolution of employee/employer conflict. *Academy of Management Review, 6,* 197-204.

Arvey, R. D. (1979). *Fairness in selecting employees.* Reading, MA: Addison-Wesley.

Barrett-Howard, E., & Tyler, T. P. (1986). Procedural justice as a criterion in allocation decisions. *Journal of Personality and Social Psychology, 50,* 296-304.

Berger, J., Zelditch, M., Anderson, B., & Cohen, B. P. (1972). Structural aspects of distributive justice: A status-value formulation. In J. Berger, M. Zelditch, & B. Anderson (Eds.), *Sociological theories in progress* (Vol. 2, pp. 21-45). Boston: Houghton Mifflin.

Bies, R. J. (1987). The predicament of injustice. The management of moral outrage. In L. L. Cummings & B. M. Staw (Eds.), *Research in organizational behavior* (Vol. 9, pp. 289-319). Greenwich, CT: JAI.

Bies, R. J., & Moag, J. S. (1986). Interactional justice: Communication criteria of fairness. In R. J. Lewicki, B. H. Sheppard, & M. H. Bazerman (Eds.), *Research on negotiation in organizations* (Vol. 1, pp. 43-55). Greenwich, CT: JAI.

Campbell, J. P., & Pritchard, R. A. (1976). Motivation theory in industrial and organizational psychology. In M. D. Dunnette (Ed.), *Handbook of industrial and organizational psychology* (pp. 63-130). Chicago: Rand McNally.

Carles, E. M., & Carver, C. S. (1979). Effects of person salience versus role salience on reward allocation in the dyad. *Journal of Personality and Social Psychology, 37,* 2071-2080.

Cohen, R. L., & Greenberg, J. (1982). The justice concept in social psychology. In J. Greenberg & R. L. Cohen (Eds.), *Equity and justice in social behavior* (pp. 1-41). New York: Academic Press.

Cosier, R. A., & Dalton, D. R. (1983). Equity theory and time: A reformulation. *Academy of Management Review, 8,* 311-319.

Crosby, F. (1976). A model of egoistical relative deprivation. *Psychological Review, 83,* 85-113.

Crosby, F. (1982). *Relative deprivation and working women.* New York: Oxford University Press.

Crosby, F. (1984). Relative deprivation in organizational settings. In B. M. Staw & L. L. Cummings (Eds.), *Research in organizational behavior* (Vol. 6, pp. 51-93). Greenwich, CT: JAI.

Dalton, D. R., & Todor, W. D. (1985a). Composition of dyads as a factor in the outcomes of workplace justice: Two field assessments. *Academy of Management Journal, 28,* 704-712.

Dalton, D. R., & Todor, W. D. (1985b). Gender and workplace justice: A field assessment. *Personnel Psychology, 38,* 133-151.

Deutsch, M. (1975). Equity, equality and need: What determines which value will be used as the basis for distributive justice? *Journal of Social Issues, 31*(3), 137-149.

Deutsch, M. (1985). *Distributive justice.* New Haven, CT: Yale University Press.

Dyer, L., & Theriault, R. (1976). The determinants of pay satisfaction. *Journal of Applied Psychology, 61,* 596-604.

Festinger, L. (1957). *A theory of cognitive dissonance.* Evanston, IL: Row, Peterson.

Folger, R. (1977). Distributive and procedural justice: Combined impact of "voice" and improvement on experienced inequity. *Journal of Personality and Social Psychology, 35,* 108-119.

Folger, R. (1986a). Rethinking equity theory: A referent cognitions model. In H. W. Bierhoff, R. L. Cohen, & J. Greenberg (Eds.), *Justice in social relations* (pp. 145-162). New York: Plenum.

Folger, R. (Chair). (1986b, April). *Fairness is more than equity: New approaches to studying organizational injustice.* Symposium presented at the first annual conference of the Society for Industrial and Organizational Psychology, Chicago.

Folger, R. (1987). Reformulating the preconditions of resentment: A referent cognitions model. In J. C. Masters & W. P. Smith (Eds.), *Social comparison, social justice, and relative deprivation: Theoretical, empirical, and policy perspectives* (pp. 183-216). Hillsdale, NJ: Lawrence Erlbaum.

Folger, R., & Greenberg, J. (1985). Procedural justice: An interpretive analysis of personnel systems. In K. M. Rowland & G. R. Ferris (Eds.), *Research in personnel and human resources management* (Vol. 3, pp. 141-183). Greenwich, CT: JAI.

Freedman, S. M., & Montanari, J. R. (1980). An integrative model of managerial reward allocation. *Academy of Management Review, 5,* 381-390.

Fry, W. R., & Cheney, G. (1981, May). *Perceptions of procedural fairness as a function of distributive preference.* Paper presented at the meeting of the Midwestern Psychological Association, Detroit.

Fry, W. R., & Leventhal, G. S. (1979, March). Cross-situational procedural preferences: A comparison of allocation preferences and equity across different social settings. In A. Lind (Chair), *The psychology of procedural justice.* Symposium conducted at the meeting of the Southwestern Psychological Association, Washington, DC.

Fuller, L. (1961). The adversary system. In H. Berman (Ed.), *Talks on American law* (pp. 10-22). New York: Vintage.

Furby, L. (1986). Psychology and justice. In R. L. Cohen (Ed.), *Justice: Views from the social sciences* (pp. 153-203). New York: Plenum.

Garland, H. (1973). The effects of piece-rate underpayment and overpayment on job performance: A test of equity theory with a new induction procedure. *Journal of Applied Social Psychology, 3,* 325-334.

Goodman, P. S., & Friedman, A. (1971). An examination of Adams' theory of inequity. *Administrative Science Quarterly, 16,* 271-288.

Greenberg, J. (1982). Approaching equity and avoiding inequity in groups and organizations. In J. Greenberg & R. L. Cohen (Eds.), *Equity and justice in social behavior* (pp. 389-435). New York: Academic Press.

Greenberg, J. (1984). On the apocryphal nature of inequity distress. In R. Folger (Ed.), *The sense of injustice* (pp. 167-188). New York: Plenum.

Greenberg, J. (1986a). Determinants of perceived fairness of performance evaluations. *Journal of Applied Psychology, 71,* 340-342. [Chapter 6, this volume.]

Greenberg, J. (1986b). Organizational performance appraisal procedures: What makes them fair? In R. J. Lewicki, B. H. Sheppard, & M. H. Bazerman (Eds.), *Research on negotiation in organizations* (Vol. 1, pp. 25-41). Greenwich, CT: JAI. [Chapter 8, this volume.]

Greenberg, J. (1987). Using diaries to promote procedural justice in performance appraisals. *Social Justice Research, 1,* 219-234. [Chapter 9, this volume.]

Greenberg, J., & Folger, R. (1983). Procedural justice, participation, and the fair process effect in groups and organizations. In P. B. Paulus (Ed.), *Basic group processes* (pp. 235-256). New York: Springer-Verlag.

Greenberg, J., & Leventhal, G. S. (1976). Equity and the use of overreward to motivate performance. *Journal of Personality and Social Psychology, 34,* 179-190.

Greenberg, J., & Ornstein, S. (1983). High status job title as compensation for underpayment: A test of equity theory. *Journal of Applied Psychology, 68,* 285-297. [Chapter 17, this volume.]

Greenberg, J., & Tyler, T. (1987). Why procedural justice in organizations? *Social Justice Research, 1,* 127-142.

Heider, F. (1958). *The psychology of interpersonal relations.* New York: John Wiley.

Heneman, H. G., III. (1985). Pay satisfaction. In K. M. Rowland & G. R. Ferris (Eds.), *Research in personnel and human resources management* (Vol. 3, pp. 115-139). Greenwich, CT: JAI.

Homans, G. C. (1961). *Social behavior: Its elementary forms.* New York: Harcourt, Brace, & World.

Jasso, G. (1980). A new theory of distributive justice. *American Sociological Review, 45,* 3-32.

LaTour, S. (1978). Determinants of participant and observer satisfaction with adversary and inquisitorial modes of adjudication. *Journal of Personality and Social Psychology, 36,* 1531-1545.

Lawler, E. E., III, & O'Gara, P. W. (1967). Effects of inequity produced by underpayment on work output, work quality, and attitudes toward the work. *Journal of Personality and Social Psychology, 51,* 403-410.

Lerner, M. J. (1977). The justice motive: Some hypotheses as to its origins and forms. *Journal of Personality, 45,* 1-52.

Lerner, M. J. (1982). The justice motive in human relations and the economic model of man: A radical analysis of facts and fictions. In V. Derlega & J. Grezlak (Eds.), *Cooperation and helping behavior: Theories and research* (pp. 121-145). New York: Academic Press.

Lerner, M. J., & Whitehead, L. A. (1980). Procedural justice viewed in the context of justice motive theory. In G. Mikula (Eds.), *Justice and social interaction* (pp. 219-256). New York: Springer-Verlag.

Leventhal, G. S. (1976a). The distribution of rewards and resources in groups and organizations. In L. Berkowitz & E. Walster (Eds.), *Advances in experimental social psychology* (Vol. 9, pp. 91-131). New York: Academic Press.

Leventhal, G. S. (1976b). Fairness in social relationships. In J. W. Thibaut, J. T. Spence, & R. C. Carson (Eds.), *Contemporary topics in social psychology* (pp. 211-239). Morristown, NJ: General Learning Press.

Leventhal, G. S. (1980). What should be done with equity theory? In K. J. Gergen, M. S. Greenberg, & R. H. Willis (Eds.), *Social exchange: Advances in theory and research* (pp. 27-55). New York: Plenum.

Leventhal, G. S., Karuza, J., & Fry, W. R. (1980). Beyond fairness: A theory of allocation preferences. In G. Mikula (Ed.), *Justice and social interaction* (pp. 167-218). New York: Springer-Verlag.

Leventhal, G. S., & Michaels, J. W. (1969). Extending the equity model: Perceptions of inputs and allocation of reward as a function of duration and quantity of performance. *Journal of Personality and Social Psychology, 12,* 303-309.

Lind, E. A., Kurtz, S., Musante, L., Walker, L., & Thibaut, J. W. (1980). Procedure and outcome effects on reactions to adjudicated resolution of conflicts of interest. *Journal of Personality and Social Psychology, 39,* 643-653.

Lind, E. A., & Tyler, T. R. (1988). *The social psychology of procedural justice.* New York: Plenum.

Mahoney, T. A. (1975). Justice and equity: A recurring theme in compensation. *Personnel, 52*(5), 60-66.

Mahoney, T. A. (1983). Approaches to the definition of comparable worth. *Academy of Management Review, 8,* 14-22.

Martin, J. (1981). Relative deprivation: A theory of distributive injustice for an era of shrinking resources. In L. L. Cummings & B. M. Staw (Eds.), *Research in organizational behavior* (Vol. 3, pp. 53-107). Greenwich, CT: JAI.

Messé, L. A. (1971). Equity in bilateral beginning. *Journal of Personality and Social Psychology, 17,* 287-291.

Mikula, G. (1980). On the role of justice in allocation decisions. In G. Mikula (Ed.), *Justice and social interaction* (pp. 127-165). New York: Springer-Verlag.

Miner, J. B. (1984). The unpaved road over the mountains: From theory to applications. *Industrial-Organizational Psychologist, 21*(2), 9-20.

Montada, L., Schmitt, M., & Dalbert, C. (1986). Thinking about justice and dealing with one's own privileges: A study of existential guilt. In H. W. Bierhoff, R. L. Cohen, & J. Greenberg (Eds.), *Justice in social relations* (pp. 125-143). New York: Plenum.

Pritchard, R. A. (1969). Equity theory: A review and critique. *Organizational Behavior and Human Performance, 4*, 75-94.

Pritchard, R. A., Dunnette, M. D., & Jorgenson, D. O. (1972). Effects of perceptions of equity and inequity on worker performance and satisfaction. *Journal of Applied Psychology, 56*, 75-94.

Reis, H. T. (1986). Levels of interest in the study of interpersonal justice. In H. W. Bierhoff, R. L. Cohen, & J. Greenberg (Eds.), *Justice in social relations* (pp. 187-209). New York: Plenum.

Schwinger, T. (1980). Just allocations of goods: Decisions among three principles. In G. Mikula (Ed.), *Justice and social interaction* (pp. 95-125). New York: Springer-Verlag.

Schwinger, T. (1986). The need principle of distributive justice. In H. W. Bierhoff, R. L. Cohen, & J. Greenberg (Eds.), *Justice in social relations* (pp. 211-225). New York: Plenum.

Sheppard, B. H. (1984). Third party conflict intervention: A procedural framework. In B. M. Staw & L. L. Cummings (Eds.), *Research in organizational behavior* (Vol. 6, pp. 141-190). Greenwich, CT: JAI.

Sheppard, B. H. (1985). Justice is no simple matter: Case for elaborating our model of procedural fairness. *Journal of Personality and Social Psychology, 49*, 953-962.

Sheppard, B. H., & Lewicki, R. J. (1987). Toward general principles of managerial fairness. *Social Justice Research, 1*, 161-176.

Stouffer, S. A., Suchman, E. A., DeVinney, L. C., Star, S. A., & Williams, R. M., Jr. (1949). *The American soldier: Vol. 1. Adjustment during Army life.* Princeton, NJ: Princeton University Press.

Thibaut, J., & Walker, L. (1975). *Procedural justice: A psychological analysis.* Hillsdale, NJ: Lawrence Erlbaum.

Thibaut, J., & Walker, L. (1978). A theory of procedure. *California Law Review, 66*, 541-566.

Törnblom, K. Y., & Jonsson, D. R. (1985). Subrules of the equality and contribution principles: Their perceived fairness in distribution and retribution. *Social Psychology Quarterly, 48*, 249-261.

Tyler, T. R., & Caine, A. (1981). The role of distributional and procedural fairness in the endorsement of formal leaders. *Journal of Personality and Social Psychology, 41*, 642-655.

Tyler, T. R., & Folger, R. (1980). Distributional and procedural aspects of satisfaction with citizen-police encounters. *Basic and Applied Social Psychology, 1*, 281-292.

Van Avermaet, E., McClintock, C., & Moskowitz, J. (1978). Alternative approaches to equity: Dissonance reduction, pro-social motivation and strategies accommodation. *European Journal of Social Psychology, 8*, 419-437.

Walker, L., Lind, E. A., & Thibaut, J. (1979). The relation between procedural justice and distributive justice. *Virginia Law Review, 65*, 1401-1420.

Walster, E., Berscheid, E., & Walster, G. W. (1973). New directions in equity research. *Journal of Personality and Social Psychology, 25*, 151-176.

Walster, E., Walster, G. W., & Berscheid, E. (1978). *Equity: Theory and research.* Boston: Allyn & Bacon.

Walton, R. W., & McKersie, R. B. (1965). *A behavioral theory of labor negotiations.* New York: McGraw-Hill.

Weick, K. E. (1966). The concept of equity in the perception of pay. *Administrative Science Quarterly, 11*, 414-439.

Weiner, N. (1980). Determinants and behavioral consequences of pay satisfaction: A comparison of two models. *Personnel Psychology, 33*, 741-757.

2

Organizational Justice

Past, Present, and Future

Social scientists have long recognized the importance of the ideals of justice as a basic requirement for the effective functioning of organizations and the personal satisfaction of the individuals they employ (Moore, 1978; Okun, 1975). Consider, for example, the significance that management scholars have accorded such organizational activities as the fair use of employment tests (Block & Dworkin, 1976), equitable payment (Jacques, 1961), the just resolution of grievances (Aram & Salipante, 1981), and the

AUTHOR'S NOTE: This chapter was originally published in the *Journal of Management,* Vol. 16, No. 2, 1990, pp. 399-432, under the title "Organizational Justice: Yesterday, Today, and Tomorrow." Copyright © 1990 by JAI Press. Reprinted by permission.

right to democratic decision making in the workplace (Locke & Schweiger, 1979). Given such diverse concerns about fairness in organizations, it is not surprising that justice has been claimed to be "the first virtue of social institutions" (Rawls, 1971, p. 3).

In view of the widespread recognition of the importance of fairness as an issue in organizations, it is understandable that theories of social and interpersonal justice have been applied to understanding behavior in organizations. It is important to note, however, that the earliest theories of social justice applied to organizations (i.e., *equity theory*, Adams, 1965; *distributive justice theory*, Homans, 1961; and *relative deprivation theory*, Stouffer, Suchman, DeVinney, Star, & Williams, 1949) were derived to test principles of justice in general social interaction, not organizations in particular. For the most part, such theories have experienced mixed and limited success when used as the basis for explaining many forms of organizational behavior (Greenberg, 1987c[1]). More recently, research has been conducted and conceptual models have been developed that are more sensitive to variables and issues directly relevant to organizational functioning. A literature has grown around attempts to describe and explain the role of fairness as a consideration in the workplace—a topic dubbed *organizational justice* (Greenberg, 1987c[1]).

Because organizational justice researchers have taken many different directions lately, the need exists to assess the field's current position and to chart its course for the future. One purpose of this chapter is to characterize the current state of research and theory development in organizational justice. Toward this end, the "today" section of this chapter will chronicle some of the major issues that are currently being addressed. This will set the stage for the "tomorrow" section that follows, in which some suggestions for the future advancement will be offered. I hope that section will stimulate useful new research and theory development. First, however, the chapter begins by looking at "yesterday" with a brief historical overview of the study of justice in organizations. This section is designed to provide essential background and to help the reader understand the conceptual underpinnings of major issues in the organizational justice literature.

YESTERDAY: FROM DISTRIBUTIVE
JUSTICE TO PROCEDURAL JUSTICE

Theorists (e.g., Greenberg, 1987c[1]; Törnblom, 1990) have distinguished between conceptualizations of justice that focus on content—the fairness of the ends achieved (*distributive justice* approaches)—and those that focus on process—the fairness of the means used to achieve those ends (*procedural justice* approaches). Although distributive justice theories are more fully developed and better known to organizational scientists, procedural justice approaches have played a major role in the recent history of organizational justice.

Equity Theory and the Distributive Justice Tradition

Historically, the equity theory of Adams (1963, 1965) has been given the greatest attention by organizational scientists interested in issues of justice (e.g., Mowday, 1987). This theory claims that people compare the ratios of their own perceived work outcomes (i.e., rewards) to their own perceived work inputs (i.e., contributions) with the corresponding ratios of a comparison other (e.g., a coworker). If the ratios are unequal, the party whose ratio is higher is theorized to be inequitably overpaid (and to feel guilty), whereas the party whose ratio is lower is theorized to be inequitably underpaid (and to feel angry). Equal ratios are postulated to yield equitable states and associated feelings of satisfaction. Individuals are theorized to adjust their own or the comparison other's actual or perceived inputs or outcomes to change unpleasant inequitable states to more pleasant equitable ones (Greenberg, 1984). These reactions may be classified as either behavioral (e.g., altering job performance) or psychological (e.g., altering perceptions of work outcomes) (Walster, Walster, & Berscheid, 1978).

Soon after the publications of Adams (1963, 1965), several empirical studies were conducted that tested various aspects of the theory (for an early review, see Pritchard, 1969). Typically, these studies hired experimental participants to work on a clerical task after leading them to believe that similarly qualified others were being paid either more than or less than themselves for doing the same work (i.e., they were either underpaid or overpaid; e.g., Andrews, 1967; Garland, 1973; Pritchard, Dunnette, & Jorgenson, 1972). In keeping with equity theory's predictions, these studies generally found that workers lowered their performance (i.e., reduced their inputs) when they were underpaid and raised their performance (i.e., increased their inputs) when they were overpaid (Adams & Freedman, 1976; Greenberg, 1982). Despite these successes, several early tests of equity theory were criticized on the grounds that some of the inequity inductions used were confounded in various ways (e.g., by challenging participants' self-esteem or by threatening their job security; Lawler, 1968; Pritchard, 1969). Despite these challenges, convincing rebuttals (Adams, 1968) in conjunction with other supportive tests of the theory using unconfounded procedures (e.g., Garland, 1973) have led reviewers to conclude that the evidence for equity theory is generally quite strong (Greenberg, 1982; Mowday, 1987).

From its beginning, many scientists embraced equity theory, an approach one prominent organizational scholar referred to as "among the more useful middle-range theories of organizational behavior" (Weick, 1966, p. 439). Because equity theory identified outcomes and inputs in quantifiable, business-related terms, its use in the study of organizational behavior was inevitable. Indeed, more than 100 studies of equity theory—most of which employed simulated work environments—were conducted in the decade after its publication (Adams & Freedman, 1976). Such empirical work, not surprisingly, resulted in later theoretical refinements (Berger, Zelditch, Anderson, & Cohen, 1972; Walster et al., 1978) and reformulations of the equity formula (e.g., Harris, 1976; Romer, 1977) that are beyond the scope of the present work (for a review of these derivative formulations, see Cohen & Greenberg, 1982).

Of the conceptual variants of equity theory that emerged, one approach that promised to be especially applicable to the study of organizational processes was its proactive counterpart, Leventhal's (1976b, 1980) *justice judgment model.* Although equity theory focused on reactions to pay inequities, Leventhal and his associates studied the conditions under which people proactively employed various justice norms (e.g., Greenberg & Leventhal, 1976). For example, it has been found that people believe that the maintenance of social harmony is promoted through the use of equal reward allocations, whereas the maximization of performance is promoted by systems (e.g., pay-for-performance plans; Heneman, 1990) that allocate outcomes equitably—that is, in proportion to relative performance (Deutsch, 1975, 1985; Leventhal, 1976a). Research showing that certain goals are believed to be facilitated by certain norms of justice is relevant to organizational behavior because it helps predict and explain administrative allocation decisions (e.g., pay raises, budget allocations) (Freedman & Montanari, 1980).

Together, Adams's reactive approach and Leventhal's proactive approach are commonly referred to as conceptualizations of distributive justice (Cohen, 1987; Törnblom, 1990) because both focus on the fairness of outcome distributions.[1] Despite the potential insight into organizational processes derived from both reactive and proactive approaches to distributive justice in the 1960s and 1970s (for reviews, see Freedman & Montanari, 1980; Greenberg, 1982), by the early 1980s these conceptualizations began to fall into disfavor (Locke & Henne, 1986). One source of frustration was equity theory's lack of specificity regarding what reactions to inequity would occur (Furby, 1986), a condition that led the author of one commentary on the state of organizational theories to include it in his "not so useful" category (Miner, 1984). At this same time, organizational scientists (e.g., Heneman, 1985; Mahoney, 1983) began to raise questions about justice in various organizational milieus that were not adequately addressed by prevailing theories of justice. Specifically, questions of how pay plans were administered and what grievance resolution practices were followed in organizations prompted concerns about fairness that were more process oriented, that is, they dealt with *how* decisions were made as opposed to *what* those decisions were. Attempting to address such questions, theorists (Folger & Greenberg, 1985; Greenberg & Folger, 1983; Greenberg & Tyler, 1987) have refocused their attention to matters of procedural justice, that is, the perceived fairness of the policies and procedures used to make decisions. Insofar as attention directed to procedural justice has dominated the attention of organizational scholars of late (e.g., Greenberg, 1987c[1]) and has generated a voluminous literature (Lind & Tyler, 1988), gaining an appreciation for the current and future directions of the field of organizational justice requires paying attention to the historical development of the concept of procedural justice.

Reorientation on Procedural Justice

A series of pioneering studies of reactions to the dispute resolution process by Thibaut and Walker (1975) in the early 1970s led to the development of their theory of procedural justice. These investigations compared people's reactions to simulated dispute resolution procedures that differed with respect to two types of control: the amount of control they offered the disputants over the procedures used to settle their grievances (referred to as *process control*) and the amount of control they had over directly determining the outcomes (referred to as *decision control*). They were especially interested in comparing highly autocratic procedures in which disputants have no control over the collection and presentation of evidence bearing on their case (low process control-low decision control conditions, such as those in the inquisitorial system used in the courts of continental Europe) and legal procedures that typically offer high degrees of input into the process (high process control-low decision control, such as in the adversarial system used in American and British courts). Research using simulated legal decisions consistently has found that verdicts resulting from procedures offering disputants process control were perceived as fairer and were better accepted than identical decisions resulting from procedures that denied process control (e.g., Walker, Lind, & Thibaut, 1979).

As additional research was conducted on this phenomenon (for reviews, see Lind & Tyler, 1988; Tyler, 1987), it became clear that this finding reflected a more general tendency across a variety of settings for procedures granting control over the process of outcome attainment to be perceived as fairer than procedures that deny process control (Greenberg & Folger, 1983). For example, research by Tyler and his associates has demonstrated the perceived fairness of input-giving procedures over mute procedures in contexts involving citizens' encounters with police officers (Tyler & Folger, 1980), students' reactions to their teachers (Tyler & Caine, 1981), and voters' evaluations of their elected officials (Tyler, Rasinski, & McGraw, 1985). Thus, it has been established that the concept of procedural justice may be more broadly applied than Thibaut and Walker (1975) originally envisioned.

Indeed, within the field of management, the practice of performance appraisals has proved to be an especially popular context for early studies whose investigators unknowingly demonstrated the applicability of procedural justice effects (for a review, see Greenberg, 1986c[8]). For example, Landy, Barnes, and Murphy (1978) found that among managerial and professional employees, perceptions of the fairness of the performance evaluations they received were highly correlated with such process variables as the opportunities to express their feelings during performance evaluations. These findings were replicated in a follow-up study (Landy, Barnes-Farrell, & Cleveland, 1980) that controlled for the possibility that employees' perceptions of the performance appraisal procedures would be influenced by the evaluations they received. Even when the outcomes of the evaluation process were partialed out, it was found that perceived fairness continued to be strongly associated with reactions to process variables. Parallel results were obtained by Dipboye and de Pontbraind (1981), who found that employees' reactions to their evaluation systems were positively related to the opportunities they believed they had to express their own viewpoints. Similarly, Lissak (1983, Field Study 1) found that Canadian soldiers believed their performance evaluations to be fairer when they were given an opportunity to provide relevant input than when no such input was permitted. Clearly, it may be concluded that input into the performance evaluation system is a key determinant of perceived fair evaluations (Greenberg, 1986c[8]).

Although Thibaut and Walker (1975) emphasized the importance of process control, the approach to procedural justice offered by Leventhal (1980; Leventhal, Karuza, & Fry, 1980) focused on other aspects of procedural justice. Specifically, Leventhal postulated that various procedural elements (e.g., the selection of decision makers, setting ground rules for evaluating potential rewards, methods of gathering information, procedures for defining the decision process, procedures for appeals, safeguards against abuse of power, and the availability of change mechanisms) are used to evaluate the fairness of outcome-distribution procedures. The fairness of the procedures, he asserted, is evaluated relative to their meeting several criteria, namely, the extent to which they suppress bias, create consistent allocations, rely on accurate information, are correctable, represent the concerns of all recipients, and are based on prevailing moral and ethical standards.

Compared with the voluminous work generated by Thibaut and Walker's approach (for a review, see Lind & Tyler, 1988), only a few studies specifically have tested Leventhal's conceptualizations. To date, research has focused on establishing the importance of the criterion of consistency (Barrett-Howard & Tyler, 1986; Fry & Cheney, 1981; Fry & Leventhal, 1979) on enhancing perceptions of fairness. In a simulated organizational setting, Greenberg (1987d[9]) found that using accurate information (in the form of diaries) as the basis of performance appraisals enhanced perceptions of the fairness of the performance evaluation method, the evaluator, and the resulting evaluations themselves. Such evidence suggests that Leventhal's approach to procedural justice may be particularly valuable when it comes to explaining fairness in organizational contexts.

TODAY: EXPANDING
THE LIMITS OF JUSTICE CONCEPTS

As reviewed above, organizational scientists are faced with a legacy of conceptual and generally supportive empirical work focusing on both distributive justice and procedural justice. Although most of the recent attention has been paid to explaining the newer concept of procedural justice, advances in distributive justice continue to occur as well. This section of the chapter will identify and describe some of the key issues that are currently addressed by organizational justice researchers. Specifically, the focus will be on five major areas: (a) distinguishing procedural and distributive justice, (b) recent theoretical advances, (c) the interpersonal aspects of procedural justice, (d) new directions in empirical tests of equity theory, and (e) justice-based explanations of organizational behavior. Because of space limitations, it will be possible to highlight only some of the major themes (for more extensive reviews, see Lind & Tyler, 1988; Törnblom, 1990).

Distinguishing Procedural
and Distributive Justice

Recent organizational research has shed light on the distinction between distributive justice and procedural justice. Specifically, these studies have empirically differentiated the elements of distributive justice and procedural justice and have identified the classes of organizational variables with which each is associated. These advances are described in this section and are summarized in Figure 2.1.

Empirically establishing the basis for the distinction. One of the most basic tasks faced by contemporary organizational justice researchers has been establishing that the distinction between distributive justice and procedural justice is not simply a theoretical heuristic but rather a real one from the perspective of the worker's phenomenology. Although several studies have determined that questionnaire measures of procedural justice and distributive justice are statistically independent of each other (Alexander & Ruderman, 1987; Tyler & Caine, 1981), it is important to determine whether employees are intuitively aware of the distinction. Two investigations have addressed this issue (Greenberg, 1986a[6]; Sheppard & Lewicki, 1987).

Sheppard and Lewicki (1987) asked a sample of managers to describe critical incidents of fair and unfair treatment by their own bosses and the principle that made these actions fair or unfair. Sixteen principles were identified, including those consistent with Leventhal's categories and Thibaut and Walker's notion of process control, as well as Adams's principle of equity. Given the general managerial context of the study, however, it was not surprising that several additional principles emerged. For example, rules regarding "providing adequate information" and "assigning challenging and meaningful work" were among those principles reported by Sheppard and Lewicki's respondents but that were not contained in earlier writings on justice. Both procedural and distributive factors were freely identified by the managers in this study. They were concerned about the equitable distribution of work assignments and job rewards as well as procedures that solicited their input, suppressed individual bias, and permitted the correction of mistakes.

Focusing on the more specific context of performance appraisal, I asked a sample of managers from several industries to describe episodes of especially fair or unfair performance appraisals (Greenberg, 1986a[6]). Seven reliable categories emerged, which another group of managers then rated with respect to their perceived importance as determinants of fair evaluations. Factor analyses of these ratings revealed that two factors (i.e.,

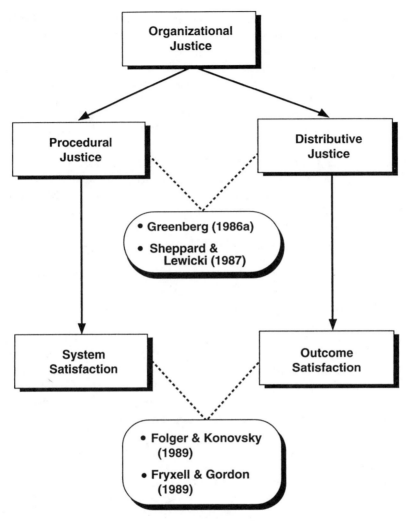

Figure 2.1. Distributive Justice Versus Procedural Justice: Summary of Evidence Empirically Supporting the Distinction and Associated Organizational Predictors

procedural determinants and distributive determinants) accounted for almost 95% of the variance. The five determinants loading highly on the procedural factor corresponded closely to those identified both by Thibaut and Walker and by Leventhal. These were (a) soliciting input prior to evaluation and using it, (b) two-way communication during interviews, (c) ability to challenge and/or rebut evaluations, (d) rater familiarity with ratee's work, and (e) consistent application of standards. The distributive justice factor consisted of two determinants theorized to reflect the fair allocation of organizational outcomes in a performance appraisal context (Greenberg, 1986b[7]), namely, receipt of ratings on the basis of performance achieved and making recommendations for salary and promotions on the basis of ratings. These findings strongly indicate that managers are aware of both distributive and procedural determinants of fairness. They also support theoretical claims regarding the existence of various elements of procedural justice (e.g., Leventhal, 1980; Thibaut & Walker, 1975).

Justice-based predictors of organizational behavior. Given that the distinction between distributive justice and procedural justice has been empirically established, the stage was set for researchers to consider how these varieties of justice relate to various organizational variables. In one of the first studies in this area, Alexander and Ruderman (1987) administered a questionnaire to approximately 2,800 employees of the federal government. They found that indexes of these employees' assessments of procedural justice were significantly related to such key measures as their trust in management, intention to turnover, evaluation of their supervisor, conflict/harmony, and job satisfaction. Moreover, with the exception of turnover intention, procedural fairness judgments accounted for significantly more variance in these dependent measures than distributive justice. Apparently, both procedural and distributive justice judgments are important, although each may be predictive of different attitudes. This idea is consistent with Tyler's (1984) research on defendants' evaluations of their courtroom experiences. Findings from this research revealed that procedural justice was strongly associated with defendants' attitudes toward the court system, whereas distributive justice was strongly associated with defendants' satisfaction with verdicts (see also Tyler, 1990; Tyler, Rasinski, & McGraw, 1985). Extrapolating from such findings, Lind and Tyler (1988) conclude that "procedural justice has especially strong effects on attitudes about institutions or authorities as opposed to the attitudes about the specific outcome in question" (p. 179). The idea that system satisfaction is related to procedural justice whereas outcome satisfaction is related to distributive justice is logical insofar as it is systems that employ procedures but outcomes that form the basis for distributions.

    This notion has received support in several organizational studies. For example, Folger and Konovsky (1989) devised measures of procedural justice and distributive justice patterned after the self-reports of perceived fair treatment obtained in my open-ended survey study (Greenberg, 1986a[6]). These measures were found to be differentially associated with various work-related outcomes in a manner paralleling Tyler's (1984) data. Specifically, perceptions of the procedures used to determine pay raises uniquely contributed to such factors as organizational commitment and trust in supervision, whereas perceptions of distributive justice were uniquely associated with one's own pay satisfaction.

Analogous results were obtained in Fryxell and Gordon's (1989) study of workers' reactions to organizational grievance systems. Using diverse samples, they found that measures of perceived procedural justice predicted satisfaction with a grievance system significantly better than measures of distributive justice. Moreover, satisfaction with unions (which helped bring about desired outcomes) was more strongly associated with perceptions of distributive justice than was satisfaction with management (which thwarted desired outcomes). The tendency for procedural justice to correlate with grievance system satisfaction was moderated by the degree to which association with the union was imposed as opposed to voluntary. Consistent with research by Tyler (1986) in nonorganizational settings, Gordon and Fryxell (1989) reported that the association between procedural justice and institutional satisfaction (grievance system satisfaction in this case) was enhanced when organizational association is imposed (such as among employees of agency shops, who are required to pay union dues). Taken together, these studies make a strong case for the relative roles of procedural justice and distributive justice in predicting work-related attitudes. Although procedural justice perceptions tend to be associated with organizational system evaluations (especially among employees who are involuntarily associated with the system), distributive justice perceptions tend to be associated with the outcomes received (see Figure 2.1).

Recent Theoretical Advances

The past few years have seen the development of two sets of theoretical ideas that promise to shed new light on existing findings in the organizational justice literature. Tyler's (1989; Lind & Tyler, 1988) *self-interest model* and *group-value model* compare major explanations of why procedural justice effects occur, and Folger's (1986, 1987b) *referent cognitions theory* (RCT) promises to integrate elements of distributive justice and procedural justice conceptualizations.

The self-interest model and the group-value model. Until recently, procedural justice researchers have been more involved in demonstrating the widespread applicability of procedural justice effects than in explaining those effects. Why is it that procedures that provide input into the making of decisions are perceived to be fairer than those that do not? Answers to this question have fallen into two categories, what Lind and Tyler (1988) refer to as the self-interest model and the group-value model.

The self-interest model, earlier referred to as the "instrumental perspective" (Tyler, 1987, p. 333), suggests that people seek control over processes because they are concerned with their own outcomes. In this regard, the opportunity to exercise voice over procedures has been explained as enhancing perceptions of procedural justice because it may lead to equitable outcomes (as suggested by Thibaut & Walker, 1978) or because it enhances control over desired outcomes (as suggested by Brett, 1986). Indeed, it has been argued that the desire to influence procedures is, in part, based on the belief that such control could yield more favorable outcomes (Greenberg & Folger, 1983).

It also has been argued that process control could enhance procedural justice because it satisfies a desire to have one's views considered, even if being heard fails to influence the decision maker as desired (Tyler, Rasinski, & Spodick, 1985). In other words, process control may enhance procedural justice not just because it is believed to have an impact on decisions but because it has value-expressive elements (Tyler, 1987)— that is, the mere expression of a preference may be positively perceived. This idea forms the basis for the group-value model (Lind & Tyler, 1988; Tyler, 1989), which stipulates that people value long-term relationships with groups (be they small work groups or large organizations), leading them to value procedures that promote group solidarity. In other words, it is not necessarily control but the promotion of within-group relationships that people value in expressions of voice. As Tyler (1989) explained,

> The group-value model argues for a broader conception of the meaning of procedural justice than is presented in the control model [of Thibaut and Walker]. It suggests that people in organizations focus on their long-term association with a group and with its authorities and institutions. People expect an organization to use neutral decision-making procedures enacted by trustworthy authorities so that, over time, all group members will benefit fairly from being members of the group. They also expect the group and its authorities to treat them in ways that affirm their self-esteem by indicating that they are valued members of the group who deserve treatment with respect, dignity, and politeness. (p. 837)

Lind and Tyler (1988) claim that both the self-interest model and the group-value model have merit and argue that it is premature to create a unified theory of procedural justice. Consistent with the self-interest model are findings that people believe that the outcomes resulting from unfair procedures are themselves unfair but only when those outcomes are trivial; more beneficial outcomes were believed to be fair regardless of the fairness of the procedure (Greenberg, 1986b[7]). Furthermore, low outcomes aroused concern about the unfair procedures used to attain them. Just as procedures were accepted when outcomes were positive in my reward allocation study (Greenberg (1987b[14]), simulated legal research has found that process control did little to enhance satisfaction when innocent verdicts were delivered (LaTour, 1978). Together, such evidence supports the self-interest model, suggesting that concerns about procedures are dictated primarily by their effects (i.e., the outcomes resulting from them). In other words, procedures are valued whenever they lead to desired results, that is, when they enhance one's self-interest.

By contrast, most of the recently reported evidence is consistent with the group-value model. Much of this research shows that the enhancement of procedural justice by process control is independent of the outcomes received, that is, "the provision of voice enhances procedural justice, even in situations in which there is little objective reason to suspect that the exercise of voice will affect decisions" (Lind & Tyler, 1988, p. 194). In support of this claim, Earley and Lind (1987) used structural equation modeling to test the role of personal control in procedural justice in both lab and field settings. In neither study was a significant causal link found between control judgments and procedural justice judgments, although the experimental manipulations significantly influenced both of these. Thus, control judgments did not cause the procedural justice judgments. Evidence for the relative importance of group considerations on justice judgments is demonstrated in a study of group decision-making practices by Miller, Jackson, Mueller, and Schersching (1987). In that study, it was found that decision fairness was more strongly associated with the extent to which the decision represented the interests of all group members than the extent to which it favored themselves. Clearly, concern about the group good was an important element of fairness, part of the general notion that justice concerns are linked to group membership (Tyler & Lind, 1990).

In a study specifically designed to test the group-value model, Tyler (1989) hypothesized that three factors unrelated to outcome or process control would influence procedural preferences and procedural justice judgments: the neutrality of the decision-making procedure, trust in decision makers (third parties), and indicators of social standing (such as expressions of politeness and respect). Interviewing Chicago citizens about their experiences with legal authorities (courts and police), Tyler found that perceived control over the process was associated with procedural justice judgments and affect toward the authorities. A greater proportion of the variance in these measures, however, was accounted for by perceptions of neutrality of treatment, trust in the authorities, and standing.

These findings are taken as evidence of the idea that fairness is related to not only just the business that people have with third parties but their relationships with them as well. They are concerned about how others make decisions, their intentions, and their interpersonal treatment.

Corroborating evidence for the group-value model has been reported in Leung and Li's (1990) survey of the attitudes of the citizens of Hong Kong about changes in the fare structure of that city's mass transit system. Consistent with the group-value model, perceptions of procedural justice were more strongly predicted by perceptions of "consideration of views" and "shows of good faith by the authorities" than by variables related to the outcome itself. Different results were obtained, however, when citizens considered certain specific positive and negative aspects of the fare structure itself. This contribution is valuable insofar as it demonstrates that group-value effects may be found in situations and cultures different from those studied by Tyler (1989). It is also important because the complex pattern of findings obtained suggests some potential boundary conditions for Tyler's model. In conclusion, although the group-value model of procedural justice has received some support, its validity remains to be established. Interest in attempting to examine the processes underlying procedural justice effects is still extremely new, however. Thus, any efforts in this direction may be considered worthwhile despite their preliminary status.

Referent cognitions theory. Folger's (1986, 1987b) RCT has been offered as an approach that promises to integrate the concepts of distributive justice and procedural justice (Folger, 1987a). The theory expands on equity theory's attempts to explain reactions to inequitable work outcomes. It distinguishes between two types of reactions: resentment reactions (theorized to result from beliefs about procedures that could be used to attain outcomes) and reactions of (dis)satisfaction (theorized to result from the relative outcomes themselves). Specifically, RCT theorizes that "in a situation involving outcomes allocated by a decision maker, resentment is maximized when people believe they *would* have obtained better outcomes if the decision maker had used other procedures that *should* have been implemented" (Cropanzano & Folger, 1989, pp. 293-294).

Experimental tests of RCT (e.g., Folger & Martin, 1986; Folger, Rosenfield, & Robinson, 1983) put participants in situations in which they failed to obtain a desirable reward because of procedures used that were either well justified or poorly justified. Referent outcomes were manipulated by indicating what different outcomes would have been attained had the procedure been different. Typically, participants who were led to believe that they would have received higher outcomes had the poorly justified procedure not been used (i.e., those in the high referent/low justification condition) expressed significant amounts of resentment, whereas those who received different outcomes for justifiable reasons were not resentful (although they were dissatisfied when the procedure yielded less desirable outcomes).

Recently, Cropanzano and Folger (1989) noted that the procedural justification manipulation in these studies may have been based on the fact that the procedures were not adequately explained to the participants (as opposed to something about the procedures themselves). Thus, in a recent experiment, they avoided this potential confounding by creating conditions in which a choice (leading to an outcome) was made by either an experimenter or the participants themselves. The greatest amount of resentment and feelings of unfair treatment occurred when the experimenter made the decision that would have brought them more favorable outcomes, a finding consistent with RCT. Procedures in which participants made their own decisions were perceived as fair regardless of what they were led to believe could have happened differently.

As Cropanzano and Folger (1989) argue, the potential value of the RCT approach lies in the greater precision it offers with respect to predicting reactions to inequities and its incorporation of procedural variables into models of unfair treatment. Specifically, they claim that

> RCT offers the conceptual basis for a true integration of distributive fairness and procedural fairness. . . . In explicitly taking into account the procedural justice practices followed by a decision maker, however, RCT indicates how outcome and procedural concerns can combine to influence the reaction a person is most likely to exhibit. (p. 297)

Because attempts to apply RCT to organizational issues have been only recent (e.g., Folger, 1987a) and because few tests of RCT in organizational settings have been published to date, its value as a tool for understanding fairness in organizations currently must be characterized as cautiously optimistic. Time will tell whether the promise offered by RCT is realized in the study of organizational justice.

The Interpersonal Aspects
of Procedural Justice

As research expanding the original conceptualizations of procedural justice (Leventhal, 1980; Thibaut & Walker, 1975) proliferates, it has become clear that perceptions of procedural justice are influenced by factors that go beyond the formal procedures used to resolve disputes or allocate rewards (Bies, 1987; Greenberg, 1990[5]). In particular, it has been demonstrated that judgments of procedural justice are influenced by two important factors: the interpersonal treatment people receive from decision makers and the adequacy with which formal decision-making procedures are explained (Bies & Moag, 1986; Tyler & Bies, 1989).

Interpersonal treatment. Several studies provide compelling evidence that people consider the nature of their treatment by others as a determinant of fairness. For example, Bies (1986) asked master of business administration (MBA) students to list the criteria they would use to evaluate the fairness of corporate recruiting procedures. Bies found that various expressions of interpersonal treatment—honesty, courtesy, timely feedback, and respect for rights—were identified along with more formal procedural justice considerations (e.g., the chance to express their own viewpoints). In a follow-up study, Bies asked another group of MBA students to describe instances of fair and unfair treatment they received during the course of employment interviews. The same four elements of interpersonal treatment were again reported, findings consistent with the first study. Concerns about the quality of interpersonal treatment received were expressed regardless of the outcome of the interview; both those who received offers and those who did not expressed the importance of the same four interpersonal factors. These findings suggest that interpersonal treatment is considered an important aspect of fair treatment independent of the outcomes resulting from that treatment.

Similar conclusions may be drawn from Tyler's (1988) research on citizens' reactions to their dealings with the police and courts. This elaborate survey study found that perceptions of honesty and ethical appropriateness (such as politeness and respect for rights) were perceived as among the most important determinants of the fairness of the treatment they received. Similar factors were identified in Lewicki's (1989) study of MBA students' assessments of the fairness of their treatment by instructors. Indeed, ethical treatment has been shown to be a key determinant of fairness across a wide variety of settings (Barrett-Howard & Tyler, 1986). In conclusion, then, it appears that the quality of the interpersonal treatment received is a major determinant of people's assessment of fair treatment.

Adequate explanations of decisions. Extending these findings, recent research has also considered the interpersonal aspects of the way decision-making procedures are enacted. Notably, Tyler and Bies (1989; based on Folger & Bies, 1989, and Leventhal, 1980) have reviewed evidence supporting the existence of five criteria related to the perceived fairness of treatment in organizations: (a) adequately considering others' viewpoints, (b) suppressing personal biases, (c) consistently applying decision-making criteria, (d) providing timely feedback about decisions, and (e) adequately explaining the basis for decisions. Recent research has focused most heavily on this last criterion, the use of adequate explanations.

The idea that it is considered fair for organizational decisions to be explained to employees is a well-established guideline in the literature on human resources management (e.g., Milkovich & Newman, 1987). Research by Bies and his associates confirms that the practice of explaining procedures enhances the fairness of the procedures themselves and the outcomes resulting from them (for reviews, see Bies, 1987; Greenberg, 1990[5]; Tyler & Bies, 1989). For example, Bies and Shapiro (1987) conducted a series of lab and field studies in which they found that people who received negative outcomes (e.g., being turned down for a job) were more likely to accept the procedures leading to them as fair when an explanation was offered than when no such explanations were provided. Similar results were also obtained by Bies and Shapiro (1988). In the domain of performance appraisal, I found analogous results (Greenberg, 1988c), namely, workers perceived their performance appraisals as fairer when monetary ratings were accompanied by written narratives explaining those ratings than when no such written explanations were given.

Extending these findings, Bies, Shapiro, and Cummings (1988) found that perceptions of procedural justice were enhanced only when explanations were believed to be *adequately* reasoned and *sincerely* communicated. For example, denied requests (e.g., rejection of a loan application) were likely to be perceived as procedurally fair when the decisions were based on logically relevant information (e.g., the use of relevant financial information; Shapiro & Buttner, 1988). Moreover, decisions based on claims of mitigating circumstances were more likely to be perceived as fair than those based on arbitrary factors (Folger et al., 1983). In addition, the more sincere an explanation for a course of action is perceived to be, the more fair those actions are believed to be (Bies et al., 1988). Taken together, such findings strongly suggest that it is not only the procedures used to determine outcomes but also explanations for those procedures that influence perceptions of procedural justice. Such verbal qualifiers of procedural action have formed the core of recently developing approaches to organizational justice based on the concept of impression management (e.g., Bies, 1987; Greenberg, 1988a[4], 1990[5]).

New Directions in Empirical
Tests of Equity Theory

Given the widespread attention accorded the concept of procedural justice in recent years, recognition of distributive justice concepts has been somewhat eclipsed. Nonetheless, research testing various tenets of equity theory continues. Compared with the late 1960s and early 1970s when equity theory research followed a popular research paradigm (i.e., giving laboratory participants false information about their own relative pay or the value of their contributions), however, the issues addressed by current investigators preclude the use of such readily available methods. Clearly, the costs of removing equity theory research from threats of amassing method-bound data have been paid by its lowered popularity as a research topic. The few tests of equity theory that have been conducted recently have taken it in some previously unexamined directions.

Inequities created by nonmonetary outcomes. Although Adams (1965) clearly recognized that various factors may constitute work outcomes (e.g., status and prestige), the ease of manipulating monetary rewards has made them the traditional target of equity theory researchers (Adams & Freedman, 1976). Researchers have also, however, tested reactions to in- equities created by various nonmonetary sources of reward.

For example, a colleague and I (Greenberg & Ornstein, 1983[17]) conducted a pair of experiments in which a high-status job title was found to serve temporarily as a reward. Specifically, a title led workers to feel equitably treated when it was given accompanying an increase in work responsibilities. In other words, the increased work expected was offset by the increased reward received in the form of the title, thereby creating an equitable state. When the title was bestowed inappropriately (i.e., when it was not earned in exchange for meritorious performance), however, it was not recognized as a reward and failed to adequately compensate participants for their extra job responsibilities, thereby leading to feelings of underpayment and associated reductions in performance. Thus, this study supported the idea that high-status job titles may function as outcomes in the equity equation.

More recent research has extended this reasoning to another source of organizational rewards, that is, the status associated with work space characteristics (e.g., large, lavishly decorated private offices). Specifically, I compared the performance of insurance underwriters who temporarily performed their jobs in the offices of either higher-status, lower-status, or equal-status coworkers (Greenberg, 1988b[15]). Reasoning that the opportunity to work in a higher-status office constituted an increase in work rewards, I expected that such individuals would report feeling over-paid and would increase their performance. Likewise, reassignment to a lower-status office was expected to be a source of underpayment, leading to decreased performance. Finally, workers in a control group performed their jobs in the office of another person of equal status and were expected to experience no change in their perceptions of payment equity and to exhibit no changes in their performance. Strong support was found for each of these predictions, thereby suggesting that the status value of offices constitutes a valid source of outcomes in the equity formula.

Further evidence of this effect was found in a related investigation (Greenberg, 1989[16]). In this study, comparisons were made between workers' reactions to various aspects of their physical work environment at two times: once after experiencing a temporary pay cut and again after their pay was reinstated. One way of justifying a reduction in pay, it was reasoned, would be to perceive greater value in other work-related rewards. Given the apparent reward value of the work environment demonstrated previously (Greenberg, 1988b[15]), I reasoned in this study that features of the work environment would be a reasonable target of such cognitive distortion. As expected, workers perceived their work environments more positively when they worked under reduced-salary conditions than when their pay was reinstated (and the need to cognitively realign the value of the nonmonetary outcomes was reduced). This evidence suggests that workers may cognitively realign the values they assign various nonmonetary rewards to justify working under equitable conditions. Not only do such findings extend the knowledge of the effect of various nonmonetary outcomes in the equity equation but also they shed light on the largely unaddressed questions about the conditions under which the cognitive realignment of information is used as a tactic of inequity reduction (Adams & Freedman, 1976).

Interpersonal and individual-level determinants of reactions to inequity. Beyond the nature of the variables creating inequitable states, researchers also have focused on the effects of interpersonal (Griffeth, Vecchio, & Logan, 1989) and intrapersonal (Huseman, Hatfield, & Miles, 1987) moderators of inequity reactions. Griffeth et al. (1989) found that a sample of part-time proofreaders were more uncomfortable being overpaid relative to another to whom they were attracted (i.e., someone who was at-titudinally similar to themselves) than someone to whom they were not attracted. Greater attempts to reduce the inequitable state were also found. Findings such as these qualify equity theory's prediction that states of overpayment may be undesirable and motivate efforts at redress. Apparently, this effect is stronger when the overpayment disadvantages a comparison person who is liked than when the overpayment disadvantages one who is not liked (see also Greenberg, 1978). Such findings add a new interpersonal dimension to equity theory.

Recent theorizing also has focused on an intrapersonal moderator of reactions to inequity. Specifically, Huseman et al. (1987) introduced the idea that people have different preferences for certain outcome/input ratios (i.e., everyone does not prefer a balanced state), a concept they term "equity sensitivity." One category of people, "equity sensitives," are theorized to respond in accordance with equity theory, to experience distress at being either overpaid or underpaid and contentment at being equitably paid. Another group, termed "benevolents," are theorized to prefer being underpaid and to enjoy generously benefiting others at their own expense. A final group, termed "entitleds," are theorized to prefer being overpaid and are interested in maximizing their outcomes. Huseman et al.'s idea, contrary to equity theory, is that equitable states are not the ideals that everyone seeks and that some people prefer states of underpayment (benevolents) and others, states of overpayment (entitleds).

As interesting as this idea may be, the evidence provided for the equity sensitivity as a stable individual difference variable remains largely untested and is seriously flawed in its derivation (Greenberg, 1987a). The major problem is that although Huseman et al. (1987) claim that preferences for other-than-equitable divisions of reward suggest the existence of an individual difference variable, it is well established that situational factors often dictate the appropriateness of norms of equality and need gratification (e.g., Deutsch, 1975; Leventhal, 1976a). Behaviors in accord with these norms should not be taken as insensitivity to the equity norm. Instead, it simply appears to be the case that different norms of justice are followed under different circumstances (Deutsch, 1975). Although many different individual difference variables have been studied in connection with distributive justice (Major & Deaux, 1982), the equity sensitivity variable—if further studied—promises to be controversial.

Justice-Based Explanations
of Organizational Phenomena

One of the most important benefits of organizational justice conceptualizations is that they may be used to explain a wide variety of organizational behaviors. Three areas in which researchers have been most active in applying justice-based explanations to organizational phenomena are managerial dispute resolution, survivors' reactions to layoffs, and sex differences in the equity-pay satisfaction relationship.

Managerial dispute resolution. Although interest in procedural justice developed out of concern over third-party dispute resolutions in legal settings (Lind & Tyler, 1988; Thibaut & Walker, 1975), the dispute resolution processes followed in organizational settings are likely to be different from those used in the courts in several ways (e.g., unlike judges, managers follow no prescribed guidelines, they are often involved in the dispute, and they usually have an ongoing relationship with the disputing parties; Kolb, 1986). As a result, managers tend to resolve disputes differently from judges: They tend to use threats to encourage resolutions (Sheppard, 1983, 1984), and they may advise the parties, encourage collaborative problem solving between them, or change the reporting relationships between the parties to avoid conflict (Kolb, 1986; Kolb & Glidden, 1986). Only recently, however, has research shown that the effects of perceived procedural justice (e.g., acceptance of even unfavorable outcomes resulting from input into the decision-making process) demonstrated in legal dispute resolution cases (see Lind & Tyler, 1988) may be found as well in instances in which people attempt to resolve disputes between parties with conflicting interests.

Karambayya and Brett (1989) asked MBA students working in groups of three to play the role of a manager and two disputing employees in each of three dispute resolution exercises. After each experience, participants completed questionnaires asking them to assess the fairness of the procedures used to affect a resolution and the fairness of the outcome itself, as well as a variety of items identifying different activities that may have occurred during the exercise. When managers attempted to resolve disputes by the use of threats or coercion, the disputing parties judged these actions and the resulting resolution to be unfair. The use of mediation procedures was judged to be procedurally fair, and the compromise solutions that typically followed from them were judged to be distributively fair. This study suggests that just as in legal settings, organizational managers acting to resolve disputes between others tend to behave in ways that differ in their perceived fairness. Specifically, "Third-party roles viewed as procedurally just are those in which a manager acting as a third party tries to mediate a resolution rather than bullying the parties into a resolution by threatening sanctions, promising benefits, or imposing ideas" (p. 703). Given the connections between perceptions of procedural justice in organizations and work-related attitudes (e.g., Folger & Konovsky, 1989), the practical impact of the various dispute resolution strategies used by Karambayya and Brett's participants may be considerable.

In contrast with the informal dispute resolution tactics used by the managers that Karambayya and Brett (1989) studied, Notz and Starke (1987) studied the behavior of people making a series of formal arbitration decisions in simulated wage-dispute settings. The study's focus was on which form of distributive justice would be used when arbitrating cases—equity or equality? When participants were free to impose any settlement they wished (conventional arbitration), they made arbitration awards consistent with equality (split-the-difference). When participants believed that one side's offer would have to be accepted (final offer arbitration), however, they based awards on equity criteria (such as the cost of living and comparable salaries). These findings suggest that people may be sensitive to several different norms of distributive justice and that preferences for these norms—equity and equality—are dictated by structural differences in the rules they are constrained to follow. Such an idea represents a new application of the earlier established notion that external situations may dictate the appropriateness of varying forms of distributive justice (Leventhal, 1976a) and that adherence to these normative standards may be used to activate certain instrumental goals (Greenberg & Cohen, 1982). In light of this analysis, the Notz and Starke (1987) study represents another current attempt to apply established conceptual notions of organizational justice to novel situations.

Survivors' reactions to layoffs. When workers are laid off, survivors (those who remain on the job) are in a good position to judge the fairness of the layoff, both distributively (i.e., who was laid off) and procedurally (i.e., how the layoff decisions were made). A program of research by Brockner and his associates (see review by Brockner & Greenberg, 1989) examines how fairness perceptions influence survivors' work behaviors and attitudes.

Participants in one laboratory experiment (Brockner, Davy, & Carter, 1985) witnessed one of their coworkers get laid off for no justifiable reason and without receiving any compensation for the work performed to that point. Relative to their laid-off colleagues, the survivors were hypothesized to feel overpaid. Consistent with equity theory predictions, the survivors reported feeling guiltier and worked harder when they witnessed such layoffs than when no layoffs occurred (i.e, when they were overpaid, as opposed to equitably paid) (see also Brockner et al., 1986).

More recently, it has been found that it is not the layoff per se but the injustice it may create that influences survivors' reactions. In a laboratory study, Brockner, Grover, Reed, DeWitt, and O'Malley (1987, Study 1) found that the act of compensating victims for their work before they were laid off effectively eliminated feelings of overpayment inequity, thereby resulting in no differences in survivors' reactions related to their witnessing a layoff. Analogous results were obtained by the same authors in a field study as well (Brockner et al., 1987, Study 2). Specifically, survivors of actual layoffs in a chain of retail stores reported feeling more committed to their organization when they believed the victims were adequately compensated than when the laid-off workers were not fairly compensated.

Taken together, the investigations by Brockner and his associates clearly showcase the value of organizational justice concepts in explaining an important organizational phenomenon. As was indicated in a recent analysis of this work (Brockner & Greenberg, 1989), the organizational justice literature suggests several additional variables germane to the layoff context that deserve investigation in future research.

Gender differences in the equity-pay satisfaction relationship. Recent research has established that the perceived fairness of pay is strongly related to pay satisfaction. For example, Berkowitz, Fraser, Treasure, and Cochran (1987) studied pay perceptions and satisfaction among a random sample of employed men. They found that the more strongly the men believed their pay was fair, the more satisfied they were with their earnings. In fact, pay equity was a stronger predictor of pay satisfaction than was the magnitude of the material benefits received. The idea that the perceived fairness of one's pay is a better predictor of pay satisfaction than the absolute amount of pay received is in keeping with evidence showing that the concepts of pay fairness and pay satisfaction are strongly related (Scarpello, 1988).

These findings are complicated by additional research showing that gender differences moderate the pay equity-satisfaction relationship (for a review, see Greenberg & McCarty, 1990[13]). Specifically, although both sexes tend to be dissatisfied with inequitable pay, women tend to be less dissatisfied (i.e., more accepting of inequitable pay) than men (Brockner & Adsit, 1986). Such evidence is consistent with other findings suggesting that people tend to believe that women are less deserving than men performing the same jobs (Jackson & Grabski, 1988)—a belief that forms the basis of the tendency for people to pay women less than men (Donnerstein, 1988).

Although many aspects of the gender-based wage gap are amenable to analysis from an organizational justice perspective (see Greenberg & McCarty, 1990[13]), particular insight may be derived from the focus on the choice of a comparison standard highlighted by the concept of relative deprivation (Crosby, 1984; Martin, 1981). This concept recognizes that feelings of satisfaction are likely to depend on the choice of a referent comparison. More recently, the concept of relative deprivation has been used to explain the high levels of job and pay satisfaction among women who are paid less than men for doing the same work (Steel & Lovrich, 1987). For example, Crosby (1982) compared the levels of job satisfaction expressed by men and women matched with respect to occupational prestige. Crosby found not only that women were paid less than men holding jobs of equal prestige but also that they felt no personal deprivation with the pay they received—what she has called "the paradox of the contented female worker" (p. 160).

A series of studies by Major and her associates has shed light on this phenomenon (for a review, see Major, 1989). For example, women expect to be paid less than men (Major & Konar, 1984), in part because they tend to compare themselves with other women who are also underpaid (Major & Forcey, 1985). Such selective exposure serves to maintain lower expectations, thereby explaining the tendency for women to not feel relatively deprived. Part of the explanation stems from prevailing social norms that tend to serve as referents against which claims of entitlement are made (Willis, 1981). Indeed, norms undervaluing the worth of "women's work" have been empirically demonstrated in recent years (e.g., Buttner & Rosen, 1987; Major & Forcey, 1985; McArthur & Obrant, 1986). To the extent that such norms dictate socially acceptable behavior, it is not surprising that women have come to accept as fair the lower pay they receive (Greenberg & McCarty, 1990[13]).

Conclusion

It is clear that recent efforts have taken the concepts of distributive justice and procedural justice far beyond their original foundations. Attempts to empirically and conceptually distinguish between these two forms of justice represent the most basic advances that have been seen. Theoretical efforts have been directed toward understanding the connections between both forms of justice and the basic psychological processes underlying each. These efforts have shown that both procedural and distributive justice formulations provide insight into understanding a wider array of organizational phenomena than originally envisioned (e.g., reactions to performance appraisals, acceptance of nonmonetary rewards, and the use of dispute resolution practices, among others). Taken together, these advances have paved the way for several promising areas of future research.

TABLE 2.1 Selected Publications Marking Stages of the Organizational Justice Life Cycle

Stage of the Life Cycle and Associated Characteristics[a]	Form of Organizational Justice	
	Distributive Justice	Procedural Justice
I. *Introduction and elaboration*		
Birth of idea	Stouffer et al. (1949)	Thibaut & Walker (1975)
	Homans (1961)	Leventhal (1980)
Extended application and definition, attempt to legitimize	Adams (1963, 1965)	Greenberg & Folger (1983) Folger & Greenberg (1985)
II. *Evaluation and augmentation*		
Critical reviews, calls for improvement, identification of moderator variables	Weick (1966) Pritchard (1969) Goodman & Friedman (1971)	Lind & Tyler (1988)
New, improved conceptualizations appear	Berger et al. (1972) Leventhal (1976a)	
III. *Consolidation and accommodation*		
Controversies wane, a few definitions are used, and books consolidate findings	Walster et al. (1978)	

[a] Based on Reichers and Schneider (1990).

TOMORROW: NEW DIRECTIONS FOR THE STUDY OF ORGANIZATIONAL JUSTICE

To lead into what the future may hold for the organizational justice literature, it may be instructive to summarize what has been established thus far and to base projections for future advances on a heuristic device known as the *life cycle of constructs* developed by Reichers and Schneider (1990). These authors postulate that scientific constructs go through three stages of development: *introduction and elaboration, evaluation and augmentation,* and *consolidation and accommodation.* Table 2.1 summarizes the various stages of the cycle and charts the development of the concepts of distributive justice and procedural justice by identifying selected publications that exemplify key characteristics of each stage.

The introduction and elaboration stage is characterized by the concept's invention or displacement from another literature. Attempts to justify the concept as important and to prove that it really exists are also part of this first stage of a concept's development. For the concept of distributive justice, introduction and elaboration is reflected by the seminal work of Stouffer et al. (1949) and Homans (1961), as well as Adams's (1963, 1965) extensions of the concept to organizational settings, where its importance has been established in the form of equity theory. For the concept of procedural justice, conceptualizations by Thibaut and Walker (1975) and Leventhal (1980) represent the earliest well-developed uses of the concept. A colleague and I (Folger & Greenberg, 1985; Greenberg & Folger, 1983) first applied the concept to organizational settings and established its importance in that context. This work defines procedural justice and attempts to establish it as a phenomenon capable of explaining various aspects of organizational behavior. As such, it meets Reichers and Schneider's (1990) description of the introduction and elaboration stage.

The second stage of construct development, evaluation and augmentation, sees the first critical reviews appearing. These may focus on problems of faulty conceptualization, measurement, and equivocal empirical findings. Moderating variables are called on to clarify the literature and to provide the basis for newly improved conceptualizations. In the distributive justice literature, early reviews of equity theory by Weick (1966), Pritchard (1969), and Goodman and Friedman (1971) addressed criticisms of the type Reichers and Schneider (1990) identified. Reconceptualizations did appear in the literature, although these were not particularly responsive to the earlier critiques. Instead, improved conceptualizations focused on other issues, such as attempts to be more specific about the nature of social comparison processes (e.g., Berger et al., 1972), adjustments of the equity formula so that it could handle negative values (e.g., Harris, 1976), and the maintenance of justice in the proactive allocation of rewards (Leventhal, 1976a). In the much newer procedural justice literature, critical reviews and attempts at identifying conceptual improvements have just begun to emerge (e.g., Lind & Tyler, 1988). Although several new conceptual directions are currently being investigated, no new fully developed reconceptualizations of procedural justice have yet appeared.

Reichers and Schneider's (1990) final stage, consolidation and accommodation, sees a reduction of controversies (and sometimes of interest in the topic). There tends to be agreement about definitions, the existence of antecedents and consequences, and the operation of various boundary conditions. Books or meta-analytic reviews consolidating the well-established findings are expected to appear. The distributive justice literature has seen such consolidation in Walster et al.'s (1978) *Equity: Theory and Research*. This work summarizes well-established findings from the equity theory literature in the form of a series of propositions and corollaries and identifies how they have been (or might be) applied to a variety of interpersonal settings. By contrast, the procedural justice literature is years away from this stage.

It is important to note that not all aspects of the distributive justice literature have been clearly established and have reached the stage of consolidation and accommodation (for an extensive review of progress in this field, see Törnblom, 1990). Certainly, the literature reviewed earlier in this chapter makes it clear that new questions continue to appear as attempts to address unresolved issues (e.g., the interrelationship between various modes of inequity reduction; Adams & Freedman, 1976; Greenberg, 1989[16]) are covered in the equity theory literature, albeit in no systematic way. It is an intriguing possibility that recent interest in equity theory has been rekindled by the burgeoning attention given to the allied concept of procedural justice. Although it may be difficult to prove the idea that interest in distributive justice is a collateral benefit of the attention given to procedural justice, it is a logical possibility that the attention given one scientific construct may influence the development of a related construct. Reichers and Schneider (1990) have considered how such a process may operate in the case of the organizational constructs of climate and culture.

Having established the relative developmental stages of the major elements of organizational justice, it is reasonable to expect various types of conceptual advances to follow in the years to come. With an eye toward facilitating this process in an orderly and organized fashion, the remainder of this chapter will outline some of the major tasks confronting organizational justice researchers. These agenda items are categorized into two major themes: methodological improvement and conceptual integration.

Methodological Improvement:
Scope, Setting, and Scaling

Serious limitations on the understanding of organizational justice are imposed because a great deal of procedural justice research may be characterized as (a) focusing on undesirable events, (b) occurring outside organizations, and (c) using ad hoc measures of perceived fairness. This state of affairs follows from conceptual developments in the field of procedural justice having been *applied to* studying organizations rather than *derived from* studying organizations. Nonetheless, serious restrictions regarding scope, setting, and scaling leave the present understanding of procedural justice in organizations highly limited and skewed.

Scope. With only a few exceptions in which inherently neutral phenomena are studied (e.g., Alexander & Ruderman, 1987; Sheppard & Lewicki, 1987), it is clearly the case that most of what is known about procedural justice is derived from studying people's reactions to negative situations. Consider these examples:

- Cropanzano and Folger (1989) measured participants' reactions to not receiving more desirable outcomes that could have been attained had a different procedure been used.
- Tyler (1984, 1987) studied citizens' reactions to encounters with police or courts (the direct or indirect result of some negative occurrence).
- Bies and Moag (1986) and Bies and Shapiro (1987) examined people's reactions to having proposals rejected and job applications denied.

Although these and other studies focusing on negative events have provided valuable insight into the meaning of procedural justice, such an approach may severely limit the understanding of procedural justice. This bias appears to be the historical result of earlier research designed to demonstrate that even negative outcomes (e.g., guilty verdicts) can be accepted if the procedures leading to them are believed to be fair (e.g., LaTour, 1978). Exchanging one negative situation for another has been a useful way of testing the generalizability of some procedural justice effects.

Now, it appears worthwhile to consider the role of procedural justice in reactions to neutral or positive outcomes. Consider some of the relatively benign organizational contexts in which procedural justice concerns may operate: for example, decisions about who will cover the phones during lunch while others are away from their desks or decisions about where the company picnic will be held. Do even such minor issues elicit concerns about procedural justice? Existing research does not provide an answer. Might such issues translate into questions of justice only when one is dissatisfied with the outcomes? Again, existing research is unclear about this. I have shown (Greenberg, 1987b[14]) that people care less about procedures when they lead to positive outcomes than to negative outcomes. In several studies, however, Tyler and Caine (1981) found the fair procedures were endorsed independently of the outcomes they brought. Might it be that when outcome distributions are believed to be fair, considerations of procedures leading to them are unimportant (Leventhal et al., 1980), or might procedural considerations be salient all the time? Rephrasing the question from a Gestalt perspective, when distributive justice is perceptually "figural," is procedural justice "ground"? It appears that the matter of *when* considerations of procedural justice become salient is far from settled and constitutes a prime candidate for future research.

Setting. Related to the scope problem is the small number of studies that have examined procedural justice among organizational employees in their organizations. The Alexander and Ruderman (1987) study and the Folger and Konovsky (1989) study are exemplary but, unfortunately, relatively unique in this regard. Other investigations have studied workers' perceptions of fairness of organizational issues not immediately confronting them (e.g., Bies et al., 1988; Greenberg, 1986a[6]; Sheppard & Lewicki, 1987). The gathering of fairness judgments among samples of working people may be a useful way of discerning some of their concerns about justice in the abstract, although it may provide limited insight into many of the organizational factors influencing their judgments.

It makes sense that aspects of work environment may influence perceptions of fairness. Differences in organizational norms and culture may affect the perceived fairness of practices known to influence procedural justice. For example, although subordinates of a manager known to have an undemocratic leadership style may accept that person's lack of consultation as normatively fair, such autocratic practices (lack of process control) coming from a more democratic, consultative manager would probably be perceived as highly unfair. Moreover, normative differences with respect to expected levels of explanation and sensitivity to interpersonal concerns also may influence people's perceptions of fairness (and possibly also the nature of their reactions to resulting unfairness). The point is that behavior relative to local organizational norms may dictate perceptions of fairness in ways that are not readily tapped in studies conducted outside of organizations.

Some promising trends may be seen in recent attempts at applying procedural justice concerns to aspects of organizational functioning that have not been previously studied. For example, Cropanzano and Folger (1991) have analyzed organizational motivation from the perspective of procedural justice. Such efforts may prove to be valuable insofar as recent major theoretical statements of motivation in organizations (e.g., Kanfer, 1990) have recognized that justice considerations are involved in employee motivation beyond the reactive quest for equity (postulated by equity theory) that traditionally has been cited for its motivational properties (Campbell & Pritchard, 1976). Another promising trend may be seen in attempts to apply procedural justice considerations to issues of employee discipline (Shapiro, 1989). Given the considerable attention that has been paid to the fairness of retribution for harm doing among philosophers (Nozick, 1974), social psychologists (Hogan & Emler, 1981), and even equity theorists (Walster et al., 1978), it is surprising that questions about the fairness of the procedures used to discipline workers have not been raised earlier. Recent efforts in this direction (e.g., Shapiro, 1989) promise not only to expand the understanding of procedural justice but also to provide a useful adjunct to the accumulated literature on employee discipline (e.g., Arvey & Jones, 1985).

The time has come to develop conceptualizations of organizational justice that are more sensitive to organizational variables. Although the existing justice conceptualizations provide a useful head start, further tests of them in organizational contexts are clearly needed to develop a truly useful understanding of organizational justice. When this is accomplished, it will be possible for theories of organizational justice to make a more meaningful contribution to the general field of social and interpersonal justice (cf. Greenberg & Tyler, 1987). To date, however, those interested in organizational justice have found greater value importing concepts for their own use than exporting conceptualizations whose merits are fully developed.

Scaling. Most studies have treated procedural justice as a dependent variable, measuring perceptions of the procedural justice of some situation. According to the listing of procedural justice studies summarized in the appendix of Lind and Tyler's (1988) book, most investigators have used single items (although a few have used two or three highly related items) specially constructed for the study and for which evidence of construct validity was not provided. Heneman (1985) has referred to such measures used in the pay satisfaction literature as ad hoc and has argued against their use on the grounds that they thwart comparisons between studies and lack construct validity. Their major benefit is that they allow questions to be tailor-made to the issues being addressed. In view of the highly disparate contexts in which procedural justice has been measured, the use of such measures is certainly understandable. To facilitate understanding of procedural justice in organizations, however, requires that a standardized measure of pay fairness be developed. Such a questionnaire could reliably tap the several dimensions of procedural justice identified as relevant to organizations in past research. The state of current procedural justice findings is such that the basis for a conceptually meaningful scale could be developed. Indeed, the time is ripe for such an endeavor to be undertaken.

The beginnings of such an effort may be seen in the scale to measure procedural justice used by Folger and Konovsky (1989). These investigators derived their 26-item measure of procedural justice from elements of procedural justice empirically established in my open-ended survey study (Greenberg, (1986a[6])), as well as from other findings in the literature (Lind & Tyler, 1988). Four factors were obtained: feedback (e.g., "gave you an opportunity to express your side"), planning (e.g., "obtained accurate information about your performance"), recourse (e.g., "make an appeal about the size of a raise"), and observation (e.g., "frequently observed your performance"). Further use of this scale ultimately will determine its usefulness as a measure of procedural justice across a variety of organizational situations (Folger and Konovsky were interested in studying reactions to pay raise decisions). Because the four factors measured were reliable and were derived on the basis of an empirical test of a conceptual position (i.e., my 1986a[6] study validating the existence of Leventhal's, 1980, procedural criteria), however, the measure appears most promising.

By contrast, all measures of justice perceptions used in organizational studies are not as well conceived. For example, the measures of distributive justice and procedural justice used by Fryxell and Gordon (1989; also Gordon & Fryxell, 1989) appear to be completely ad hoc and lacking in theoretical justification. For example, one of their so-called distributive justice items was "The grievance procedure lets me stand up for what I think is right, even if it's not popular" (Fryxell & Gordon, 1989, p. 857). It may be argued that such an item may be better conceived of as a procedural justice item because it asks for judgments about a procedure allowing the free expression of ideas, rather than outcomes. The intent is not to criticize this study per se but to provide an example of how a more carefully derived measure of justice perceptions could have avoided questions such as those raised here. Using a carefully constructed standardized measure of organizational justice not only could have avoided such questions but also could have enhanced the comparability of findings across studies.

One of the better uses to which a measure of organizational justice could be put would be to compare and distinguish between perceptions of fairness and related concepts, such as perceptions of satisfaction. Although several would argue that satisfaction and fairness are strongly related (e.g., Dyer & Theriault, 1976), evidence suggests that some persons distinguish between pay satisfaction and pay fairness (Scarpello, 1988). Although the two concepts may be related, findings from referent cognitions theory (Folger, 1986, 1987b) suggest that people may not feel resentful about being unfairly treated but may still feel dissatisfied with the outcomes they receive. Obviously, the meaning of fairness relative to related concepts has not yet been fully explored. The use of a standardized measure of organizational fairness would be of considerable assistance in helping explicate the position of justice perceptions in the larger nomological net.

The Need for Conceptual Integration

If advances in the area of organizational justice are to occur, it is clear that some degree of conceptual integration is necessary. Although Lind and Tyler (1988) claim that it might be premature to dismiss some of the various processes offered as explanations of procedural justice effects, the time appears right for some conceptual housekeeping.

Unification of similar phenomena. First, it appears necessary for procedural justice researchers to pay greater attention to threats of reinventing the wheel by failing to give adequate recognition to earlier discoveries that are essentially identical. As a case in point, consider the following similar sets of findings disclosed in the present review:

- Sheppard and Lewicki (1987): In an open-ended questionnaire, managers expressed the importance of "not harming others" as an element of fairness.
- Bies (1986): A group of MBA students identified "courteous treatment" as a determinant of fair corporate recruiting procedures.
- Tyler (1989): Citizens of Chicago highly rated "politeness" and "respect" as determinants of their fair treatment by civil authorities.
- Karambayya and Brett (1989): Managers' attempts at resolving conflicts were rated as fair by disputing parties when the managers refrained from "bullying" them into a solution.

It is reasonable to interpret all of these findings as showing the same thing, namely, that fairness demands treating others with civility and dignity. For this reason, it would be unreasonable for investigators finding essentially similar results to claim that their results are unique. Although some facets of some findings may be unique, it is currently at least as important for researchers to thoroughly compare and explain the connections between their own findings and earlier work as it is to announce a novel result. Conceptual progress may be attained by looking for similarities as well as for differences.

A good example of this may be seen in the literature just cited. Although Bies (1987) and Tyler (1987) have independently developed their understanding of the role of interpersonal dignity as a determinant of procedural fairness, it is encouraging that they have combined forces (Tyler & Bies, 1989) to create a more unified approach to understanding the interpersonal context of procedural justice (see also Folger & Bies, 1989). Although this is precisely the approach being advocated, such integration will inevitably lead to the orphaning and abandonment of the penultimate constructs that led to the integration (in this case, interactional justice, Bies & Shapiro, 1987, and the value-expressive model, Tyler, 1987). The immediate effect of such integration may be confusion regarding the status of the discarded concepts, although conceptual integration promises to minimize confusion in the long run. Meanwhile, given the active involvement of researchers in the evaluation and augmentation stage of development (cf. Reichers & Schneider, 1990), the threat of conceptual overlap is quite real.

Interconnecting procedural and distributive justice: Focus on consequences of justice violations. There is yet another sense in which a plea for conceptual unification may be voiced, namely, establishing the connections between distributive justice and procedural justice. Although Folger's (1986, 1987b) referent cognitions theory has made some inroads in this regard, it is clear that more integrative efforts are needed. Evidence showing that procedural justice factors accounted for more variance in perceptions of fairness than distributive justice factors (e.g., Alexander & Ruderman, 1987; Tyler & Caine, 1981) was important insofar as it helped highlight the value of the procedural justice concept and subjected it to further study. Such findings, however, should not be taken as evidence of the unimportance of distributive justice factors in organizations. Indeed, the equity theory literature makes it clear that workers are quite sensitive to discrepancies in the relative differences in their receipt of outcomes. Currently established is that another collection of factors—a wide group of procedural factors—is also responsible for perceptions of fairness.

To date, however, it has not been shown how people respond to procedurally created unfairness. Although researchers may know that various classes of procedural variables may be perceived as fair or unfair, we do not yet know how these attitudes translate into behavior. Although it has been shown that people may respond to work-based inequities in many different ways, we know little, if anything, about how people respond to procedural injustices. In other words, the behavioral consequences of procedural justice violations need to be established. Do different procedural justice violations lead to different reactions? Are these similar to or different from reactions to distributive justice violations, both affectively and behaviorally? As long as we remain content with perceptions of fairness as the primary dependent variable (replete with its earlier noted problems), it is not likely that the procedural justice concept will meet its potential for explaining people's behavior in work situations.

After the behavioral effects of procedural justice violations are established, it will be possible to understand how distributive and procedural justice are interrelated. In other words, the grounds for establishing the conceptual connections between procedural justice and distributive justice may be through their consequences. The need exists, then, to study procedural justice as an antecedent, determining its consequences on behavior. The current focus on the antecedents of justice judgments has highlighted the difference between distributive justice and procedural justice, inasmuch as each is defined by a different set of factors. Only when we have studied the different impact of these forms of justice, however, will it be possible to fully appreciate the importance of justice as a guiding force in organizations.

CONCLUSION

The 1990s promise to be a decade in which the viability of organizational justice as a meaningful organizational construct will be fully realized. The definitional work of the 1960s and 1970s, along with the qualifications and elaborations offered in the 1980s, has set the stage for what promises to be an era in which issues of justice and fairness—in many diverse forms—will rise to the top of the field of organizational behavior's collective research agenda. For this to occur, there first must be some serious improvements in the way organizational justice researchers operate. By offering some guidance regarding a variety of critical issues, this chapter ideally will help bring to fruition the promise of the concept of organizational justice.

NOTE

1. This generic use of the term *distributive justice* should not be confused with Homans's (1961) more specific, although not inconsistent, conceptualization from which Adams's (1965) equity theory was derived.

REFERENCES

Adams, J. S. (1963). Toward an understanding of inequity. *Journal of Abnormal and Social Psychology, 67,* 422-436.

Adams, J. S. (1965). Inequity in social exchange. In L. Berkowitz (Ed.), *Advances in experimental social psychology* (Vol. 2, pp. 267-299). New York: Academic Press.

Adams, J. S. (1968). Effects of overpayment: Two comments on Lawler's paper. *Journal of Personality and Social Psychology, 10,* 315-316.

Adams, J. S., & Freedman, S. (1976). Equity theory revisited: Comments and annotated bibliography. In L. Berkowitz & E. Walster (Eds.), *Advances in experimental social psychology* (Vol. 9, pp. 43-90). New York: Academic Press.

Alexander, S., & Ruderman, M. (1987). The role of procedural and distributive justice in organizational behavior. *Social Justice Research, 1,* 177-198.

Andrews, I. R. (1967). Wage inequity and job performance: An experimental study. *Journal of Applied Psychology, 51,* 39-45.

Aram, J. D., & Salipante, P. F., Jr. (1981). An evaluation of organizational due process in the resolution of employee/employer conflict. *Academy of Management Review, 6,* 197-204.

Arvey, R. D., & Jones, A. P. (1985). The use of discipline in organizational settings: A framework for future research. In L. L. Cummings & B. M. Staw (Eds.), *Research in organizational behavior* (Vol. 7, pp. 367-408). Greenwich, CT: JAI.

Barrett-Howard, E., & Tyler, T. (1986). Procedural justice as a criterion in allocation decisions. *Journal of Personality and Social Psychology, 50,* 296-304.

Berger, J., Zelditch, M., Anderson, B., & Cohen, B. P. (1972). Structural aspects of distributive justice: A status-value formulation. In J. Berger, M. Zelditch, & B. Anderson (Eds.), *Sociological theories in progress* (pp. 21-45). Boston: Houghton Mifflin.

Berkowitz, L., Fraser, C., Treasure, F. P., & Cochran, S. (1987). Pay, equity, job gratifications, and comparisons in pay satisfaction. *Journal of Applied Psychology, 72,* 544-551.

Bies, R. J. (1986, August). Identifying principles of interactional justice: The case of corporate recruiting. In R. J. Bies (Chair), *Moving beyond equity theory: New directions in research on justice in organizations.* Symposium conducted at the meeting of the Academy of Management, Chicago.

Bies, R. J. (1987). The predicament of injustice: The management of moral outrage. In L. L. Cummings & B. M. Staw (Eds.), *Research in organizational behavior* (Vol. 9, pp. 289-319). Greenwich, CT: JAI.

Bies, R. J., & Moag, J. S. (1986). Interactional justice: Communication criteria of fairness. In R. J. Lewicki, B. H. Sheppard, & M. H. Bazerman (Eds.), *Research on negotiation in organizations* (Vol. 1, pp. 43-55). Greenwich, CT: JAI.

Bies, R. J., & Shapiro, D. L. (1987). Interactional fairness judgments: The influence of causal accounts. *Social Justice Research, 1,* 199-218.

Bies, R. J., & Shapiro, D. L. (1988). Voice and justification: Their influence on procedural fairness judgments. *Academy of Management Journal, 31,* 676-685.

Bies, R. J., Shapiro, D. L., & Cummings, L. L. (1988). Causal accounts and managing organizational conflict: Is it enough to say it's not my fault? *Communication Research, 15,* 381-399.

Block, N. J., & Dworkin, G. (1976). *The IQ controversy: Critical readings.* New York: Pantheon.

Brett, J. M. (1986). Commentary on procedural justice papers. In R. J. Lewicki, B. H. Sheppard, & M. H. Bazerman (Eds.), *Research on negotiation in organizations* (Vol. 1, pp. 81-90). Greenwich, CT: JAI.

Brockner, J., & Adsit, L. (1986). The moderating impact of sex on the equity-satisfaction relationship: A field study. *Journal of Applied Psychology, 71,* 585-590.

Brockner, J., Davy, J., & Carter, C. (1985). Layoffs, self-esteem, and survivor guilt: Motivational, affective, and attitudinal consequences. *Organizational Behavior and Human Decision Processes, 36,* 229-244.

Brockner, J., & Greenberg, J. (1989). The impact of layoffs on survivors: An organizational justice perspective. In J. Carroll (Ed.), *Applied social psychology and organizational settings* (pp. 45-75). Hillsdale, NJ: Lawrence Erlbaum.

Brockner, J., Greenberg, J., Brockner, A., Borotz, J., Davy, J., & Carter, J. (1986). Layoffs, equity theory, and work performance: Further evidence on the impact of survivor guilt. *Academy of Management Journal, 29,* 373-384.

Brockner, J., Grover, S., Reed, T., DeWitt, R., & O'Malley, M. (1987). Survivors' reactions to layoffs: We get by with a little help for our friends. *Administrative Science Quarterly, 32,* 526-541.

Buttner, E. H., & Rosen, B. (1987). The effects of labor shortages on starting salaries for sex-typed jobs. *Sex Roles, 17,* 59-71.

Campbell, J. P., & Pritchard, R. D. (1976). Motivation theory in industrial and organizational psychology. In M. D. Dunnette (Ed.), *Handbook of industrial and organizational psychology* (pp. 63-130). Chicago: Rand McNally.

Cohen, R. L. (1987). Distributive justice: Theory and research. *Social Justice Research, 1,* 19-40.

Cohen, R. L., & Greenberg, J. (1982). The justice concept in social psychology. In J. Greenberg & R. L. Cohen (Eds.), *Equity and justice in social behavior* (pp. 1-41). New York: Academic Press.

Cropanzano, R., & Folger, R. (1989). Referent cognitions and task decision autonomy: Beyond equity theory. *Journal of Applied Psychology, 74,* 293-299.

Cropanzano, R., & Folger, R. (1991). Procedural justice and worker motivation. In R. M. Steers & L. W. Porter (Eds.), *Motivation and work behavior* (5th ed., pp. 131-143). New York: McGraw-Hill.

Crosby, F. (1982). *Relative deprivation and working women.* New York: Oxford University Press.

Crosby, F. (1984). Relative deprivation in organizational settings. In B. M. Staw & L. L. Cummings (Eds.), *Research in organizational behavior* (Vol. 6, pp. 51-93). Greenwich, CT: JAI.

Deutsch, M. (1975). Equity, equality, and need: What determines which value will be used as the basis for distributive justice? *Journal of Social Issues, 31*(3), 137-149.

Deutsch, M. (1985). *Distributive justice: A social-psychological perspective.* New Haven, CT: Yale University Press.

Dipboye, R. L., & de Pontbraind, R. (1981). Correlates of employee reactions to performance appraisals and appraisal systems. *Journal of Applied Psychology, 66,* 248-251.

Donnerstein, M. (1988). Pay equity evaluations of occupations and their bases. *Journal of Applied Social Psychology, 18,* 905-925.

Dyer, L., & Theriault, R. (1976). The determinants of pay satisfaction. *Journal of Applied Psychology, 61,* 596-604.

Earley, P. C., & Lind, E. A. (1987). Procedural justice and participation in task selection: The role of control in mediating justice judgments. *Journal of Personality and Social Psychology, 52,* 1148-1160.

Folger, R. (1986). Rethinking equity theory: A referent cognitions model. In H. W. Bierhoff, R. L. Cohen, & J. Greenberg (Eds.), *Justice in social relations* (pp. 145-162). New York: Plenum.

Folger, R. (1987a). Distributive and procedural justice in the workplace. *Social Justice Research, 1,* 143-160.

Folger, R. (1987b). Reformulating the preconditions of resentment: A referent cognitions model. In J. C. Masters & W. P. Smith (Eds.), *Social comparison, justice, and relative deprivation: Theoretical, empirical, and policy perspectives* (pp. 183-215). Hillsdale, NJ: Lawrence Erlbaum.

Folger, R., & Bies, R. J. (1989). Managerial responsibilities and procedural justice. *Employee Responsibilities and Rights Journal, 2,* 79-90.

Folger, R., & Greenberg, J. (1985). Procedural justice: An interpretive analysis of personnel systems. In K. M. Rowland & G. R. Ferris (Eds.), *Research in personnel and human resources management* (Vol. 3, pp. 141-183). Greenwich, CT: JAI.

Folger, R., & Konovsky, M. (1989). Effects of procedural and distributive justice on reactions to pay raise decisions. *Academy of Management Journal, 32,* 115-130.

Folger, R., & Martin, C. (1986). Relative deprivation and referent cognitions: Distributive and procedural justice effects. *Journal of Applied Psychology, 22,* 531-546.

Folger, R., Rosenfield, D., & Robinson, T. (1983). Relative deprivation and procedural justification. *Journal of Personality and Social Psychology, 45,* 268-273.

Freedman, S. M., & Montanari, J. R. (1980). An integrative model of managerial reward allocation. *Academy of Management Review, 5,* 381-390.

Fry, W. R., & Cheney, G. (1981, August). *Perceptions of procedural fairness as a function of distributive preference*. Paper presented at the meeting of the Midwestern Psychological Association, Detroit, MI.

Fry, W. R., & Leventhal, G. S. (1979, August). Cross-situational procedural preferences: A comparison of allocation preferences and equity across different settings. In A. Lind (Chair), *The psychology of procedural justice*. Symposium presented at the meeting of the American Psychological Association, Washington, DC.

Fryxell, G. E., & Gordon, M. E. (1989). Workplace justice and job satisfaction as predictors of satisfaction with union and management. *Academy of Management Journal, 32*, 851-866.

Furby, L. (1986). Psychology and justice. In R. L. Cohen (Ed.), *Justice: Views from the social sciences* (pp. 153-203). New York: Plenum.

Garland, H. (1973). The effects of piece-rate underpayment and overpayment on job performance: A test of equity theory with a new induction procedure. *Journal of Applied Social Psychology, 3*, 325-334.

Goodman, P. S., & Friedman, A. (1971). An examination of Adams' theory of inequity. *Administrative Science Quarterly, 16*, 271-288.

Gordon, M. E., & Fryxell, G. E. (1989). Voluntariness of association as a moderator of the importance of procedural and distributive justice. *Journal of Applied Social Psychology, 19*, 993-1009.

Greenberg, J. (1978). Allocator-recipient similarity and the equitable division of rewards. *Social Psychology Quarterly, 41*, 337-341.

Greenberg, J. (1982). Approaching equity and avoiding inequity in groups and organizations. In J. Greenberg & R. L. Cohen (Eds.), *Equity and justice in social behavior* (pp. 389-435). New York: Academic Press.

Greenberg, J. (1984). On the apocryphal nature of inequity distress. In R. Folger (Ed.), *The sense of injustice* (pp. 167-188). New York: Plenum.

Greenberg, J. (1986a). Determinants of perceived fairness of performance evaluations. *Journal of Applied Psychology, 71*, 340-342. [Chapter 6, this volume.]

Greenberg, J. (1986b). The distributive justice of organizational performance evaluations. In H. W. Bierhoff, R. L. Cohen, & J. Greenberg (Eds.), *Justice in social relations* (pp. 337-351). New York: Plenum. [Chapter 7, this volume.]

Greenberg, J. (1986c). Organizational performance appraisal procedures: What makes them fair? In R. J. Lewicki, B. H. Sheppard, & M. H. Bazerman (Eds.), *Research on negotiation in organizations* (Vol. 1, pp. 25-11). Greenwich. CT: JAI. [Chapter 8, this volume.]

Greenberg, J. (1987a). *Equity sensitivity: A situational alternative to the meta-construct*. Unpublished manuscript, Ohio State University, Columbus.

Greenberg, J. (1987b). Reactions to procedural injustice in payment distributions: Do the means justify the ends? *Journal of Applied Psychology, 72*, 55-61. [Chapter 14, this volume.]

Greenberg, J. (1987c). A taxonomy of organizational justice theories. *Academy of Management Review, 12*, 9-22. [Chapter 1, this volume.]

Greenberg, J. (1987d). Using diaries to promote procedural justice in performance appraisals. *Social Justice Research, 1*, 219-234. [Chapter 9, this volume.]

Greenberg, J. (1988a). Cultivating an image of justice: Looking fair on the job. *Academy of Management Executive, 2*, 155-158. [Chapter 4, this volume.]

Greenberg, J. (1988b). Equity and workplace status: A field experiment. *Journal of Applied Psychology, 73*, 606-613. [Chapter 15, this volume.]

Greenberg, J. (1988c, August). Using social accounts to manage impressions of performance appraisal fairness. In J. Greenberg & R. J. Bies (Cochairs), *Communicating fairness in organizations*. Symposium presented at the meeting of the Academy of Management, Anaheim, CA.

Greenberg, J. (1989). Cognitive re-evaluation of outcomes in response to underpayment inequity. *Academy of Management Journal, 32,* 174-184. [Chapter 16, this volume.]

Greenberg, J. (1990). Looking fair vs. being fair: Managing impressions of organizational justice. In B. M. Staw & L. L. Cummings (Eds.), *Research in organizational behavior* (Vol. 12, pp. 111-157). Greenwich, CT: JAI. [Chapter 5, this volume.]

Greenberg, J., & Cohen, R. L. (1982). Why justice? Normative and instrumental interpretations. In J. Greenberg & R. L. Cohen, (Eds.), *Equity and justice in social behavior* (pp. 437-469). New York: Academic Press.

Greenberg, J., & Folger, R. (1983). Procedural justice, participation, and the fair process effect in groups and organizations. In P. B. Paulus (Ed.), *Basic group processes* (pp. 235-256). New York: Springer-Verlag.

Greenberg, J., & Leventhal, G. S. (1976). Equity and the use of overreward to motivate performance. *Journal of Personality and Social Psychology, 34,* 179-190.

Greenberg, J., & McCarty, C. L. (1990). Comparable worth: A matter of justice. In G. R. Ferris & K. M. Rowland (Eds.), *Research in personnel and human resources management* (Vol. 8, pp. 265-301). Greenwich, CT: JAI. [Chapter 13, volume.]

Greenberg, J., & Ornstein, S. (1983). High status job title as compensation for underpayment: A test of equity theory. *Journal of Applied Psychology, 68,* 285-297. [Chapter 17, this volume.]

Greenberg, J., & Tyler, T. R. (1987). Why procedural justice in organizations? *Social Justice Research, 1,* 127-142.

Griffeth, R. W., Vecchio, R. P., & Logan, J. W., Jr. (1989). Equity theory and interpersonal attraction. *Journal of Applied Psychology, 74,* 394-401.

Harris, R. J. (1976). Handling negative inputs: On the plausible equity formulae. *Journal of Experimental Social Psychology, 12,* 194-209.

Heneman, H. G., III. (1985). Pay satisfaction. In K. M. Rowland & G. R. Ferris (Eds.), *Research in personnel and human resources management* (Vol. 3, pp. 115-139). Greenwich, CT: JAI.

Heneman, R. L. (1990). The merit pay process. In G. R. Ferris & K. M. Rowland (Eds.), *Research in personnel and human resources management* (Vol. 8, pp. 205-264). Greenwich, CT: JAI.

Hogan, R., & Emler, N. P. (1981). Retributive justice. In M. Lerner & S. C. Lerner (Eds.), *The justice motive in social behavior: Adapting to times of scarcity and change* (pp. 125-143). New York: Plenum.

Homans, G. C. (1961). *Social behavior: Its elementary forms.* New York: Harcourt, Brace, & World.

Huseman, R. C., Hatfield, J. D., & Miles, E. W. (1987). A new perspective on equity theory: The equity sensitivity construct. *Academy of Management Review, 12,* 222-234.

Jackson, L. A., & Grabski, S. V. (1988). Perceptions of fair pay and the gender wage gap. *Journal of Applied Social Psychology, 18,* 606-625.

Jacques, E. (1961). *Equitable payment.* New York: John Wiley.

Kanfer, R. (1990). Motivation theory and industrial/organizational psychology. In M. D. Dunnette & L. M. Hough (Eds.), *Handbook of industrial and organizational psychology* (2nd ed., Vol. 1, pp. 75-170). Palo Alto, CA: Consulting Psychologists Press.

Karambayya, R., & Brett, J. M. (1989). Managers handling disputes: Third-party roles and perceptions of fairness. *Academy of Management Journal, 32,* 687-704.

Kolb, D. M. (1986). Who are organizational third parties and what do they do? In R. J. Lewicki, B. H. Sheppard, & M. H. Bazerman (Eds.), *Research on negotiation in organizations* (Vol. 1, pp. 207-278). Greenwich, CT: JAI.

Kolb, D. M., & Glidden, P. (1986). Getting to know your conflict options. *Personnel Administrator, 31*(6), 77-90.

Landy, F. J., Barnes, J. L., & Murphy, K. R. (1978). Correlates of perceived fairness and accuracy of performance evaluation. *Journal of Applied Psychology, 63,* 751-754.

Landy, F. J., Barnes-Farrell, J., & Cleveland, J. N. (1980). Perceived fairness and accuracy of performance evaluation: A follow-up. *Journal of Applied Psychology, 65,* 355-356.

LaTour, S. (1978). Determinants of participant and observer satisfaction with adversary and inquisitorial modes of adjudication. *Journal of Personality and Social Psychology, 36,* 1531-1545.

Lawler, E. E. (1968). Equity theory as a predictor of productivity and work quality. *Psychological Bulletin, 70,* 596-610.

Leung, K., & Li, W. K. (1990). Psychological mechanisms of process control effects. *Journal of Applied Psychology, 75,* 613-620.

Leventhal, G. S. (1976a). The distribution of rewards and resources in groups and organizations. In L. Berkowitz & E. Walster (Eds.), *Advances in experimental social psychology* (Vol. 9, pp. 91-131). New York: Academic Press.

Leventhal, G. S. (1976b). Fairness in social relationships. In J. W. Thibaut, J. T. Spence, & R. C. Carson (Eds.), *Contemporary topics in social psychology* (pp. 211-239). Morristown, NJ: General Learning Press.

Leventhal, G. S. (1980). What should be done with equity theory? In K. J. Gergen, M. S. Greenberg, & R. H. Willis (Eds.), *Social exchange: Advances in theory and research* (pp. 27-55). New York: Plenum.

Leventhal, G. S., Karuza, J., & Fry, W. R. (1980). Beyond fairness: A theory of allocation preferences. In G. Mikula (Ed.), *Justice and social interaction* (pp. 167-218). New York: Springer-Verlag.

Lewicki, R. J. (1989, August). The management of classroom justice: Instructor evaluations and concern for fairness. In C. Martin (Chair), *Procedural fairness theory and research: Applications to human resource management.* Symposium presented at the meeting of the Academy of Management, Washington, DC.

Lind, E. A., & Tyler, T. (1988). *The social psychology of procedural justice.* New York: Plenum.

Lissak, R. I. (1983). *Procedural fairness: How employees evaluate procedures.* Unpublished doctoral dissertation, University of Illinois, Urbana-Champaign.

Locke, E. A., & Henne, D. (1986). Work motivation theories. In C. L. Cooper & I. Robertson (Eds.), *International review of industrial and organizational psychology: 1986* (pp. 1-35). New York: John Wiley.

Locke, E. A., & Schweiger, D. M. (1979). Participation in decision making: One more look. In B. M. Staw (Ed.), *Research in organizational behavior* (Vol. 1, pp. 265-339). Greenwich, CT: JAI.

Mahoney, T. A. (1983). Approaches to the definition of comparable worth. *Academy of Management Review, 8,* 14-22.

Major, B. (1989). Gender differences in comparisons and entitlement: Implications for comparable worth. *Journal of Social Issues, 45,* 99-116.

Major, B., & Deaux, K. (1982). Individual differences in justice behavior. In J. Greenberg & R. L. Cohen (Eds.), *Equity and justice in social behavior* (pp. 43-76). New York: Academic Press.

Major, B., & Forcey, B. (1985). Social comparisons and pay evaluations: Preferences for same-sex and same-job wage comparisons. *Journal of Applied Psychology, 21,* 393-405.

Major, B., & Konar, E. (1984). An investigation of sex differences in pay expectations and their possible causes. *Academy of Management Journal, 27,* 777-792.

Martin, J. (1981). Relative deprivation: A theory of distributive injustice for an era of shrinking resources. In L. L. Cummings & B. M. Staw (Eds.), *Research in organizational behavior* (Vol. 3, pp. 53-107). Greenwich, CT: JAI.

McArthur, L. Z., & Obrant, S. W. (1986). Sex biases in comparable worth analyses. *Journal of Applied Social Psychology, 16,* 757-770.

Milkovich, G. T., & Newman, J. M. (1987). *Compensation* (2nd ed.). Plano, TX: Business Publications.

Miller, C. E., Jackson, P., Mueller, J., & Schersching, C. (1987). Some social psychological effects of group decision rules. *Journal of Personality and Social Psychology, 52,* 325-332.

Miner, J. B. (1984). The unpaved road over the mountains: From theory to application. *The Industrial/Organizational Psychologist, 21*(2), 9-20.

Moore, B. (1978). *Injustice: The social bases of obedience and revolt.* White Plains, NY: M. E. Sharpe.

Mowday, R. T. (1987). Equity theory predictions of behavior in organizations. In R. M. Steers & L. W. Porter (Eds.), *Motivation and work behavior* (4th ed., pp. 89-110). New York: McGraw-Hill.

Notz, W. W., & Starke, F. A. (1987). Arbitration and distributive justice: Equity or equality? *Journal of Applied Psychology, 72,* 359-365.

Nozick, R. (1974). *Anarchy, state, and utopia.* New York: Basic Books.

Okun, A. M. (1975). *Equality and efficiency: The big tradeoff.* Washington, DC: Brookings Institution.

Pritchard, R. A. (1969). Equity theory: A review and critique. *Organizational Behavior and Human Performance, 4,* 75-94.

Pritchard, R. D., Dunnette, M. D., & Jorgenson. D. O. (1972). Effects of perceptions of equity and inequity on worker performance and satisfaction. *Journal of Applied Psychology, 56,* 75-94.

Rawls, J. (1971). *A theory of justice.* Cambridge, MA: Harvard University Press.

Reichers, A. E., & Schneider, B. (1990). Climate and culture: Life cycles of constructs. In B. Schneider (Ed.), *Organizational climate and culture* (pp. 5-39). San Francisco: Jossey-Bass.

Romer, D. (1977). Limitations in the equity theory approach: Toward a resolution of the "negative inputs" controversy. *Personality and Social Psychology Bulletin, 3,* 228-231.

Scarpello, V. (1988, August). *Pay satisfaction and pay fairness: Are they the same?* Paper presented at the meeting of the Society for Industrial/Organizational Psychology, Dallas, TX.

Shapiro, D. L. (1989). *Managing marginal employees: An examination of the effect of threats, impression management tactics, and cultural differences to disciplinary problems in the workplace.* Unpublished manuscript, University of North Carolina, Chapel Hill.

Shapiro, D. L., & Buttner, H. B. (1988, August). *Adequate explanations: What are they, and do they enhance procedural justice under severe outcome circumstances?* Paper presented at the meeting of the Academy of Management, Anaheim, CA.

Sheppard, B. H. (1983). Managers as inquisitors: Some lessons from the law. In M. H. Bazerman & R. J. Lewicki (Eds.), *Negotiation in organizations* (pp. 193-213). Beverly Hills, CA: Sage.

Sheppard, B. H. (1984). Third-party conflict intervention: A procedural framework. In B. M. Staw & L. L. Cummings (Eds.), *Research in organizational behavior* (Vol. 6, pp. 141-190). Greenwich, CT: JAI.

Sheppard, B. H., & Lewicki, R. J. (1987). Toward general principles of managerial fairness. *Social Justice Research, 1,* 161-176.

Steel, B. S., & Lovrich, N. P., Jr. (1987). Comparable worth: The problematic politicization of a public personnel issue. *Public Personnel Management, 18,* 23-36.

Stouffer, S. A., Suchman, E. A., DeVinney, L. C., Star, S. A., & Williams, R. M., Jr. (1949). *The American soldier: Vol. 1. Adjustment during army life.* Princeton, NJ: Princeton University Press.

Thibaut, J., & Walker, L. (1975). *Procedural justice: A psychological analysis.* Hillsdale, NJ: Lawrence Erlbaum.

Thibaut, J., & Walker, L. (1978). A theory of procedure. *California Law Review, 66,* 541-566.

Törnblom, K. Y. (1990). The social psychology of distributive justice. In K. Scherer (Ed.), *The nature and administration of justice: Interdisciplinary approaches* (pp. 45-70). Cambridge, UK: Cambridge University Press.

Tyler, T. R. (1984). The role of perceived injustice in defendants' evaluation of their courtroom experience. *Law and Society Review, 18,* 51-74.

Tyler, T. R. (1986). When does procedural justice matter in organizational settings? In R. J. Lewicki, B. H. Sheppard, & M. H. Bazerman (Eds.), *Research on negotiation in organizations* (Vol. 1, pp. 7-23). Greenwich, CT: JAI.

Tyler, T. R. (1987). Conditions leading to value-expressive effects in judgments of procedural justice: A test of four models. *Journal of Personality and Social Psychology, 52,* 333-344.

Tyler, T. R. (1988). What is procedural justice? *Law and Society Review, 22,* 301-335.

Tyler, T. R. (1989). The psychology of procedural justice: A test of the group-value model. *Journal of Personality and Social Psychology, 57,* 830-838.

Tyler, T. R. (1990). *Why people follow the law: Procedural justice, legitimacy, and compliance.* New Haven, CT: Yale University Press.

Tyler, T. R., & Bies, R. J. (1989). Beyond formal procedures: The interpersonal context of procedural justice. In J. Carroll (Ed.), *Advances in applied social psychology: Business settings* (pp. 77-98). Hillsdale, NJ: Lawrence Erlbaum.

Tyler, T., & Caine, A. (1981). The role of distributive and procedural fairness in the endorsement of formal leaders. *Journal of Personality and Social Psychology, 41,* 643-655.

Tyler, T. R., & Folger, R. (1980). Distributional and procedural aspects of satisfaction with citizen-police encounters. *Basic and Applied Social Psychology, 1,* 281-292.

Tyler, T. R., & Lind, E. A. (1990). Intrinsic versus community-based justice models: When does group membership matter? *Journal of Social Issues, 46,* 83-94.

Tyler, T. R., Rasinski, K., & McGraw, K. (1985). The influence of perceived injustice on support for political authorities. *Journal of Applied Social Psychology, 15,* 700-725.

Tyler, T. R., Rasinski, K., & Spodick, N. (1985). The influence of voice on satisfaction with leaders: Exploring the meaning of process control. *Journal of Personality and Social Psychology, 48,* 72-81.

Walker, L., Lind, E. A., & Thibaut, J. (1979). The relation between procedural justice and distributive justice. *Virginia Law Review, 65,* 1401-1420.

Walster, E., Walster, G. W., & Berscheid, E. (1978). *Equity: Theory and research.* Boston: Allyn & Bacon.

Weick, K. E. (1966). The concept of equity in the perception of pay. *Administrative Science Quarterly, 11,* 414-439.

Willis, T. A. (1981). Downward comparison principles in social psychology. *Psychological Bulletin, 90,* 245-271.

3

The Social Side of Justice in Organizations

W hat constitutes the fair treatment of people in organizations? During the past three decades, several different approaches have characterized the focus of scientists examining this important question. For many years, the study of fairness in organization was dominated by a *distributive justice* orientation, an approach that focused on outcomes—both how allocators distributed them and how recipients reacted to those allocations (Greenberg, 1987b[1]). Conceptualizations such as Adams's (1965) equity theory and Leventhal, Karuza, and Fry's (1980) allocation preference

AUTHOR'S NOTE: This chapter was originally published in *Justice in the Workplace* (R. Cropanzano, Ed.), pp. 79-103, under the title "The Social Side of Fairness: Interpersonal and Informational Classes of Organizational Justice." Copyright © 1993 by Lawrence Erlbaum Associates. Reprinted by permission.

theory typify this orientation (for reviews, see Greenberg, 1982, 1987b[1], 1990c[2]).

As this perspective gained dominance, an independent approach to the study of justice began to develop in Thibaut and Walker's (1975) pioneering studies of reactions to the procedures used to reach decisions in dispute resolution contexts. Following this lead, researchers became interested in expanding the distributive justice orientation to include consideration of the processes by which outcomes are determined—that is, by adopting a procedural justice orientation (e.g., see Greenberg & Folger, 1983; Greenberg & Tyler, 1987). Since the 1980s, studies of procedural justice have rejuvenated both research and conceptual interest in matters of organizational justice, in large part because of the widespread applicability that such approaches have had in explaining a variety of organizational phenomena (Folger & Greenberg, 1985; Greenberg, 1990c[2]). For example, research on procedural justice has shed considerable conceptual light on such important organizational concerns as performance appraisals (e.g., Greenberg, 1986[6], 1987a[14]), employee compensation (e.g., Miceli & Lane, 1991), survivors' reactions to layoffs (e.g., Brockner & Greenberg, 1990), and managerial dispute resolution (e.g., Karambayya & Brett, 1989).

One by-product of this considerable level of activity has been growing recognition that the original focus of both distributive and procedural justice is overly narrow in its emphasis on structural matters (Greenberg & McCarty, 1990; Tyler & Bies, 1990). Existing theories and research have tended to focus on the mechanisms by which distributive and procedural justice are accomplished. For example, distributive justice researchers have focused a considerable amount of attention on questions such as, "When are various distributive norms situationally appropriate?" (e.g., see Greenberg & Cohen, 1982; Törnblom, 1990). Procedural justice researchers popularly considered, "What procedural elements (e.g., voice in decision making, consistency of treatment, and the like) enhance the fairness of reward allocations?" (e.g., Greenberg, 1986[6], 1987b[1]). This popular focus on matters of how fairness may be structured, although important, has come at the expense of recognizing another important source of fairness perceptions—namely, the social determinants of fairness.

Beginning in the late 1980s, several researchers have noted that when people are asked to report what constitutes unfair treatment, their responses focused on interpersonal rather than structural factors. For example, reports of inconsiderate, impolite treatment, and lack of consideration for others' feelings have been obtained in several open-ended questionnaire studies tapping perceived determinants of fairness (e.g., Messick, Bloom, Boldizar, & Samuelson, 1985; Mikula, Petrik, & Tanzer, 1990), and the importance of these factors has been established in examinations of retrospective accounts of fair treatment in a variety of organizational contexts (Bies & Moag, 1986; Tyler, 1986). Taken together, these studies provide strong agreement that the quality of interpersonal treatment one receives constitutes another source of perceived fairness, one that is not immediately recognized by the prevailing emphasis on the structural aspects of outcome distributions and procedures.

The purpose of this chapter is to elucidate the status of these social determinants of justice. Given their prevalence in several contemporary investigations of organizational justice (e.g., Greenberg, 1990a[10], 1991a, 1993, 1994), such a task should prove beneficial by providing a useful platform from which to clarify and understand these factors. Toward this end, I begin the chapter by summarizing the current conceptual confusion regarding the interpersonal aspects of justice. I then seek to eliminate this confusion by proposing a rudimentary taxonomy that positions these social determinants relative to existing categories of justice. This sets the stage for reviewing some of the most recent empirical findings on the social determinants of justice. Because this research raises critical questions about the psychological mechanisms theorized to account for the impact of the social determinants of justice, the next section of the chapter focuses on these processes. The chapter then concludes by summarizing the current status of the social side of organizational justice.

CONCEPTUAL CONFUSION REGARDING
THE STATUS OF SOCIAL ASPECTS OF JUSTICE

In one of the earliest conceptual statements regarding the social determinants of justice, Bies and Moag (1986) identified the term *interactional justice* to refer to people's sensitivity to "the quality of interpersonal treatment they [people] receive during the enactment of organizational procedures" (p. 44). It was Bies's (1986; Bies & Shapiro, 1987) contention that interactional justice should be understood as separated from procedural justice on the grounds that it represents the enactment of procedures rather than the development of procedures themselves.

Although others agreed that these so-called interactional factors were important—indeed, they were repeatedly identified in open-ended questionnaire studies of justice determinants (e.g., Messick et al., 1985; Sheppard & Lewicki, 1987)—they disagreed that the enactment of procedures was not truly a part of the procedural justice concept itself (Lind & Tyler, 1988). For example, I (Greenberg, 1990c[2]; Greenberg & McCarty, 1990) argued that so-called interactional justice may be best understood as an interpersonal aspect of procedural justice and that the concept of procedural justice should be broadened to accommodate interpersonally based procedures. (This is in addition to the structural determinants of procedural justice imposed by Leventhal et al., 1980—consistency, lack of bias, accuracy, correctability, representativeness, and ethicality.) As a clue that the separate concept of interactional justice has given way to recognition that there is an interpersonal side of procedural justice, one need only consider the recent writings of Bies (e.g., Folger & Bies, 1989; Greenberg, Bies, & Eskew, 1991). Notably, Tyler and Bies (1990) eschewed the term *interactional justice* in favor of "the interpersonal context of procedural justice" (p. 81) and noted that procedural fairness judgments are influenced, in part, by the interpersonal treatment one receives.

Taking an intermediate position, Mikula et al. (1990) claimed that there is merit in recognizing both that interactional justice is a separate concept and that it may be subsumed under procedural justice. As they put it,

> It strikes us that both viewpoints are equally reasonable as long as one focuses exclusively on social situations of judgment and decision-making (e.g., allocation decisions . . .)—as the majority of justice research has done in the past. In those cases, interpersonal treatment relates mostly to the enactment of procedures. However . . . studies suggest a broader concept of interpersonal treatment which goes beyond situations of judgement and decision-making and includes all kinds of interactions and encounters. If one agrees to such a broad concept, it seems better to regard the manner of interpersonal treatment as an independent subject of justice evaluations rather than to subsume it under the concept of procedure. (p. 143)

Underlying Mikula et al.'s (1990) position is the notion that the justice of interpersonal treatment goes beyond the simple enactment of procedures; it also deals with the making of allocation decisions. Similarly, it was Bies and Moag's (1986) original contention that interpersonal treatment is an intermediary between procedures and outcome distributions. As such, it appears that the interpersonal aspects of justice—which thus far have been appreciated only from a procedural justice perspective—are also involved in the distributive side of justice. Indeed, it is this incompleteness of conceptualization that has led to the confusion and the controversy described here. It is my contention that what has been referred to as interactional justice may be legitimately recognized as a part of procedural justice because, under certain circumstances, it is. Likewise, it is also sometimes separated from procedural concerns and is an aspect of distributive justice. In my opinion, the confusion lies in that the distinction between procedures and outcomes, although applied to the structural aspects of justice, has not yet been applied to the social aspects of justice. In other words, although theorists have concentrated on the procedural aspects of the social determinants of justice, they have not explicitly recognized the corresponding distributive aspects of the social determinants of justice. With this in mind, a taxonomy is proposed that seeks to clarify the role of social factors in conceptualizations of justice, one that integrates these factors into the existing distinction between procedures and distributions already popularized in the justice literature (Greenberg, 1987b[1], 1990c[2]; Greenberg & Folger, 1983).

A TAXONOMY OF JUSTICE CLASSES

I propose a taxonomy that is designed to highlight the distinction between the structural and social determinants of justice by noting their place in each of the two established types of justice—distributive and procedural. I begin by defining the dimensions from which the taxonomy is composed. Then, four justice classes are identified by crosscutting the two dimensions. By highlighting the types of behaviors associated with each of the resulting justice classes, I intend to clarify the existing confusion concerning the interpersonal aspects of justice.

Defining Dimensions

The proposed taxonomy is formed by crosscutting two independent dimensions: (a) category of justice—procedural and distributive—and (b) focal determinants—structural and social. As established earlier and described in great detail elsewhere (e.g., Greenberg, 1987b[1]; Walker, Lind, & Thibaut, 1979), distributive justice refers to the perceived fairness of outcome distributions (Homans, 1961), whereas procedural justice refers to the fairness of the procedures used to determine those outcomes (Folger & Greenberg, 1985; Thibaut & Walker, 1975). In essence, the difference is based on the distinction between content and process that is basic to many of the social and philosophical approaches to the study of justice (for a review, see Cohen & Greenberg, 1982).

The distinction between structural and social determinants is based on the immediate focus of just action. In the case of structural determinants, justice is sought by focusing on the environmental context within which interaction occurs. By contrast, the social determinants of justice focus on the treatment of individuals. Thus, although the structural determinants ensure fairness by structuring a decision-making context, the social determinants ensure fairness by concentrating on the interpersonal

TABLE 3.1 A Taxonomy of Justice Classes

	Category of Justice	
Focal Determinant	Procedural	Distributive
Structural	Systemic justice	Configural justice
Social	Informational justice	Interpersonal justice

treatment one receives. Accordingly, the act of following a prevailing rule of justice (e.g., distributing reward equitably; Leventhal, 1976) is structurally fair; the act of treating others in an open and honest fashion (e.g., providing adequate social accounts of decisions; Bies, 1987; Greenberg, 1990b[5]) is socially fair. This distinction is analogous to one made in the conflict resolution literature (e.g., Neale & Bazerman, 1991) between solutions that focus on structure (e.g., the setting of a superordinate goal) and those that focus on interpersonal processes (e.g., teaching people to communicate more effectively).

Admittedly, at this point, these defining dimensions of the taxonomy may appear to be a bit abstract and in need of further elaboration. As the various justice classes are described in the following section, however, considerable substance is added to the skeleton provided thus far.

Justice Classes

A taxonomy of justice is formed with classes created by combining categories of justice with focal determinants of justice. The names given to the resulting classes are shown in Table 3.1.

Systemic justice. I use the term *systemic justice* to refer to the variety of procedural justice that is accomplished via structural means. This is the class of justice that was originally studied by procedural justice scholars. For example, Thibaut and Walker (1975) noted that procedural justice requires structuring the dispute resolution context such that disputants are given control over the process by which a resolution is sought.

The systemic justice class is also represented by Leventhal's (1980) proposed rules to evaluate the fairness of allocation procedures. Specifically, he claimed that fairness demands imposing procedures that allow for allocation decisions to be made such that they (a) are consistent across people and time, (b) disallow expressions of bias, (c) are based on accurate information, (d) provide opportunities to modify and reverse decisions, (e) represent the concerns of all parties, and (f) are compatible with prevailing moral and ethical standards. These are all ways of structuring the context such that procedural justice is obtained. As such, they are examples of acts that promote systemic justice.

Configural justice. I use the term *configural justice* to refer to the variety of distributive justice that is accomplished via structural means. This class of justice has been popularly studied by sociologists (e.g., Törnblom, 1990) and social psychologists (Deutsch, 1975) interested in the pattern of resource allocations perceived as fair under various circumstances—hence, the term *configural.*

Distributions of reward may be structured either by forces to conform to existing social norms (e.g., equity, equality, and need have been popularly studied; Deutsch, 1975; Leventhal, 1976) or by the desire to attain some instrumental goal (e.g., promoting productivity or minimizing conflict; Greenberg & Cohen, 1982). These are all ways of structuring the context of reward allocations such that certain distributive patterns result. As such, they are examples of acts that promote configural justice.

Informational justice. I use the term *informational justice* to refer to the social determinants of procedural justice. Hence, informational justice may be sought by providing knowledge about procedures that demonstrate regard for people's concerns. Research has shown that an effective way of doing this is by providing people adequate social accounts of the pro-cedures used to determine desired outcomes (Bies, 1987). Because it is typically the open sharing of information that promotes this class of justice, the term *informational* is used to identify it.

Information about procedures may take many forms. For example, research has shown that MBA job candidates believed that corporate recruiters treated them fairly to the extent that they presented honest and candid information and reasonable justifications for the decisions they made (Bies & Moag, 1986). Similarly, Bies and Shapiro (1987, 1988) found that people who received negative outcomes (such as being denied a job or having a proposal rejected) were more likely to accept those results as fair when they received a reasonable explanation regarding the procedure used than when no such justification was provided. The role of informational justice also has been demonstrated in the domain of performance appraisal. Notably, I had workers rate the fairness of the performance appraisals they received and compared the ratings of those whose numerical evaluations were accompanied by written narratives explaining their ratings (the outcome, in this case) with those who received no such explanation (Greenberg, 1991b). As expected, significantly higher perceptions of fairness were obtained when explanations were provided than when they were not. Thus, the use of explanations regarding the procedures used to determine performance ratings enhanced the perceived fairness of those ratings.

For explanations to be perceived as fair, however, they must also be recognized as genuine in intent (i.e., not merely ingratiatory) and based on sound reasoning. For example, fairness judgments tend to be enhanced when explanations are believed to be communicated without any ulterior motives (Bies, Shapiro, & Cummings, 1988), based on information that is logical to the outcome distribution at hand (Shapiro & Buttner, 1988), and based on legitimate factors (e.g., claims of mitigating circumstances as opposed to arbitrary judgments; Folger, Rosenfield, & Robinson, 1983). Taken together, such research suggests that the social aspect of procedural justice—that is, informational justice—constitutes an important element of reactions to procedural injustice.

Interpersonal justice. I use the term *interpersonal justice* to refer to the social aspects of distributive justice. Interpersonal justice may be sought by showing concern for individuals regarding the distributive outcomes they received. By contrast to informational justice, which focuses on knowledge of the procedures leading to outcomes, interpersonal justice focuses on the consequences of those outcomes directly. Empirical support for the distinction may be drawn from my study of the explanations given to account for employee performance ratings (Greenberg, 1991b). In this investigation, evidence of distinct categorical differences was found between explanations that focused on providing information relevant to the rating (informational justice) and those that focused on expressions of remorse for the outcomes themselves (interpersonal justice).

Several examples of interpersonal justice variables may be noted. For example, Bies (1986) found that job candidates who were displeased with the outcomes they received (i.e., they were turned down) believed those outcomes to be fairer when the authority figure demonstrated concern for their plight than when no such concern was communicated. In another context, Tyler (1988) found that citizens' reactions to dealings with police and courts were highly influenced by the sensitivity shown to their problems by authorities. Namely, ostensible displays of politeness and respect for citizens' rights enhanced their perceptions of fair treatment by authorities. Finally, Mikula et al.'s (1990) open-ended questionnaire research tapping people's perceptions of fair and unfair treatment also identified several behaviors that fall into this category. For example, it may be said that complaints of "letting somebody down" and "selfish behavior" reflect a type of failure to meet one's social obligations to a distribution of effort. As such, they represent violations of interpersonal justice.

It also makes sense to look at apologies as a tactic for enhancing interpersonal justice (see also Bies, 1987; Greenberg, 1990b[5]). Because they involve expressions of remorse, apologies help harm doers distance themselves from the negative effects of their actions (Tedeschi & Norman, 1985). My research showed that apologies tend to be included in the written narratives that accompany performance appraisals and are most frequently given to low performers (Greenberg, 1991b). I also found that the low-rated employees who received apologies for their low ratings accepted those evaluations as more fair than those who failed to receive apologies. Such findings are consistent with additional evidence from other contexts showing that apologies are an effective means of reducing expressions of anger (Baron, 1990; Ohbuchi, Kameda, & Agarie, 1989).

Discussion

One of the major benefits of this taxonomy is that it expands current understanding of the nature of the social determinants of justice beyond that provided by the current work on interactional justice (e.g., Bies & Moag, 1986; Bies & Shapiro, 1987). Indeed, the taxonomy proposes a solution to the current conceptual confusion regarding the status of interactional justice as a separate category of justice versus an element of procedural justice. Because the definition of interactional justice refers to the enactment of organizational procedures, it is clear that the social determinants of justice are involved in *both* procedural justice (i.e., the procedures used to determine outcomes) and distributive justice (i.e., the outcome resulting from enacting those procedures). Indeed, the present taxonomy distinguishes between those social determinants of justice that deal with procedures (informational justice) and those that deal with outcomes (interpersonal justice). In so doing, this taxonomy not only clarifies the role of the social determinants of justice but does so in a manner that symmetrically expands the existing distributive-procedural dichotomy.

An important by-product of recognizing both the distributive and procedural aspects of the social determinants of justice—that is, the interpersonal and informational justice classes—is that it promises to stimulate needed research. Traditionally, interpersonal justice has been less widely studied than its procedural counterpart, informational justice. I hope that by separating these justice classes from each other, the stage is set for conducting research that closely examines the separate effects of each one. Toward this end, given the advances made in recently completed research (presented in the following section), attention to the social determinants of justice promises to be the subject of increased empirical and conceptual activity.

RESEARCH ON THE ORGANIZATIONAL IMPACT OF SOCIAL DETERMINANTS OF JUSTICE

Although several studies already cited help define the distinction between the informational and interpersonal justice classes, additional recent research examines the effect of these factors on various aspects of organizational behavior. In particular, three different domains have been studied to date—employee theft, acceptance of a corporate smoking ban, and employee reactions to corporate layoffs. Findings in each of these areas are summarized next.

Employee Theft

On the basis of the assumption that employees would engage in petty theft as a means of redressing an underpayment inequity, I undertook two experimental studies—a field quasi experiment and a follow-up laboratory study—that examined the extent to which the social determinants of justice mitigated theft reactions to underpayment inequity. Participants in the first study (Greenberg, 1990a[10]) were employees of three different manufacturing plants owned by the same parent company. The employees of all three plants, mostly clerical workers and low-level manufacturing operatives, had similar demographic characteristics and had no opportunities to communicate with each other. In response to a cash-flow crisis caused by unexpectedly lost contracts, the company had decided that it was necessary to engage in the cost-cutting response of reducing the pay of all employees in two of the three plants by 15% for 10 weeks. (These were the plants whose employees manufactured the products no longer needed because of the lost contracts.) The employees in these two plants received less pay than they had been receiving although they were expected to perform at a comparable level—hence, a naturalistic manipulation of underpayment inequity had occurred (Adams, 1965).

With the cooperation of the parent company, the experimenter manipulated the manner in which the pay cut was explained to the workers in the two affected plants. Employees at one plant, selected at random, received an explanation that was high in both informational and interpersonal justice (in the present taxonomy, a high social justice condition). Employees of the other plant received an explanation that was low on both these dimensions (low social justice condition). Specifically, in the high social justice condition, employees were provided with a great deal of information about the need for the layoffs (an elaborate and lengthy presentation involving the use of charts and graphs to detail the nature of the problem and the necessity of taking the action). They were also presented repeated expressions of remorse over the negative outcomes (e.g., "Will it hurt? Of course! But it will hurt us all alike. . . . It really hurts me to do this, and the decision didn't come easily"). By contrast, employees in the low social justice condition were given only minimal information about the need for the layoffs and its justification; the basis for the decision was not described. Moreover, only the most perfunctory expressions of apology or remorse were voiced. Thus, by manipulating the statements of company officials, either high levels or low levels of both informational and interpersonal justice were introduced. Finally, because no pay cuts were necessitated in the third plant, its employees constituted the control group.

The major dependent measure was the rate of employee theft. This was the company's standard measure of "shrinkage," the percentage of inventory unaccounted for by known uses (e.g., sales, waste, etc.). These measures were collected by persons blind to the study. Data were collected on a weekly basis during the 30-week study—10 weeks before the pay cuts were instituted, 10 weeks during the pay cut period, and 10 weeks after normal pay was reinstated. As expected by equity theory, the workers whose pay was reduced (i.e., underpaid workers) responded to the resulting underpayment inequity by stealing—a way of attempting to raise their outcomes in an unauthorized manner. After the pay was reinstated, the theft rate returned to its lower, pre-pay cut levels. By contrast, those in the control group showed no changes in theft rate throughout the study.

Of particularly interest is how much the employees stole as a function of the nature of the information and interpersonal treatment they received. Employees who received low levels of information presented in an insensitive manner stole approximately 8% (compared with a base rate of approximately 3%), whereas those who received high levels of information presented in a highly sensitive manner stole slightly more than 4%. This difference was not only statistically significant but also financially significant for the company that bore the cost of this undesirable behavior. Those receiving the low social justice manipulations reported that they were treated more inequitably than those who received the negative outcomes but who were presented high social justice manipulations. Those in the high social justice condition, however, expressed no more inequitable treatment than those who were not underpaid (those in the control group). In addition, the data show that many of those in the low social justice condition responded to the inequity they experienced in another way as well—namely, by quitting their jobs. Specifically, although more than 25% of the workers in the low social justice condition resigned in response to the pay cut, only about 2% did so in the high social justice condition (compared with 0% in the control group). In summary, these data clearly demonstrate that low levels of informational and interpersonal justice encourage expressions of inequity and several forms of behavioral redress—pilfering (to increase outcomes) and resigning (to leave the field).

Given that this initial field quasi experiment used manipulations that combined both informational and interpersonal justice, a follow-up study was conducted in a laboratory setting in which the independent effects of the informational and interpersonal factors could be assessed independently (Greenberg, 1993[11]). The participants were undergraduates who were promised an established fair pay rate, $5 per hour, to perform a clerical task. After performing the task, a random half of the participants were told that they would be paid the $5 promised them, whereas the remaining participants were told they would be paid only $3. Informational justice was manipulated by varying the quality of the information used as the basis for establishing this rate of pay. Specifically, the high informational justice conditions were characterized by (a) the use of directly acquired information (b) from an expert source (c) who is identified (d) that is double-checked with an independent source. By contrast, the low informational justice manipulations relied on (a) the use of hearsay information (b) from a person of undisclosed expertise (c) who is not identified (d) that is not independently verified. Remarks meeting these criteria were tailored to the underpaid and equitably paid conditions separately. For example, in the underpayment/high informational justice condition, participants were told:

> While you were working, I found out from my supervisor that our research sponsor is really only paying $3 instead of the $5 you were promised. As you can see from this document [experimenter shows participant fake budget figures], this is the amount that was planned in the original budget proposal. To make sure, I also called the project's budget officer and was reassured of this figure. Because of a typographical error, some participants did get $5, but this was a mistake. Starting now, you can get only $3.

By contrast, in the underpayment/low informational justice condition, participants were told:

> While you were working, I heard from someone in the hall that our research sponsor is really only supposed to be paying $3, instead of the $5 you were promised. As a result, that's what I'll be paying you.

Following the administration of the informational justice manipulation, additional comments were made that created the interpersonal justice manipulation. These remarks varied in the degree of caring and sensitivity shown the participants with respect to their pay rate. Specifically, the high interpersonal justice conditions were characterized by (a) repeated expressions of remorse (or satisfaction) and (b) attempts to dissociate from (or associate with) the outcome. Low sensitivity conditions were characterized by (a) expressions of disinterest with the participants' outcomes and (b) claims of greater concern with one's own personal outcomes. Remarks meeting these criteria were tailored to the underpaid and equitably paid conditions separately. For example, in the underpayment/high interpersonal justice condition, participants were told:

> You really got a bad deal and I feel very sorry for you. I know it's only a $2 difference, but I feel awful for misleading you. Please recognize that it's not my fault and that I would pay you more if I could. You seem like such a nice person, I really hate to have to do this to you. I don't want to upset you. It's probably not much consolation, but I feel very badly about this myself.

By contrast, in the underpayment/low interpersonal justice condition, participants were told:

> That's the way it is; I don't make the rules around here. I really don't care how much you get paid. I don't care too much about how much others get; I'm more concerned about how much I get paid myself.

After the final interpersonal sensitivity remarks were made, the experimenter told the participants that he had to rush down the hall to run another experimental session. With this, he reached into his hip pocket and removed a handful of $1 bills, quarters, nickels, dimes, and pennies, and placed this money on a nearby desk. The experimenter's seemingly disorganized state helped create the impression that he was unaware of the exact amount of money he put on the table. In keeping with this image, he said,

> I have to go down the hall now to begin another session, so [reaching into his pocket] I'll just have to leave you some money to pay yourself with. I don't know how much is here, but it looks like there's more than enough for you. Just take the $5 ($3) you are supposed to be paid and leave the rest on the table.

This procedure made it possible for participants to take as much money as they wanted without believing that the experimenter would be able to tell how much was actually taken. Because in actuality, however, a total of

$10.42 was available (7 $1 bills, 6 quarters, 11 dimes, 12 nickels, and 22 pennies), it was possible to determine exactly how money was taken.

The results clearly showed that the amount of pay taken was dependent on payment equity in conjunction with the justice manipulations. For example, although no appreciable theft occurred among participants who were equitably paid, the amount of theft was considerable among those who were underpaid. Nevertheless, the amount of money underpaid workers took varied as a function of the informational justice and the interpersonal justice manipulations. Although the effect of these two factors did not interact with each other, each factor contributed to a reduction in the amount of money taken. Theft was reduced when levels of informational justice were high rather than low and when levels of interpersonal justice were high rather than low. In fact, when both factors were high, theft rate was lowest, and when both factors were low, theft rate was highest. In other words, each type of justice contributed additively to a reduction in theft behavior stimulated by the surprise instigation of inequitable treatment.

Acceptance of a Corporate Smoking Ban

Given how clear-cut the effects of interpersonal and informational justice have been shown to be on mitigating theft reactions to underpayment inequity, another study was undertaken to determine the extent to which the observed effects were generalizable to other types of negative behaviors. With this in mind, I tested the effectiveness of social justice manipulations on another important variable associated with effective organizational functioning—namely, acceptance of a corporate smoking ban (Greenberg, 1994[12]). Just as theft can cost companies a great deal, so too can the failure of workers to accept a smoking ban—especially if otherwise good workers who happen to smoke find the ban unacceptable and quit their jobs as a result. The research was undertaken with an interest in asking whether the introduction of social justice variables would enhance workers' acceptance of a corporate smoking ban.

Extrapolating from the previous research on employee theft (Greenberg, 1990a[10], 1993[11]), I had reason to believe that the manipulations I had been using to mitigate theft reactions to underpayment could also be used to help facilitate acceptance of a corporate smoking ban. This notion was tested in the following manner. In meetings conducted by corporate officials, employees of a clerical services company were told that the company was about to introduce a companywide smoking ban. Effective the following week, there would be a total ban on smoking on all company premises. Because the meetings were conducted in separate rooms, I had an opportunity to present separate groups of employees with different degrees of information about the reasons for the smoking ban and in ways that demonstrated different degrees of social sensitivity. The manipulations were similar to the ones used in the theft laboratory study (Greenberg, 1993[11]). Specifically, in the informational justice condition, employees either were presented with a great deal of information about the costs of smoking, the health and danger risks involved, and so on (the high informational justice condition) or were given limited and superficial information about the negative effects of smoking on the company and its employees (the low informational justice condition). In addition, this information was presented in a manner in which either considerable social sensitivity was shown about the potential difficulty involved with giving up smoking on the job (the high interpersonal justice condition) or little sensitivity was shown to the feelings of those affected (the low interpersonal justice condition).

In addition, because the smoking ban (unlike the pay cut that occurred in the earlier studies) did not affect all workers in the same way, an opportunity presented itself to study the manner in which the hypothesized effects may be qualified by the severity of the outcome. To do this, an independent variable (termed *outcome severity*) was composed by noting whether workers smoked on the job and, if so, how much. Dichotomizing the distribution of the number of cigarettes smoked, levels of the variable were created by distinguishing between those who smoked less than the median amount (light smokers) and those who smoked more than the median amount (heavy smokers). One of the key dependent measures dealt with "acceptance of the smoking ban," an internally consistent group of three items tapping workers' willingness to go along with the ban.

Among the results, most notably, there was evidence for an egocentric bias, that is, the more severe the outcome (i.e., the more the worker smoked), the less the ban was accepted. This is consistent with several of my earlier studies in which it was found that what is fair is what benefits oneself (Greenberg, 1983, 1987c[9]). This was qualified, however, by the informational justice and interpersonal justice manipulations. Each of these factors interacted with the severity variable but not with each other. As in the theft studies, each factor contributed some to the acceptance of the smoking ban; their combined effects were additive.

This effect, however, was most pronounced among heavy smokers, that is, those who were most adversely affected by the ban. In other words, among heavy smokers, the introduction of high levels of informational justice and interpersonal justice effectively raised the acceptance rate of the smoking ban to levels approaching those of light smokers and non-smokers. The effects of these variables were less pronounced among light smokers. Even more extreme, nonsmokers' acceptance of the ban was not at all influenced by the social justice manipulations; their level of acceptance was already asymptotically high. Hence, I concluded from this study not only that the effects I noted for theft also occurred for acceptance of a corporate smoking ban, thereby showing generalizability, but also, with respect to when the effects occurred, that the mitigating effects were greatest among those who were most adversely affected. From a practical perspective, this may be considered quite useful because these were the workers who were most harmed—hence, the ones who were in greatest danger of quitting. Noting that these were, in fact, the participants who were most likely to benefit from the social justice manipulations is encouraging with respect to the practical implications of the work.

These findings do not imply that the manipulations had no effects on nonsmokers; indeed they did. Although nonsmokers were not affected by the information and the sensitivity in their acceptance of the ban, they were affected when it came to recognizing the fairness of the procedure the company used to introduce the smoking ban. In fact, with respect to ratings of fairness, all participants agreed that the use of detailed information presented in a socially sensitive manner enhanced perceptions of the fairness of the way the smoking ban was instituted. Fairness perceptions were enhanced by increases in informational justice and increases in interpersonal justice. Each factor contributed to some of the variance in perceived fairness; the greatest levels of fairness were recognized when the levels of both variables were high.

At this point, an ethical aside is in order regarding the conduct of this study. The procedure called for participants to receive one of four instructional sets (2 levels of informational justice × 2 levels of interpersonal justice) and then to complete the questionnaire. Although it would have been ideal, from an experimental perspective, to include a measure of actual compliance with the smoking ban, or perhaps acceptance of the ban at some time in the future, it was considered ethically necessary to use a procedure that would have otherwise invalidated the interpretation of such data. Specifically, because the earlier theft research (Greenberg, 1990a[10], 1993[11]) established that a substantial benefit was associated with administering high levels of both the informational and interpersonal justice manipulations, it would have been considered ethically inappropriate to release any participants until they had actually been exposed to these treatments. As a result, the experimental sessions were not ended until all employees were thoroughly debriefed and then given the high levels of whatever variables were not earlier administered. Because such treatment was known to yield beneficial outcomes, it was essential for them to be provided to all employees after they were temporarily withheld (i.e., before the questionnaire was completed). To release them in advance of such debriefing, although essential for the collection of compliance data, may have caused the employees undue stress and cost the company the consequences of such negative reactions. From a cost-benefit perspective, it was clearly essential to refrain from using any procedure that would have knowingly sustained employees' experienced distress.

Minimizing Negative
Responses to Layoffs

Yet another domain in which the effects of social justice variables have been examined is reactions to layoffs among both victims and survivors (see Konovsky & Brockner, 1993). In this connection, a series of questionnaire studies by Brockner et al. (1994) and an experimental investigation of mine (Greenberg, 1991a) paint a consistent picture of the beneficial effects of high levels of social justice variables.

In the first study by Brockner et al. (1994), victims of layoffs completed a questionnaire in which they indicated the extent to which they were given advance notice regarding their layoffs (an informational justice variable), the extent to which they were offered benefits that eased the financial costs of the layoffs, and their desire for governmental regulations designed to protect workers from layoffs. It was found that the less advance notice that was given (i.e., the less informational justice was recognized), the more the participants favored governmental regulation, especially when the financial effects of the layoffs were great. In other words, when minimal warning was given about the use of an undesirable procedure, people expressed a preference for actions that would minimize a recurrence of such situations.

In their follow-up study, Brockner et al. (1994) sent a questionnaire to employees who survived the layoffs of some of their fellow employees at the same organization. This time, the social justice measures included three intercorrelated questionnaire items tapping both interactional justice (e.g., clarity of the explanations given for the layoffs) and interpersonal justice (e.g., the extent to which layoff victims had news of the layoffs delivered in "a nice way"). The dependent measure consisted of judgments of organizational commitment. An interaction pattern similar to that of the previous study was found in these two studies as well. In other words, a significantly lower level of organizational commitment was expressed by survivors who believed that the layoff victims were treated in a socially unfair manner, especially when they believed that the effects of the layoffs were particularly severe (measured in percentage of persons laid off).

The pattern of findings in these studies is consistent despite the different measures. These findings are also similar to the pattern of interaction noted in my study of workers' reactions to a corporate smoking ban (Greenberg, 1994[12]). In that study too, the most negative effects were found among those who experienced the most severe outcomes (i.e., the heaviest smokers) when the level of social justice was lowest. Clearly then, a consistent pattern of evidence shows that the reactions to social justice variables are qualified by the nature of the consequences involved. This makes sense when one considers that informational and interpersonal justice manipulations are, after all, designed to reduce the consequences of outcomes. As such, the interaction pattern may be taken as a summary of the combination of conditions under which negative reactions to negative treatment may be effectively mitigated. From this perspective, it makes a great deal of sense to find that the combination of poor treatment and poor outcomes sets the stage for the most negative reactions.

Although the Brockner et al. (1994) results are of interest, their questionnaire did not separate the effects of interpersonal and informational factors. As such, the individual contributions of these variables to reactions to layoffs remains to be determined. Moreover, because Brockner et al. measured but did not manipulate social justice variables, their correlational study does not permit direct assessment of the causal effects of social justice variables.

An experimental study of mine eliminated these problems (Greenberg, 1991a). The participants in this investigation were employees of an assembly plant who were asked to write brief narratives about what it was like to work for their company. Their responses were collected twice— once 6 weeks before any layoffs occurred and again immediately after company layoff notices were distributed. The layoff notices were prepared in a fashion following from the independent manipulations of informational and interpersonal justice established in other investigations in this area (Greenberg, 1990a[10], 1993[11], 1994[12]). In other words, the informational justice variable was characterized by providing either lengthy explanations regarding the company's economic problems and the necessity for the layoff (high informational justice condition) or limited statements of the problems involved (low informational justice condition). This information was combined with varying expressions of sympathy for the workers: either sincere expressions of sorrow for having to take this action (high interpersonal justice condition) or rather cool, detached statements regarding the business necessity of the action (low interpersonal justice condition). This information was presented to supplement notices indicating either that they were being laid off themselves (victim condition) or that some other company employees (survivor condition) were being laid off. (This information was, of course, true.)

The primary data consisted of raters' assessments of the affective tone of the workers' descriptive comments concerning their jobs. Data were available both before and immediately after the layoffs for both victims and survivors. The overall pattern of findings was remarkably similar to that obtained in my study of workers' reactions to a smoking ban (Greenberg, 1994[12]). In fact, parallels can be drawn between those who were not directly adversely affected (nonsmokers and survivors) and those who were directly adversely affected (smokers and layoff victims). Specifically, I found that descriptions of the company became more negative following the layoffs. Consistent with a self-serving, egoistic perspective, however (Greenberg, 1983, 1987c[9]), after the layoffs the victims expressed even greater negative reactions than the survivors. In addition, among the victims, the negative reactions were mitigated by the use of statements high in levels of informational and interpersonal justice. Indeed, the most negative reactions occurred among victims of layoffs receiving low levels of both informational and interpersonal justice. Although the survivors of layoffs were less strongly affected by the social justice manipulations, they were affected in the same relative pattern. For ethical purposes, the participants were thoroughly debriefed as in the smoking ban study (Greenberg, 1994[12]), that is, by receiving any beneficial treatments that were earlier denied.

Summary

These findings not only conceptually corroborate those of Brockner et al. (1994) but also extend the generalizability of several earlier studies showing a similar pattern of findings regarding the effects of informational and interpersonal justice. This research makes it clear that high levels of both informational and interpersonal justice, alone and/or together, are effective in mitigating the undesirable behavioral and attitudinal reactions to negative outcomes. Whether it was theft reactions to underpayment inequity, acceptance of a corporate smoking ban, or employees' affective reactions toward their companies following layoffs, providing employees with complete explanations regarding the procedures used in a way that showed sensitivity toward their unfortunate situations effectively reduced their negative reactions. These manipulations reduced levels of theft, promoted acceptance of the smoking ban among those who were most adversely affected, and lowered negative affect toward the company following layoffs.

THEORETICAL QUESTIONS AND IMPLICATIONS

The taxonomy and research just reviewed highlight several critical conceptual issues in need of further development. In particular, several theoretical questions and implications raised by this work may be identified. The remainder of this chapter addresses two of these: (a) the processes underlying the mitigating influences of informational and interpersonal justice and (b) the juxtaposition of the present approach with the group-value model of procedural justice (Lind & Tyler, 1988).

Processes Underlying the Mitigating Influences of Informational and Interpersonal Justice: Some Possibilities

Given the high degree of consistency with which the mitigating effects of social justice variables have been observed across a variety of phenomena, it is appropriate to ask why the effect occurs. In other words, what are the underlying processes involved? Given the statistically significant interactions found between the social justice manipulations and the reaction measures, it may be said that the social justice variables moderate the relationship between the negative outcomes and the negative reactions (Baron & Kenny, 1986). The exact nature of the processes responsible for yielding different reactions to unfavorable outcomes is unclear, however. Indeed, as Baron and Kenny noted, the use of moderators sometimes leads to positing the existence of various mediational processes. In the present case, four possibilities with respect to the nature of the mediational processes may be identified.

First, it may be the case that the social justice manipulations work by reducing the negativity of the outcome (Bies, 1987). Therefore, to the extent that the negative outcomes are made to seem not so bad, it is not surprising that the reactions may be not so negative. Evidence for this possibility is provided by my employee theft field quasi experiment (1990a[10]). Participants in that study expressed the greatest degree of payment inequity under the conditions in which the most extreme inequity reduction behaviors occurred (that is, when social justice was low). To the extent that the social justice manipulations influenced perceptions of outcome fairness, it follows that reactions to outcome fairness would be qualified. Thus, the most negative behaviors occurred when the most inequitable payment was given—that is, when the lowest levels of social justice variables were administered. Despite this, the nature of the data made it impossible to test this effect directly. Specifically, because the behavioral reactions measured (i.e., theft rates) were collected at the aggregate level, they could not be correlated with individual perceptions of payment equity. As a result, it is not yet possible to claim that social justice manipulations moderate reactions to negative outcomes by virtue of their qualifying the perceived fairness or negativity of those outcomes.

Second, it may be the case that the social justice manipulations work by qualifying people's willingness to respond in a negative fashion. Although people might continue to suffer from the negative outcomes, the social justice manipulations may minimize people's willingness to express themselves negatively. Indeed, previous research has shown that people do not always show discernible responses to felt inequities (Greenberg, 1984) and that direct inequity-reducing actions are not always taken even when inequitable conditions are recognized (Greenberg, 1987c[9]; Mark & Folger, 1984). In cases in which authorities have displayed high degrees of social justice (attempting to justify the harm and minimize its impact), it makes sense that victims would feel somewhat obligated to refrain from expressing themselves in a disruptive manner. Likewise, an authority's ostensible displays of disregard for one's plight might stimulate, if not instigate, a disgruntled subordinate's willingness to respond in a negative fashion. As such, it may be that the processes of modeling (Bandura, 1986) and/or reciprocating others' behaviors (Gouldner, 1960) may account for the observed tendency for social justice manipulations to mitigate negative reactions to negative outcomes. In the absence of any direct tests of this possibility, however, this notion must remain within the realm of speculation.

A third possibility is that the social justice manipulations may influence, to some extent, both the level of outcome negativity experienced and the willingness to express oneself negatively in a simultaneous fashion. In other words, it is recognized that the first two possibilities are not mutually exclusive. Indeed, to the extent that one process occurs, it is possible that the other might also be triggered. Thus, some degree of moderation of both the negativity of the outcome and the willingness to respond in a negative fashion might occur. Evidence in support of this possibility is lacking at this time, however.

A fourth possibility is that one social justice manipulation may influence the outcome negativity expressed and that the other may influence the willingness to express oneself negatively. For example, it might be that the sharing of information reduces the level of negative outcomes experienced, whereas the ostensible shows of concern for the outcomes received reduce the willingness to react negatively. Similarly, the reverse might also be possible, namely, the sharing of information may reduce the willingness to react negatively, whereas the ostensible shows of concern for the outcomes received might reduce the negativity of the outcomes.

Although direct support for this possibility has yet to be demonstrated, some preliminary findings are available to suggest that people's perceptions of fairness do, in fact, differentiate between the informational and interpersonal justice classes. For example, when laboratory participants (Greenberg, 1993[11]) were asked to rate the fairness of the procedures used to determine their pay, the only differentiating factor was the degree of informational justice shown (procedures were perceived as significantly fairer under high informational justice conditions than under low informational justice conditions). Similarly, when these same participants were asked to rate the fairness of the experimenter's treatment of them, the only differentiating factor was the degree of interpersonal justice shown (the treatment was perceived as significantly fairer under high interpersonal justice conditions than under low interpersonal justice conditions). To the extent that people are capable of differentiating between the various determinants of fairness, it is possible that each social justice class might be individually responsible for acting on a separate determinant of the reactions. Once again, however, in the absence of any direct evidence bearing on this possibility, it must remain within the realm of conjecture.

Juxtaposition to the Group-Value
Model of Procedural Justice

In recent years, some key insights into the processes responsible for reactions to procedural injustices have been provided by the group-value model (Lind & Tyler, 1988; Tyler & Lind, 1992). Because some of these processes may be involved in the effects I have described here, I am devoting some space to discussing this approach vis-à-vis the present work. As becomes apparent, despite considerable agreement, some key sources of disagreement are noted that help to underscore the major assumptions of the present conceptualization.

During the past decade, questions about the mechanisms underlying the operation of procedural justice effects have been answered in both the social control and the value-expressive opportunities they provide (Tyler, 1987). Fair distribution procedures are recognized as such because they either enhance one's control over desired outcomes (the control explanation; Thibaut & Walker, 1975) or because they provide an opportunity to strengthen long-term relationships with authority figures (the group-value explanation; Lind & Tyler, 1988). Although both control and non-control factors are clearly involved (e.g., see Lind, Kanfer, & Earley, 1990), mounting evidence (e.g., Tyler, 1989) suggests that control is not the only reason why people prefer to have input into the decisions affecting them. Specifically, the model suggests that because people in organizations focus on their long-term associations with authorities, they expect organizations "to use neutral decision-making procedures enacted by trustworthy authorities" and to treat them "with respect, dignity, and politeness" so that, through time, all group members will benefit fairly from being members of the group (Tyler, 1989, p. 837). Beyond neutrality and trust, the group-value model also specifies that group standing is also critical to fairness judgments. Elaborating on this, Lind (1988) said,

> To the extent that procedures provide signs that the perceiver has full status in the group, the procedures will be seen as fair. Thus, procedural justice will be high when the procedure emphasizes the importance of the person and the importance the group accords to the person's concerns and rights. The model therefore predicts that procedural fairness will be high for procedures that promote respectful or polite treatment or that dignify the concerns of people involved, because such treatment symbolizes full status in the group. Conversely, procedures that are perfunctory, undignified, or impolite in the way they treat people are status-threatening and likely to be seen as unfair. (p. 14)

Consistent with the group-value model, studies have shown that perceptions of fairness are related to the extent to which decision outcomes reflect the views of those involved (Miller, Jackson, Mueller, & Schersching, 1987) and show signs of good faith by the authorities involved (Leung & Li, 1990; Tyler, 1989).

These descriptions and this evidence make it clear that fairness is enhanced by the types of behaviors described by the informational and interpersonal justice classes identified in the present work. Clearly, I agree with Lind and Tyler (1988) that the social factors represent important determinants of fair treatment. I also acknowledge their suggestion that the underlying mechanism for perceptions of fairness in this case may be identification with group values. In other words, treating people with dignity and respect may make them feel welcome as members of a group or organization to which they value belonging.

Nevertheless, I believe it is important to qualify Lind and Tyler's (1988) position by adding that the social determinants reflect not only the fairness of the procedures but also the fairness of distributions themselves. Typically, it is not formal procedures but individual actions taken that reflect concern for one's rights and well-being. For example, an individual who knowingly allocates insufficient quantities of needed resources to others, and who does so in a calculated, calloused fashion (e.g., by saying, "Take this pittance, it's all I'm going to give you") is following a distributive practice that is unfair in both its enactment and its outcomes. Strictly speaking, no procedural violations may have occurred—if, for example, prevailing norms dictated that it was acceptable for the allocator to make distributive decisions without seeking others' input (Greenberg, Eskew, & Miles, 1991). Thus, although I agree with Lind (1988) that perfunctory, undignified, and impolite actions may be procedurally unfair, so too are many distributive acts that are showcased in similar fashion. Because often distributive behaviors are not the result of any formal procedural guidelines but rather the result of an individual's decision making (e.g., Leventhal, 1980), it would be misleading to infer that such negative treatment would not be judged to be unfair. Indeed, it is not only the fairness of procedures but the fairness of outcomes themselves that demand the use of socially fair treatment. With this, I simply restate one of my major themes of this chapter—namely, that undesirable social treatment should be recognized as an element not only of procedural justice but of distributive justice as well.

Having stated this, I reiterate a point I made earlier (Greenberg, 1990c[2]): With all the recent attention paid to procedural justice, researchers run the risk of forgetting about distributive justice. The need to integrate both the procedural and distributive aspects of justice (including the social and structural determinants of each), I believe, is essential. Any social scientist who claims to study one aspect of justice without paying attention to the other is surely guilty of premature specialization. Given that definitions of procedural justice encompass distributive justice, separating one from the other is a most delicate operation—one that should be taken no more lightly than a surgeon operating on one half of the brain while neglecting the other half!

CONCLUSION

By elucidating the social determinants of fairness in organizations in this chapter, I have attempted to make advances along several important fronts. Given that people frequently cite various elements of social interaction when describing episodes of fair and unfair treatment, this chapter sought to provide a useful framework for more precisely understanding the nature of these perceptions. Beyond this, the same conceptual taxonomy promises to be a useful tool for (a) clarifying existing confusion regarding the status of social determinants of justice relative to the prevailing procedural-distributive distinction and (b) highlighting newly identified justice classes in need of further research attention. Despite several conceptual ambiguities unearthed by these analyses (which themselves promise to expand the boundaries of conceptual thought about organizational justice), it is clear that the traditional emphasis on the structural determinants of justice has painted an incomplete picture of organizational justice. I hope that on the basis of the arguments made in this chapter, the social determinants of justice—which previously have been recognized in an unsystematic fashion—will now be legitimized as a coherent, systematic complement to the structural determinants of both procedural and distributive justice.

REFERENCES

Adams, J. S. (1965). Inequity in social exchange. In L. Berkowitz (Ed.), *Advances in experimental social psychology* (Vol. 2, pp. 267-299). New York: Academic Press.

Bandura, A. (1986). *Social foundations of thought and action.* Englewood Cliffs, NJ: Prentice Hall.

Baron, R. A. (1990). Countering the effects of destructive criticism: The relative efficacy of four interventions. *Journal of Applied Psychology, 75,* 235-245.

Baron, R. M., & Kenny, D. A. (1986). The moderator-mediator variable distinction in social psychological research: Conceptual, strategic, and statistical considerations. *Journal of Personality and Social Psychology, 51,* 1173-1182.

Bies, R. J. (1986, August). Identifying principles of interactional justice: The case of corporate recruiting. In R. J. Bies (Chair), *Moving beyond equity theory: New directions in research on justice in organizations.* Symposium conducted at the meeting of the Academy of Management, Chicago.

Bies, R. J. (1987). The predicament of injustice: The management of moral outrage. In L. L. Cummings & B. M. Staw (Eds.), *Research in organizational behavior* (Vol. 9, pp. 289-319). Greenwich, CT: JAI.

Bies, R. J., & Moag, J. S. (1986). Interactional justice: Communication criteria of fairness. In R. J. Lewicki, B. H. Sheppard, & M. H. Bazerman (Eds.), *Research on negotiation in organizations* (Vol. 1, pp. 43-55). Greenwich, CT: JAI.

Bies, R. J., & Shapiro, D. L. (1987). Interactional fairness judgments: The influence of causal accounts. *Social Justice Research, 1,* 199-218.

Bies, R. J., & Shapiro, D. L. (1988). Voice and justification: Their influence on procedural fairness judgments. *Academy of Management Journal, 31,* 676-685.

Bies, R. J., Shapiro, D. L., & Cummings, L. L. (1988). Causal accounts and managing organizational conflict: Is it enough to say it's not my fault? *Communication Research, 15,* 381-399.

Brockner, J., & Greenberg, J. (1990). The impact of layoffs on survivors: An organizational justice perspective. In J. Carroll (Ed.), *Applied social psychology and organizational settings* (pp. 45-75). Hillsdale, NJ: Lawrence Erlbaum.

Brockner, J., Konovsky, M., Cooper-Schneider, R., Folger, R., Martin, C., & Bies, R. J. (1994). Interactive effects of procedural justice and outcome negativity on victims and survivors of job loss. *Academy of Management Journal, 37,* 397-409.

Cohen, R. L., & Greenberg, J. (1982). The justice concept in social psychology. In J. Greenberg & R. L. Cohen (Eds.), *Equity and justice in social behavior* (pp. 1-41). New York: Academic Press.

Deutsch, M. (1975). Equity, equality, and need: What determines which value will be used as the basis for distributive justice? *Journal of Social Issues, 31*(3), 137-149.

Folger, R., & Bies, R. J. (1989). Managerial responsibilities and procedural justice. *Employee Responsibilities and Rights Journal, 2,* 79-90.

Folger, R., & Greenberg, J. (1985). Procedural justice: An interpretive analysis of personnel systems. In K. M. Rowland & G. R. Ferris (Eds.), *Research in personnel and human resources management* (Vol. 3, pp. 141-183). Greenwich, CT: JAI.

Folger, R., Rosenfield, D., & Robinson, T. (1983). Relative deprivation and procedural justification. *Journal of Personality and Social Psychology, 45,* 268-273.

Gouldner, A. W. (1960). The norm of reciprocity: A preliminary statement. *American Sociological Review, 25,* 161-179.

Greenberg, J. (1982). Approaching equity and avoiding inequity in groups and organizations. In J. Greenberg & R. L. Cohen (Eds.), *Equity and justice in social behavior* (pp. 389-435). New York: Academic Press.

Greenberg, J. (1983). Overcoming egocentric bias in perceived fairness through self-awareness. *Social Psychology Quarterly, 46,* 152-156.

Greenberg, J. (1984). On the apocryphal nature of inequity distress. In R. Folger (Ed.), *The sense of injustice* (pp. 167-188). New York: Plenum.

Greenberg, J. (1986). Determinants of perceived fairness of performance evaluations. *Journal of Applied Psychology, 71,* 340-342. [Chapter 6, this volume.]

Greenberg, J. (1987a). Reactions to procedural injustice in payment distributions: Do the means justify the ends? *Journal of Applied Psychology, 72,* 55-61. [Chapter 14, this volume.]

Greenberg, J. (1987b). A taxonomy of organizational justice theories. *Academy of Management Review, 12,* 9-22. [Chapter 1, this volume.]

Greenberg, J. (1987c). Using diaries to promote procedural justice in performance appraisals. *Social Justice Research, 1,* 219-234. [Chapter 9, this volume.]

Greenberg, J. (1990a). Employee theft as a reaction to underpayment inequity: The hidden cost of pay cuts. *Journal of Applied Psychology, 75,* 561-568. [Chapter 10, this volume.]

Greenberg, J. (1990b). Looking fair vs. being fair: Managing impressions of organizational justice. In B. M. Staw & L. L. Cummings (Eds.), *Research in organizational behavior* (Vol. 12, pp. 111-157). Greenwich, CT: JAI. [Chapter 5, this volume.]

Greenberg, J. (1990c). Organizational justice: Yesterday, today, and tomorrow. *Journal of Management, 16,* 399-432. [Chapter 2, this volume.]

Greenberg, J. (1991a). *Social fairness and employees' reactions to layoffs.* Manuscript submitted for publication.

Greenberg, J. (1991b). Using explanations to manage impressions of performance appraisal fairness. *Employee Responsibilities and Rights Journal, 4,* 51-60.

Greenberg, J. (1993). Stealing in the name of justice: Informational and interpersonal moderators of theft reactions to underpayment inequity. *Organizational Behavior and Human Decision Processes, 54,* 81-103. [Chapter 11, this volume.]

Greenberg, J. (1994). Using socially fair treatment to promote acceptance of a work site smoking ban. *Journal of Applied Psychology, 79,* 288-297. [Chapter 12, this volume.]

Greenberg, J., Bies, R. J., & Eskew, D. E. (1991). Establishing fairness in the eye of the beholder: Managing impressions of organizational justice. In R. Giacalone & P. Rosenfeld (Eds.), *Applied impression management: How image making affects managerial decisions* (pp. 111-132). Newbury Park, CA: Sage.

Greenberg, J., & Cohen, R. L. (1982). Why justice? Normative and instrumental interpretations. In J. Greenberg & R. L. Cohen (Eds.), *Equity and justice in social behavior* (pp. 437-469). New York: Academic Press.

Greenberg, J., Eskew, D. E., & Miles, J. A. (1991, August). *Adherence to participatory norms as a moderator of the fair process effect: When voice does not enhance procedural justice.* Paper presented at the meeting of the Academy of Management, Miami, FL.

Greenberg, J., & Folger, R. (1983). Procedural justice, participation, and the fair process effect in groups and organizations. In P. B. Paulus (Ed.), *Basic group processes* (pp. 235-256). New York: Springer-Verlag.

Greenberg, J., & McCarty, C. (1990). The interpersonal aspects of procedural justice: A new perspective on pay fairness. *Labor Law Journal, 41*, 580-586.

Greenberg, J., & Tyler, T. R. (1987). Why procedural justice in organizations? *Social Justice Research, 1*, 127-142.

Homans, G. C. (1961). *Social behavior: Its elementary forms.* New York: Harcourt, Brace, & World.

Karambayya, R., & Brett, J. M. (1989). Managers handling disputes: Third-party roles and perceptions of fairness. *Academy of Management Journal, 32*, 687-704.

Konovsky, M., & Brockner, J. (1993). Managing victim and survivor layoff reactions: A procedural justice perspective. In R. Cropanzano (Ed.), *Justice in the Workplace* (pp. 133-154). Hillsdale, NJ: Lawrence Erlbaum.

Leung, K., & Li, W. K. (1990). Psychological mechanisms of process control effects. *Journal of Applied Psychology, 75*, 613-620.

Leventhal, G. S. (1976). The distribution of rewards and resources in groups and organizations. In L. Berkowitz & E. Walster (Eds.), *Advances in experimental social psychology* (Vol. 9, pp. 91-131). New York: Academic Press.

Leventhal, G. S. (1980). What should be done with equity theory? In K. J. Gergen, M. S. Greenberg, & R. H. Willis (Eds.), *Social exchange: Advances in theory and research* (pp. 27-55). New York: Plenum.

Leventhal, G. S., Karuza, J., & Fry, W. R. (1980). Beyond fairness: A theory of allocation preferences. In G. Mikula (Ed.), *Justice and social interaction* (pp. 167-218). New York: Springer-Verlag.

Lind, E. A. (1988, August). *Theoretical controversy in procedural justice: Self-interest and group-volume models of perceived fairness in legal, political, and organizational contexts.* Paper presented at the meeting of the American Psychological Association, Atlanta, GA.

Lind, E. A., Kanfer, R., & Earley, P. C. (1990). Voice, control, and procedural justice: Instrumental and noninstrumental concerns in fairness judgments. *Journal of Personality and Social Psychology, 59*, 952-959.

Lind, E. A., & Tyler, T. (1988). *The social psychology of procedural justice.* New York: Plenum.

Mark, M. M., & Folger, R. (1984). Responses to relative deprivation: A conceptual framework. *Review of Personality and Social Psychology, 5*, 192-218.

Messick, D. M., Bloom, S., Boldizar, J. P., & Samuelson, C. D. (1985). Why we are fairer than others. *Journal of Experimental Social Psychology, 21*, 480-500.

Miceli, M. P., & Lane, M. C. (1991). Antecedents of pay satisfaction: A review and extension. In K. M. Rowland & G. R. Ferris (Eds.), *Research in personnel and human resources management* (Vol. 9, pp. 235-309). Greenwich, CT: JAI.

Mikula, G., Petrik, B., & Tanzer, N. (1990). What people regard as unjust: Types and structures of everyday experiences of injustice. *European Journal of Social Psychology, 20*, 133-149.

Miller, C. E., Jackson, P., Mueller, J., & Schersching, C. (1987). Some social psychological effects of group decision rules. *Journal of Personality and Social Psychology, 52*, 325-332.

Neale, M. A., & Bazerman, M. H. (1991). *Cognition and rationality in negotiation.* New York: Free Press.

Ohbuchi, K., Kameda, M., & Agarie, N. (1989). Apology as aggression control: Its role in mediating appraisal of and response to harm. *Journal of Personality and Social Psychology, 56*, 219-227.

Shapiro, D. L., & Buttner, H. B. (1988, August). *Adequate explanations: What are they, and do they enhance procedural justice under severe outcome circumstances?* Paper presented at the meeting of the Academy of Management, Anaheim, CA.

Sheppard, B. H., & Lewicki, R. J. (1987). Toward general principles of managerial fairness. *Social Justice Research, 1*, 161-176.

Tedeschi, J. T., & Norman, N. (1985). Social power, self-presentation, and the self. In B. R. Schlenker (Ed.), *The self and social life* (pp. 293-322). New York: McGraw-Hill.

Thibaut, J., & Walker, L. (1975). *Procedural justice: A psychological analysis.* Hillsdale, NJ: Lawrence Erlbaum.

Törnblom, K. Y. (1990). The social psychology of distributive justice. In K. Scherer (Ed.), *The nature and administration of justice: Interdisciplinary approaches* (pp. 45-70). Cambridge, UK: Cambridge University Press.

Tyler, T. R. (1986). When does procedural justice matter in organizational settings? In R. J. Lewicki, B. H. Sheppard, & M. H. Bazerman (Eds.), *Research on negotiation in organizations* (Vol. 1, pp. 7-23). Greenwich, CT: JAI.

Tyler, T. R. (1987). Conditions leading to value-expressive effects in judgments of procedural justice: A test of four models. *Journal of Personality and Social Psychology, 52*, 333-344.

Tyler, T. R. (1988). What is procedural justice? *Law and Society Review, 22*, 301-335.

Tyler, T. R. (1989). The psychology of procedural justice: A test of the group-value model. *Journal of Personality and Social Psychology, 57*, 830-838.

Tyler, T. R., & Bies, R. J. (1990). Beyond formal procedures: The interpersonal context of procedural justice. In J. Carroll (Ed.), *Advances in applied social psychology: Business settings* (pp. 77-98). Hillsdale, NJ: Lawrence Erlbaum.

Tyler, T. R., & Lind, E. A. (1992). A relational model of authority in groups. In M. Zanna (Ed.), *Advances in experimental social psychology* (Vol. 25, pp. 115-191). San Diego, CA: Academic Press.

Walker, L., Lind, E. A., & Thibaut, J. (1979). The relation between procedural justice and distributive justice. *Virginia Law Review, 65*, 1401-1420.

PART II

Perceiving Fairness on the Job
THE ROLE OF IMPRESSION MANAGEMENT

MOST social scientists conceive of justice as a normative ideal—the state created by acting in a way commensurate with normative standards of fairness. As lay people often use the term, however, justice is more of a target attribution—that is, a desired characteristic, one who "is fair." When we speak of others, say instructors or police officers, as "being fair," we mean to imply that they are the type of person who would behave in a certain, fair manner. To the extent that people are so perceived, I theorized, they may derive power associated with restricting the range of attributions responsible for their behavior. As such, supervisors perceived as fair by subordinates may be trusted and believed when it is reported that financial problems preclude the possibility of a raise. Supervisors perceived as unfair, however, may be challenged in response to a similar claim. This reasoning suggests that it may be to one's advantage not only to *be fair* but also to *look fair* in the eyes of others. In other words, perceptions of fairness may be understood as an impression management process.

The two chapters in this part of the book adopt this impression management orientation. In Chapter 4, originally prepared for an audience of executives, I outline the basics of an impression management approach to justice. I also summarize the findings of a simple survey highlighting a key idea: People believe it is more important to look fair than to actually be fair. This is somewhat akin to the old question about the noise made by the tree falling in the forest when no one is present to hear it. Does fairness really matter when one is not credited for it? Maybe it is an oversimplification, but in the world of organizations at least, fairness seems to count most when others are able to recognize it.

In Chapter 5, I expand this theme, presenting a full-blown conceptualization of organizational justice as an impression management process. I begin by presenting evidence arguing that fairness is, in fact, a desired social identity and that people seek to present themselves as fair, both to themselves and others. Then I review various tactics that can be used to cultivate an image of fairness and summarize case studies demonstrating some of these techniques in action. I conclude this chapter by discussing the implications of adopting an impression management-based approach to organizational justice.

4
—

How Do People Manage
Impressions of Organizational Justice?

Certainly, it appears that being fair is a central interest among today's managers, concerned as they must be about providing "equal employment opportunities," adhering to "fair labor practices," and offering "a fair day's pay for a fair day's work." Just as judges promote fairness in the legal system and referees and umpires ensure that sporting events are played fairly, managers are responsible for upholding both their company's and society's views of fairness by guaranteeing the fair treatment of employees

AUTHOR'S NOTE: This chapter was originally published in the *Academy of Management Executive,* Vol. 2, No. 2, 1988, pp. 155-157, under the title "Cultivating an Image of Justice: Looking Fair on the Job." Copyright © 1988 by the Academy of Management. Reprinted by permission.

(Mark & Greenberg, 1987). Despite this, however, it remains unclear what those responsible for the day-to-day management of organizations think constitutes fair behavior.

Not surprisingly, just as legal scholars and philosophers cannot agree on what fairness *really* is in any absolute sense, social scientists have relied on studying justice as it is perceived to be—that is, what is fair is in the eye of the beholder (Cohen, 1986). In organizations, in which the differing perspectives, interests, and goals of supervisors and subordinates might offer each access to different sources of information (as well as different biases on the same information), uncertainties about what is perceived as fair are likely to arise (Greenberg, 1987[1]). As a result, we may expect that seasoned managers trying to be fair may learn to focus on what others believe to be fair, thereby cultivating an impression of fairness rather than striving toward any abstract sense of morality. Indeed, when interviewing executives on the topic of organizational justice, I learned that in business organizations, fairness was often a matter of impression management. As one senior vice president of a *Fortune* 500 firm confided in me, "What's fair is whatever the workers think is fair. My job is to convince them that what's good for the company is fair for them as individuals."

Hearing this sentiment echoed by others, I began to suspect that fairness—as viewed by corporate management—was perhaps as much a matter of image as it was a matter of morality, that is, "looking fair" may be at least as important as actually "being fair." After all, even the best-intentioned, most fair-minded manager may fail to win the approval of subordinates who are not convinced of his or her fairness. Given this, I may ask the following two questions: (a) Are managers more concerned about looking fair or actually being fair? and (b) What do managers do to cultivate impressions of fairness?

THE IMPORTANCE OF
LOOKING FAIR: SURVEY EVIDENCE

To learn what managers thought about fairness, a survey was conducted among 815 managers throughout the United States, 328 of whom managed travel bureaus and 487 of whom managed retail stores. One group of three highly intercorrelated questions asked them how concerned they were about *actually being fair* in their treatment of subordinates (e.g., "On the job, how concerned are you about how fairly you treat your subordinates?"). A second group of three highly intercorrelated questions asked the managers how concerned they were about *appearing*

TABLE 4.1 What Can Managers Do to Appear to Be Fair?

Response	Frequency
1. Announce all pay raises and promotions	81%
2. Explain how pay raises are determined	76%
3. Allow workers participation in decisions	55%
4. Explain why work assignments are made	43%

to be fair (e.g., "On the job, how concerned are you about leaving an impression on subordinates that you treated them fairly?"). The responses to all questions could range from 1 (not at all concerned) to 9 (extremely concerned).

Statistically, the two sets of questions were independent of each other (Pearson correlation coefficient = .06), suggesting that managers considered looking fair and being fair to be two distinct concepts. More important, the responses to these two questions were significantly different: Managers expressed greater concern about appearing to be fair (mean scale value = 7.9) than actually behaving fairly (mean scale value = 6.1).

Given that looking fair was found to be so highly important to the sample, I asked respondents a follow-up, open-ended question that focused on what they specifically did or could do to look fair: "In your present position, describe one thing you think you might be able to do to make your subordinates think you are treating them fairly." After idiosyncratic responses were eliminated, six students categorized the remaining responses into categories, the most popular of which are shown in Table 4.1.

As these results make clear, the managers in this survey emphasized the importance of being open, public, participative, and nonsecretive in their actions. Subordinates would think managers were fair if they openly and honestly considered their viewpoints. The managers emphasized that looking fair did not necessarily mean disguising unfair acts to make them appear fair. Usually, it meant just making sure that others knew that what was going on was open and aboveboard. Communicating fair intentions was critical.

WAYS OF LOOKING
FAIR: A TAXONOMY

The findings of this survey study may be categorized according to a simple taxonomy, as shown in Table 4.2. The classification scheme differentiates between the things managers do to look fair (behavioral acts)

TABLE 4.2 Looking Fair: A Taxonomy and Examples

	Behavioral Acts	*Social Accounts*
Outcomes	Announcing pay raises and promotions publicly	Explaining why certain work assignments must be made
Processes	Allowing workers participation in decisions	Explaining how pay raises are determined

and things they *say* to look fair (*social accounts*). It also distinguishes between the means by which things are done (*process*) and the end results themselves (*outcomes*).

Starting in the upper-left corner of Table 4.2, readers may identify those things workers do to emphasize the fairness of organizational outcomes. Announcing annual pay raises and promotions by posting the information on a bulletin board or publishing it in a company newsletter makes the outcomes of the organization's decision-making processes public. Such a practice may well lead all employees to believe that the organization has nothing to hide—there are no secret deals, no favoritism (Greenberg & Folger, 1983).

Similar impressions of justice may be inculcated in various organizational processes dictating *how* things are done (lower-left corner of Table 4.2). For example, various participatory decision-making plans, such as management-by-objectives programs and the Scanlon plan, fall into this category. The use of employee suggestion systems and flextime programs may also be seen as systematic attempts to give workers input into decisions affecting them (Folger & Greenberg, 1985). Research on comparative law has shown that the legal systems believed to be the fairest are those (such as in the United States) in which the litigants have the greatest control over how their trials are conducted (e.g., freedom to select their attorneys, opportunities to present evidence, etc.; Thibaut & Walker, 1975). Analogously, participatory decision-making systems in organizations may be believed to be fairer than more autocratic procedures. As such, astute managers may be quick to "market" these plans, incorporating what they communicate about the fairness of the company into its corporate image, both internal and external.

As the taxonomy notes, looking fair may be enhanced not only through what is done but also through what is said (see right side of Table 4.2). Research has shown that when it comes to perceptions of justice, words may speak just as loudly as actions. For example, a recent study found that workers believe a performance rating accompanied by an explanation of that rating is fairer than a rating with no accompanying explanation

(Greenberg, 1991). Likewise, Bies and Shapiro (1987) found that employees whose proposals and plans were rejected by higher management were more likely to feel that they were treated fairly if an explanation for the decision was given than if no explanation was forthcoming. By emphasizing the fairness-creating value of explanations, such findings fit in well with the taxonomy. Indeed, explanations of outcomes—such as *what* and *why* certain job assignments were made—and processes—such as *how* management goes about deciding pay raises—are useful mechanisms for promulgating impressions of fairness.

REAPING THE BENEFITS OF LOOKING FAIR

So far, I have identified and categorized a variety of things that managers may do and say to appear fair. To understand these tactics more clearly it helps to consider why they are done. What are the benefits of looking fair? What are managers trying to accomplish by looking fair? Although it is difficult to identify accurately an individual's true motives, social psychological theory suggests some likely benefits of appearing to be fair.

One benefit is the added influence and power managers are likely to gain among subordinates who believe they are fair people (Tedeschi & Melburg, 1984). Generally speaking, people admire fair-mindedness in others. Such liking may well strengthen a manager's power base by encouraging subordinates to comply with the manager to gain their approbation (French & Raven, 1959). The attribution of fairness similarly may enhance a manager's credibility—just as it does for a judge. A manager who is perceived as fair is one who can be trusted; he or she is consistent, lacks ulterior motives, and, as such, gains important power to manage (Tedeschi & Norman, 1985).

A manager with a reputation for fairness might gain not only a direct power advantage but an indirect one as well. Many managerial decisions are made on the basis of information that is unknown to subordinates, thereby making the matter of its potential fairness ambiguous. When such a decision is made by a manager who has gained a reputation for being fair, one may expect it to be accepted more readily by subordinates than if it is made by a manager with less of a reputation for fairness. In the face of ambiguity, a manager may draw on his or her reputation to reassure workers of the fairness of the manager's decisions. The admonition to "trust me" may well be honored when it comes from a manager with an accepted track record of fairness. Thus, a reputation for fairness may help give a manager the benefit of the doubt in ambiguous or novel situations (Tedeschi & Melburg, 1984).

The benefits of fairness discussed thus far derive from the manager's enhanced organizational power base. It also should be noted that others' beliefs in one's fairness may help reinforce one's identity and self-esteem. Research has shown that people sometimes make decisions designed to convince themselves of their own fairness (Greenberg, 1983). This is especially true of those who strongly endorse the Protestant work ethic (Greenberg, 1979). A manager's self-image as a fair person may well be reinforced by workers who respond to the image of fairness the manager portrays.

It would be an oversight to conclude this chapter without also noting the organizational benefits of looking fair. Just as an individual may seek a reputation as fair-minded, so too might an entire organization strive for an image as a place that treats its employees and its customers fairly. An organization with an established "culture of fairness" might reap the benefits of attracting (and maintaining) the best job candidates and capturing the business of customers who are impressed by that corporate image (Greenberg, 1990[5]). Advertising campaigns promoting the good-will the organization has created for the community at large may well be interpreted as self-promotional efforts at creating a corporate image of fairness (Packard, 1959).

BEYOND FAIRNESS

Although this chapter has focused on the ways managers cultivate impressions of fairness, it would be misleading to assume that such impressions are always identifiable as single, preeminent concerns. I do not mean to imply that managers are always concerned about looking fair or that fairness is the most desired attributional concern in organizations. It is likely, however, that managers' interest in looking fair manifests itself in indirect ways. For example, attempting to be politically expedient in giving performance appraisals and conciliatory in negotiation situations may well be recognized as specialized forms of fair self-presentations. Indeed, research has shown that managers *are* concerned about the impressions of fairness they make in such contexts (Greenberg, 1986[6]; Longenecker, Gioia, & Sims, 1987). Certainly, more needs to be known about what forms presentations of fairness may take in various organizational contexts. For now, however, it seems a useful beginning toward understanding the role of fairness in organizations to leave practicing managers with a sense of self-consciousness about the importance placed on looking fair.

REFERENCES

Bies, R. J., & Shapiro, D. L. (1987). Interactional fairness judgments: The influence of causal accounts. *Social Justice Research, 1,* 199-218.

Cohen, R. L. (Ed.). (1986). *Justice: Views from the social sciences.* New York: Plenum.

Folger, R., & Greenberg, J. (1985). Procedural justice: An interpretive analysis of personnel systems. In K. M. Rowland & G. R. Ferris (Eds.), *Research in personnel and human resources management* (Vol. 3, pp. 141-183). Greenwich, CT: JAI.

French, J. R. P., & Raven, B. (1959). The bases of social power. In D. Cartwright (Ed.), *Studies in social power* (pp. 118-149). Ann Arbor: University of Michigan Press.

Greenberg, J. (1979). Protestant ethic endorsement and the fairness of equity inputs. *Journal of Research in Personality, 13,* 81-90.

Greenberg, J. (1983). Self-image vs. impression-management in adherence to distributive justice standards: The influence of self-awareness and self-consciousness. *Journal of Personality and Social Psychology, 44,* 5-19.

Greenberg, J. (1986). Determinants of perceived fairness of performance evaluations. *Journal of Applied Psychology, 71,* 340-342. [Chapter 6, this volume.]

Greenberg, J. (1987). A taxonomy of organizational justice theories. *Academy of Management Review, 12,* 9-22. [Chapter 1, this volume.]

Greenberg, J. (1990). Looking fair vs. being fair: Managing impressions of organizational justice. In B. M. Staw & L. L. Cummings (Eds.), *Research in organizational behavior* (Vol. 12, pp. 111-157). Greenwich, CT: JAI. [Chapter 5, this volume.]

Greenberg, J. (1991). Using explanations to manage impressions of performance appraisal fairness. *Employee Responsibilities and Rights Journal, 4,* 51-60.

Greenberg, J., & Folger, R. (1983). Procedural justice, participation, and the fair process effect in groups and organizations. In P. B. Paulus (Ed.), *Basic group processes* (pp. 235-256). New York: Springer-Verlag.

Longenecker, C. O., Gioia, D. A. & Sims, H. P., Jr. (1987). Behind the mask: The politics of employee appraisal. *Academy of Management Executive, 1,* 183-194.

Mark, M., & Greenberg, J. (1987, January). Evening the score. *Psychology Today,* pp. 44-50.

Packard, V. (1959). *The status seekers.* New York: David McKay.

Tedeschi, J. T., & Melburg, V. (1984). Impression management and influence in the organization. In S. B. Bachrach & E. E. Lawler (Eds.), *Research in the sociology of organizations* (Vol. 3, pp. 31-58). Greenwich, CT: JAI.

Tedeschi, J. T., & Norman, N. (1985). Social power, self-presentation, and the self. In B. R. Schlenker (Ed.), *The self and social life* (pp. 293-322). New York: McGraw-Hill.

Thibaut, J., & Walker, L. (1975). *Procedural justice: A psychological analysis.* Hillsdale, NJ: Lawrence Erlbaum.

5

Looking Fair on the Job

Does It Really Matter?

In conjunction with a training exercise on developing managerial skills, I recently asked a group of managers, "What should your subordinates think about you in order for you to function effectively as a supervisor?" As evidenced by the following sample of responses, one of the most commonly expressed themes centered on the importance of being perceived as fair.

AUTHOR'S NOTE: This chapter was originally published in *Research in Organizational Behavior* (B. M. Staw & L. L. Cummings, Eds.), Vol. 12, pp. 111-157, under the title "Looking Fair vs. Being Fair: Managing Impressions of Organizational Justice." Copyright © 1990 by JAI Press. Reprinted by permission.

To close a sale I have to get both the salesman and the customer to think they're being treated fairly. (Used car sales manager)

Almost anything I decide about office policy can be accepted if the staff thinks I've treated them fairly. (Office manager at an insurance company)

If my crew doesn't think I'm fair, it's all over, I can't get anything done. (Crew chief for a rural electric cooperative)

My teachers and students can think whatever they want about me, so long as they think I'm fair. (Assistant principal of a high school)

Even those who prefer to dismiss these self-reports as unscientific data have to admit that the sentiments expressed reflect a commonly espoused concern about the importance of fairness. Indeed, if news headlines of the late 1980s linking certain political and religious figures to morally unethical behaviors have taught anything, it is that the mere *appearance* of an impropriety may be sufficient to erode a powerful figure's base of support, precipitating a fall from grace. What the managers in my training class seem to be saying is similar: Appearing to be fair helps get the job done.

Although the importance of looking fair on the job was expressed prominently by my managerial sample, the theme of impression management has been given little attention by the prevailing reactive content theories of organizational justice (Greenberg, 1987a[1]), such as equity theory (Adams, 1965) or relative deprivation theory (e.g., Crosby, 1984), which traditionally have focused on the reactions of workers paid more than or less than comparably qualified others (e.g., for reviews, see Greenberg, 1982, 1987a[1]; Mowday, 1987). This is not to say that purely anecdotal evidence provides the only inspiration for studying the appearance of fairness in organizations. On the contrary, a shift has been noted in recent social science theorizing away from intrapsychic theories (such as equity theory) toward more interpersonal approaches—in reports both of social psychological processes (e.g., Tetlock, 1985; Tetlock & Manstead, 1985) and of organizational phenomena (e.g., Chatman, Bell, & Staw, 1986; Gardner & Martinko, 1988; Giacalone & Rosenfeld, 1987, 1990). As theorists (e.g., Bies, 1987b; Reis, 1981) begin to explore justice from an impression management perspective (Schlenker, 1980), it appears that the study of organizational justice is beginning its journey along this tide.

This chapter advances an impression management orientation toward organizational justice. Such an approach is offered in the interest of promoting theoretical pluralism (Feyerabend, 1970)—encouraging the study of organizational justice from more than one point of view. As such, it is intended not to completely supplant more traditional approaches but rather to provide an alternative that accounts for a broader array of organizational justice concerns. Toward this end, this chapter will examine research and theory relevant to three core issues within the impression management literature (Tetlock, 1985; Tetlock & Manstead, 1985). Specifically, this chapter will consider (a) the extent to which fairness is a desired social identity, (b) the possible targets of fair impressions, and (c) the tactics used to achieve a fair identity. Following this, the implications of these analyses for future research and theory development will be considered. Before turning to this, however, I will begin by reviewing some germane background issues.

BACKGROUND: JUSTICE
AS AN IMPRESSION MANAGEMENT ISSUE

To set the stage for the presentation to follow, three background issues will be discussed. First, I will review the intrapsychic tradition of studying organizational justice and point out some of its limitations. Then, I will outline the alternatives offered by an impression management approach. Last, earlier conceptualizations of justice showing an appreciation for impression management processes will be reviewed.

The Intrapsychic Tradition
of Equity Theory and Its Limitations

According to my taxonomy of organizational justice theories (Greenberg, 1987a[1]), the predominant approach to studying justice in organizations has been Adams's (1965) equity theory. Rooted in the tradition of psychological balance theories (e.g., Festinger, 1957; Heider, 1958), equity theory offers an intrapsychic explanation of behavior that focuses on the cognitive and motivational processes of the individual. Specifically, the theory proposes that workers will experience a state of inequity whenever they perceive that the ratios of their own job rewards (*outcomes*) to job contributions (*inputs*) are unequal to the corresponding ratios of some comparison others. The person favored by any imbalance is expected to feel guilty from the resulting "overpayment inequity," whereas the under-benefited worker is expected to feel angry from the resulting "underpayment inequity." These negative states are theorized to cause tension, motivating attempts to restore a more desirable, balanced condition: equity (Walster, Walster, & Berscheid, 1978). Such efforts may be behavioral (such as by raising or lowering one's work contributions; e.g., Pritchard, Dunnette, & Jorgenson, 1972) and/or psychological (such as by reassessing the perceived value of one's work outcomes; e.g., Greenberg, 1989[16])—both of which have been studied in organizations (for reviews, see Greenberg, 1982; Mowday, 1987).

The research inspired by equity theory has left a formidable legacy in the archives of organizational behavior (e.g., see Adams & Freedman, 1976; Greenberg, 1982). Since then, however, interest in equity theory has waned (Greenberg, 1987a[1]; Reis, 1986), with one observer relegating it to the ranks of the "not so useful" theories of organizational behavior (Miner, 1984). One likely reason for equity theory's decline in popularity may be the acceptance of accumulated criticisms regarding its internal validity (e.g., Furby, 1986; Greenberg, 1984; Schwab, 1980). For example, the theory has been criticized on the grounds that (a) the conceptual status of many job elements as outcomes or inputs (e.g., decision-making power and status) is ambiguous (e.g., Goodman & Friedman, 1971; Tornow, 1971); (b) the experimental procedures commonly used to manipulate states of inequity are confounded and subject to alternative explanations (e.g., Pritchard, 1969); (c) the hypothesized mediational role of the affective state, *inequity distress,* is unsupported (e.g., Greenberg, 1984); and (d) the interrelationship between modes of inequity resolution is conceptually ambiguous (e.g., Adams & Freedman, 1976; Greenberg, 1989). Such criticisms have resulted in some proposed structural reformulations of equity theory (e.g., Cosier & Dalton, 1983; Harris, 1976) and the introduction of derivative approaches (e.g., Berger, Zelditch, Anderson, & Cohen, 1972; Folger, 1986).

A more frequently expressed reason for disenchantment with equity theory (e.g., Bies, 1987b; Greenberg, 1987a[1])—and one more relevant to this chapter—is its limited capacity to explain the broad array of factors that define justice as a concern in organizations (Folger & Greenberg, 1985; Greenberg, 1987a[1]). One particular criticism is that equity theory fails to consider how perceptions of justice are influenced by the procedures through which outcomes are determined (Leventhal, 1980). This limitation has resulted in many attempts to broaden the domain of organizational justice (Greenberg, 1987a[1]) to include *procedural justice* variables focusing on *how* outcomes are determined (for reviews, see Folger & Greenberg, 1985; Greenberg & Tyler, 1987; Lind & Tyler, 1988). For example, research has shown that the procedures used to appraise employees (Greenberg, 1986a[6], 1986c[8], 1987b[9]), supervise them (Sheppard & Lewicki, 1987), and resolve conflicts between them (Sheppard, 1984, 1985) are at least as important as determinants of perceived fairness and job satisfaction as the outcomes resulting from these procedures (see also Alexander & Ruderman, 1987).

Equity theory also has been cited for ignoring the social contexts in which assessments of fairness are made. For example, although research derived from equity theory has focused on reactions to payment inequities (Greenberg, 1982) and on allocations of organizational resources (Freedman & Montanari, 1980), more recent research has revealed that people think of fairness as behaviors that go far beyond these limited responses and focus on interpersonal considerations, such as the things people say to one another (Messick, Bloom, Boldizar, & Samuelson, 1985). In this regard, Bies (1987b) has characterized people making fairness judgments as "intuitive jurists" (Fincham & Jaspars, 1980; Hamilton, 1980), seeking to understand *why* certain events occurred, instead of dispassionate, "intuitive scientists" (Kelley, 1967), or "intuitive accountants" (Bies, 1987b), analytically balancing their mental ledgers of outcomes and inputs. This approach is used to introduce the notion of *interactional justice*—the fairness of the interpersonal treatment people receive (Bies & Moag, 1986)—as the basis for studying the role of information presentation of perceived justice. To date, research inspired by the interactional justice approach has found that the explanations given for why outcome decisions are reached may influence workers' reactions to the perceived fairness of layoffs (Brockner & Greenberg, 1989), hiring decisions (Bies, 1986b; Shapiro & Buttner, 1988), performance ratings (Greenberg, 1988b), and the acceptance or rejection of proposals (Bies & Shapiro, 1987, 1988; Bies, Shapiro, & Cummings, 1988).

It may be concluded from this brief review that although equity theory, with its emphasis on intrapsychic processes, has fallen into disfavor among organizational scholars, interest in the topic of organizational justice remains very much alive and has seen a resurgence, stimulated largely by the social context-sensitive procedural and interactional approaches (for a review, see Greenberg, 1987a[1]). This chapter proposes a thematic focus to the study of organizational justice on the basis of the concept of impression management.

An Impression Management Alternative

Schlenker (1980) has defined impression management as "the conscious or unconscious attempt to control images that are projected in real or imagined social interactions" (p. 6). This chapter argues that workers are concerned about projecting an image of themselves as fair and that they engage in many tactics to do so. In so doing, I will present impression management as an explanatory concept that helps integrate disparate issues and approaches to organizational justice while at the same time broadening the core knowledge of research on impression management (Tetlock & Manstead, 1985).

The idea that people say and do things to create desired identities in the eyes of others has a rich tradition in the social sciences (e.g., Cooley, 1902; James, 1890; see also the historical review by Scheibe, 1985). The theme of impression management has evolved in contemporary times from the observational research of the sociologist (e.g., Austin, 1961; Goffman, 1959) to the laboratory of the experimental social psychologist (Schlenker, 1980; Tedeschi, 1981), and more recently to the field studies of the organizational psychologist (Gardner & Martinko, 1988; Giacalone & Rosenfeld, 1987). Basic to the impression management approach is Tetlock's idea that people operate as "intuitive politicians" (Bell & Tetlock, 1989; Tetlock, 1985; Tetlock & Manstead, 1985) who seek to convince themselves and others that they possess desired characteristics. As Moberg (1977) put it, "Politicians must avoid having their behavior attributed by others to a particular intent (illegitimate or self-serving motives). They may do so first by 'creating the impression' that they have legitimate motives" (p. 1). Such political astuteness may be keenly important in organizations. Indeed, the importance of cultivating a proper image has been associated with organizational phenomena as widespread as leadership (Tedeschi & Melburg, 1984), performance appraisal (Longenecker, Sims, & Gioia, 1987), goal setting (Huber, Latham, & Locke, 1989), and career development (Chatman et al., 1986). With the present work, the field of organizational justice may be added to those in which an impression management perspective has been introduced.

The impression management approach to organizational justice explicitly recognizes that fairness is in the eye of the beholder. In hierarchical organizations, the different interests, goals, and access to information of individuals at different levels are likely to lead to different beliefs about what constitutes fair procedures and outcomes (Greenberg, 1987a[1]). Accordingly, a manager who does what he or she believes to be fair—whatever that may be—may learn that others are not necessarily likewise convinced. To some extent, organizational justice may require impressing others with one's fairness. If different organizational perspectives offer different views of morally, ethically, and socially appropriate behaviors (Cavanagh, Moberg, & Velasquez, 1981), it may be in the best interest of effective management to be sensitive to others' perspectives on fairness. As I noted elsewhere, "even the best-intentioned, most 'fair-minded' manager may fail to win the approval of subordinates who are not convinced of his or her fairness" (Greenberg, 1988a[4], p. 155). Thus, the impression management view of organizational justice conceives of fairness as a label for a set of attributions regarding adherence to appropriate standards of conduct that enhances one's self-image and/or one's projected social image. How these images operate and their value as a managerial tool will be discussed in this chapter.

Earlier Applications of Impression Management to Justice

Impression management interpretations of justice behavior are not completely new (e.g., see Bies, 1987b; Reis, 1981). The theme of impression management has been introduced indirectly to the justice literature on several earlier occasions—once as an alternative interpretation of equity theory findings and once as the result of a movement to study justice as a normative value.

The self-esteem challenge to equity theory. Ironically, although not always characterized as such, some of the earliest and most persistent critiques of equity theory research were predicated on an impression management interpretation. Specifically, the prototypical early experimental tests of equity theory (e.g., Adams & Rosenbaum, 1962) manipulated overpayment by leading subjects to believe that they were unqualified for the job they were about to do but that they would be hired anyway and paid at the advertised rate (which, of course, was inappropriately high). This manipulation has been criticized on the grounds that it may have threatened workers' self-esteem (Lawler, 1968; Pritchard, 1969). Accordingly, the possibility cannot be ruled out that the high levels of performance that followed this manipulation were the result of workers' attempts to dem-onstrate to themselves and their employers that they were actually quite capable despite their apparent underqualifications. In other words, participants' reactions to the inequity may have been caused by attempts to manage impressions of themselves (to both themselves and their superiors), rather than attempts to minimize distress resulting from the inequity.

Support for the self-esteem explanation is provided in a role-playing investigation by Andrews and Valenzi (1970). Participants in this study were asked to report how they would feel if they were involved in a qualifications-challenging situation such as that in the Adams and Rosenbaum study. Although none of the participants expressed awareness of a wage inequity, approximately 44% noted that their self-esteem would be threatened. Although further debate on the construct validity of inequity manipulations has continued (for reviews, see Greenberg, 1982; Schwab, 1980), the self-esteem criticism was an important one. It represents the earliest efforts to propose an impression management explanation for what was initially theorized as an intrapsychic process.

Normative and instrumental "uses" of justice. An analogous appreciation for impression management influences on justice behavior followed in the 1970s as theorists began to conceive of justice as a social norm. Spearheading this movement, Sampson (1975) argued that "by nature, man is not an equity theorist" (p. 49). Specifically, eschewing the intrapsychic perspective, he contended that "equity is not as much a psychological law about human nature as it is a psychological outcome of the culture's economic socialization practices" (p. 58). This theorizing ushered in the beginning of a series of conceptualizations about *justice norms* guiding the allocation of resources—social rules specifying "criteria that define certain distributions of rewards and resources as fair and just" (Leventhal, 1976, p. 94). Initially, to the norm of equity, Sampson (1975) added a second justice norm: equality. Later theorists added a third norm: need (Deutsch, 1975; Leventhal, 1976), and the list of justice norms proliferated to 6 (Lerner, 1977), 9 (Lerner, 1980), and 17 (Reis, 1984, 1986).

Such efforts were, in part, directed toward answering the question "Which norm, when?" Such research has shown that the selection of a justice norm often depends on the goal of the allocator (for a review, see Greenberg & Cohen, 1982). At the risk of oversimplifying the conclusions of this research, I characterize the findings as this: A preference for *equitable* allocations (to each according to merits) predominates when an allocator's goal is to foster economic productivity, *equal* allocations (to each the same) are made when the preservation of harmony is the desired goal, and *need*-based allocations (to each according to legitimate need) result when the allocator's goal is to foster personal welfare and development (see Deutsch, 1975, 1985; Leventhal, 1976). This sphere of investigation helps underscore the point that prevailing social rules help define actions made in the name of justice.

Implicit within the normative approach to justice is the idea that adherence to normative standards is dictated by prevailing social forces. The person who follows a normative prescription may be motivated reactively, out of recognition of the pressures to conform to justice norms (Allen, 1982). It also has been postulated that such behavior is motivated proactively, by the belief that behaving in a certain manner provides a path toward attaining other goals. Writing on this topic, a colleague and I (Greenberg & Cohen, 1982) have argued that many acts performed in the name of fairness actually may be motivated by the desire to attain other goals—what we called *instrumental* acts.

Parallel to prosocial behaviors, which are not necessarily motivated by an underlying concern for altruism (Schwartz, 1977), ostensibly fair behaviors may not necessarily be motivated by an ultimate concern for justice. Justice may be a penultimate state on the way to an ultimate goal (Greenberg, 1986b[7]). Leventhal (1976) articulated this point clearly when he asserted that

> it is likely that an allocator who distributes rewards equitably does so more because he desires to maximize long-term productivity than because he desires to comply with an abstract standard of justice. His decisions are based on an expectancy that equitable distributions of reward will elicit and sustain high levels of motivation and performance. (p. 96)

As such, Leventhal (1980) distinguishes between acts motivated out of a concern for justice per se, "fair behavior," and those derived from other motives, "quasi-fair behavior." The possibility that the justice-restoring effects of an action may be epiphenomenal, motivated apart from moral or ethical considerations, is basic to the argument that people may internalize expectations about the effects of behaving fairly and do so to meet these expectations. In other words, justice may be "used" as the mechanism for attaining other goals. Although it is difficult to prove the existence of a specific motive underlying behavior, evidence suggests that people sometimes engage in ostensibly fair actions for expressed reasons that do not reflect any concern for fairness at all. For example, I found that equitable divisions of reward were made by persons claiming to be trying to maximize their own gain or the gain of others (Greenberg, 1978). Thus, people may be implicitly aware that their adherence to a justice norm may reflect "an attempt to gain the unique pattern of instrumental benefits that is associated with following that norm" (Leventhal, 1976, p. 95).

The underlying point is that many acts are performed behind a veneer of justice. If so, then one may ask how norms of justice are sustained. It may be argued that justice norms remain intact *because* of their instrumental value. Norms of justice facilitate social system goals (Greenberg & Cohen, 1982). Justice norms may be used to promote the social welfare of individuals and society by providing an orderly way for resources to be distributed. As noted, "justice works" (p. 457); norms create explanations that guide behaviors in directions that are reinforced by society. Moreover, justice is socially rewarding; people are rewarded for treating others fairly (Walster et al., 1978). Indeed, research has shown that people often closely adhere to justice standards whenever they believe that others can reward them socially for doing so (e.g., Morse, Gruzen, & Reis, 1976;

Reis & Gruzen, 1976; Rivera & Tedeschi, 1976). Such conformity to justice norms not only is individually rewarding (Allen, 1982) but also facilitates social interaction in general by making interaction more predictable (Thibaut & Kelley, 1959). Given this background, the stage is now set for analyzing the role of justice in some of the core questions of the impression management literature.

FAIRNESS AS A DESIRED SOCIAL IDENTITY

Probably the most basic core question asked among impression management theorists is what types of identities people seek (Tetlock, 1985; Tetlock & Manstead, 1985). Although it may be tempting to answer this question by positing that people seek socially desirable identities, such a response fails to consider the broad cultural and historical differences that may exist in definitions of desirability (Schlenker, 1980). Moreover, it is overly simplistic in that people sometimes seek identities that are not positive. Even identities emphasizing toughness, dangerousness, helplessness, weakness, and dependency, Jones and Pittman (1982) claim, may be effective as means of gaining social approval and power.

There can be little doubt that the characteristic of fairness is recognized as desirable. Probably the most basic evidence in support of this idea is provided by Anderson's (1968) study in which students rated 555 personality traits on scales ranging from 0 (*least favorable or desirable*) to 6 (*most favorable or desirable*). Although the trait "fair" was not among those rated, Anderson found that related traits received high ratings of favorability (e.g., "honest," $M = 5.55$; "honorable," $M = 5.07$; "ethical," $M = 4.76$). In addition, the trait "unfair" was rated as extremely undesirable ($M = 1.07$). Such evidence clearly reflects the abstract positive connotations of fairness and the negative connotations of unfairness as personal characteristics.

Beyond such abstractions, a case can be made for fairness as a social identity. As Reis (1981) has noted, the desire to be seen as virtuous and fair is implicit within Jones and Pittman's (1982) class of self-presentational strategies known as *exemplification*. An exemplifier is one who "seeks to project integrity and moral worthiness" (p. 245). Because of the conceptual overlap between fairness and exemplification as identities, it has been claimed that perceiving oneself as an exemplifier may be understood as an attempt to project an image of fairness (Reis, 1981).

More direct evidence of a widespread motive to shape dispositional beliefs about fairness is provided by survey research highlighting the central position of fairness as a work value. For example, recent survey research has shown that a concern about fairness on the job is one of the most prevalent life values noted among a wide variety of workers (e.g., Cornelius, Ullman, Meglino, Czajka, & McNeely, 1985; Ravlin & Meglino, 1987). Although other investigations reveal individual differences in the specific structure of fairness values (e.g., Rasinski, 1987), it appears safe to claim that fairness is a desired value. Identities that are valued on the job may well be those that stimulate the greatest efforts to be attained.

Other evidence that fairness is a social identity comes from the finding that people perceive themselves as fairer than others. In six studies conducted in the United States and the Netherlands, Messick and his associates (Liebrand, Messick, & Wolters, 1986; Messick et al., 1985) found that participants reported behaviors thought to be fair as more characteristic of themselves than of others, believing that they more often did fair things and less often did unfair things. Given the general tendency for people to attribute desirable characteristics to themselves (Miller & Ross, 1975), such self-serving perceptions of one's own fairness may be taken as evidence of the social desirability of fair identities.

The most direct evidence of fairness as a desired identity in organizations is provided by my survey of 815 managers (Greenberg, 1988a[4]). Participants were asked two sets of questions: one set inquiring how concerned they were about *actually being fair* on the job and another set asking how concerned they were about *appearing to be fair* on the job. Managers expressed greater concern about appearing fair than actually being fair. Moreover, the two sets of questions were not significantly correlated with each other, suggesting that managers distinguished between looking fair and being fair.

These findings provide a useful adjunct to this chapter by directly revealing that the desire to cultivate an impression of fairness is of great concern to managers. The findings also suggest that this concern operates at the level of conscious awareness. This is not to say, however, that such self-consciousness is a necessary precondition for fair impression management to occur (Schlenker, 1980; Tetlock & Manstead, 1985). Indeed, theorists have contended that impression management efforts may be the result of well-learned scripts (Jones & Pittman, 1982; Schlenker, 1980) and that ostensible reactions to inequities may be the result of enacting such scripts (Greenberg, 1984). Furthermore, it may be argued that questionnaire responses regarding the importance of fairness may themselves represent attempts by participants to present themselves favorably to an authority figure (Alexander & Rudd, 1981). Notwithstanding these limitations, it appears safe to assume that the attribution of fairness is a desired individual identity in organizational settings.

TARGETS OF FAIR IDENTITIES

Accepting that fairness is a desired social identity, I continue my analysis by asking, "To whom are identities of fairness presented?" At the risk of oversimplification, I may answer as follows: oneself and others. Although external audiences (such as bosses, teachers, and judges) are usually emphasized in the study of impression management (e.g., Baumeister, 1982; Jones & Pittman, 1982), there is also widespread acceptance of the idea that people seek to cultivate certain impressions of themselves for themselves (e.g., Greenwald & Breckler, 1985; Schlenker, 1986). As I will review here, the justice literature has recognized the importance of both internal and external targets of an image of fairness.

In keeping with the distinction that justice norms may be either normative or instrumental (Greenberg & Cohen, 1982), Tetlock (1985) has drawn a parallel distinction between impression management efforts that are *principled* (i.e., intended to satisfy internalized standards) and those that are *pragmatic* (i.e., concerned with establishing good relationships with others). Many of the same situational variables (e.g., degree of public scrutiny) and dispositional variables (e.g., self-consciousness) identified as mediating the choice of principled versus pragmatic goals (Greenwald & Breckler, 1985; Tetlock, 1985) also have been identified as moderators of both reactions to inequity and the choice of a justice standard (Reis, 1981).

Others as Targets: Pragmatic Identities

One such situational variable concerns the public scrutiny of one's behavior. A commonly used experimental technique to distinguish intrapsychic explanations from impression management explanations of behavior involves manipulating the degree to which participants believe their behavior is under public scrutiny (Tetlock & Manstead, 1985). The underlying rationale is that behaviors designed to impress others occur only when people believe that others can observe their behavior.

Several studies of reactions to inequity have relied on this manipulation (for a review, see Reis, 1981). For example, Rivera and Tedeschi (1976) compared participants' reactions to overpayment inequity using a simple paper-and-pencil measure and an elaborate lie detector (the "bogus pipeline"; Jones & Sigall, 1971). Overpaid participants reported feeling more guilt than equitably paid participants when they believed their true feelings could not be detected (in the paper-and-pencil condition) than when the lie detector encouraged them to express their true feelings. Had the overpayment inequity induction actually led to feelings of guilt, there would have been no reason to suspect that differences in the face validity of the instrument used to measure such guilt would have made any difference. Yet because the socially desirable guilt response (one *should* feel guilty for being overpaid) was more prevalent when participants believed they could misrepresent their true feelings with impunity, it appears that the reactions expressed may be more the result of the desire to appear socially acceptable to the experimenter than the desire to express their true feelings. Such findings have been taken as support for the idea that responses to equitable treatment may be based on people's impression management concerns, "contrary to the postulated intra-psychic processes that have been proposed as mediating post-allocation responses" (Rivera & Tedeschi, 1976, p. 899).

A similar tendency for verbal reactions to overpayment to reflect impression management interests has been found by Morse et al. (1976). Participants in this experiment justified overpayment conditions by exaggerating claims of task difficulty to a greater degree when they expected their self-reports to be shared with the experimenter than when they expected them to remain anonymous. Several additional studies (reviewed by Reis, 1981) likewise show that publicly visible reactions to overpayment take the socially desirable form of ostensibly demonstrating dissatisfaction with overpayment more than responses made in private.

Analogous evidence using the public-private distinction is found in the literature on the allocation of reward. By comparing the responses of participants made publicly and privately, this literature has repeatedly found that "subjects incorporate the perceived standards of significant others who are aware of their behavior" (Reis, 1981, p. 276). For example, Lane and Messé (1971) found that dyad members who expected to be introduced to each other were less likely to take advantage of each other by taking self-interested shares of reward than those who were not identified. Related research has found that allocators attempt to present themselves favorably to recipients by dividing reward equally among them (Leventhal, Michaels, & Sanford, 1972), especially when they expect recipients to be aware of their decisions (Reis & Gruzen, 1976). Expecting to meet the recipient of an allocation decision also leads people to favor equal allocations, even when an equity-based allocation may be justified by their higher inputs (Austin & McGinn, 1977; Shapiro, 1975). Equal divisions of reward also tend to be made whenever allocators expected to be evaluated by another whose impressions are valued, such as one's spouse (Schoeninger & Wood, 1969), coworkers (Friedman & Goodman, 1974), or friends (Austin, 1980). Presumably, making a more self-serving response would be antagonistic to an interest in making a favorable self-presentation. In summary, studies of reward allocation behaviors suggest that equal divisions of reward are made in the interest of promoting favorable impressions of oneself.

It is important to point out that such favorable impressions may not necessarily be impressions of fairness. By not taking advantage of others and not wishing to confront those they have harmed, participants are at least demonstrating an interest in avoiding conflicts likely to arise from discriminatory behavior (Deutsch, 1975; Leventhal, 1976). That they are trying to impress others with their fairness is less apparent. For this to be the case, participants would have had to internalize the normative appropriateness of equal allocations. To the extent that their behaviors may have been motivated by an interest in avoiding conflict, their impression management interests, although considerable, may have focused on identities other than fairness. Accepting the inherent ambiguities regarding exactly what behaviors may be fair in any situation (e.g., Reis, 1986), however, one may posit that participants in these studies may just be seeking to minimize their costs in the experimental situation, to "get out of it" as inexpensively as possible. Given the low value of the stakes involved, it is not surprising to find experimental participants willing to forgo financial reward in favor of social reward—especially when they can do so by following a justice norm, such as equality (Greenberg, 1978).

Despite this caveat, evidence exists that certain justice behaviors may be the result of specific attempts to cultivate impressions of fairness. Rather than dealing with the impressions created in the minds of others, the investigations examining explicit attempts at cultivating impressions of fairness have focused on the self as a target of fair impressions.

Oneself as Target: Principled Identities

Experimental research making the self salient as a target of impression management typically follows the practice of making participants "objectively self-aware" (Duval & Wicklund, 1972; Wicklund, 1975) by having them confront their reflections in a mirror. According to the theory of objective self-awareness, the self-focused attention created by this manipulation heightens self-critical judgments. People become more aware of the discrepancies between their own behavior and ideal standards, thereby making them more sensitive to normative values (Vallacher & Solodky, 1979).

Evidence that self-awareness moderates reactions to inequity has been found by Reis and Burns (1982). These investigators found that overpaid participants were more productive when they performed a task in the presence of a mirror than in the absence of a mirror. Related findings were also obtained by Gibbons and Wicklund (1982, Experiment 4). Given that equity theory predicts increased outputs in response to overpayment inequity, the higher level of inputs following overpayment by self-aware participants than by not self-aware participants suggests that reactions to overpayment inequity are heightened by states of self-awareness. Being self-aware heightened participants' sensitivity to the state of inequity they experienced. Although these findings show that self-awareness increases responsiveness to states of inequity, they do not reveal anything about participants' proactive concerns about adhering to justice standards.

Such a connection has been established, however, in several studies investigating the role of self-awareness on adherence to justice standards. In one study (Greenberg, 1980), participants who were made self-aware while dividing earned rewards between themselves and a competitor showed greater concern for making equitable allocations (i.e., divisions proportional to inputs) than participants who were not self-aware. The mirror-induced self-awareness led higher-input participants to keep more reward for themselves and lower-input participants to keep less reward for themselves than that kept by those not self-aware. Moreover, self-aware participants expressed greater concern about having made the appropriate allocation response than those who were not self-aware. In another study (Greenberg, 1983a), participants rated making fair payments as more important when they were self-aware than when they were not self-aware. Self-aware participants in this study were more prone than those who were not self-aware to reject as unfair all inequitable allocation decisions, even those that benefited themselves.

Thus far, it has been established that states of self-awareness enhance adherence to personal standards of justice. The previous section of this chapter reported that people are also concerned with creating a favorable impression on others. As a result, it is possible that the two interests may conflict. Indeed, the inherent ambiguity associated with the fairness of any given response may make different reward allocation norms (e.g., equity, equality, and need; Deutsch, 1975) justifiable as normatively appropriate (Leventhal, 1976). As a result, a potentially fair response may not necessarily be one that is best accepted. For example, although conditions may be such that the prevailing standard of justice is the equity norm (such as when competitive, profit-oriented conditions exist; Deutsch, 1975), it cannot be assumed that the most favorable impressions may be created by adhering to this norm. This is the case when a reward allocator expects to have future interaction with a poor-performing corecipient. Impressing such individuals, research has shown (Austin & McGinn, 1977; Reis & Gruzen, 1976; Shapiro, 1975), dictates the use of equal allocations—responses that promote interpersonal harmony (Leventhal et al., 1972). As a result, the normative behaviors required to satisfy one's internal standards of justice may be inconsistent with those needed to cultivate a favorable self-image. The resolution of such conflicts appears to be based on the relative strength of the various forces.

To test this notion I (Greenberg, 1983b, Experiment 1) studied how participants respond to such conflicts by manipulating self-awareness (mirror presence or absence) in conjunction with impression management concerns (expectation of meeting a lower-input person). In keeping with my earlier study (Greenberg, 1980), participants who were self-aware tended to make equitable allocations and to report that behaving fairly was more important to them than those who were not self-aware. Also as predicted, those who expected to meet their low-input competitors tended to make equal allocations (Shapiro, 1975). When self-aware participants expected to meet their low-input competitors, however, a conflict occurred between making a favorable impression on oneself (by allocating the reward equitably—that is, in proportion to relative contributions) and on the other person (by allocating the reward equally). Participants tended to resolve this conflict by favoring either one norm or the other; they were almost equally divided in their preference for equity and equality, making few compromise solutions. Apparently, participants were divided as to the relative strength of their impression management targets. Some adhered to self-standards by allocating rewards equitably; others presented themselves favorably to recipients by allocating rewards equally.

The possibility of an individual difference variable moderating the choice of competing allocation rules is suggested by the attention given to the distinction between public and private self-consciousness in the impression management literature (e.g., Greenwald & Breckler, 1985; Tetlock & Manstead, 1985). The self-consciousness scale developed by Fenigstein, Scheier, and Buss (1975) distinguishes between public self-consciousness—a concern for oneself as a social object (high scorers are concerned about the impressions they make on others), and private self-consciousness—awareness of the covert, personal aspects of oneself (high scorers are attuned to their internal standards; for a review, see Carver & Scheier, 1981).

Reasoning that differences in public versus private self-consciousness may have moderate reactions to the self-image versus impression management conflict in Experiment 1, I conducted a follow-up study (Greenberg, 1983b, Experiment 2). This investigation re-created the conflict conditions for participants who were highly public self-conscious (scored high on public self-consciousness and low on private self-consciousness) and those who were highly private self-conscious (scored high on private self-consciousness and low on public self-consciousness). I reasoned that persons in these extreme groups would resolve the conflict between internal standards of justice and the pressure to present oneself favorably to others in ways commensurate with their predispositions. As expected, participants followed the equity norm most closely when they were made highly self-aware (by the presence of a mirror) *and* were dispositionally predisposed to follow their internal standards (the highly private self-conscious group). Analogously, the strongest adherence to the equality norm occurred when highly public self-conscious participants were not made self-aware. Participants in this condition expressed less concern about doing what seemed fair to themselves than participants in any of the other conditions. Accordingly, it appears that concerns for fairness and adherence to justice norms are influenced by *both* personal and situational factors operating additively to dictate the salience of justice norms.

These findings have been conceptually replicated in a study obtaining opposite behavioral results. Creating a situation in which equality was normatively appropriate instead of equity (joint cooperation was emphasized; Deutsch, 1975), Kernis and Reis (1984) had participants allocate rewards after performing a task on which they were led to believe they were more productive. They found that the equality norm was followed by participants who were highly private self-conscious but that the equity norm was followed by participants who were highly public self-conscious. Although these findings are behaviorally opposite mine (Greenberg, 1983b, Experiment 2), they are conceptually identical.

The reason involves manipulations used in the two studies dictating the appropriateness of different norms of justice to fulfill internal and external standards. Specifically, to make salient internal standards, I used a competitive context that made the equity norm appropriate (Greenberg, 1983b), whereas Kernis and Reis (1984) used a cooperative context that made the equality norm appropriate. (For a discussion of the situational factors dictating the appropriateness of various justice norms, see Deutsch, 1975; Greenberg & Cohen, 1982; Lerner, 1977; Leventhal, 1976.) Furthermore, to make salient external standards, I led participants to believe that they would get to meet a low-input corecipient (Greenberg, 1983b), thereby encouraging the use of equal allocations to avoid conflict and cultivate that person's favor (Reis & Gruzen, 1976; Shapiro, 1975). By contrast, Kernis and Reis (1984) explicitly encouraged participants to consider each person's relative contributions when allocating the money between them, that is, equity was encouraged to please the experimenter. Despite these different sets of internal and external standards, both studies yielded conceptually identical patterns of results. To wit, both studies show that private self-consciousness enhanced adherence to internal standards and that public self-consciousness enhanced adherence to external standards.

Although these findings were obtained in two separate studies in which situational factors defined different justice standards as normatively appropriate, they provide the type of experimental convergence that enhances confidence in the underlying theoretical interpretation. (For further discussion, see also Carver & Scheier, 1985.)

To summarize, the research reviewed here makes a clear case for the importance of the self as a target of identities of fairness. People like to think of themselves as fair, particularly those who are predisposed to think about their personal standards and/or when discrepancies from those standards are made salient situationally. Taking these findings together with the evidence showing people's sensitivity toward impressing others with fairness, I may safely conclude that concerns about fair impression management are directed both inward, toward one's self-image, and outward, toward one's social image.

TACTICS OF PROMOTING FAIR IDENTITIES

On the basis that people are interested in impressing both themselves and others with their fairness, a question arises as to how they go about creating such impressions. Although "almost all behaviors and appearances potentially convey information about the self and may be used as a self-presentational strategy" (Schneider, 1981, p. 26), theorists have concentrated on studying the influence of verbal claims about the self. Particularly in organizations, language is recognized as the tool through which managers explain and rationalize their actions (Pfeffer, 1981) and has been studied as such (e.g., Gardner & Martinko, 1988). The potential influence of statements about oneself has been noted explicitly by Schlenker (1980) in his treatise on impression management: "Through public descriptions of the traits they possess, the things they are accountable for, and the ways they view the world, people can secure identities that maximize the public esteem in which they are held and the outcomes they receive" (p. 91). Similarly, survey research on the tactics of organizational politics has noted that managerial personnel explicitly identify things said to cultivate and maintain a favorable image in organizations— such as sensitivity to organizational norms—as a popular tactic of gaining organizational influence (Allen, Madison, Porter, Renwick, & Mayes, 1979). Apparently, people seek to "explain themselves" to others by presenting themselves in ways that create, promote, and maintain desired social identities (Tedeschi & Reiss, 1981b).

This is known as *self-presentation,* "a set of behaviors designed by an actor to establish particular identities in the eyes of various audiences"

(Tedeschi & Norman, 1985, p. 293). Following Tedeschi's lead (e.g., Tedeschi & Melburg, 1984; Tedeschi & Norman, 1985), this chapter's discussion of impression management tactics will distinguish between self-presentations that are *defensive* (i.e., designed to mend a spoiled identity) and *assertive* (i.e., initiated to establish a particular identity). The next two sections will discuss the defensive and assertive tactics used to manage impressions of fairness.

Defensive Tactics:
Identity-Threatening Predicaments

Theorists have conceived social situations as involving challenges to people's self-images, raising questions about the legitimacy of one's claim to an image. For example, as Schlenker (1980) put it, "Life is a constant series of tests in which we are called on to substantiate our claims through personal performance or some other means" (p. 99). When an event occurs that casts unwanted aspersions on someone's character, that person is said to be in a *predicament*. Specifically, Schlenker has defined predicaments as "situations in which events have undesirable implications for the identity-relevant images actors have claimed or desire to claim in front of real or imagined audiences" (p. 125). In keeping with the work of Bies (1987b), situations in which an injustice is perceived to have occurred may be characterized as "predicaments of injustice" for those associated with it. The severity of a predicament depends not only on the undesirability of the event but also on the actor's responsibility for the event (Bell & Tetlock, 1989; Tetlock, 1985). Schlenker expressed this clearly when he characterized responsibility as "the adhesive that links an actor to an event and attaches appropriate sanctions to the actor that deserves it" (p. 126). Given this, it is not surprising that the major tactics for extricating oneself from social predicaments are attributional in nature (Snyder, 1985).

Building on the pioneering sociological work of Austin (1961) and Scott and Lyman (1968), Schlenker (1980) identified two broad classes of remedial tactics used to reduce the negative repercussions of a predicament: *accounts* and *apologies*. Although Tedeschi and his associates (e.g., Tedeschi & Melburg, 1984; Tedeschi & Norman, 1985; Tedeschi & Reiss, 1981b) have expanded this list, accounts and apologies remain the most commonly researched tactics for defending against social predicaments. Accordingly, I will now consider how accounts and apologies may be used to help minimize threats to one's self-identity as a fair person.

Accounts. Accounts are explanations designed to remove an actor from a predicament. They provide information about an event that either lessens one's responsibility for it and/or lessens the apparent severity of the consequences (Schlenker, 1980; Tedeschi & Reiss, 1981a). Two types of accounts have been identified: excuses and justifications. An excuse allows actors to deny or minimize responsibility for a predicament; a justification attempts to reduce the negative consequences of a predicament (Austin, 1961; Scott & Lyman, 1968).

More precisely, excuses are "explanations in which individual acknowledge that their conduct was somehow bad, wrong, or inappropriate, but attempted to minimize their personal responsibility or culpability for it" (Tetlock, 1985, p. 215). Several theorists (e.g., Fincham & Jaspars, 1980; Snyder, 1985; Snyder, Higgins, & Stucky, 1983) have claimed that excuses will lessen one's apparent responsibility for an event if it can be demonstrated that the causes of the event were external and/or unintentional. Both internality and intentionality have been studied as general attributional categories (e.g., Weiner, 1974), and they have been shown to influence justice behavior (Greenberg, 1984; Kidd & Utne, 1978; Utne & Kidd, 1980).

Explanations suggesting that an actor's behavior was not volitional but the result of externally imposed demands (e.g., "my hands were tied by economic pressures") tend to minimize one's perceived responsibility for the effects of that behavior (Heider, 1958). Moreover, events believed to be externally caused (such as competitive events won as a result of luck as opposed to skill) tend *not* to be rewarded in a manner that credits people differentially for their inputs—that is, equitably (Cohen, 1974; Greenberg, 1980; Wittig, Marks, & Jones, 1981). Furthermore, reward distributions following from externally caused outcomes are perceived to be less fair than those resulting from conditions in which people are responsible for having caused their outcomes (Greenberg, 1980). Similarly, research has found that people are more responsive to inequities that others have intentionally created than those that are unintentional (e.g., Greenberg & Frisch, 1972; Leventhal, Weiss, & Long, 1969). For example, participants are more likely to reallocate rewards to redress overpayment or underpayment inequities if these were believed to be intentionally rather than unintentionally created (Garrett & Libby, 1973). Taken together, these findings suggest that attributions of internal and intentional causality heighten people's sensitivity to injustices.

In keeping with this, a stream of research by Bies and his associates has examined the influence of claims of mitigating circumstances on feelings of injustice (for a review, see Bies, 1987b). A mitigating circumstance lessens one's responsibility for an event, often by imposing explanations of external and unintentional causality (Weiner, 1974), thereby excusing an actor for any resulting injustice. Research by Bies et al. (1988) content analyzed the retrospective accounts workers gave of their bosses' reasons for denying their requests, revealing six types of mitigating circumstances. The most frequently cited mitigating circumstance was the worker's own behavior (e.g., incompetence), followed by claims of budgetary constraints, controls imposed by higher levels of management, limitations of a political nature, restrictions due to formal company policy, and inconsistencies with company norms. The mitigating circumstance judged most adequate had to do with company norms (e.g., "traditionally, our company has never allowed this"). Judged least adequate were explanations based on the current political environment (e.g., "it would be politically incorrect to do this now"). In fact, claims of mitigating circumstances based on such political considerations were judged no more adequate than reports of no mitigating circumstances at all.

In several laboratory studies, Bies and Shapiro (1987, Studies 1 and 2; 1988, Study 1) studied the effects of claims of mitigating circumstances (e.g., an economic depression) on reactions to unfavorable organizational events (e.g., budget cutbacks). Such accounts were found to reduce people's feelings of having been unfairly treated relative to others receiving the same outcomes but who were not given accounts of mitigating circumstances. Follow-up research in field settings also has found that accounts of mitigating conditions enhanced perceptions of fairness of naturally occurring negative outcomes, such as the rejection of a proposal of organizational funding (Bies & Shapiro, 1987, Study 3; 1988, Study 2; Bies et al., 1988), rejection of an application for employment (Bies & Moag, 1986), poor performance ratings (Greenberg, 1988b), and layoffs (Brockner & Greenberg, 1989). The point of these studies is that accounts of mitigating circumstances discourage persons disappointed by managerial decisions from attributing malevolent motives to the decision maker (i.e., eliminating a worst-case reading of the situation), thereby facilitating acceptance of the outcomes (Bies, 1989).

Further research has shown that excuses may most effectively facilitate outcome acceptance when they are perceived as adequate. For example, Bies and Shapiro (1987, Studies 2 and 3) found that the perceived adequacy of the reasons for claiming mitigating circumstances was significantly more important as a determinant of perceived fair treatment than the claim itself (e.g., an explanation couched as adverse economic conditions). Similarly, Folger and his associates (e.g., Folger & Martin, 1986; Folger, Rosenfield, & Robinson, 1983) found that the feelings of discontent resulting from procedural changes creating unfavorable outcomes were reduced only when an adequate explanation was given for the changes. Recent evidence also suggests that "good" excuses (e.g., claims of mitigating circumstances) were more effective than "bad" excuses (e.g., no mitigating circumstances) or no excuses at all in alleviating the anger of victims of another's harm doing (Weiner, Amirkhan, Folkes, & Varette, 1987). These findings are consistent with evidence from the impression management literature showing that the acceptance of excuses requires them to be perceived as genuine (Jones, 1964) and not habitual (Snyder et al., 1983).

What constitutes an adequate excuse? Several recent studies shed light on this question. For example, Shapiro and Buttner (1988) found that explanations for rejected loan requests that were *logical* (i.e., based on relevant financial information) were perceived as adequate and that such explanations enhanced perceptions of procedural justice. Several additional studies have found that the apparent *sincerity* of an excuse is another determinant of its perceived adequacy. For example, Bies (1987b; Bies et al., 1988) found that the greater the perceived sincerity of a supervisor's reasons for rejecting workers' requests, the more liked the supervisor was and the more fair those supervisors' actions were perceived to be. Additional research has shown that sincere explanations were found to facilitate social exchange in another way—by discouraging the use of disruptive conflict (Baron, 1988). Indeed, organizational explanations perceived to be ingenuine and manipulative in intent have been found to be associated with disliking for the person offering the explanations and the unfairness of the resulting actions (Greenberg & Ornstein, 1983[17]). As such, explanations that are based on logical information and that show sincerity appear to be the most effective in enhancing the perceived fairness of outcomes and the procedures that led to them. Although several additional factors may moderate these effects (Bies, 1987b), the studies reported here suggest some promising candidates for refining conceptualizations of adequate excuses.

To summarize, evidence supports the idea that excuses can influence the perceived fairness of events. People are most likely to redress inequities that are believed to be under internal control and the result of intentional acts. In addition, the perceived fairness of undesirable outcomes has been found to be enhanced by claims of mitigating circumstances. Verbal excuses—specifically, those perceived to be adequate—enhance perceptions of fairness. Adequate excuses are ones that are logical and that are believed to be sincere.

Another category of accounts is *justifications*. In contrast to excuses, in which one dissociates oneself from a predicament, justifications are "explanations in which the actor takes responsibility for the action, but denies that it has the negative quality that others might attribute to it"

(Tedeschi & Reiss, 1981b, p. 281). Predicaments can be resolved if the actor's blameworthy behavior has been explained away in an acceptable manner. Hence, justifications also have been referred to as "techniques of neutralization" (Sykes & Matza, 1957). Schlenker (1980) describes several ways of reducing the severity of a predicament. Among these are (a) changing the focus of social comparisons and (b) appealing to superordinate goals. The justice-related implications of each of these tactics will be discussed.

People often justify identity-threatening actions by claiming that "everyone else does it." Individuals making such a claim seem to be implying that their actions are normatively acceptable and that singling them out for their behavior would be unfair. Although reference standards are emphasized in many theories of organizational justice (e.g., Adams, 1965; for a review, see Greenberg, 1987a[1]), Bies (1987b) indicates that only a few studies have examined the effects of justifications based on social comparisons—what he terms "referential accounts" (p. 301).

Two studies focused on social comparisons that were temporally based (Albert, 1977). For example, Bies (1986a) found that people who had proposals rejected by their bosses were more likely to accept this outcome as fair if they believed the boss might approve their proposal subsequently. Future comparisons apparently facilitated workers' acceptance of the fairness of negative outcomes. Similarly, I found that references to future outcomes (e.g., "I hope you will do better next time") were made by managers in 16.22% of the narratives they gave to explain their subordinates' performance ratings (Greenberg, 1988b). Compared with subordinates receiving no such messages, those who received messages making reference to future outcomes rated their performance evaluations as more fair. Apparently, communications raising the prospect of future positive outcomes were effective in enhancing the perceived fairness of current negative outcomes.

An alternative source of temporal comparisons is information regarding what *could* have happened (Kahneman & Tversky, 1982). For example, some of the managers in my study (Greenberg, 1988b) informed subordinates that their outcomes could have been worse (e.g., "I could have given you a lower rating"). Research by Folger and his associates (e.g., Folger & Martin, 1986; Folger et al., 1983) has found that people's reactions to injustices are influenced by their beliefs about outcomes that could have occurred (for a review, see Folger, 1986). Specifically, when participants were told that a change in procedures could have led to lower outcomes than they currently received, they reported less discontent than when more desirable outcomes could have resulted. Apparently, believing that "things could have been worse" was accepted as justification for the procedural changes that adversely affected their outcomes.

Another technique of justification calls for presenting the incident in the context of attempts to achieve superordinate goals. A father who claims to punish his children "for their own good," for example, may be seen as justifying his actions by embedding them within a more desirable or acceptable context. Likewise, organizations faced with having to lay off employees may justify the decision on the grounds of economic necessity and ostensibly display their good intentions by promoting their retraining or outplacement services. Such "reframing" as "ideological accounts" (Bies, 1987b, p. 300) helps redefine questionable actions or outcomes as morally acceptable (Lofland, 1969). Tedeschi and Reiss (1981b) note that events may be justified by appealing to higher authorities (e.g., organizational policies), loyalties (e.g., group norms), humanistic values (e.g., peace), ideology (e.g., nationalism), and—of current interest—norms of justice (e.g., equity).

How are appeals to norms of justice used to justify one's actions? Tedeschi and Reiss (1981b) explain that someone's failure to work as contracted or failure to pay for work done may be justified on the grounds that such acts could exacerbate unfair conditions. For example, workers who believe they have been underpaid may seek to restore an equitable state by lowering their performance or going on strike (Greenberg, 1982). Indeed, evidence that such labor actions are justified by recourse to superordinate goals of justice is readily provided by the words often seen on the picket signs carried by striking workers: "Justice on the job," "A fair day's pay for a fair day's work," or most simply, "Unfair!"

In a previous study (Greenberg, 1988b), I found that managers gave ideologically based explanations of performance to 11.22% of the subordinates whose work they evaluated. An explanation such as "This rating is good for you; it'll show you there's room for improvement" fits into this category. Such explanations were given primarily to subordinates whose work was rated as average or good and less frequently to those rated either higher or lower than this. Such ideological justifications enhanced workers' perceptions of the fairness of the evaluations they received relative to those who received no descriptive explanation for their performance ratings. Similarly, Bies (1986a) found that workers' willingness to work harder for bosses who rejected their proposals was facilitated by the use of ideologically based accounts.

To recapitulate, people attempt to justify unacceptable actions by getting others to believe that the future holds more favorable outcomes and that these outcomes are required to attain superordinate goals. Such beliefs facilitate the perceived fairness of unacceptable outcomes.

Apologies. In addition to accounts (excuses and justifications), apologies are also used to extricate oneself from an impression management predicament. Following from Goffman (1971), Tedeschi and Norman (1985) define apologies as "confessions of responsibility for negative events which include some expression of remorse" (p. 299). Apologies are designed to convince an audience that although the actor accepts blame for the un- desirable event, any attributions made on the basis of it would not be accurate. According to Schlenker (1980), successful apologies convince others that the harmdoer's actions "should not be considered a fair representation of what the actor is 'really like' as a person" (p. 154) and permit them to "leave the undesirable event behind and present a reformed identity to the audience" (p. 157). The mechanisms of apology can range from a perfunctory saying "pardon me," typically for minor harmful acts, to complex statements adding expressions of remorse, offers of help, requests for forgiveness, and the use of self-castigation, usually reserved for acts with more serious consequences (Schlenker & Darby, 1981).

One mechanism for gaining the acceptance of one's apologies is to perform penance and to offer to compensate one's victims (Goffman, 1971). In a series of studies, a colleague and I (O'Malley & Greenberg, 1983) found that persons who admitted their harmdoing and voluntarily offered to compensate their victims were believed by female participants to require smaller payments as fair restitution than those who did not offer any such penance. The act of voluntarily admitting responsibility was apparently accepted as a "down payment" toward undoing wrongdoing, thereby necessitating smaller amounts of additional compensation. In other words, lower amounts of compensation were believed to be fair costs to be borne by those who already partially compensated their victims by voluntarily admitting their wrongdoing. The tendency for other acts of remorse to induce leniency has been shown in several additional studies (e.g., Schwartz, Kane, Joseph, & Tedeschi, 1978).

How accepting others are of one's apologies depends, no doubt, on the severity of the deviation from acceptable standards. Kelman (1973) has distinguished between deviations from standards of *morality* (e.g., harming others or society in general), likely to elicit feelings of guilt and remorse, and deviations from standards of *propriety* (e.g., failing to behave in accord with one's particular position or role identity), likely to elicit embarrassment and shame. Evidence from simulated legal settings suggests that harsher fines may be administered to deter moral violations than to deter violations of standards of propriety (Kalven & Zeisel, 1966). Similarly, post hoc analyses of sporting events suggests that more serious penalties (e.g., suspensions) are reserved for unfair acts (i.e., procedural justice violations) that threaten the moral character of the game (e.g., recruitment violations and serious fights), whereas more lenient penalties (e.g., foul shots in basketball) are used to regulate the orderly progress of the game (Brickman, 1977; Greenberg, Mark, & Lehman, 1985; Mark & Greenberg, 1987). Such sanctions may be understood as society's mechanisms for institutionalizing restitution from those who do not voluntarily yield to more subtle social pressures.

In my investigation of the explanations given for performance evaluations, I have studied apologies (also referred to as "penitential accounts" by Bies, 1987b) in organizations (Greenberg, 1988b). Apologies (e.g., "I am sorry to have to give you such a low rating") were given as the prevalent explanation of performance ratings in 13.41% of the cases studied. These represented the most popular category of explanation given to workers in the lowest performance categories ("poor" and "needs improvement"). Although workers receiving such low ratings tended to be dissatisfied with their evaluations, an apologetic explanation for the rating enhanced workers' feelings that their ratings were fair, relative to those who were not offered any such apology.

In summary, both accounts (including excuses and justifications) and apologies have been shown to be effective mechanisms for defending against the threat of an identity of unfairness. Verbal behaviors offered to excuse, justify, or apologize for one's actions can enhance the perceived fairness of those actions and the social acceptance of the actor.

Assertive Tactics:
Identity-Enhancing Situations

As noted earlier, self-presentational efforts are directed not only toward defending against identity-threatening predicaments but also toward promoting identity-enhancing situations. Variously referred to as *assertive* tactics (Tedeschi & Norman, 1985), *offensive* attributions (Tetlock, 1985), and *acclaiming* tactics (Schlenker, 1980), impression management theorists have recognized the existence of proactive efforts directed toward seeking approval for behavior in a meritorious way. Following the lead of D'Arcy (1963), theorists have distinguished between *entitlings*—attempts to gain responsibility for positive events and their consequences—and *enhancements*—attempts to augment the positive implications of one's actions (e.g., Schlenker, 1980; Tedeschi & Norman, 1985; Tedeschi & Reiss, 1981a; Tetlock, 1985). As the following sections illustrate, both entitling actions and enhancements are used as tactics to enhance one's image of fairness.

Entitlings. Imagine supervisors who believe they behaved responsibly by appraising subordinates' performance following all the procedural rules (e.g., giving worker input into the decision) and distributive practices (e.g., rating commensurate with work performed) recognized as prerequisites for fair performance appraisals (Greenberg, 1986a[6], 1986c[8]). Nevertheless, they feel their praiseworthy actions are not being recognized by their subordinates or their superiors. This situation may be said to create a "predicament of image projection" (Tedeschi & Reiss, 1981a, p. 8) for the supervisors, who will desire to gain credit for their actions by getting others to attribute the characteristic of fairness to them. The behaviors directed at prompting these attributions are referred to as entitlings (D'Arcy, 1963). As such, entitlings are the opposite of excuses: The former actions attempt to maximize one's responsibility for positive events, whereas the latter attempt to minimize one's responsibility for negative events (Tedeschi & Reiss, 1981a).

What do managers do to enhance their perceived responsibility for fair outcomes? In what fairness-entitling actions do they engage? Some answers are provided in a previous study (Greenberg, 1988a[4]) in which I asked a sample of 815 managers to describe one thing they thought they could do to make their subordinates think they treated them fairly. The responses fell into four categories derived by crosscutting things done to look fair (*behavioral acts*) and things said to look fair (*social account*) with the means by which things are done (*process*) and the end results themselves (*outcomes*). Specifically, 81% of the respondents reported that they could enhance their image of fairness by "publicly announcing all pay raises and promotions"—a behavioral act focusing on outcomes. "Allowing workers to participate in decision making," a response reported by 55% of the sample, exemplifies a behavioral act focusing on organizational processes. Social accounts also focused on outcomes, such as "explanations of why certain work assignments must be made" (43% frequency), and processes, such as "how pay raises are determined" (76% frequency). Managers were apparently aware of several tactics they could use to promote fair self-attributions. Although it remains to be determined how often managers actually use these tactics and how effective these tactics ultimately may be in cultivating fair impressions, it is instructive to note the range of potentially entitling actions managers believed were possible.

Although earlier research has focused on various organizational outcomes and processes perceived as fair (for a review, see Folger & Greenberg, 1985), my findings (Greenberg, 1988a[4]) extend this work by showing that managers are aware of the things they can do to promote the *impression* of fairness. In other words, managers appear to be aware of what they have to do or say to *look fair*. Entitlings may be understood as representing tactics for promoting one's image of fairness—*intuitive self-marketing plans,* if you will.

Astute managers who plan to reap the benefits of fair dispositional characteristics may carefully select behaviors that help cultivate desired impressions in the minds of relevant others. Allen et al. (1979) implicitly make this point in reporting their findings regarding the popularity of various techniques of organizational politics (which they conceive of as tactics for gaining organizational influence). Among the most frequently obtained responses were "attempts to create and maintain a favorable self-image." These included responses such as developing a reputation for being thoughtful and honest—attributions similar to those in Jones and Pittman's (1982) exemplification category, as well as less cognitive acts, such as good grooming.

The organizational politician was also noted for drawing attention to successes, including ones for which the individual was not directly responsible (Allen et al., 1979). Schlenker (1980) refers to this as the "association principle," the tendency to associate oneself with desirable images. Managers claimed this was done sometimes by taking credit for another's accomplishments and often by making misleading statements or not crediting the appropriate source of one's ideas. It is indeed a curious (and, to my knowledge, untested) possibility that one may use a practice of such a dubious ethical nature to foster an image of oneself as a fair individual. Given the importance of justice as a tool of organizational politics (Cavanagh et al., 1981), however, it would not be surprising to find people attempting to solicit at least partial credit for implementing well-received organizational plans. In fact, anticipating this, team leaders may well wish to gain their team members' support by allowing them to share the credit for their group's accomplishments—thereby giving them an opportunity to "bask in the reflected glory" of their joint accomplishments (Richardson & Cialdini, 1981).

Enhancements. In addition to attempting to credit themselves with positive events, people also attempt to persuade others that an ambiguous event was positive or that an ostensibly positive event really was *very* positive. Such efforts at augmenting the positive implications of one's actions are known as enhancements and represent a second category of assertive impression management tactics (Tedeschi & Norman, 1985). Just as entitling actions are the opposite of excuses, enhancements may be understood to be the opposite of justifications (Tedeschi & Reiss, 1981a).

The key to enhancing self-presentations is information. It is therefore not surprising that in their study of managers' use of organizational politics, Allen et al. (1979) found that "information presentation" was one of the most popularly reported techniques. Managers claimed to selectively withhold and distort information to influence others. In the case of influence through fair self-promotion, managers may be likely to take advantage of inherently ambiguous consensual definitions of fairness by presenting information that enhances the perceived fairness of their actions (Backman, 1985). By selectively presenting information about an ambiguous event, managers may be helping consensually define the "truth" about it for those who are involved with interpreting it. In other words, managers may attempt to negotiate an impression of themselves as fair (Backman, 1985; Schlenker, 1980). This possibility is in keeping with the idea that social constructions help define moral conduct—including a sense of fairness (Backman, 1985). Similarly, the concept of leadership also has been presented as a "negotiated identity" that is socially constructed (Tedeschi & Melburg, 1984). The underlying idea is that many salient realities confronting people in organizations are socially constructed (Weick, 1979). People respond to what they believe, and information is the key to manipulating beliefs. Therefore, it is not surprising that the selective presentation of information—enhancement behavior—is such a useful tool of organizational politics.

There appear to be many ways organizational agents can enhance the ostensible fairness of their intentions, thereby helping others define their perceived reality as fair. For example, public pronouncements (such as press releases, policy statements, and advertising campaigns) and internal memorandums (such as announcements made in writing or at meetings and statements in company newsletters) may be recognized as tools used to promote fairness at the organizational level. Similarly, annual reports have been interpreted as tools to influence interested parties in an organization's image (e.g., Salancik & Meindl, 1984; Staw, McKechnie, & Puffer, 1983). At the individual level, managers may behave analogously by selectively detailing their decisions and by feeding leaks of fair actions through opinion leaders and informal channels of communication (Katz, 1957). The organizational performance appraisal interview may be understood as another vehicle through which the fairness of a manager's actions may be communicated (Greenberg, 1986c[8]).

It is, in fact, quite likely that an organization that institutes an ostensibly fair, nurturant policy (e.g., a nonlayoff agreement) may seek to enhance the intended benefits by promoting it both internally, to employees, and externally, via institutional advertising. Advertising also may be used by organizations to promote their goodwill gestures toward their customers. For example, one large word processing software firm has reproduced in print ads its monthly telephone bills totaling $169,848.22 for toll-free customer support lines ("What's So Special," 1988). The ad, which juxtaposes the bill with a check for the amount signed by the company president, may be understood as an attempt to enhance the company's image of concern for its customers. The benefits to be derived from the "we're fair, we care" image may well rival, if not exceed, those directly associated with the administration of the policy itself (Greenberg, 1988a[4]). The possibility that such efforts represent intentional attempts at impression management is inherent in Thompson's (1967) notion of *prospective rationality:* "Organizations act rationally to increase their evaluations or ratings by others on whom they are dependent" (p. 65).

Impression Management
Strategies: Reputation Building

I conclude this part of the chapter on tactics with a final point: All the impression management tactics described here are designed to have an immediate, short-term effect on one's perceived identity. Tedeschi and his associates (e.g., Tedeschi & Melburg, 1984; Tedeschi & Norman, 1985) distinguish between these short-term tactics and *strategies*—behaviors designed to have long-term consequences on impressions.

Strategic impression management "typically involves a variety of tactical behaviors cumulatively directed toward establishing a particular identity in the eyes of others" (Tedeschi & Norman, 1985, p. 296). As such, impression management strategies have the effect of *reputation building.* An individual who repeatedly convinces others of his or her fairness eventually may develop a reputation as a fair person. Relative to the person-specific and transitory identities resulting from the tactics described to this point, reputations are "typically functional for multiple audiences (or targets), [and] are effective across various situations" (Tedeschi & Norman, 1985, p. 297). They are, therefore, much more powerful tools, opening up a wider world of influence. For this reason, a person's acquisition of a good reputation may be seen as an investment that yields long-term gains in social influence (Schlenker, 1980). Accordingly, the benefits of behaving fairly may be derived not only from the immediate impact of the actions themselves but also from the cumulative impact of the impression that the actor is himself or herself "a fair person." To my knowledge, there are, unfortunately, no direct empirical tests of this process as it applies to the development of reputations of fairness. Given the likely effect of reputations of fairness, such research appears to be quite useful.

IMPLICATIONS OF AN IMPRESSION
MANAGEMENT VIEW OF ORGANIZATIONAL JUSTICE

The issues discussed thus far have some interesting implications and raise some important questions for the study of organizational justice. Implications and questions focusing on four issues will be raised here: (a) the sincerity of fair impressions, (b) organizational influences on fair identities, (c) the benefits and liabilities of fair impression, and (d) the management of impressions of organizational justice.

On the Sincerity of
Looking Fair: Hollow Justice?

If the research and conceptual ideas introduced in this chapter combine to make any single point, it is surely that *looking fair* is a distinct concern from *being fair*. Certainly, people may behave fairly because they are motivated by an interest in doing the right thing, believing that the cumulative effect of fair behavior benefits everyone in the long run (Lerner, 1977; Walster et al., 1978). Indeed, the value of justice and morality at the organizational level has been expressed eloquently by the philosopher John Rawls (1971), who referred to justice as "the first virtue of social institutions, as truth is of systems of political thought" (p. 3), and equally powerfully by the sociologist Charles Perrow (1972): "The common purpose of an organization must always be a moral purpose, and to inculcate this moral purpose into the very fiber of the organization and into the members of it is the only meaningful task of the executive" (p. 77). I do not challenge this position. Rather, I seek to expand the point by noting that people may facilitate the process of fostering morality by promoting their own fairness. Such a sentiment is not completely new to management thinking, as Chester Barnard (1938), the former president of AT&T, argued more than a half century ago: "Wholesale general persuasion in the form of salesmanship and advertising" (p. 144) is needed to persuade employees of the moral character of executives' actions. The various assertive tactics described in this chapter may be understood as mechanisms for ensuring agreement about the importance of one's fair actions.

In addition, people may strive to attain the benefits of being recognized as fair but without actually behaving fair. Such self-promotions of fairness lacking in substance may be referred to as *hollow justice*. Any mere veneer of fairness may function as effectively as any more deeply rooted concern for moral righteousness as long as it is not perceived to be manipulative. A perceived intentional "using" of fairness as a tool of manipulation is likely to backfire when such insincerity is suspected (as indicated by research on the ingratiator's dilemma; e.g., Jones, 1964; Liden & Mitchell, 1988; Ralston, 1985). In a demonstration of this effect, participants in two experiments (Greenberg & Ornstein, 1983[17]) reported feeling equitably paid when they were compensated for added job responsibilities by being given a high-status job title. When they suspected that their supervisor may have given them the title to trick them into thinking they were fairly compensated, however, they rebelled—attributing malicious motives to the supervisor, perceiving they were underpaid, and dramatically lowering their job performance.

Although some may seek to further their selfish interests by wrapping their malevolent motives around the mantle of justice—particularly political leaders (DiQuattro, 1986)—it is not necessary to assume deceptive motives to embrace an impression management view of justice. In this regard, I should not be represented as echoing the sentiments of Philip Stanhope, the earl of Chesterfield, who in 1749 said, "Without some dissimulation, no business can be carried out at all" (cited in Rheingold, 1988, p. 88). Impression management theorists are quick to point out, and I agree, that people's tactical efforts at presenting themselves favorably to others should *not* be confused with lying (Schlenker, 1980; Tedeschi & Rosenfeld, 1981). The image one puts forth may be sincere in that it accurately reflects the actor's self-image, or it may represent dissembling. Not all inaccurate self-presentations may be consciously duplicitous, however; some may represent identities actors believe they have, if only through wishful thinking (Baumeister, 1982). Generally speaking,

> People need to believe attributions designed to protect their sense of self-worth (otherwise the attributions do not serve their "intended" motivational function), but people do not need to believe attributions designed to protect their public or social identities (we can offer explanations for conduct that impresses others favorably, but that we do not really believe to be true). (Tetlock, 1985, p. 222)

A key determinant of the sincerity of one's projected image is the degree of clarity surrounding the appropriateness of the behavior in question (Baron, 1988; Snyder, 1985). The inherent ambiguity regarding what constitutes fairness makes it possible for many actions to be presented as fair. The ambiguous nature of fairness has been established in several open-ended questionnaires focusing specifically on organizational behaviors (e.g., Greenberg, 1986a[6]; Sheppard & Lewicki, 1987) and general social interaction (Liebrand et al., 1986; Messick et al., 1985). This condition makes it possible for people to couch their behaviors (including their verbal remarks) as justice without intentional dishonesty. People may well believe that certain acts are fair that others cannot accept as such (Baumeister, 1982). In other words, fairness may be a socially constructed reality (Bies, 1987b; Weick, 1979). The idea that fairness is a desired label that people seek to attach to their behaviors is one of the most important implications of an impression management interpretation of justice (Bies, 1987b). Understanding the processes through which labels of fairness are attached and removed (an approach that has been recommended for the study of leadership by Tedeschi & Melburg, 1984) opens up an entirely new direction for research on organizational justice. Such an approach clearly identifies a host of research questions different from an approach assuming that the underlying motive behind an act of justice is the desire to relieve the negative emotions brought on by an inequitable payment (Greenberg, 1987a[1]).

One example of the type of new questions likely to emerge is a shift in research on individual differences in justice behavior. Traditionally, researchers have studied how differences in such variables as sex, personality, and nationality relate to intolerance for inequities and the preference for various normative standards of justice (for a review, see Major & Deaux, 1982). An impression management perspective suggests the introduction of variables based on *self-presentational styles* (Arkin, 1981), such as determinants of sensitivity toward engendering disapproval for unfairness relative to garnering approval for fairness and preferences for various defensive and assertive techniques of fair impression management. Knowing about such variables furthers the understanding of the mechanisms by which impressions of fairness are cultivated.

Organizational Influences on Fair Identities

It has been shown that people seek to present themselves as fair to others and to themselves. Superimposing these findings on organizational contexts identifies some interesting and important unanswered questions.

For one, it would be instructive to know if certain organizational figures are more salient than others as sources of self-presentational concerns. Typically, higher-status persons are more inclined to be targets of impression management efforts (Gardner & Martinko, 1988). In organizations, this phenomenon is complicated because one's actions are likely to have impact on—or, at least, be known by—multiple constituencies (Ralston, 1985). In many cases, what may be done to impress one party with one's own fairness may be antagonistic to cultivating another's impressions of fairness. For example, in keeping with the research reviewed here, managers may seek to divide available monies for pay raises equally among their subordinates to minimize the interpersonal strain that merit-based, equitable divisions may create (Leventhal, 1976). In so doing, however, managers run the risk of displeasing other workers, particularly high-input workers who would have benefited from equitable divisions of reward. To impress such individuals with fairness may require making a different response. Further complicating the example, supervisors also may face pressure from their superiors to follow other rules of fairness. In cases of conflicting expectations among multiple constituencies, it may be expected that the target selected for impression management purposes will be the target whose impressions are most highly valued (Schlenker, 1980). In organizations, this may well be that person believed to control the most valued resources.

This situation is complicated by the possibility that different organizational constituencies may be sensitive to qualitatively different manifestations of fairness. In other words, the aspect of an individual's behavior needed to cultivate an image of fairness may vary for different target persons. For example, a middle manager may seek to convince subordinates that he or she behaved fairly by giving them a voice in the decisions regarding the staffing of office telephones during lunch hours (e.g., "Someone has to monitor the phones during lunch, and rather than assign one of you to do so, I'll let you decide among yourselves who should do it."). This same manager may have to convince superiors that he or she behaved fairly by presenting the personnel assignment decision in a manner consistent with other organizational units (e.g., "As done elsewhere in our company, I delegated this decision to the workers themselves."). Thus, a manager may be able to satisfy the fairness demands of multiple constituencies by simply focusing explanations on different aspects of the same behavior. In this example, the manager would emphasize to the subordinates that he or she allowed them to make the decision themselves (i.e., emphasizing the procedural fairness criterion of voice in decision making; Greenberg & Folger, 1983), whereas to the superior, the manager would emphasize that in performing the same behavior, the manager conformed to organizational policy (i.e., emphasizing the distributional equality of the outcome). By selectively reporting one's behavior, it may be possible to convince several targets of one's fairness. (Of course, to the extent that an actor's image of fairness is reputational, persons interacting with that actor are likely to attribute his or her actions to fair motives simply because of that person's reputation. He or she would receive the benefit of the doubt about being fair.)

In addition, consider how social pressures in organizations impose subtle limitations on efforts at positive self-presentation. In particular, the tendency to play up one's organizational fairness may be limited by fears of presenting oneself immodestly. The practice of immodestly attempting to manipulate desired impressions may sometimes backfire (such as when the actions are perceived as exaggerated and ethically inappropriate), resulting in an undesirable image—a self-promotor's paradox (Ashforth & Gibbs, 1990). As a result, the risks of being caught in the act of ostensibly manipulating impressions may be especially likely to be accepted by those who believe their potentially positive impression-forming actions would otherwise go unnoticed. Persons who believe that others will come to know of their desirable actions tend to be less self-aggrandizing than those who do not (Baumeister & Jones, 1978). To the extent that existing mechanisms of organizational communication (e.g., the announcement of actions in a company newsletter) ensure the transmittal of managers' fair actions, managers may be reluctant to engage in further self-promotional efforts. Instead, managers convinced of public acceptance of their actions may reinforce their subordinates' attributions of their fairness through their humility. In so doing, they may be benefiting from the secondary impression of modesty as well as the calculated impression of fairness (Schneider, 1981). As Schlenker (1980) put it, "Successful people can afford to be modest and thus acquire images of success and humility" (p. 193).

Benefits and Liabilities of Fair Impressions

Impression management theorists (e.g., Tedeschi & Reiss, 1981a; Tetlock & Manstead, 1985) have pointed out several benefits of favorable self-presentations that apply quite well to self-presentations of fairness (Greenberg, 1988a[4]). Several possible liabilities and limitations are also associated with attempting to cultivate an image of fairness.

Benefits. One benefit of a fair identity is that it may reinforce a person's self-identity and sense of self-esteem (Greenwald & Breckler, 1985). People sometimes do things to convince themselves of their fairness (Greenberg, 1983a), particularly those individuals who strongly endorse the Protestant work ethic (Greenberg, 1979). An internalized belief in a just world (Lerner, 1980) is likely to be reinforced by actions that help define oneself as fair. Indeed, research has shown that self-image maintenance is a potent determinant of fair behavior (Greenberg, 1980, 1983a, 1983b).

In addition to these intrapsychic benefits, fair identities also may help individual organizational functioning by enhancing managers' power bases. In fact, Tedeschi and Norman (1985) explicitly contend that self-presentations may be interpreted as influence attempts. Managers perceived as fair may gain power advantages through several mechanisms.

To the extent that fair behaviors are admired (Messick et al., 1985) and liking encourages compliance with managers to gain their approbation (French & Raven, 1959), attributions of fairness may strengthen managers' power bases. Similarly, managers' power may be enhanced by their subordinates' beliefs in their fairness because of widely held associations between fairness and credibility (Liebrand et al., 1986; Messick et al., 1985). Just as the power of fair judges is derived from their perceived lack of ulterior motives and consistent application of the law, so too may managers' reputations for credibility and trustworthiness facilitate their power to supervise (Tedeschi & Melburg, 1984; Tedeschi & Norman, 1985; Tedeschi & Reiss, 1981a).

An indirect power advantage also may be gained by managers believed to be fair. As has been noted earlier in this chapter, the fairness of many managerial decisions is ambiguous to subordinates because they are made on the basis of unknown information. Managers with reputations for fairness (or, at least, those who have temporarily impressed others with their fairness) may meet fewer challenges to their authority than others who lack the reputational power of fairness. In ambiguous situations, managers may rely on their reputations for fairness to convince subordinates of the fairness of their actions. Managers who have demonstrated themselves to be fair in the past may well derive power from the acceptance of their admonitions to "trust me, I'll be fair." In other words, a reputation for fairness may help give managers the benefit of the doubt in situations in which judgments of fairness may not be easily made—a process similar to the issuance of "idiosyncrasy credit" (Hollander, 1964) noted in the study of leadership emergence in small groups.

In addition, fair social identities may facilitate functioning at the organizational level. An organizational-level image of fairness—that is, a corporate culture of fairness—may help attract and retain the best qualified job candidates, as well as customers who are attracted by the company's positive image (Greenberg, (1988a[4]). Indeed, Murray and Montanari (1986) have argued that the public will recognize and support socially responsive firms, that is, those that fulfill society's moral and ethical expectations. To the extent that this is true, then benefits of identities of corporate fairness may also be realized in marketing indicators (e.g., percentage of market share) as well as management indicators (e.g., degree of job satisfaction). Promotional efforts that position corporations as fair-minded to their employees, the surrounding economic community, and the environment may be the result of efforts to cultivate a corporate image of fairness (Greenberg, 1988a[4]). (As an example, one may note the frequent advertisements by large oil companies promoting their efforts at eliminating, rather than contributing to, environmental pollution.)

Schwoerer and Rosen (1989) have found that job applicants' impressions of prospective employers were enhanced by brochures promoting the organizations as committed to a doctrine encouraging "fair treatment to all employees." Corporate values, including those emphasizing justice and morality, have been recognized as core elements of organizational culture (Deal & Kennedy, 1982).

In addition to individuals seeking to convince themselves (the private self) or specific external audiences (the public self) of their fairness, organizations provide an opportunity for people to seek adherence to superordinate goals, norms of justice accepted collectively by reference groups. Greenwald and Breckler (1985) use the term *collective self* to refer to an individual's internalization of the goals of a group with whom he or she is identified, the "we-aspect" of one's identity. Although it is often assumed that internalization of reference groups' standards account for public self-presentations (a "situated identity" position; Alexander & Rudd, 1981), the possibility that workers directly may seek to impress the collective self with their fairness remains untested. Some relevant research has shown that people may frame accounts of their behavior in highly ideological terms (e.g., "this is the right thing to do because it helps us—the company"), making reference to loftier collective goals to meet more immediate needs (see Bies, 1987b).

Sensitivity to the collective self might not be equal at all organizational levels. Specifically, it may be speculated that higher-level organizational officials, presidents, and CEOs tend to be held most responsible for achieving collective standards of fairness. The perspective afforded by their positions may empower them to consider justice from a collective viewpoint more than others whose lower levels in the hierarchy encourage them to focus on more individual-level concerns. Position power, in fact, may well reflect one's level of interest in collective concerns about justice (Tedeschi & Norman, 1985).

Liabilities. In addition to the benefits associated with an image of fairness, there also may be some liabilities that are not immediately obvious to those who strive to attain that image. For one, the responsibilities of one's image sometimes may jeopardize one's social standing (Schlenker, 1980). Consider, for example, the plight of certain political and religious figures (former President Nixon and TV evangelists Bakker and Swaggart come to mind) whose alleged indiscretions have publicly disgraced them. Because these individuals' identities were defined primarily by their lofty moral standing, it would not be surprising to find them more disgraced for their actions than others who never sought, by virtue of their position or their actions, a reputation for moral purity.

A challenged identity is, perhaps, most threatened when it forms the core of one's public image. A parallel to the concept of *status liability* (Wiggins, Dill, & Schwartz, 1965) is apparent. Just as a high-status person may receive the most credit for positive outcomes and take the most blame for negative outcomes, a similar process may be operating with respect to self-presentations. Persons whose primary social identities are invested in a certain image not only may receive the most approval for events affirming that identity but also may receive the most disapproval for events challenging that identity (Schlenker, 1980). Thus, although images of fairness may be quite valuable organizational tools, some costs may also be associated with maintaining them.

Just as individuals may bear costs associated with having a fair identity, so too may institutions bear similar costs—and in an analogous manner. For example, because the American news media are expected to fairly and dispassionately report stories to the public, press accounts of news events that are biased or that proactively create rather than reactively report stories sometimes instigate public outcries of injustice. Such was the case, for example, when press reports surfaced prior to the 1988 U.S. presidential election that questioned Republican vice presidential candidate Dan Quayle's motives for joining the National Guard (allegedly, to avoid being drafted and serving in a military unit in Vietnam). One poll taken at that time found that 55% of those surveyed believed the press coverage was unfair ("Poll," 1988). Such assessments may well be partly responsible for the growing public disenchantment with the mass media (Roberts & Maccoby, 1985). Given that the American press is an institution histori-cally associated with safeguarding justice and democracy, public sensi-tivity to potentially unfair actions on its part (e g., claims of overzealously hounding a political candidate) may be readily understood as an instance of an institution's liability for its reputation. In other words, just as "holier than thou" individuals might be held to a higher moral standard than mere mortal souls, so too may institutions sanctioned with responsibility for ensuring public well-being be expected to face harsh disapproval when they appear to have violated the very rights they are empowered to protect.

Another personal liability associated with having a reputation for being fair may be the burden of having to justify one's actions as fairness rather than any other criteria, such as one's own preferences (B. R. Schlenker, personal communication, June 26, 1988). If a fair person is who you *are* in the eyes of others, your projected identity, then it may be seen as insufficient for you to account for your actions in ways that do not assert this identity. Others will be looking for and expect to find an explanation couched as fairness and may be dissatisfied by any other type of explanation.

In fact, an intriguing possibility is that failure to assert the identity regularly may actually weaken the identity itself. Such obligations to justify actions as fair (i.e., pressures to live up to one's reputation) may be burdensome in that they force one to express one's actions in the language of justice (e.g., "I did it this way because it took everyone's relative contributions into account") and may restrict the use of other explanatory mechanisms, such as personal choice (e.g., "I did it this way because I wanted to"). In other words, to reap the benefits of a fair identity, a person may have to pay for it with restricted behavioral (or at least, rhetorical) options required to maintain that identity. (This process is analogous to the press agent's efforts to put clients into situations that help reassert their public images—such as getting the playboy millionaire to be seen in the presence of a beautiful starlet at a chic night spot. To maintain his appeal as a box office draw, the playboy is expected to present himself in a manner consistent with the image created for him—whether he wants to or not!)

Managing—and Mismanaging—Impressions
of Organizational Fairness: Case Studies

Given that scientists and practitioners have only recently begun to recognize and appreciate the full range of organizational behaviors associated with organizational justice, it is not too surprising to find few published cases in which issues of fair impression management are explicitly analyzed. Yet with increased frequency, recent treatises on corporate morality are beginning to pay attention to the matter of impressions of fairness, if only in passing (e.g., Jackall, 1988; Walton, 1988). In addition, two recent cases explicitly focus on concerns about fair impressions created in organizations. One highlights the successful management of fair impressions; the other, unsuccessful management.

Successful impression management: Introducing a new performance appraisal system at Cyanamid. In 1986, the American Cyanamid Company introduced a new performance appraisal system companywide following a successful experiment in the company's Medical Research Division during the previous 3 years (Gellerman & Hodgson, 1988). After reducing an unworkable 10-point scale to an easier 3-point scale and eliminating forced-distribution expectations, claims that the scale was unfair were greatly reduced. In fact, during the last year of the study (1986), 63% of the workers using the new system reported that it fairly assessed their performance, compared with only 24% in a control group using the old system. On the basis of such findings, the new system was adopted in 1986 for all the company's 11,500 U.S. employees.

Although the company planned on introducing the new system companywide regardless of the study's findings, the positive reaction of workers in the company's Medical Research Division was cited as justification for introducing the system. These findings were then widely disseminated throughout the company in an attempt at publicizing the new system's fairness—and the company's fairness in basing the system's introduction on such successful trial outcomes. Such an ostensible effort at showing the company's concern for introducing an established perceived-fair practice was seen as consistent with CEO George J. Sella Jr.'s commitment toward humanizing the corporate culture and improving the quality of life for the company's employees. These actions also have been credited for fostering workers' acceptance of the new system. (Indeed, it is difficult to ascertain the extent to which acceptance of the new system is based on employees' genuine regard for the system's own characteristics uncontaminated by the company's ballyhoo regarding its greatness.) Cyanamid's efforts at impressing its workforce with the company's interest in introducing proved-fair procedures provides an excellent example of the concern for cultivating fair impressions described in this chapter.

Unsuccessful impression management: The firing of the Ohio State University's football coach. By contrast to the Cyanamid case, not all organizational changes are managed in a manner perceived as fair. An excellent example is provided by Lewicki's (1988) analysis of claims of unfairness resulting from the firing of the Ohio State University's head football coach, Earle Bruce, in November 1987.

The case begins when the university's president, Edward Jennings, fired Bruce in the middle of the coach's contract, one week before the 1987 season's final game (against its arch rival, the University of Michigan). Claiming that such personnel matters required secrecy, President Jennings gave little or no information to the public regarding his reasons for Coach Bruce's surprise dismissal (the coach had repeatedly led his team to 9-3 seasons—a good, but not impressive, record). The firing subsequently led the university's athletic director to resign in protest, Bruce to bring suit against the university (resulting in a $471,000 settlement), the university president to lose a great deal of goodwill for his actions (publicly decried as unfair), and the coach to emerge as a sympathetic victimized hero.

In analyzing this incident, Lewicki (1988) noted that public organizations with highly visible performance and large public constituencies (such as in this case) need to be sensitive to the perceived fairness of their actions. Clearly, in this case, the university president was not sensitive enough to issues of perceived fairness. Specifically, by failing to disclose adequate reasons behind the coach's firing, the university may be seen as violating the public's consensually perceived rights of full disclosure and its right to question undesirable actions. Although there were no actual legal rights to such information in this case, the disclosure of such information would have been useful in facilitating the public's acceptance of the decision as a fair one. Lewicki claimed that by not providing such information, the university violated the public's right to know, thereby providing an incident of ineffective management of social accounts resulting in perceptions of unfairness. Certainly, the effects of such actions on alumni donations, fan support, and the recruitment of future players and coaches—although unknown at the time—may be taken as useful indicators of the long-term effect of such mismanagement.

Synthesis. Despite their many differences, the Cyanamid case and the Ohio State University case clearly underscore the importance of impressions of fairness in organizations. It was the promoted appearance of fairness that facilitated acceptance of Cyanamid's new performance appraisal system and the ostensible unfairness of the manner of the coach's firing that led to public disapproval of the university president. Just because Cyanamid's new performance appraisal system does a better job of evaluating workers, or even if President Jennings actually had just cause for firing Coach Bruce, it was the *way* in which the information was presented in both cases that appears to have been so responsible for the reactions that resulted. Thus, as I have been saying throughout this chapter: It is the management of an impression of fairness that is so greatly responsible for the reactions that result from one's behavior.

CONCLUSION

Can it be said that concerns about impressing others with one's fairness are preeminent in organizations or that fairness is the most important attributional goal sought by subordinates, managers, or organizations? Although any claims to these effects may represent overstatements, the salience of concerns about fairness cannot be ignored. Unfortunately, organizational scientists have largely overlooked impression management issues as they pertain to organizational fairness. Long limited by the domination of a narrow perspective about justice, they have not been able to capture the richness of this topic. With these remarks, it is hoped that the field of organizational behavior will expand its views of organizational justice and redirect at least some of its efforts away from being fair and toward looking fair.

As in the case of earlier efforts at applying an impression management perspective to social phenomena traditionally studied by intrapsychic theories (Tetlock & Manstead, 1985), my interest has been in encouraging the study of organizational justice from an alternative point of view. I believe the departure from the historically prevalent reactive content frameworks (e.g., equity theory and relative deprivation theory) for studying organizational justice (Greenberg, 1987a[1]) outlined here provides a more perceptive approach into a broader range of issues of organizational justice than heretofore may have been considered. As such, the time appears to have come for equity theory, the reigning theory of organizational justice, to release its hegemony over the field. Such a shift in paradigms would be in keeping with a reorientation that took place in social psychology from the 1960s to the 1970s, "a shift from motivational/drive models of cognitions, behaviors, and internal states to information processing, attribution models of such phenomena" (Bem, 1972, p. 43). This shift that Bem referred to is also in evidence in the field of organizational behavior (e.g., Salancik & Pfeffer, 1978). The field of organizational justice has been slow to catch up with this movement, however (Greenberg, 1987a[1]). I hope that the impression management orientation advanced in this chapter will encourage some new directions in organizational justice research and theory development that embrace the intrapsychic orientation.

Before concluding, I must caution readers against the temptation toward interpreting an element of irony in this chapter—namely, that one would act manipulatively in the name of fairness. To be sure, there is nothing inherently Machiavellian about wanting to appear fair. Concerns about the perceived fairness of one's own actions reflect a social sensitivity that may be no more deceitful than any other self-presentational efforts (such as dressing to impress others or treating people in a kind manner to win their friendship). Of course, although any calculated impression may be motivated by unethical interests (e.g., the slick con job of the snake oil salesman), there is no reason to suspect that fairness as a desired identity is any more likely to be associated with the deceitful intentions of those who pursue it than any other identity. To the (I hope) many readers to whom this caveat may seem unnecessary and overly defensive, my reply is that it is not aimed at you. Rather, it is intended to reassure those inclined to treat justice as a cherished virtue that risks tarnishing by tampering with it (Bellah, Madsen, Sullivan, Swidler, & Tipton, 1985) that any concern for nurturing justice fails to render it less pure.

I opened this chapter by arguing that practicing managers may have greater awareness of the importance of fair social identities than most organizational scientists who study fairness. In closing, it is hoped that the impression management perspective advanced on these pages will stimulate the efforts of those who study organizational behavior to catch up with the consensual beliefs of those who practice it.

REFERENCES

Adams, J. S. (1965). Inequity in social exchange. In L. Berkowitz (Ed.), *Advances in experimental social psychology* (Vol. 2, pp. 267-299). New York: Academic Press.

Adams, J. S., & Freedman, S. (1976). Equity theory revisited: Comments and annotated bibliography. In L. Berkowitz & E. Walster (Eds.), *Advances in experimental social psychology* (Vol. 9, pp. 43-90). New York: Academic Press.

Adams, J. S., & Rosenbaum, W. B. (1962). The relationship of worker productivity to cognitive dissonance about wage inequities. *Journal of Applied Psychology, 46,* 161-164.

Albert, S. (1977). Temporal comparison theory. *Psychological Review, 84,* 485-503.

Alexander, C. N., Jr., & Rudd, J. (1981). Situated identities and response variables. In J. T. Tedeschi (Ed.), *Impression management theory and social psychological research* (pp. 83-103). New York: Academic Press.

Alexander, S., & Ruderman, M. (1987). The role of procedural and distributive justice in organizational behavior. *Social Justice Research, 1,* 177-198.

Allen, R. W., Madison, D. L., Porter, L. W., Renwick, P. A., & Mayes, B. T. (1979). Organizational politics: Tactics and characteristics of its actors. *California Management Review, 22,* 77-83.

Allen, V. L. (1982). Effect of conformity pressure on justice behavior. In J. Greenberg & R. L. Cohen (Eds.), *Equity and justice in social behavior* (pp. 187-215). New York: Academic Press.

Anderson, N. H. (1968). Likableness ratings of 555 personality-trait words. *Journal of Personality and Social Psychology, 9,* 272-279.

Andrews, L. R., & Valenzi, E. R. (1970). Overpay inequity of self-image as a worker: A critical examination of an experimental induction procedure. *Organizational Behavior and Human Performance, 5,* 266-276.

Arkin, R. M. (1981). Self-presentational styles. In J. T. Tedeschi (Ed.), *Impression management theory and social psychological research* (pp. 311-333). New York: Academic Press.

Ashforth, B. E., & Gibbs, B. (1990). The double-edge of organizational legitimation. *Organizational Science, 1,* 177-194.

Austin, J. L. (1961). *Philosophical papers.* London: Oxford University Press.

Austin, W. (1980). Friendship and fairness: Effects of type of relationship and task performance on choice of distribution rules. *Personality and Social Psychology Bulletin, 6,* 402-407.

Austin, W., & McGinn, N. C. (1977). Sex differences in choice of distribution rules. *Journal of Personality, 45,* 379-394.

Backman, C. W. (1985). Identity, self-presentation, and the resolution of moral dilemmas: Toward a social psychological theory of moral behavior. In B. R. Schlenker (Ed.), *The self and social life* (pp. 261-289). New York: McGraw-Hill.

Barnard, C. (1938). *The functions of the executive.* Cambridge, MA: Harvard University Press.

Baron, R. A. (1988). Attributions and organizational conflict: The mediating role of apparent sincerity. *Organizational Behavior and Human Decision Processes, 41,* 111-127.

Baumeister, R. F. (1982). A self-presentational view of social phenomena. *Psychological Bulletin, 91,* 3-26.

Baumeister, R. F., & Jones, E. E. (1978). When self-presentation is constrained by the target's knowledge: Consistency and compensation. *Journal of Personality and Social Psychology, 36,* 608-618.

Bell, N. E., Tetlock, P. E. (1989). The intuitive politician and the assignment of blame in organizations. In R. A. Giacalone & P. Rosenfeld (Eds.), *Impression management in the organization* (pp. 105-123). Hillsdale, NJ: Lawrence Erlbaum.

Bellah, R. N., Madsen, R., Sullivan, W. M., Swidler, A., & Tipton, S. M. (1985). *Habits of the heart.* New York: Harper & Row.

Bem, D. J. (1972). Self-perception theory. In L. Berkowitz (Ed.), *Advances in experimental social psychology* (Vol. 6, pp. 42-66). New York: Academic Press.

Berger, J., Zelditch, M., Anderson, B., & Cohen, B. P. (1972). Structural aspects of distributive justice: A status-value formulation. In J. Berger, M. Zelditch, & B. Anderson (Eds.), *Sociological theories in progress* (Vol. 2, pp. 21-45). Boston: Houghton Mifflin.

Bies, R. J. (1986a). *The delivery of bad news in organizations: Strategies and tactics.* Unpublished manuscript, Northwestern University, Evanston, IL.

Bies, R. J. (1986b, August). Identifying principles of interactional justice: The case of corporate recruiting. In R. J. Bies (Chair), *Moving beyond equity theory: New directions in research on organizational justice.* Symposium presented at the meeting of the Academy of Management, Chicago.

Bies, R. J. (1987a). Beyond "voice": The influence of decision-maker justification and sincerity on procedural fairness judgments. *Representative Research in Social Psychology 17,* 3-14.

Bies, R. J. (1987b). The predicament of injustice: The management of moral outrage. In L. L. Cummings & B. M. Staw (Eds.), *Research in organizational behavior* (Vol. 9, pp. 289-319). Greenwich, CT: JAI.

Bies, R. J. (1989). Managing conflict before it happens: The role of accounts. In M. A. Rahim (Ed.), *Managing conflict: An interdisciplinary approach* (pp. 83-91). New York: Praeger.

Bies, R. J., & Moag, J. S. (1986). Interactional justice: Communications criteria of fairness. In R. J. Lewicki, B. H. Sheppard, & M. H. Bazerman (Eds.), *Research on negotiation in organizations* (Vol. 1, pp. 43-55). Greenwich, CT: JAI.

Bies, R. J., & Shapiro, D. L. (1987). Interactional fairness judgments: The influence of causal accounts. *Social Justice Research, 1,* 199-218.

Bies, R. J., & Shapiro, D. L. (1988). Voice and justification: Their influence on procedural fairness judgments. *Academy of Management Journal, 31,* 676-685.

Bies, R. J., Shapiro, D. L., & Cummings, L. L. (1988). Causal accounts and managing organizational conflict: Is it enough to say it's not my fault? *Communication Research 15,* 381-399.

Brickman, P. (1977). Crime and punishment in sports and society. *Journal of Social Issues, 33,* 140-164.

Brockner, J., & Greenberg, J. (1989). The impact of layoffs on survivors: An organizational justice perspective. In J. Carroll (Ed.), *Advances in applied social psychology: Business settings* (pp. 45-75). Hillsdale, NJ: Lawrence Erlbaum.

Carver, C. S., & Scheier, M. F. (1981). *Attention and self-regulation: A control-theory approach to human behavior.* New York: Springer-Verlag.

Carver, C. S., & Scheier, M. F. (1985). Aspects of self and the control of behavior. In B. R. Schlenker (Ed.), *The self and social life* (pp. 146-174). New York: McGraw-Hill.

Cavanagh, G. F., Moberg, D. J., & Velasquez, M. (1981). The ethics of organizational politics. *Academy of Management Review, 6,* 363-374.

Chatman, J. A., Bell, N. E., & Staw, B. M. (1986). The managed thought: The role of self-justification and impression management in organizational settings. In D. Gioia &

H. Sims (Eds.), *The thinking organization: Dynamics of organizational social cognition* (pp. 191-214). San Francisco: Jossey-Bass.

Cohen, R. L. (1974). Mastery and justice in laboratory dyads: A revision and extension of equity theory. *Journal of Personality and Social Psychology, 29,* 464-474.

Cooley, C. H. (1902). *Human nature and the social order.* New York: Charles Scribner's Sons.

Cornelius, E. T., Ullman, J. C., Meglino, B. M., Czajka, J., & McNeely, B. (1985, November). *A new approach to the study of worker values and some preliminary results.* Paper presented at the meeting of the Southern Management Association, Orlando, FL.

Cosier, R. A., & Dalton, D. R. (1983). Equity theory and time: A reformulation. *Academy of Management Review, 8,* 311-319.

Crosby, F. (1984). Relative deprivation in organizational settings. In B. M. Staw & L. L. Cummings (Eds.), *Research in organizational behavior* (Vol. 6, pp. 51-93). Greenwich, CT: JAI.

D'Arcy, E. (1963). *Human acts: An essay in their moral evaluation.* New York: Oxford University Press.

Deal, T. E., & Kennedy, A. A. (1982). *Corporate cultures.* Reading, MA: Addison-Wesley.

Deutsch, M. (1975). Equity, equality and need: What determines which value will be used as the basis for distributive justice? *Journal of Social Issues, 31,* 137-149.

Deutsch, M. (1985). *Distributive justice.* New Haven, CT: Yale University Press.

DiQuattro, A. (1986). Political studies and justice. In R. L. Cohen (Ed.), *Justice: Views from the social sciences* (pp. 85-116). New York: Plenum.

Duval, S., & Wicklund, R. A. (1972). *A theory of objective self-awareness.* New York: Academic Press.

Fenigstein, A., Scheier, M. F., & Buss, A. H. (1975). Public and private self-consciousness: Assessment and theory. *Journal of Consulting and Clinical Psychology, 43,* 522-527.

Festinger, L. (1957). *A theory of cognitive dissonance.* Evanston, IL: Row, Peterson.

Feyerabend, P. K. (1970). How to be a good empiricist: A plea for tolerance in matters epistemological. In B. A. Brody (Ed.), *Readings in the philosophy of science* (pp. 55-77). Englewood Cliffs, NJ: Prentice Hall.

Fincham, F. D., & Jaspars, J. M. (1980). Attribution of responsibility: From man the scientist to man the lawyer. In L. Berkowitz (Ed.), *Advances in experimental social psychology* (Vol. 13, pp. 81-138). New York: Academic Press.

Folger, R. (1986). Rethinking equity theory: A referent cognitions model. In H. W. Bierhoff, R. L. Cohen, & J. Greenberg (Eds.), *Justice in social relations* (pp. 145-162). New York: Plenum.

Folger, R., & Greenberg, J. (1985). Procedural justice: An interpretive analysis of personnel systems. In K. M. Rowland & G. R. Ferris (Eds.), *Research in personnel and human resources management* (Vol. 3, pp. 141-183). Greenwich, CT: JAI.

Folger, R., & Martin, C. (1986). Relative deprivation and referent cognitions: Distributive and procedural justice effects. *Journal of Experimental Social Psychology, 22,* 531-546.

Folger, R., Rosenfield, D., & Robinson, T. (1983). Relative deprivation and procedural justifications. *Journal of Personality and Social Psychology, 45,* 268-273.

Freedman, S. M., & Montanari, J. R. (1980). An integrative model of managerial reward allocation. *Academy of Management Review, 5,* 381-390.

French, J. R. P., Jr., & Raven, B. (1959). The bases of social power. In D. Cartwright (Ed.), *Studies in social power* (pp. 118-149). Ann Arbor: University of Michigan Press.

Friedman, A., & Goodman, P. S. (1974). *The effect of individualizing pay and secrecy about pay on salary allocations.* Unpublished manuscript, Hebrew University, Jerusalem.

Furby, L. (1986). Psychology and justice. In R. L. Cohen (Ed.), *Justice: Views from the social sciences* (pp. 153-203). New York: Plenum.

Gardner, W. L., & Martinko, M. J. (1988). Impression management: An observational study linking audience characteristics with verbal self-presentations. *Academy of Management Journal, 31,* 42-65.

Garrett, J. B., & Libby, W. L., Jr. (1973). Role of intentionality in mediating responses to inequity in the dyad. *Journal of Personality and Social Psychology, 28,* 21-27.

Gellerman, S. W., & Hodgson, W. G. (1988). Cyanamid's new take on performance appraisal. *Harvard Business Review, 66*(3), 36-37, 40-41.

Giacalone, R. A., & Rosenfeld, P. (1987). Impression management concerns and reinforcement interventions. *Group & Organization Studies, 12,* 445-453.

Giacalone, R. A., & Rosenfeld, P. (Eds.). (1990). *Impression management in the organization.* Hillsdale, NJ: Lawrence Erlbaum.

Gibbons, F. X., & Wicklund, R. A. (1982). Self-focused attention and helping behavior. *Journal of Personality and Social Psychology, 43,* 462-474.

Goodman, P. S., & Friedman, A. (1971). An examination of Adam's theory of inequity. *Administrative Science Quarterly, 16,* 271-288.

Goffman, E. (1959). *The presentation of self in everyday life.* Garden City, NY: Anchor Doubleday.

Goffman, E. (1971). *Relations in public.* New York: Basic Books.

Greenberg, J. (1978). Effects of reward value and retaliative power on allocation decisions: Justice, generosity, or greed? *Journal of Personality and Social Psychology, 36,* 367-379.

Greenberg, J. (1979). Protestant ethic endorsement and the fairness of equity inputs. *Journal of Research in Personality, 13,* 81-90.

Greenberg, J. (1980). Attentional focus and locus of performance causality as determinants of equity behavior. *Journal of Personality and Social Psychology, 38,* 579-585.

Greenberg, J. (1982). Approaching equity and avoiding inequity in groups and organizations. In J. Greenberg & R. L. Cohen (Eds.), *Equity and justice in social behavior* (pp. 389-435). New York: Academic Press.

Greenberg, J. (1983a). Overcoming egocentric bias in perceived fairness through self-awareness. *Social Psychology Quarterly, 46,* 152-156.

Greenberg, J. (1983b). Self-image versus impression management in adherence to distributive justice standards: The influence of self-awareness and self-consciousness. *Journal of Personality and Social Psychology, 44,* 5-19.

Greenberg, J. (1984). On the apocryphal nature of inequity distress. In R. Folger (Ed.), *The sense of injustice* (pp. 167-188). New York: Plenum.

Greenberg, J. (1986a). Determinants of perceived fairness of performance evaluations. *Journal of Applied Psychology, 71,* 340-342. [Chapter 6, this volume.]

Greenberg, J. (1986b). The distributive justice of organizational performance evaluations. In H. W. Bierhoff, R. L. Cohen, & J. Greenberg (Eds.), *Justice in social relations* (pp. 337-351). New York: Academic Press. [Chapter 7, this volume.]

Greenberg, J. (1986c). Organizational performance evaluations: What makes them fair? In R. J. Lewicki, B. H. Sheppard, & M. H. Bazerman (Eds.), *Research on negotiation in organizations* (Vol. 1, pp. 25-41). Greenwich, CT: JAI. [Chapter 8 , this volume.]

Greenberg, J. (1987a). A taxonomy of organizational justice theories. *Academy of Management Review, 12,* 9-22. [Chapter 1, this volume.]

Greenberg, J. (1987b). Using diaries to promote procedural justice in performance appraisals. *Social Justice Research, 1,* 219-234. [Chapter 9, this volume.]

Greenberg, J. (1988a). Cultivating an image of justice: Looking fair on the job. *Academy of Management Executive, 2,* 155-158. [Chapter 4, this volume.]

Greenberg, J. (1988b, August). Using social accounts to manage impressions of performance appraisal fairness. In J. Greenberg & R. J. Bies (Cochairs), *Communicating fairness in organizations.* Symposium presented at the meeting of the Academy of Management, Anaheim, CA.

Greenberg, J. (1989). Cognitive re-evaluation of outcomes in response to underpayment inequity. *Academy of Management Journal, 32,* 174-184. [Chapter 16, this volume.]

Greenberg, J., & Cohen, R. L. (1982). Why justice? Normative and instrumental interpretations. In J. Greenberg & R. L. Cohen (Eds.), *Equity and justice in social behavior* (pp. 437-469). New York: Academic Press.

Greenberg, J., & Folger, R. (1983). Procedural justice, participation, and the fair process effect in groups and organizations. In P. B. Paulus (Ed.), *Basic group processes* (pp. 235-256). New York: Springer-Verlag.

Greenberg, J., Mark, M. M., & Lehman, D. (1985). Equity and justice in sports and games. *Journal of Sports Behavior, 8,* 18-33.

Greenberg, J., & Ornstein, S. (1983). High status job title as compensation for underpayment: A test of equity theory. *Journal of Applied Psychology, 68,* 285-297. [Chapter 17, this volume.]

Greenberg, J., & Tyler, T. R. (1987). Why procedural justice in organizations? *Social Justice Research, 1,* 127-142.

Greenberg, M. S., & Frisch, D. M. (1972). Effect of intentionality on willingness to reciprocate a favor. *Journal of Experimental Social Psychology, 8,* 99-111.

Greenwald, A. G., & Breckler, S. J. (1985). To whom is the self presented? In B. R. Schlenker (Ed.), *The self and social life* (pp. 126-145). New York: Academic Press.

Hamilton, V. L. (1980). Intuitive psychologist or intuitive lawyer? Alternative models of the attribution process. *Journal of Personality and Social Psychology, 39,* 767-772.

Harris, R. J. (1976). Handling negative inputs: On the plausible equity formulae. *Journal of Experimental Social Psychology, 12,* 194-209.

Heider, F. (1958). *The psychology of interpersonal relations.* New York: John Wiley.

Hollander, E. P. (1964). *Leaders, groups, and influence.* New York: Oxford University Press.

Huber, V. L., Latham, G. P., & Locke, E. A. (1989). The management of impressions through goal setting. In R. A. Giacalone & P. Rosenfeld (Eds.), *Impression management in the organization* (pp. 203-217). Hillsdale, NJ: Lawrence Erlbaum.

Jackall, R. (1988). *Moral mazes.* New York: Oxford University Press.

James, W. (1890). *The principles of psychology* (Vol. 1). New York: Henry Holt.

Jones, E. E. (1964). *Ingratiation.* New York: Appleton-Century-Crofts.

Jones, E. E., & Pittman, T. S. (1982). Toward a general theory of strategic self-presentation. In J. Suls (Ed.), *Psychological perspectives on the self* (Vol. 1, pp. 231-262). Hillsdale, NJ: Lawrence Erlbaum.

Jones, E. E., & Sigall, H. (1971). The bogus pipeline: A new paradigm for measuring affect and attitude. *Psychological Bulletin, 76,* 349-364.

Kahneman, D., & Tversky, A. (1982). Availability and the simulation heuristic. In D. Kahneman, P. Slovik, & A. Tversky (Eds.), *Judgment under uncertainty: Heuristics and biases* (pp. 201-208). Cambridge, UK: Cambridge University Press.

Kalven, J., & Zeisel, H. (1966). *The American jury.* Boston: Little, Brown.

Katz, E. (1957). The two-step flow of communication. *Public Opinion Quarterly, 21,* 61-78.

Kelley, H. H. (1967). Attribution theory in social psychology. In D. Levine (Ed.), *Nebraska Symposium on Motivation* (Vol. 15, pp. 55-88). Lincoln: University of Nebraska Press.

Kelman, H. C. (1973). Violence without moral restraint: Reflections on the dehumanization of victims and victimizer. *Journal of Social Issues, 29,* 25-61.

Kernis, M., & Reis, H. T. (1984). Self-consciousness, self-awareness, and justice in reward allocation. *Journal of Personality, 52,* 58-70.

Kidd, R. F., & Utne, M. K. (1978). Reactions to inequity: A prospective on the role of attributions. *Law and Human Behavior, 2,* 301-312.

Lane, I. M., & Messé, L. A. (1971). Equity and the distribution of rewards. *Journal of Personality and Social Psychology, 20,* 1-17.

Lawler, E. E., III. (1968). Equity theory as a predictor of productivity and work quality. *Psychological Bulletin, 70,* 596-610.

Lerner, M. J. (1977). The justice motive: Some hypotheses as to its origins and forms. *Journal of Personality, 45,* 1-52.

Lerner, M. J. (1980). *The belief in a just world.* New York: Plenum.

Leventhal, G. S. (1976). The distribution of rewards and resources in groups and organizations. In L. Berkowitz & E. Walster (Eds.), *Advances in experimental social psychology* (Vol. 9, pp. 91-131). New York: Academic Press.

Leventhal, G. S. (1980). What should be done with equity theory? In K. J. Gergen, M. S. Greenberg, & R. H. Willis (Eds.), *Social exchange: Advances in theory and research* (pp. 27-55). New York: Plenum.

Leventhal, G. S., Michaels, J. W., & Sanford, C. (1972). Inequity and interpersonal conflict: Reward allocation and secrecy about reward as methods of preventing conflict. *Journal of Personality and Social Psychology, 23,* 88-102.

Leventhal, G. S., Weiss, T., & Long, G. (1969). Equity, reciprocity, and reallocating rewards in the dyad. *Journal of Personality and Social Psychology, 13,* 300-305.

Lewicki, R. J. (1988, August). The public face of justice: Ineffective management of an organizational justice problem. In J. Greenberg & R. J. Bies (Cochairs), *Communicating fairness in organizations.* Symposium presented at the meeting of the Academy of Management, Anaheim, CA.

Liden, R. C., & Mitchell, T. R. (1988). Ingratiatory behaviors in organizational settings. *Academy of Management Review, 13,* 572-587.

Liebrand, W. B. G., Messick, D. M., & Wolters, F. J. M. (1986). Why we are fairer than others: A cross-cultural replication and extension. *Journal of Experimental Social Psychology, 22,* 590-604.

Lind, E. A., & Tyler, T. R. (1988). *The social psychology of procedural justice.* New York: Plenum.

Lofland, J. (1969). *Identities and deviance.* Englewood Cliffs, NJ: Prentice Hall.

Longenecker, C. O., Sims, H. P., Jr., & Gioia, D. A. (1987). Behind the mask: The politics of employee appraisal. *Academy of Management Executive, 1,* 183-193.

Major, B., & Deaux, K. (1982). Individual differences in justice behavior. In J. Greenberg & R. L. Cohen (Eds.), *Equity and justice in social behavior* (pp. 43-76). New York: Academic Press.

Mark, M. M., & Greenberg, J. (1987, January). Evening the score. *Psychology Today, 20,* 44-50.

Messick, D. M., Bloom, S., Boldizar, J. P., & Samuelson, C. D. (1985). Why we are fairer than others. *Journal of Experimental Social Psychology, 21,* 480-500.

Miller, D. T., & Ross, M. (1975). Self-serving biases in the attribution of causality: Fact or fiction? *Psychological Bulletin, 82,* 213-225.

Miner, J. B. (1984). The unpaved road over the mountains: From theory to applications. *Industrial/Organizational Psychologist, 21*(2), 9-20.

Moberg, D. J. (1977, April). *Organizational politics: Perspective from attribution theory.* Paper presented at the meeting of the American Institute for Decision Sciences, Chicago.

Morse, S. J., Gruzen, J., & Reis, J. T. (1976). The nature of equity restoration: Some approval-seeking considerations. *Journal of Experimental Social Psychology, 12,* 1-8.

Mowday, R. T. (1987). Equity theory predictions of behavior in organizations. In R. M. Steers & L. W. Porter (Eds.), *Motivation and work behavior* (4th ed., pp. 89-110). New York: McGraw-Hill.

Murray, K. B., & Montanari, J. R. (1986). Strategic management of the socially responsible firm: Integrating management and marketing theory. *Academy of Management Review, 11,* 815-827.

O'Malley, M. N., & Greenberg, J. (1983). Sex differences in restoring justice: The down payment effect. *Journal of Research in Personality, 17,* 174-185.

Perrow, C. (1972). *Complex organizations.* Glenview, IL: Scott, Foresman.

Pfeffer, J. (1981). Management as symbolic action. In L. L. Cummings & B. M. Staw (Eds.), *Research in organizational behavior* (Vol. 3, pp. 1-52). Greenwich, CT: JAI.

Poll: News on Quayle is unfair. (1988, August 29). *Columbus Dispatch*, p. 2A.

Pritchard, R. (1969). Equity theory: A review and critique. *Organizational Behavior and Human Performance, 4,* 75-94.

Pritchard, R., Dunnette, M. D., & Jorgenson, D. O. (1972). Effects of perceptions of equity and inequity on worker performance and satisfaction. *Journal of Applied Psychology, 56,* 75-94.

Ralston, D. A. (1985). Employee ingratiation: The role of management. *Academy of Management Review, 10,* 447-487.

Rasinski, K. A. (1987). What's fair is fair—or is it? Value differences underlying public views about social justice. *Journal of Personality and Social Psychology, 53,* 201-211.

Ravlin, E. C., & Meglino, B. M. (1987). Effects of values on perception and decision making: A study of alternative work value measures. *Journal of Applied Psychology, 72,* 666-673.

Rawls, J. (1971). *A theory of justice.* Cambridge, MA: Harvard University Press.

Reis, H. T. (1981). Self-presentation and distributive justice. In J. T. Tedeschi (Ed.), *Impression management theory and social psychological research* (pp. 269-291). New York: Academic Press.

Reis, H. T. (1984). The multidimensionality of justice. In R. Folger (Ed.), *The sense of injustice* (pp. 25-61). New York: Plenum.

Reis, H. T. (1986). Levels of interest in the study of interpersonal justice. In H. W. Bierhoff, R. L. Cohen, & J. Greenberg (Eds.), *Justice in social relations* (pp. 187-209). New York: Plenum.

Reis, H. T., & Burns, L. B. (1982). The salience of the self in responses to inequity. *Journal of Experimental Social Psychology, 18,* 464-475.

Reis, H. T., & Gruzen, J. (1976). On mediating equity, equality, and self-interest: The role of self-presentation in social exchange. *Journal of Experimental Social Psychology, 12,* 487-503.

Rheingold, H. (1988). *They have a word for it.* Los Angeles: Jeremy P. Tarcher.

Richardson, K. D., & Cialdini, R. B. (1981). Basking and blasting: Tactics of indirect self-presentation. In J. T. Tedeschi (Ed.), *Impression management theory and social psychological research* (pp. 41-53). New York: Academic Press.

Rivera, A. N., & Tedeschi, J. T. (1976). Public versus private reactions to positive inequity. *Journal of Personality and Social Psychology, 34,* 895-900.

Roberts, D. F., & Maccoby, N. (1985). Effects of mass communication. In G. Lindzey & E. Aronson (Eds.), *Handbook of social psychology* (3rd ed., Vol. 2, pp. 539-598). New York: Random House.

Salancik, G. R., & Meindl, J. R. (1984). Corporate attributions as strategic illusions of management control. *Administrative Science Quarterly, 29,* 238-254.

Salancik, G. R., & Pfeffer, J. (1978). A social information processing approach to job attitudes and task design. *Administrative Science Quarterly, 23,* 224-253.

Sampson, E. E. (1975). On justice as equality. *Journal of Social Issues, 31,* 45-64.

Scheibe, K. E. (1985). Historical perspectives on the presented self. In B. R. Schlenker (Ed.), *The self and social life* (pp. 33-64). New York: McGraw-Hill.

Schlenker, B. R. (1980). *Impression management: The self-concept, social identity, and interpersonal relations.* Belmont, CA: Brooks/Cole.

Schlenker, B. R. (1986). Self-identification: Toward an integration of the private and public self. In R. Baumeister (Ed.), *Public self and private self* (pp. 21-62). New York: Springer-Verlag.

Schlenker, B. R., & Darby, B. W. (1981). The use of apologies in social predicaments. *Social Psychology Quarterly, 44,* 271-278.

Schneider, D. J. (1981). Tactical self-presentations: Toward a broader conception. In J. T. Tedeschi (Ed.), *Impression management theory and social psychological research* (pp. 23-40). New York: Academic Press.

Schoeninger, D. W., & Wood, D. W. (1969). Comparison of married and ad hoc mixed-sex dyads negotiating the division of a reward. *Journal of Experimental Social Psychology, 5,* 483-499.

Schwab, D. P. (1980). Construct validity in organizational behavior. In B. M. Staw & L. L. Cummings (Eds.), *Research in organizational behavior* (Vol. 2, pp. 3-43). Greenwich, CT: JAI.

Schwartz, G., Kane, T., Joseph, J., & Tedeschi, J. T. (1978). The effects of remorse on reactions to a harm-doer. *British Journal of Social and Clinical Psychology, 17,* 293-297.

Schwartz, S. (1977). Normative influences on altruism. In L. Berkowitz (Ed.), *Advances in experimental social psychology* (Vol. 10, pp. 222-279). New York: Academic Press.

Schwoerer, C., & Rosen, B. (1989). Effects of employment-at-will policies and compensation policies on corporate image and job pursuit intentions. *Journal of Applied Psychology, 74,* 653-656.

Scott, M. B., & Lyman, S. M. (1968). Accounts. *American Sociological Review, 33,* 46-62.

Shapiro, D. L., & Buttner, E. H. (1988, August). *Adequate explanations: What are they, and do they enhance procedural justice under severe outcome circumstances?* Paper presented at the meeting of the Academy of Management, Anaheim, CA.

Shapiro, E. G. (1975). Effect of expectation of future interaction on reward allocation in dyads: Equity or equality? *Journal of Personality and Social Psychology, 31,* 873-880.

Sheppard, B. H. (1984). Third party conflict intervention: A procedural framework. In B. M. Staw & L. L. Cummings (Eds.), *Research in organizational behavior* (Vol. 6, pp. 141-190). Greenwich, CT: JAI.

Sheppard, B. H. (1985). Justice is no simple matter: Case for elaborating our model of procedural fairness. *Journal of Personality and Social Psychology, 49,* 953-962.

Sheppard, B. H., & Lewicki, R. J. (1987). Toward general principles of managerial fairness. *Social Justice Research, 1,* 161-176.

Snyder, C. R. (1985). The excuse: An amazing grace? In B. R. Schlenker (Ed.), *The self and social life* (pp. 235-289). New York: McGraw-Hill.

Snyder, C. R., Higgins, R. L., & Stucky, R. J. (1983). *Excuses: Masquerades in search of social grace.* New York: John Wiley.

Staw, B. M., McKechnie, P. I., & Puffer, S. M. (1983). The justification of organizational performance. *Administrative Science Quarterly, 28,* 582-600.

Sykes, G., & Matza, D. (1957). Techniques of neutralization: A theory of delinquency. *American Journal of Sociology, 22,* 664-670.

Tedeschi, J. T. (Ed.). (1981). *Impression management theory and social psychological research.* New York: Academic Press.

Tedeschi, J. T., & Melburg, V. (1984). Impression management and influence in the organization. In S. B. Bachrach & E. J. Lawler (Eds.), *Research in the sociology of organizations* (Vol. 3, pp. 31-58). Greenwich, CT: JAI.

Tedeschi, J. T., & Norman, N. (1985). Social power, self-presentation, and the self. In B. R. Schlenker (Ed.), *The self and social life* (pp. 293-322). New York: McGraw-Hill.

Tedeschi, J. T., & Reiss, M. (1981a). Identities, the phenomenal self, and laboratory research. In J. T. Tedeschi (Ed.), *Impression management theory and social psychological research* (pp. 3-22). New York: Academic Press.

Tedeschi, J. T., & Reiss, M. (1981b). Verbal strategies in impression management. In C. Antaki (Ed.), *The psychology of ordinary explanations of social behaviour* (pp. 271-309). London: Academic Press.

Tedeschi, J. T., & Rosenfeld, P. (1981). Impression management theory and the forced compliance situation. In J. T. Tedeschi (Ed.), *Impression management theory and social psychological research* (pp. 147-177). New York: Academic Press.

Tetlock, P. E. (1985). Toward an intuitive politician model of attribution processes. In B. R. Schlenker (Ed.), *The self and social life* (pp. 203-234). New York: McGraw-Hill.

Tetlock, P. E., & Manstead, A. (1985). Impression management versus intrapsychic explanations in social psychology: A useful dichotomy? *Psychological Review, 92,* 59-77.

Thibaut, J. W., & Kelley, H. H. (1959). *The social psychology of groups.* New York: John Wiley.

Thompson, J. D. (1967). *Organizations in action.* New York: McGraw-Hill.

Tornow, W. W. (1971). The development and application of an input-outcome moderator test on the perception and reduction of inequity. *Organizational Behavior and Human Performance, 6,* 614-638.

Utne, M. K., & Kidd, R. F. (1980). Attribution and equity. In G. Mikula (Ed.), *Justice and social interaction* (pp. 63-93). New York: Springer-Verlag.

Vallacher, R. A., & Solodky, M. (1979). Objective self-awareness, standards of evaluation and moral behavior. *Journal of Experimental Social Psychology, 15,* 252-262.

Walster, E., Walster, G. W., & Berscheid, E. (1978). *Equity: Theory and research.* Boston: Allyn & Bacon.

Walton, C. C. (1988). *The moral manager.* Cambridge, MA: Ballinger.

Weick, K. E. (1979). *The social psychology of organizing* (2nd ed.). Reading, MA: Addison-Wesley.

Weiner, B. (1974). Achievement motivation as conceptualized by an attribution theorist. In B. Weiner (Ed.), *Achievement motivation and attribution theory* (pp. 3-48). Morristown, NJ: General Learning Press.

Weiner, B., Amirkhan, J., Folkes, V. S., & Varette, J. A. (1987). An attributional analysis of excuse giving: Studies of a naive theory of emotion. *Journal of Personality and Social Psychology, 52,* 316-324.

What's so special about WordPerfect? (1988, March). *Personal Computing,* 100-103, 107-109, 113, 115-116.

Wicklund, R. A. (1975). Objective self-awareness. In L. Berkowitz (Ed.), *Advances in experimental social psychology* (Vol. 8, pp. 233-275). New York: Academic Press.

Wiggins, J. A., Dill, F., & Schwartz, R. D. (1965). On "status liability." *Sociometry, 28,* 197-209.

Wittig, M. R., Marks, G., & Jones, G. A. (1981). The effects of luck versus effort attributions on reward allocations to self and other. *Personality and Social Psychology Bulletin, 7,* 71-78.

PART III

Performance Appraisals

EVALUATING OTHERS FAIRLY

OF all the organizational contexts in which superiors and subordinates interact, I have always thought of the performance appraisal as one particularly rich in opportunities for matters of justice (and injustice) to arise. For example, judgments of fairness may focus on the outcomes of the appraisal process, that is, the rating itself or the pay raise resulting from it. Fairness judgments also may focus on the processes used to determine those outcomes, such as the subordinates' opportunities to provide valid information as the basis for deriving performance ratings. In other words, both distributive justice and procedural justice are highly relevant when it comes to organizational performance appraisals.

In Chapter 6, I empirically demonstrate this point in a study that asks a most basic question: What makes a performance evaluation fair? Through an iterative process of posing open-ended questions and following up with focused questionnaires, both the distributive and procedural components of performance appraisals were derived. Moreover, specific elements of both forms of justice were identified. The findings of this study lend empirical support to theoretical conceptualizations that argue for the conceptual independence of distributive and procedural justice and that claim the importance of various elements of fair procedures.

Chapters 7 and 8 were meant to be companion pieces examining the underlying processes that make performance appraisals fair both distributively and procedurally. In Chapter 7, I assert that fair appraisals need to be understood from two distributive perspectives: the extent to which performance ratings reflect the quality of one's performance and the extent to which organizational rewards are distributed in accordance with performance ratings. An empirical study is presented in support of the importance of both these distributive justice contexts. Then, in Chapter 8, I dissect the performance appraisal process, identifying tasks within which matters of procedural justice are likely to arise. Specifically, the importance of fair procedures is discussed as it applies to three key tasks: the gathering of performance data, the evaluation of that information, and the communication of evaluations during interviews. Last, I discuss how using fair procedures may help eliminate some of the well-established biases associated with the appraisal process.

Chapter 9 presents the results of a laboratory study specifically designed to test the effectiveness of a procedure—diary keeping—on promoting impressions of fair appraisal procedures. I found that in a laboratory setting, participants performing a simple clerical task perceived their performance ratings as fairer when they came from someone who observed their work and ostensibly recorded notes in a diary than when no such care was taken. In addition to their obvious applied implications, these results are discussed with respect to the strong case they make for using accurate information as the basis for evaluating work performance fairly.

—

6

—

What Makes a Performance Evaluation Fair?

W hat makes a performance evaluation perceived as fair? In view of the potential importance of fair evaluations in determining workers' acceptance of appraisal systems (Dipboye & de Pontbraind, 1981; Lawler, 1967), this is a significant question. Two approaches to the answer may be identified.

Traditional views of justice in organizational settings, such as equity theory (Adams, 1965), have focused on the relative ratio of a worker's outcomes of his or her inputs to some standard of comparison as the basis for assessing the fairness of a relationship (for a review, see Greenberg,

AUTHOR'S NOTE: This chapter was originally published in the *Journal of Applied Psychology,* Vol. 71, No. 2, pp. 340-342, under the title "Determinants of Perceived Fairness of Performance Evaluations." Copyright © 1986 by the American Psychological Association. Reprinted by permission.

1982). This *distributive justice* perspective focuses on the fairness of the evaluations received relative to the work performed. Workers may, in fact, assess the fairness of their appraisals by comparing the relative ratings they received in return for the work they contributed (Greenberg, 1986a[7]).

Additional evidence suggests, however, that beliefs about fair performance evaluations may also be based on the procedures by which the evaluations are determined apart from the ratings received (see Greenberg, 1986b[8]). This *procedural justice* perspective focuses on the fairness of the evaluation procedures used to determine the ratings. For example, in organizational questionnaire studies, Landy and his associates (Landy, Barnes, & Murphy, 1978; Landy, Barnes-Farrell, & Cleveland, 1980) found that the fairness of performance evaluations was related to several process variables (e.g., the opportunity to express feelings when evaluated) regardless of the rating outcomes themselves. Several laboratory studies have also shown the importance of procedural variables on the perceived fairness of performance appraisal systems (Greenberg, 1987[9]; Kanfer, Sawyer, Earley, & Lind, 1987).

Although several correlates of perceived fairness in performance appraisals have been revealed by Landy et al. (1978), their study was designed to examine the influence of process variables and, as such, paid little attention to the potential contribution of distributive factors as determinants of appraisal fairness. Moreover, by using a closed-format questionnaire in which the potential correlates of fairness were identified a priori (although on no apparent theoretical basis), it was not possible for participants to identify any other aspects of the appraisal process that may have contributed to their perception of its fairness. To avoid these limitations, the present study used an open-ended questionnaire method as the basis for identifying the determinants of perceived fair performance appraisals. This practice follows in the tradition of several other attempts to identify perceived fair managerial practices (e.g., Bies & Moag, 1986; Sheppard & Lewicki, 1987).

METHOD

Sample

The research sample consisted of a total of 217 middle managers employed in three different industrial groups: cable-TV companies located throughout the United States ($n = 95$), wholesale pharmaceutical distributing companies located primarily in the Midwest ($n = 80$), and credit unions in the state of Ohio ($n = 42$). Demographically, the overall sample was 78% male, 94% white, and 88% college educated, with an average tenure with their present organizations of 4.5 years. Virtually all the sample claimed to have had at least 30 experiences in receiving and 30 experiences in giving formal performance evaluations.

Procedure and Analytic Technique

The participants in all three subsamples took part in the study in conjunction with their participation in management training seminars.[1] Separate subsets of the overall sample were used in each of the four phases of the study. Each subset contained a roughly proportional number of participants from each of the three subgroups. The division into subsets was made on the basis of the availability of groups at various times in their training schedules, although the scheduling of participants to these events was decided at random.

In the response generation phase of the study, 56 participants were asked to think of an incident in which they received either a particularly fair or unfair performance evaluation on their job. They were then asked to write down the one most important factor that made it so fair or unfair. These responses were paraphrased and abstracted into simple statements and reworded in the fair direction by the experimenter. The phrases were then typed on index cards.

The categorization phase consisted of giving the cards to a group of 40 participants from the same sample who were asked to sort them into similar groupings following the unstructured Q-sort technique (Stephenson, 1953), that is, no predetermined number of categories was specified. To generate a homogeneous composite of these sortings that reduced the number of idiosyncratic statements, the criterion of retaining statement clusters that showed at least 75% common overlap was used. For a response category to be defined, a set of two or more statements had to be grouped together by at least 75% of the participants. Given that no a priori number of categories was imposed (the obtained range was 3 to 13), this level of agreement is considered to be a high one in Q-sort research (Stephenson, 1953). This procedure reduced the 56 original statements (1 from each of 56 respondents) to 18 statements falling into seven different categories (containing a range of from 2 to 4 statements each). The within-category rate of interrater agreement ranged from 75% (30 of 40 participants put the same group of statements in one category) to 100%, with an average within-category agreement rate of 88%.

In the cross-validation phase of the study, 46 additional participants categorized the 18 statements back into the seven categories. Because of the earlier elimination of idiosyncratic statements, participants were

TABLE 6.1 Factor Loadings and Mean Importance Ratings of Determinants of Fair
Performance Appraisals

Determinant	Factor loading		Importance rating	
	1	2	M	SD
Procedural factors				
Soliciting input prior to evaluation and using it	.46	.09	6.1	1.2
Two-way communication during interview	.67	.10	5.8	1.5
Ability to challenge/rebut evaluation	.66	.15	4.9	2.0
Rater familiarity with ratee's work	.59	.18	5.1	1.6
Consistent application of standards	.55	.20	6.9	1.5
Distributive factors				
Receipt of rating based on performance achieved	.25	.70	7.1	0.9
Recommendation for salary/promotion based on rating	.15	.61	7.2	1.3

NOTE: $N = 75$.

highly successful in performing these ratings, with a hit rate of 98.6% (of
828, only 12 were misclassified).

In the importance-rating phase of the study, another group of 75
participants from the same sample were asked to rate the importance of
each of the seven categories as determinants of fair evaluations. A 9-point
bipolar scale with end points labeled 1 (*not at all important*) and 9 (*extremely
important*) was used.

RESULTS

Responses to the seven questionnaire items were factor analyzed using
the principal-factors technique and a varimax rotation. The first two
factors accounted for 94.7% of the variance, and a third added less than
1%. The factor loadings are displayed in Table 6.1.

The five items that loaded highly on Factor 1, but not on Factor 2,
clearly appear to reflect procedural dimensions of fairness and are so
labeled in Table 6.1. In addition, two items that loaded highly on Factor
2, but not on Factor 1, appeared to reflect distributive dimensions of
fairness.[2] Although the observed pattern of factor loadings is clear, the
relatively small sample size on which the ratings were based ($N = 75$)
makes these loadings more unstable than would be desirable.

The mean importance ratings of each of the statements also appear in
Table 6.1. A one-way repeated measures analysis of variance comparing the
importance of the distributive factors and the procedural factors revealed

no significant difference, $F(1, 449) = 1.24$. Within-participants comparisons between the five procedural factors revealed no overall difference in their perceived importance, $F(4, 296) < 1.00$. Similarly, the ratings of the two distributive factors were not rated as significantly different from each other, $F(1, 74) < 1.00$.

DISCUSSION

The results provide empirical support for several theoretical conceptualizations of procedural justice that have postulated the importance of various determinants of fair procedures. For example, two of the factors identified in this study, ability to challenge and/or rebut evaluations and consistent application of standards, correspond closely with Leventhal, Karuza, and Fry's (1980) identification of appeals procedures and consistency of allocation practices as determinants of fair procedures for the distribution of resources. Similarly, the soliciting input factor and the two-way communication factor identified here reflect Thibaut and Walker's (1975) concern for process control (the opportunity to influence the information that will be used to make decisions)—a concept central to their theory of procedural justice. Although support already exists showing the importance of the Leventhal et al. (1980) and the Thibaut and Walker (1975) determinants of procedural justice (for a review, see Folger & Greenberg, 1985), the present findings highlight their potential applicability to performance appraisal contexts.

These findings also provide strong support to conceptual attempts to expand procedural justice conceptualizations by applying them to organizational settings in general (Greenberg & Folger, 1983) and performance appraisal situations in particular (Greenberg, 1986b[8]). Findings that the use of diaries enhances the perceived fairness of performance appraisals (Greenberg, 1987[9]) corroborate identification of the rater familiarity with ratee's work factor identified in this study inasmuch as the supervisor's keeping of a performance diary may be seen as increasing his or her familiarity with the ratee's performance. The importance of rater familiarity as a determinant of fair appraisals revealed in this study corroborates Landy et al.'s (1978) significant correlation between fairness ratings and a questionnaire item tapping supervisor's knowledge of performance. It is also consistent with the expressed importance of rater familiarity as a determinant of valid performance appraisals (e.g., Ilgen & Barnes-Farrell, 1984).

There are several additional ways in which the present findings corroborate and extend other studies of procedural justice in organizational settings. Most generally, these findings support the existence of both procedural and distributive determinants of fairness in organizations found in Alexander and Ruderman's (1987) large-scale survey study. More specifically, several studies inspired by Thibaut and Walker's (1975) theory have found that procedures giving employees input into the performance appraisal system are seen as fairer than those that do not (Kanfer et al., 1987; Lissak, 1983). The present study complements these findings by showing that workers are aware of the importance of soliciting and using worker input as a precondition of fair appraisals.

The two distributive factors identified in this study closely correspond to my distributive justice-based analysis of performance appraisals (Greenberg, 1986a[7]). In this connection, support was found for two distinct channels of influence as determinants of distributive justice—the relationship between performance and rating and that between rating and subsequent administrative action. The significant correlation between perceived fairness and the Landy et al. (1978) item "Is action plan related to performance weakness?" reflects a similar sensitivity to distributive factors. The finding that distributive factors were rated as important as procedural factors as determinants of fairness suggests that researchers and theorists should not allow distributive factors to get lost in the shadow of the recent attention paid to procedural determinants of fairness. Both procedural and distributive factors need to be taken into account in any thorough conceptualization of justice in organizational settings.

In closing, a note of caution is in order with respect to the generalizability of the results. Although three different managerial groups were used in this study, the great similarity between them does not allow a conclusion that the same factors would emerge in different populations or that they would have the same relative importance. Indeed, the present results, despite their strong fit with existing research and theory, must be considered limited to the population used in the study. Future research is needed to determine the extent to which other factors would emerge as determinants of fairness in different populations.

NOTES

1. Because all three samples were similar demographically and identical results were obtained for each sample separately, no distinction is made between the three subsamples used in this study.

2. Support for the identification of these factors was derived using a cross-validation procedure similar to that used for the generation of the items. A group of 56 undergraduate students at a

Midwestern university reverse-sorted the seven statements into two categories—procedural factors (concerning the fairness of the evaluation procedure) and distributive factors (concerning the fairness of the resulting evaluation). Of the 392 total categorizations, 385 were accurate, resulting in a hit rate of 98.2%, thus supporting the identification of the factors.

REFERENCES

Adams, J. S. (1965). Inequity in social exchange. In L. Berkowitz (Ed.), *Advances in experimental social psychology* (Vol. 2, pp. 267-299). New York: Academic Press.

Alexander, S., & Ruderman, M. (1987). The role of procedural and distributive justice in organizational behavior. *Social Justice Research, 1,* 177-198.

Bies, R. J., & Moag, J. S. (1986). Interactional justice: Communicating criteria of fairness. In R. J. Lewicki, B. H. Sheppard, & M. H. Bazerman (Eds.), *Research on negotiation in organizations* (Vol. 1, pp. 43-55). Greenwich, CT: JAI.

Dipboye, R. L., & de Pontbraind, R. (1981). Correlates of employee reactions to performance appraisals and appraisal systems. *Journal of Applied Psychology, 66,* 248-251.

Folger, R., & Greenberg, J. (1985). Procedural justice: An interpretive analysis of personnel systems. In K. M. Rowland & G. R. Ferris (Eds.), *Research in personnel and human resources management* (Vol. 3, pp. 141-183). Greenwich, CT: JAI.

Greenberg, J. (1982). Approaching equity and avoiding inequity in groups and organizations. In J. Greenberg & R. L. Cohen (Eds.), *Equity and justice in social behavior* (pp. 389-435). New York: Academic Press.

Greenberg, J. (1986a). The distributive justice of organizational performance evaluations. In H. W. Bierhoff, R. L. Cohen, & J. Greenberg (Eds.), *Justice in social relations* (pp. 337-351). New York: Plenum. [7]

Greenberg, J. (1986b). Organizational performance appraisal procedures: What makes them fair? In M. H. Bazerman, R. J. Lewicki, & B. H. Sheppard (Eds.), *Research on negotiation in organizations* (Vol. 1, pp. 25-41). Greenwich, CT: JAI. [8]

Greenberg, J. (1987). Using diaries to promote procedural justice in performance appraisals. *Social Justice Research, 1,* 219-234. [9]

Greenberg, J., & Folger, R. (1983). Procedural justice, participation, and the fair process effect in groups and organizations. In P. B. Paulus (Ed.), *Basic group processes* (pp. 235-256). New York: Springer-Verlag.

Ilgen, D. R., & Barnes-Farrell, J. L. (1984). *Performance planning and evaluation.* Chicago: SRA.

Kanfer, R., Sawyer, J., Earley, P. C., & Lind, E. A. (1987). Participation in task evaluation procedures: The effects of influential opinion expression and knowledge of evaluative criteria on attitudes and performance. *Social Justice Research, 1,* 235-249.

Landy, F. J., Barnes, J. L., & Murphy, K. R. (1978). Correlates of perceived fairness and accuracy of performance evaluation. *Journal of Applied Psychology, 63,* 751-754.

Landy, F. J., Barnes-Farrell, J. L., & Cleveland, J. N. (1980). Perceived fairness and accuracy of performance evaluation: A follow-up. *Journal of Applied Psychology, 65,* 355-356.

Lawler, E. E. (1967). The multi-trait multi-rater approach to measuring managerial job performance. *Journal of Applied Psychology, 51,* 369-381.

Leventhal, G. S., Karuza, J., & Fry, W. R. (1980). Beyond fairness: A theory of allocation preferences. In G. Mikula (Ed.), *Justice and social interaction* (pp. 167-218). New York: Springer-Verlag.

Lissak, R. I. (1983). *Procedural fairness: How employees evaluate procedures.* Unpublished doctoral dissertation, University of Illinois, Urbana-Champaign.

Sheppard, B. H., & Lewicki, R. J. (1987). Toward general principles of procedural fairness. *Social Justice Research, 1,* 161-176.
Stephenson, W. (1953). *The study of behavior.* Chicago: University of Chicago Press.
Thibaut, J., & Walker, L. (1975). *Procedural justice: A psychological analysis.* Hillsdale, NJ: Lawrence Erlbaum.

—

7

—

The Distributive Justice
of Performance Evaluations

Traditionally, concern about matters of justice and fairness among scientists interested in organizational behavior has focused on ways of determining equitable payment and assessing behavioral and attitudinal reactions to inequitable payment (Greenberg, 1982). This orientation toward money as the primary medium through which justice is studied is reflected in much of the organizational literature (e.g., Vecchio, 1982). At the same time, however, there also appears to be a growing recognition

AUTHOR'S NOTE: This chapter was originally published in *Justice in Social Relations* (H. W. Bierhoff, R. L. Cohen, & J. Greenberg, Eds.), pp. 337-351, under the title "The Distributive Justice of Organizational Performance Evaluations." Copyright © 1986 by Plenum Publications. Reprinted by permission.

that matters of justice are involved in several nonfinancial exchanges taking place within organizations (see Nord, 1980). The chapter by Martin (1986) and the chapter by Crosby (1984) in an organizationally oriented serial represent excellent examples of this trend. Much of my work on procedural justice (e.g., Folger & Greenberg, 1985; Greenberg, 1986b[8]) also reflects an appreciation for the idea that considerations of justice are involved in many forms of nonmonetary social exchange in organizations.

The present chapter is in keeping with this orientation. It represents an outgrowth of my conceptual statements (Folger & Greenberg, 1985; Greenberg & Folger, 1983; Greenberg & Tyler, 1987) and empirical reports (Greenberg, 1986a[6], 1986b[8], 1987[9]) demonstrating how concerns about justice manifest themselves in one particular aspect of organizational life—performance appraisal. Specifically, this chapter will present some new conceptualizations of distributive justice that are relevant to performance appraisal situations and some data that bear on them. The focus will be on *distributive justice*—the fairness of evaluations received—as opposed to *procedural justice*—the fairness of the procedures on which those evaluations are based, a topic treated in detail elsewhere (Greenberg, 1986b[8]). After presenting these ideas, their implications, both for conceptualizations of justice and for organizational theory and practice, will be discussed.

DISTRIBUTIVE JUSTICE IN
THE CONTEXT OF PERFORMANCE APPRAISAL

One day not long ago, one of my students, in an obviously distressed state, came to my office. She found a grade of D on her university grade report despite having received positive performance feedback all term long. On further investigating this situation, I found that I actually had given the student a grade of A but that a clerical error in another office was responsible for the much lower grade she received. After arranging for an official correction of the student's grade, I began thinking about how typical the problem faced by this student probably was—at least as it may exist in the minds of offended parties.

Although the student in this story was actually the innocent victim of a clerical error, anyone who has ever taught probably has encountered students who believed the final grade they received was not representative of the quality of work they performed. In many ways, this claim is similar to that voiced by workers who complain that the pay raises they receive are not commensurate with their positive performance evaluations. Their

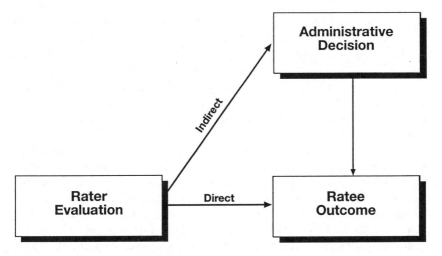

Figure 7.1. Channels of Influence in Organizational Performance Appraisal Systems

distress, of course, can be readily understood in equity theory's claim that persons receiving outcomes (a final grade in the case of the student and a pay raise in the case of the worker) lower than merited by their inputs (their academic performance or job performance, respectively) will feel angry (Adams, 1965; Walster, Walster, & Berscheid, 1978).

Channels of Influence in Appraisal Systems

As appealing as this reasoning may be, it overlooks an important aspect of the situation (one that came up in discussion with the distressed student)—namely, whether the performance evaluation is viewed as an outcome in itself or as an input that demands certain other associated outcomes for equity to be established. An illustration summarizing the structural elements of justice in a performance evaluation situation is shown in Figure 7.1. The diagram shows two distinct channels of influence operating in a performance appraisal system: a direct one and an indirect one. Evaluations can either operate as outcomes themselves or serve as intermediate steps through which administrative decisions, operating as outcomes, are made.

Consider how these processes may have been operating in the case of the distressed student. The student thought that I believed her to be performing at a high level of proficiency. If this evaluation is taken as a direct outcome—an intrinsic reward (Deci, 1975)—the student would be positively influenced. She would feel proud and happy that she performed well and pleased the evaluating authority figure. As it was (and often is the case), however, the positive evaluation was not responded to as an end in itself. Instead, it operated indirectly, as a secondary reinforcer that should have led to a positive administrative decision that accurately reflected the positive evaluation. In this sense, the evaluation operated more as an input than as an outcome. By defining her inputs as positive, an expectation was created for receipt of an administrative reward that reflected that evaluation.

I have encountered the same phenomenon in some of my organizational consulting experiences. Workers are often distressed at not being paid in a manner consistent with their evaluations. Knowing that this happens (sometimes because of economic difficulties within their organizations), supervisors sometimes give low performance ratings merely to justify the low pay raises they know will be forthcoming. The cost of doing this, of course, is borne by the worker's job development. "Why," a worker might ask, "if I am doing everything correctly, am I receiving a poor evaluation?" Using the evaluation to justify the outcome may bring about an immediate reward-performance congruity, but because the performance feedback is inaccurate, it might also be detrimental to employee training and development (Wexley & Latham, 1981).

These illustrations highlight some fundamental, yet often overlooked, points about justice in work organizations, especially the role of performance evaluations in assessing the justice of organizational outcomes. By focusing on the relationship between performance evaluations and distributive justice, this chapter intends to shed some new light on both the study of justice and the study and practice of organizational phenomena.

Performance Appraisal and Organizational Justice

By *performance appraisal,* I am referring to "the process by which an organization measures and evaluates an individual employee's behavior and accomplishments for a finite time period" (DeVries, Morrison, Shullman, & Gerlach, 1981, p. 2). It is a process that occurs in one form or another in most contemporary business and government organizations (Bernardin & Beatty, 1984). Although performance evaluations are used to help develop employees' skills and to facilitate the making of personnel decisions, it is safe to say that much of industry's concern about performance appraisals comes as a reaction to attempts to comply with recent legislation and court rulings demanding the use of *fair* appraisal procedures. Although it is beyond the scope of this chapter to detail the performance appraisal process and the legal rulings bearing on it (the

TABLE 7.1 Performance Appraisal: Steps, Legal Considerations, and Organizational
Justice Issues

Performance Appraisal Steps[a]	Legal Considerations[b]	Organizational Justice Issues
1. Conduct job analysis. 2. Develop appraisal instruments.	Evaluations must be based on the work actually done. Instruments must tap job-relevant criteria.	
3. Select raters. 4. Train raters. 5. Measure performance.	Raters must be familiar with the work and the rating scales and must have an opportunity to observe and measure the ratees' performances.	Procedural justice: Appraisal procedures should be free from biasing influences.
6. Share appraisal with ratee. 7. Set new performance goals. 8. Reward or punish performance.	Qualifications for pay raises, promotions, and transfers must be publicized. Personnel decisions must be justified by a valid performance appraisal procedure.	Distributive justice: Administrative decisions should be commensurate with appraisal outcomes.

[a] Adapted from Latham and Wexley (1981).
[b] Adapted from Klasson, Thompson, and Luben (1980).

interested reader is referred to Latham & Wexley, 1981), Table 7.1 summarizes this information vis-à-vis their corresponding organizational justice concerns.

As this table shows, the appraisal phases in which job information is collected (steps 1 and 2) and performance ratings are made (steps 3 through 5) are conceptualized as bearing more on matters of procedural justice than distributive justice (and are analyzed by Greenberg, 1986b[8]). Those phases of the performance appraisal process in which evaluations are communicated and appropriate administrative actions are taken (steps 6 through 8) relate most clearly to distributive justice—the focus of this chapter. Indeed, laws such as the 1978 Civil Service Reform Act clearly require personnel actions to be based on employees' (validly assessed) job skills and qualifications (see Klasson, Thompson, & Luben, 1980). Using the terminology of justice researchers, distributive justice requires administrative decisions to be commensurate with appraisal outcomes. In the following sections of this chapter, I will analyze the conceptual complexities involved in implementing these requirements.

TABLE 7.2 A Classification System of Evaluations as Outcomes

Level of Analysis	Terminality of Evaluation	
	Penultimate (Evaluations leading to other outcome judgments)	Ultimate (Evaluations as end-state judgments)
Psychological	Attributional mediation of performance	Communication of self-worth and value
Organizational	Administrative decisions (e.g., salary, promotion, entry into training programs)	Communication of career potential

A TAXONOMY OF ORGANIZATIONAL
PERFORMANCE EVALUATIONS AS OUTCOMES

In many ways, the performance evaluations received in work settings can be understood as outcomes in the sense of the term suggested by equity theory. They are received in recognition of workers' accomplishments. A positive evaluation is, after all, rewarding and a negative one is punishing, regardless of whether or not it is followed up by appropriate administrative actions. In fact, the high status that workers are accorded from positive evaluations are specifically identified by Adams (1965) as an outcome. As I have already noted, however, a performance evaluation may not always function as an outcome directly (recall Figure 7.1). It may be direct in that the positive evaluation can function as an end in itself. Alternatively, it can function indirectly by leading to the administration of other rewards. Table 7.2 will help examine more closely the implications of these direct and indirect avenues of influence by presenting a classification system of evaluations as outcomes.

This simple taxonomy is composed of two dimensions: terminality of evaluation and level of analysis. The *terminality* dimension is used to distinguish between how final, or terminal, the evaluations are as outcomes. A distinction is made between penultimate outcomes and ultimate outcomes. An evaluation operating as a *penultimate outcome* is one that leads to other outcome judgments. An *ultimate outcome* is one that functions as an end state in itself. A distinction is also made with respect to the level of analysis by which outcomes can operate: outcomes that influence employees' organizational standing and those that influence their psychological state.

For example, a positive evaluation would be considered a penultimate outcome if it serves as the basis of a subsequent organizational decision to give the good worker a high pay raise or a promotion. At a more psychological level, attributions of performance causality may be considered penultimate outcome evaluations. These are judgments about what causes a person's behavior, judgments that lead to subsequent judgments about what the person is like as a worker. These correspondent inferences (Jones & Davis, 1965) are penultimate relative to more general performance judgments. (For example, the evaluation that someone produced twice as many units as the average employee may lead to the judgment that he or she is a good worker.)

Evaluations can also operate as ultimate outcomes. As such, they operate as end-state judgments in themselves. A positive evaluation of a worker's performance can function at a psychological level of impact by communicating the rater's beliefs about the worker's worth to the organization. A positive evaluation may mean a good feeling for the worker (Leskovec, 1967). From an organizational perspective, a positive evaluation can have a related positive impact by communicating something encouraging about the employee's future with the organization.

In the case of evaluations as ultimate outcomes, they may be expected to operate like any other outcome in the equity equation. This expectation stands although performance evaluations have not previously been studied as outcomes from an equity theory perspective. Even more interesting situations emerge by considering how performance evaluations may function indirectly, as penultimate outcomes. Before proceeding further with this analysis, it is necessary to engage in a slight digression to clarify an important underlying assumption.

THE INPUT-DEFINING FUNCTION
OF ORGANIZATIONAL PERFORMANCE EVALUATIONS

The ambiguity of performance standards on many jobs may make it difficult, if not impossible, for workers to know exactly how well or poorly they are working. (This is contrasted with laboratory studies, in which explicit input feedback is provided.) In this sense, it can be said that the *evaluation serves an input-defining function.* Cognitive theories of motivation, such as expectancy theory (e.g., Vroom, 1964) suggest that *expectancy* (the perceived link between effort and performance) and *instrumentality* (the perceived link between performance and reward) contribute to motivation. As illustrated in Figure 7.2, performance appraisal may be seen as playing an important role in defining the quality of one's inputs. If workers do not know how good a "good job" is, performance appraisals may help workers to define the quality of their inputs, which may, in turn, create outcome expectations.

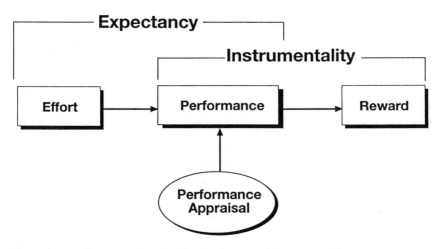

Figure 7.2. Performance Appraisal in the Context of Expectancy Theory

It is precisely in this connection that concerns about distributive justice arise. An organizational authority agent who appraises performance can lead workers to accept as legitimate the assessment of the workers' performances. The appraiser who does this, in effect, creates expectations for outcomes. If these ultimate outcomes (pay) match the appraisals, then the reward received will be seen as fair. If they do not match, they will likely be seen as unfair. This is what equity theory predicts.

PERFORMANCE EVALUATIONS AS ULTIMATE
AND PENULTIMATE OUTCOMES: RESEARCH EVIDENCE

Several of my previous studies address these predictions. These investigations simultaneously demonstrate how evaluations may operate as ultimate and penultimate outcomes.

Using Performance Evaluations to
Qualify Reactions to Monetary Outcomes

In one study (Greenberg, 1984), 176 college students performed a clerical task that had an ambiguous performance referent—one that made it difficult for them to be able to tell how well or poorly they were doing until they were told. Specifically, the task consisted of copying numbers from a printed list onto a computer coding form, a task found to be highly susceptible to acceptance of false performance feedback in several earlier studies (e.g., Greenberg, 1977). Twice during their work periods, participants were given either positive or negative performance evaluations. Specifically, they were told that they had been performing either "much better than" or "much worse than" most others.

The terminality of the evaluation was also manipulated. This was accomplished either by paying participants for their work or by not paying them at all. It was reasoned that a monetary payment would make the evaluations operate as penultimate outcomes—ones whose satisfaction would be gauged relative to the ultimate outcomes, the monetary payment. As equity theory suggests, payment outcomes congruent with evaluations (acting, in this case, as inputs) would lead to more positive reactions than incongruent states. By contrast, no monetary payments would make the evaluations operate as outcomes themselves. As a hedonic comparison (Brickman & Bulman, 1977), workers would be expected to be more satisfied with positive evaluations than with negative ones. With this in mind, an outcome manipulation was designed in which participants received either higher pay than expected, lower pay than expected, or no pay, with none expected.

The dependent variable of interest was a satisfaction index. It consisted of a cluster of highly intercorrelated questionnaire measures assessing overall satisfaction with the experiment, satisfaction with the experimenter, and fairness of treatment in the experiment. The pattern of mean satisfaction-index scores as a function of payment (outcome terminality) and performance evaluation is shown in Figure 7.3.

These results support the above outlined hypotheses. Specifically, participants were more satisfied with high pay than low pay overall, but this was qualified by the evaluation they received. Participants were more satisfied with their low pay when they believed it followed from poor performance evaluations than from good ones. In fact, no workers were more upset than poorly paid good workers. Although the effect was not as great for highly paid workers, the high payment following from a poor evaluation lowered satisfaction relative to highly paid workers who were positively evaluated, although not to a statistically significant degree. These findings are perfectly in keeping with equity theory's predictions regarding the balance of outcomes and inputs as a determinant of satisfaction (see Walster et al., 1978).

The more interesting aspect of these findings resides in the case in which evaluations served as ultimate outcomes (i.e., the no-pay condition). In this case, satisfaction was found to be as high or as low as it was when pay and performance evaluations were congruent. High evaluations seemed to serve as positive outcomes in themselves, making workers feel highly satisfied. Low evaluations seemed to serve as negative outcomes in

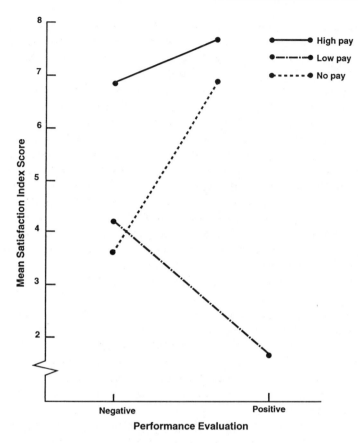

Figure 7.3. Mean Levels of Reported Satisfaction as a Function of Performance Evaluation and Payment Level (Greenberg, 1984)

themselves, making workers feel dissatisfied. These data, then, show how evaluations of performance can serve as ultimate outcomes themselves or as penultimate outcomes (acting as inputs, creating expectations for monetary rewards).

Using Performance Evaluations to Qualify Reactions to Job Titles as Outcomes

Another illustration of this phenomenon can be seen in two studies (Greenberg & Ornstein, 1983[17]). These investigations, only a small portion of which will be reported here, were designed to demonstrate a related idea about the ambiguity of high-status job titles—whether they operated as outcomes or as inputs.

The participants in these investigations were college students who performed a proofreading task in exchange for pay. In the earned title condition, participants were told that they had performed well. This good performance, they were told, earned them the title of "senior proofreader" and the added responsibility of checking others' work during an additional hour for which they would not be paid. In the unearned title condition, the title and the extra work were given but without any performance evaluation serving as the basis of the decision. In two experiments, by the end of the final work period, participants in the unearned title condition were performing at a significantly lower level than their counterparts in the earned title condition. The difference between the two conditions was that a positive performance evaluation preceded the decision to grant the high-status job title and the associated responsibilities in the earned title condition. In other words, participants performed at a higher level when they were given a high-status job title and a positive evaluation than when they were given just the high-status job title without any performance evaluation.

The positive performance evaluation justified the higher status and added responsibilities, leading workers to feel their treatment was equitable and to maintain a consistently high level of performance. The performance evaluation made the high status appear real and accepted as genuine. Without any evaluation, however, participants ultimately believed that the experimenter was manipulative—giving them a meaningless title in an attempt to justify the increased inputs expected of them. This illustrates another sense in which evaluations may serve as indirect influences on outcomes. The evaluation justified the bestowal of high status as legitimate and warranted, thereby legitimizing the expected increase in inputs. The granting of the identical status without an appraisal led participants to challenge the subsequent rewards. Simply put, the evaluation information qualified the effects of other outcomes. To summarize, these studies show that performance evaluations can alter perceptions of inputs and outcomes, therefore altering perceptions of distributive justice.

IMPLICATIONS

If the foregoing analyses have any value, it is to be found in their implications both for conceptualizations of distributive justice and for organizational theory and practice. This closing section will discuss these implications.

Implications for
Conceptualizations of Distributive Justice

One of the primary implications of studying distributive justice in the context of performance appraisals is that doing so highlights the importance of several previously neglected aspects of distributive justice. Most basic in this regard is the suggestion that performance evaluations can function as outcomes in affecting people's perceptions of distributive justice. This is a contribution not only in that it redirects attention from more traditionally studied monetary outcomes but also in that it qualifies our understanding of monetary outcomes. The research summarized in this chapter clearly demonstrates that the perceived meaning of pay and reactions to pay may be qualified by beliefs about the performance evaluations through which that pay appears to have been determined. As a result, caution needs to be exercised in (a) interpreting the results of field studies in which there are different payment outcomes and (b) generalizing from simple laboratory studies in which payment outcomes are manipulated in the absence of performance evaluations. The present conceptualization may be viewed as a call for further investigation into the interrelationships among different forms of distributive outcomes in general and between performance evaluations and pay in particular.

One of the most perplexing problems in studying equity and distributive justice in complex organizational settings is the inherent ambiguities involved in distinguishing between outcomes and inputs (Tornow, 1971). The present chapter suggests that performance evaluations can operate either as outcomes (directly or indirectly), as inputs (i.e., information justifying employees' claims to future outcomes), or as both. This state of affairs raises serious questions about the validity of attempts to study complex organizational exchanges from the same structural model used for studying simple dyadic interaction. If outcomes and inputs, as the basic building blocks, are rendered uninterpretable, what orientation to studying distributive justice can supplant it? Although it may be premature to answer this question definitively at this time, a promising approach is suggested by the work of Mikula (1986). His unstructured approach to assessing the perceived determinants of distributive justice in social situations may be useful to offering insight into complex distributive questions, just as Sheppard's (1984) unstructured interviewing approach to organizational bargaining has proved useful in explaining complex procedural questions.

Another implication of the present conceptualization for future work on distributive justice is that a wider level of analysis—perhaps an organizational level—may be useful. Although Reis (1986) notes the importance of the level of analysis issue, Brickman, Folger, Goode, and Schul's

(1981) arguments about levels of analysis are most relevant here. Their suggestion that justice at the individual level does not ensure justice at a broader societal level applies well to the present application of distributive justice. A macro perspective on justice at an organizational level would force attention away from concerns of individual evaluation decisions to overall evaluation-decision histories and policies. Such an orientation, it may be claimed, would be more sensitive to the complexities of distributive justice in organizational settings suggested in this chapter than more traditional micro-level approaches.

Implications for
Organizational Theory and Practice

Performance appraisal practitioners have emphasized the importance of basing evaluations on observable incidents of work behavior (Carroll & Schneier, 1982). If a performance evaluation is considered as an outcome and the work behavior as relevant inputs, then it follows from equity theory that the recommended evaluation-behavior linkage would promote distributive justice. Another common recommendation—and legal requirement (Klasson et al., 1980)—is to make administrative decisions commensurate with evaluations (DeVries et al., 1981). In the present terminology, the evaluation is a secondary, or penultimate, outcome. It serves to define expectations of forthcoming personnel decisions. Functionally, then, it serves as an input, requiring a match with ultimate outcomes to be distributively just. To combine these points, it would be correct to suggest that distributive justice requires congruence between perceptions of performance excellence, resulting performance evaluations, and personnel actions made on the basis of those evaluations.

One of the most effective things supervisors (using the terminology shown in Figure 7.2) could do during performance appraisal interviews would be to strengthen employees' instrumentality beliefs. Supervisors should attempt to make sure that employees have well-defined beliefs about what outcomes they may expect to receive for the work they do. Although these contingencies are formally spelled out in some pay plans (such as the piecework system), it is incumbent on supervisors working under less formal reward contingency systems to promote beliefs in reliable reward-performance contingencies. In an attempt to foster instrumentality beliefs, managers may be required to stipulate clearly what the relevant job behaviors and rewards are—a key component of any performance evaluation interview (Carroll & Tosi, 1973). Just as important, it is critical for managers to make it possible for those instrumentalities to materialize. Instrumentality beliefs about receiving certain raises in response to certain production increases communicated during performance appraisal interviews may be effective only insofar as they can be expected to be met. If an organization has a history of not meeting its promises, then not only might immediate dissatisfaction result, but also it may be difficult to establish believable instrumentality perceptions in the future. This point also further illustrates the potential value of studying the justice of performance appraisal from an organizationwide perspective.

It may be expected that many of the adverse reactions to organizational inequities noted as reactions to monetary-based inequities (such as withdrawal, dissatisfaction, and impaired performance; see Greenberg, 1982) would also result from evaluation-based inequities. Moreover, it may be speculated that some portion of the global dissatisfaction expressed as inequity in some studies (e.g., Finn & Lee, 1972) may be the result of reactions to unfair performance evaluations. Given the highly sensitive nature of the performance evaluation process, it is quite likely to be a substantial part of expressions of organizational dissatisfaction that are based on claims of injustice.

REFERENCES

Adams, J. S. (1965). Inequity in social exchange. In L. Berkowitz (Ed.), *Advances in experimental social psychology* (Vol. 2, pp. 267-299). New York: Academic Press.

Bernardin, H. J., & Beatty, R. W. (1984). *Performance appraisal: Assessing human behavior at work.* Boston: Kent.

Brickman, P., & Bulman, R. J. (1977). Pleasure and pain in social comparison. In J. M. Suls & R. L. Miller (Eds.), *Social comparison processes* (pp. 149-186). Washington, DC: Hemisphere.

Brickman, P., Folger, R., Goode, E., & Schul, Y. (1981). Microjustice and macrojustice. In M. Lerner & S. C. Lerner (Eds.), *The justice motive in social behavior* (pp. 173-204). New York: Plenum.

Carroll, S. J., & Schneier, C. E. (1982). *Performance appraisal and review systems.* Glenview, IL: Scott, Foresman.

Carroll, S. J., Jr., & Tosi, H. L. (1973). *Management by objectives: Applications and research.* New York: Macmillan.

Crosby, F. (1984). Relative deprivation in organizational settings. In B. M. Staw & L. L. Cummings (Eds.), *Research in organizational behavior* (Vol. 6, pp. 51-94). Greenwich, CT: JAI.

Deci, E. L. (1975). *Intrinsic motivation.* New York: Plenum.

DeVries, D. L., Morrison, A. M., Shullman, S. L., & Gerlach, M. L. (1981). *Performance appraisal on the line.* New York: John Wiley.

Finn, R. H., & Lee, S. M. (1972). Salary equity: Its determination, analysis, and correlates. *Journal of Applied Psychology, 56,* 283-292.

Folger, R., & Greenberg, J. (1985). Procedural justice: An interpretive analysis of personnel systems. In K. M. Rowland & G. R. Ferris (Eds.), *Research in personnel and human resources management* (Vol. 3, pp. 141-183). Greenwich, CT: JAI.

Greenberg, J. (1977). The Protestant work ethic and reactions to negative performance evaluations on a laboratory task. *Journal of Applied Psychology, 62,* 682-690.

Greenberg, J. (1982). Approaching equity and avoiding inequity in groups and organizations. In J. Greenberg & R. L. Cohen (Eds.), *Equity and justice in social behavior* (pp. 389-435). New York: Academic Press.

Greenberg, J. (1984). *Performance evaluations as penultimate outcomes: A preliminary study.* Unpublished manuscript, Ohio State University, Columbus.

Greenberg, J. (1986a). Determinants of perceived fairness of performance evaluations. *Journal of Applied Psychology, 71,* 340-342. [Chapter 6, this volume.].

Greenberg, J. (1986b). Organizational performance appraisal procedures: What makes them fair? In R. J. Lewicki, B. H. Sheppard, & M. H. Bazerman (Eds.), *Research on negotiation in organizations* (Vol. 1, pp. 25-41). Greenwich, CT: JAI. [Chapter 8, this volume.].

Greenberg, J. (1987). Using diaries to promote procedural justice in performance appraisals. *Social Justice Research, 1,* 219-234. [Chapter 9, this volume.].

Greenberg, J., & Folger, R. (1983). Procedural justice, participation, and the fair process effect in groups and organizations. In P. B. Paulus (Ed.), *Basic group processes* (pp. 235-256). New York: Springer-Verlag.

Greenberg, J., & Ornstein, S. (1983). High status job title as compensation for underpayment: A test of equity theory. *Journal of Applied Psychology, 68,* 285-297. [Chapter 17, this volume.].

Greenberg, J., & Tyler, T. (1987). Why procedural justice in organizations? *Social Justice Research, 1,* 127-142.

Jones, E. E., & Davis, K. E. (1965). From acts to dispositions: The attribution process in social perception. In L. Berkowitz (Ed.), *Advances in experimental social psychology* (Vol. 2, pp. 118-156). New York: Academic Press.

Klasson, C. R., Thompson, D. E., & Luben, G. L. (1980). How defensible is your performance appraisal system? *Personnel Administrator, 25,* 77-83.

Latham, G. P., & Wexley, K. N. (1981). *Increasing productivity through performance appraisal.* Reading, MA: Addison-Wesley.

Leskovec, E. (1967). A guide for discussing the performance appraisal. *Personnel Journal, 46,* 150-152.

Martin, J. (1986). When expectations and justice do not coincide: Blue-collar visions of a just world. In H. W. Bierhoff, R. L. Cohen, & J. Greenberg (Eds.), *Justice in social relations* (pp. 317-335). New York: Plenum.

Mikula, G. (1986). The experience of injustice: Toward a better understanding of its phenomenology. In H. W. Bierhoff, R. L. Cohen, & J. Greenberg (Eds.), *Justice in social relations* (pp. 103-124). New York: Plenum.

Nord, W. R. (1980). The study of organizations through a resource-exchange paradigm. In K. J. Gergen, M. S. Greenberg, & R. H. Willis (Eds.), *Social exchange: Advances in theory and research* (pp. 119-139). New York: Plenum.

Reis, H. T. (1986). Levels of interest in the study of interpersonal justice. In H. W. Bierhoff, R. L. Cohen, & J. Greenberg (Eds.), *Justice in social relations* (pp. 187-225). New York: Plenum.

Sheppard, B. H. (1984). Third party conflict intervention: A procedural framework. In B. M. Staw & L. L. Cummings (Eds.), *Research in organizational behavior* (Vol. 6, pp. 141-190). Greenwich, CT: JAI.

Tornow, W. W. (1971). The development and application of an input-outcome moderator test on the perception and reduction of inequity. *Organizational Behavior and Human Performance, 6,* 614-638.

Vecchio, R. P. (1982). Predicting worker performance in inequitable settings. *Academy of Management Review, 7,* 103-110.

Vroom, V. H. (1964). *Work and motivation.* New York: John Wiley.

Walster, E., Walster, G. W., & Berscheid, E. (1978). *Equity: Theory and research.* Boston: Allyn & Bacon.

Wexley, K. N., & Latham, G. P. (1981). *Developing and training human resources in organizations.* Glenview, IL: Scott, Foresman.

8
___

The Procedural Justice
of Performance Evaluations

Several years ago, I supervised the internship of a graduate student placed in a white-collar organization in an Ohio city. As part of his project, the student was responsible for interviewing the employees about their reactions to their company's performance appraisal system. How did they feel about the way they were evaluated? Unfortunately, their responses were far from positive. Almost unanimously, the employees complained that there appeared to be no established basis for the evalua-

AUTHOR'S NOTE: This chapter was originally published in *Research on Negotiation in Organizations* (R. J. Lewicki, B. H. Sheppard, & M. H. Bazerman, Eds.), Vol. 1, pp. 25-41, under the title "Organizational Performance Appraisal Procedures: What Makes Them Fair?" Copyright © 1986 by JAI Press. Reprinted by permission.

tions they received. They had little idea about what they did that influenced the evaluations they received, who made the evaluations, and how they were determined. As one might expect, the workers reported considerable concern about this state of affairs. As discouraging as conditions appeared to have been in this one company, studies surveying employees' reactions to their appraisal systems suggest that they are far from exceptional (Carroll & Schneier, 1982).

One way of interpreting these workers' complaints is through insight offered by research and theory on *procedural justice* (Thibaut & Walker, 1975). Essentially, this perspective focuses on the perceived fairness of the procedures used in making decisions (see Tyler, 1986). Although this perspective was initially applied to decision making in dispute resolution situations, originally by Thibaut and Walker (1975), and later by researchers such as Lind (1982) and Sheppard (1984), I have more recently attempted to apply the concept to understanding a variety of organizational phenomena as well (e.g., Folger & Greenberg, 1985).

Drawing on this background (and bolstered by the organizational experiences reported in the opening paragraph), I was intrigued by the possibility that the study of procedural justice could be applied to a wider range of phenomena than had previously been the case—especially organizational phenomena. In attempting to apply the concept of procedural justice to a variety of organizational phenomena, earlier work uncovered good evidence that concerns about fair procedures have an effect on compensation systems, participatory decision-making processes, and dispute resolution systems, as well as performance evaluation systems—the focus of the current research (Folger & Greenberg, 1985; Greenberg & Folger, 1983). In these reviews and in other work (Greenberg, 1986[7]), I have suggested some ways in which procedural justice may be involved in the performance evaluation process (see Folger & Greenberg, 1985).

The purpose of this chapter is to elaborate on how theory and research on procedural justice can be used to help understand the performance appraisal process and how insights from studying these processes can be used to further the understanding of procedural justice. A framework will be provided describing several different types of performance appraisal procedures that can be interpreted from a procedural justice perspective. Specifically, the chapter will focus on procedures for (a) employee input, (b) enhancing the accuracy of performance data, and (c) minimizing rater bias. Research evidence bearing on each of these types of procedures and the implications of this evidence for organizational practice will be presented. Before doing this, however, this chapter begins by taking a closer look at the nature and importance of procedural justice as it applies to understanding organizational performance appraisals.

PROCEDURAL JUSTICE: ITS NATURE
AND IMPORTANCE IN EVALUATING PERFORMANCE

In most organizations, once or twice a year supervisors use some rating scales to evaluate the performance of those employees under their supervision and then communicate these appraisals to these employees—a process known as performance appraisal, or performance evaluation (for a detailed review, see Bernardin & Beatty, 1984; Latham & Wexley, 1981). To better appreciate how performance appraisal can be explained from a procedural justice perspective, this section will provide a description of what procedural justice is and its potential importance in understanding performance appraisal.

Concerns about justice in organizations and organizational processes have been voiced in many contexts, ranging from interest in making "fair" personnel selection decisions (Arvey, 1979), to "justly" settling labor disputes (Walton & McKersie, 1965) and negotiating "equitable" wage settlements (Mahoney, 1975). For the most part, however, writing on organizational justice tends to focus on issues of *distributive justice* (Homans, 1961), that is, the perceived fairness of organizational outcome distributions, and on reactions to those distributions (for reviews, see Freedman & Montanari, 1980; Greenberg, 1982). More frequently overlooked, although equally important, is an orientation toward studying the rules and procedures by which organizational decisions are made, referred to as *procedural justice* (Thibaut & Walker, 1975). The distinction between distributive justice and procedural justice focuses on differences between the ends or consequences of organizational outcome states—*what* the outcomes are—and the means or processes used to determine those outcomes—*how* those outcomes are determined (for more on this distinction, see Walker, Lind, & Thibaut, 1979).

The most basic research question bearing on the current topic is what makes a performance evaluation appear to be fair. Is it *what* you get or *how* you get it, or both, that makes an evaluation seem fair?

A well-established fact of organizational life is that many employees, and often their unions, believe their appraisal systems are unfair (Levine, 1975). They often resist appraisal systems because they believe these systems measure performance inaccurately and reflect supervisory biases (Ilgen & Barnes-Farrell, 1984). Evidence suggests that it may well be the *procedures* used to make the appraisal—and *not* just the outcome of the appraisal itself (the evaluation)—that determine how fair appraisals are perceived to be.

Some initial evidence in support of this idea is provided by two studies by Landy and his associates (Landy, Barnes, & Murphy, 1978; Landy, Barnes-Farrell, & Cleveland, 1980). In the first study, these researchers questioned more than 700 managerial and professional employees of a large manufacturing company about the nature of their performance evaluations and their reactions to them. They found that the perceived fairness of the appraisal system was positively correlated with procedural variables, such as the frequency of evaluation and the opportunity to express their personal feelings. In a follow-up study, the same pattern of results was found regardless of the ratings the workers received (Landy et al., 1980). In other words, performance outcomes failed to moderate workers' perceptions of evaluation procedures. A fair evaluation is one that contains certain procedural elements, regardless of the content of the evaluations themselves.

Delving more specifically into this topic, I completed a study designed to assess exactly what determines the perceived fairness of performance evaluations. A survey was conducted among 128 pharmacists and wholesale drug salespeople, respondents who reported having considerable experience in both giving and receiving performance evaluations. Of interest to the present topic, they were asked to give the *one* most important determinant of a fair performance evaluation. Their answers were summarized in direct phrases, typed on cards, and sorted by 45 undergraduate student judges into three categories: *procedural reasons* (e.g., having an opportunity to have a say in the rating procedure); *distributive reasons* (e.g., getting a high rating for doing good work); and *other reasons* (anything that did not fall into these other categories).

The judges were trained in the meaning of the categories and were able to make reliable categorizations. A stringent criterion of categorization was used: If more than three judges disagreed with the categorization made by the others, that item was put into a separate "uncertain" category. Even using this stringent criterion (more than 90% agreement), only 2% of the responses showed this much disagreement and were not reliably categorized.

Fifty-six percent of the responses fell into the procedural category. This means that the majority of subjects believed that it was *how* their evaluations were determined that made them fair. Some typical responses were, "I should be evaluated by someone who knows my work," and "I should have a chance to speak in my own behalf." Thirty-nine percent focused on distributive matters, such as "If I'm the best worker, I should get the best ratings—that's fair." Only 3% were reliably categorized as something else.

These results reveal that procedural variables are important in determining the fairness of evaluations. With this background, the next step was to take a closer look at exactly what procedures may serve to enhance perceptions of procedural justice and how they operate. The diversity of responses to the open-ended question used in this survey study made it difficult to uncover any specific procedural variables likely to influence justice perceptions. Some insight into what these variables may be, however, is suggested by the literature on procedural justice and by some of the litigation regarding performance appraisal (Schneier, 1978).

Specifically, in his conceptualization of procedural justice, Leventhal (1980; Leventhal, Karuza, & Fry, 1980) has identified several procedural rules theorized to enhance perceptions of procedural justice. Among these are three particular rules that appear to be most applicable to performance appraisal contexts: the correctability rule, the accuracy rule, and the bias suppression rule.

The correctability rule refers to a person's opportunities to correct the information used in making a decision. In the context of performance appraisal procedures, Leventhal's notion of correctability recognizes the potential importance of *input-giving procedures,* appraisal methods in which workers are given an opportunity to provide their supervisors with information about their own performance. Implementation of this rule is consistent with the rationale underlying litigation emphasizing the importance of employees being able to initiate personnel actions on their own (Klasson, Thompson, & Luben, 1980).

Another rule identified by Leventhal is the accuracy rule, a rule requiring that decisions be based on the most *accurate information* possible. In performance appraisal procedures, it is expected that fair procedures are ones based on accurate information. In a similar vein, some legal rulings (e.g., *Brito v. Zia,* 1973) have emphasized the importance of documenting appraisal decisions on accurately collected performance information (Cascio & Bardin, 1981).

Last is Leventhal et al.'s (1980) bias suppression rule. In performance appraisal terms, the attainment of procedural justice may require the *minimization of bias in performance ratings.* The importance of rater training as a tool of bias reduction has long been recognized by the courts as a requirement of fair performance evaluations (Kleiman & Durham, 1981).

As this analysis suggests, there may be good a priori reason to study the role of procedural justice in each of three different categories of performance appraisal procedures. In other words, there is adequate rationale to suspect that certain aspects of performance appraisal procedures may enhance perceptions of procedural justice. These include (a) procedures that increase ratees' inputs into the evaluation process, (b) procedures that enhance the accuracy of the information used in making evaluations, and (c) procedures that discourage raters' motivations to bias their evaluations. Each of these three procedural elements will be examined more closely in the sections to follow. In some cases, the role of the procedural elements will be demonstrated with direct empirical evidence; in some other cases, it will be extrapolated from existing studies originally conducted with other topical foci; and in still others, it merely will be speculated. As such, the remaining sections of the chapter will simultaneously review existing knowledge regarding procedural justice in performance appraisals and set an agenda for future research and theory building.

INPUT-GIVING PROCEDURES

One well-established finding from Thibaut and Walker's (1975) research on procedural justice in legal settings is that outcomes are believed to be more fair when the persons affected by them have a say in the procedures by which they are determined (e.g., LaTour, 1978; Lind, Kurtz, Musante, Walker, & Thibaut, 1980). Considerable organizational evidence also suggests that participation in decision making enhances the perceived fairness of and acceptance of the decisions (Folger & Greenberg, 1985; Maier, 1970).

Input into the performance appraisal process may take several forms in organizations. By conceptualizing performance appraisals as a simple three-step process, three different stages at which input may be provided are identified and discussed below.

Information-Gathering Stage

In one of the first stages of performance appraisal, information about ratees is gathered (either objective, subjective, or memory-based; Borman, 1978; Cooper, 1981). At this stage, workers can have input by having the opportunity to provide information about their performance (such as pointing out and/or explaining what they have done). Several studies indicate that evaluations are believed to be fairer when workers are given an opportunity to provide some input into the evaluation process.

For example, in a field questionnaire, Dipboye and de Pontbraind (1981) found that employees' feelings about their appraisal system were positively associated with their beliefs about the opportunity to express inputs. Two studies directly manipulated input. In part of his dissertation at the University of Illinois, Lissak (1983, Field Study 1) compared the reactions of Canadian soldiers who had an opportunity to write narratives about their performance with those who did not. Kanfer, Sawyer, Earley, and Lind (1987) did the same thing in a laboratory study. They compared the behavioral and attitudinal reactions of undergraduate student workers who had the opportunity to offer information about their own performance to their supervisor with those who did not. Both investigations reported that providing input into the evaluation procedure enhanced job satisfaction and perceived fairness. Moreover, Kanfer et al. found that high input into the evaluation process enhanced job performance (but only when performance criteria were made explicit).

Evaluation Judgment Stage

Procedural justice also may be important in the evaluation judgment stage. Of course, if the appraisals are self-appraisals, then direct input is provided. Research has shown that workers are often more satisfied with self-appraisal procedures than supervisory appraisals (Bassett & Meyer, 1968). Overall, evaluations are better accepted if they contain at least some self-evaluations, as opposed to being based entirely on supervisory judgments (Teel, 1978).

It is not surprising that self-appraisals are usually positively biased— perhaps because of the desire to present oneself favorably and perhaps because of the addition of self-relevant information (cf. research on the actor-observer divergence in attribution; Watson, 1982). Regardless, it appears safe to speculate that self-appraisals are believed to be fairer than appraisals made without ratees' own evaluations. In the absence of research in this area, however, this supposition is merely speculative.

The Interview Stage

Another form of input may be provided at the evaluation interview stage. During this stage, input may take the form of making it possible for the ratee to respond to the rater's feedback. The opportunity for two-way communication may be seen as an input-providing mechanism. The success of so-called problem-solving approaches to performance appraisal interviews (Maier, 1976) is probably because the opportunity to react to the evaluation makes it seem fairer. Although the ultimate evaluation decision may have been made already, the opportunity to speak on one's own behalf, to defend oneself, to set the record straight, may effectively enhance feelings of fairness. The mechanisms underlying these potentially beneficial effects of "voice" have been discussed at length by Greenberg and Folger (1983).

DIARIES: PROCEDURES ENHANCING
THE ACCURACY OF PERFORMANCE DATA

As mentioned earlier, it is not only input into the evaluation procedures that influences fairness but also the information-gathering techniques themselves that are important. For appraisal procedures to be perceived as fair, they must be based on accurate records and information (Leventhal, 1980). In actual practice, however, supervisors often appraise performance on the basis of little or no information. Many times, it is only a vague memory of the impression, and not objective information, that forms the basis for the performance rating (Ilgen & Feldman, 1983). For fair ratings to result, however, the behavioral basis of these evaluations must be made salient.

Practitioners have developed a technique to do this: *the diary.* Studies have shown that when raters take notes and write down critical incidents of work behavior, the resulting ratings are less biased and more reliable (see Bernardin & Buckley, 1981).

Research Evidence

A study (Greenberg, 1987[9]) provides evidence that the use of diaries also makes evaluations seem fair. The participants in this study were management students who had to perform a clerical task. The participants expected to be evaluated for their performance after they finished. They performed the task for one half hour, during which the experimenter—in two of the conditions—entered the workroom three times.

In the *diary condition,* the experimenter observed the workers' performance on two occasions and took notes ostensibly concerning their performance. In the *observation condition,* the experimenter watched for the same amount of time but did not keep a diary. In a *control condition,* no observations were made at all.

After these observations. the experimenter gave participants either *positive feedback,* telling them that they did better than average; *negative feedback,* telling them that they did worse than average; or *neutral feedback,* telling them that they performed about the same as others.

There were four main dependent variables that through factor analysis were summarized by two groups of two questions each. The *procedural justice index* consisted of questions dealing with the perceived satisfaction of the evaluation procedure and the perceived fairness of the evaluation procedure. The *distributive justice index* consisted of questions dealing with the perceived satisfaction with the evaluation outcome and the perceived fairness of the evaluation outcome.

As in several other studies (e.g., Alexander & Ruderman, 1987; Tyler & Caine, 1981), these two measures were found to be independent. For both indexes, there were significant main effects of evaluation procedure and evaluation outcome but no significant interaction. Specifically, the more accurate information-gathering procedure (the diary) enhanced the perceived fairness of the resulting outcomes. The effect of the outcomes not only was independent of procedures but also accounted for significantly less variance in ratings.

In addition, participants rated their liking for the experimenter and their liking for the task itself. These were highly intercorrelated and were combined to form a *generalized liking index*. A significant interaction was obtained between evaluation outcome and evaluation procedure such that procedures did not influence participants' affective reactions when the evaluations were positive or negative. The evaluation procedures, however, were found to be sensitive to affective reactions only when evaluations were neutral. Under this condition, evaluators and tasks were much better liked when a diary procedure was used than when less accurate and thorough information-gathering procedures were used.

Implications

From a practical perspective, these findings suggest that the use of diaries may be a useful way of leading workers to believe that their evaluation procedures are fair. Given the emphasis on using accurately documented performance information as the basis of evaluations stipulated in the 1978 Civil Service Reform Act (Chapter 43 of Title 5, U.S. Code) and by the Equal Employment Opportunity Commission (cf. Schneier, 1978), it appears that diaries may be an effective way of enhancing *perceived* compliance with regulations. Case law (e.g., *Allen v. City of Mobile*, 1971) similarly has supported the use of diaries documenting evidence of substandard performance to be used to justify the dismissal of poor employees. These legal regulations and precedents together with the present results suggest that the use of diaries may facilitate the attainment of justice from both a legal-institutional perspective and an individual-phenomenological perspective.

Conceptually, the findings support the claim that information-gathering procedures can be used to enhance perceived procedural justice. Just as a legal case is perceived to be fair if the procedures used to try the case are valid, so too may appraisal decisions be seen as fair if they are based on thoroughly and accurately collected information (Leventhal, 1976).

Of course, accurate information can still be misused and lead to invalid ratings if the rater is motivated to bias the evaluations. This suggestion leads to the third procedural element identified earlier: bias-minimizing procedures.

BIAS-MINIMIZING PROCEDURES

Traditionally, industrial-organizational psychologists have paid a great deal of attention to the causes of and methods for minimizing bias in performance appraisal systems (Landy & Zedeck, 1983). For the most part, they have focused their attention on the rating instruments used— scale format issues (e.g., Cooper, 1981). Although it is true that the *tools* used to evaluate performance may be important contributors to rating bias, issues of fairness are likely to be linked to the *policies and procedures* that encourage bias, rather than to the instruments themselves. Several potential sources of procedural bias in performance appraisals will be discussed—biases caused by incomplete and inaccurate information, rater motivation, and indeterminate evaluation policies and standards.

Incomplete and Inaccurate Information

The possibility that performance ratings may be biased by incomplete and inaccurate information has been well established in the performance evaluation literature. Specifically, many of the currently popular infor- mation-processing approaches to performance appraisal (e.g., Borman, 1978; Cooper, 1981; Ilgen & Feldman, 1983) explicitly focus on raters' tendencies to select, generate, organize, and integrate information bear- ing on performance ratings. This work suggests that potentially relevant information is often either omitted or distorted in the rating process not only because of raters' limited cognitive capacity to process information but also because of biases in the initial availability of relevant information (Carroll & Schneier, 1982).

Performance ratings may often be based on incomplete or sketchy performance information (Ilgen & Feldman, 1983). Given the multiple job responsibilities of most supervisors, it is not unusual to find that they are frequently too busy to know as much as they should about the subordinates they are evaluating—particularly supervisors who exercise a broad span of control (Steers & Lee, 1983). Under such circumstances, performance ratings may be based on highly incomplete, "undersampled" information: the type that may be particularly susceptible to bias, such as the illusory halo error (Cooper, 1981). Not surprisingly, employees have been known to resist appraisal systems that are based on inaccurate or exceptionally incomplete information, especially when the consequences of the appraisal are great (Nash & Carroll, 1975).

Some insight into this evidence is provided by Leventhal's (1980) suggestion that the thoroughness of information gathering is one of the key defining elements of procedural justice, a supposition supported by several validity studies (Fry & Cheney, 1981; Fry & Leventhal, 1979). Unfortunately, there appears to be no research directly attempting to assess the perceived fairness of evaluation procedures as a function of the completeness and accuracy of the information forming the basis of the resulting evaluation. It is tempting, however, to speculate that the perceived unfairness of evaluation methods depends at least in part on the accuracy and completeness of the information on which the evaluation judgment is based. As my previously mentioned diary study shows (Greenberg, 1987[9]), supervisors who at least give the appearance of attempting to gather thorough and accurate information will be perceived as fairer evaluators.

Rater Motivation

Bias in appraisals also may be caused by the rater's motivation to bias evaluations in some manner. The motivation to bias ratings may differ according to the rater's role or organizational position relative to the ratee. For example, raters sometimes claim that it is unfair for them to be evaluated by their peers—coworkers who are often biased to give low ratings, especially when the existing reward structure is competitive (Kane & Lawler, 1978). A similar tendency to deflate performance ratings also may occur among supervisors who, as is sometimes claimed by labor unions, selectively negatively bias the ratings of those who openly question management's labor practices (Levine, 1975).

In addition to these biases toward rating deflation, supervisors sometimes may be motivated to inflate their subordinates' performance ratings. This may be especially so whenever giving high ratings helps promote the rater's image as one who is doing an effective job of employee development. In other words, whenever a rater's own performance effectiveness is defined (at least in part) by his or her own effectiveness in eliciting high performance from subordinates, then giving subordinates a high rating may constitute an indication of the rater's own effectiveness. In several studies (Greenberg, 1984, 1985), I have referred to this tendency as the *self-serving bias* in performance appraisal.

I obtained a clue that such a phenomenon exists in a field study using as participants administrators at a technical college (Greenberg, 1984). Responses on part of a larger questionnaire showed that supervisors' ratings of their subordinates were positively correlated with their self-reported contribution to that person's performance. The more they felt they were responsible for a worker's performance, the higher the performance rating they gave.

Why is this? Two possible explanations are immediately suggested by the dialogue between Miller (1978) and Bradley (1978). One possibility is that it results from a *perceptual bias*—an attempt to protect and/or enhance one's self-image. Another possibility is that it is a *response bias* —an attempt to cultivate a favorable impression on another. Although that other may potentially be other raters (Mitchell & Klimoski, 1984) or ratees themselves (Latham & Wexley, 1981), the target of impression management considered in this study was the rater's supervisor.

Raters giving subordinates a high rating may enhance their superior's belief that they are doing a good job. If one's subordinates are doing well, then that person is doing a good job of bringing them along. So, rating them highly may be seen as a reflection of one's own competence. Not only would the supervisor be impressed, but also raters would feel good about themselves. (This is not to deny the possibility that under different circumstances, a self-serving interest would motivate raters to adapt a particularly tough response style.) It is possible—indeed, likely—that both concerns may be salient. Under certain circumstances, it is possible that self-image concerns and impression management concerns may be differentially salient to raters. Raters are frequently themselves the targets of ratings by others in the organizational hierarchy, their own superiors. Accordingly, they are subject not only to concerns about self-image management but also to concerns about the impressions they make on their own superiors.

To test these ideas, a laboratory study (Greenberg, 1985) was conducted using undergraduate business students who served as evaluating supervisors of others who performed a clerical task. Half the participants were led to believe that they were being evaluated with respect to their ability to promote the effectiveness of their subordinates, and the other half were not. Also manipulated was the nature of participants' contact with the subordinates: Some were given an opportunity to help them improve their work, some were given an opportunity to have casual conversations with them, and still others had no contact with their subordinates.

The primary dependent variable of interest was participants' evaluations of workers' performance. Participants gave higher performance ratings to subordinates when they gave them some suggestions for improvement than when they had only social contact with the ratees or no contact at all. This finding constituted support for the self-serving bias. In other words, participants who associated themselves with ratees' performance tended to rate that performance higher than those who did not. This effect was found regardless of whether ratees' performance improved, declined, or remained unchanged following the informational contact.

Several sources of evidence converge to suggest that the observed self-serving bias was the result of a perceptual bias rather than a response bias. It was reasoned that self-serving evaluations would be made only when the nature of the contact between the rater and the ratee was such that the ratee could possibly benefit from the rater's assistance. In the absence of guidance, no opportunity to enhance one's self-image is provided. Accordingly, support for the perceptual bias explanation is provided by the finding that inflated ratings following informational contact with ratees resulted only for rating dimensions that were relevant to the rater's potential sphere of influence during the study. As further evidence for the perceptual bias explanation, performance inflation was observed regardless of whether participants expected to be evaluated for their effectiveness in getting their subordinates to function effectively. If the effect were only because of participants' attempts to influence their superiors' impressions of them (i.e., a response bias), then it would not be expected to manifest itself in the absence of evaluation by superiors.

Several practical procedural suggestions stem from this work. For one, the findings suggest that the role of evaluator and trainer should be separated. Organizational policies and procedures that confuse these roles could be precisely the conditions under which the self-serving bias is found. As Meyer, Kay, and French (1965) said some three decades ago, "It seems foolish to have a manager serving in the self-conflicting role as a counselor . . . when, at the same time, he is presiding as a judge over the same employee's salary action case" (p. 127). Separate evaluators and trainers would make not only for more valid evaluations but, consequently, for potentially fairer ones as well.

Indeterminate Evaluation
Policies and Standards

Finally, I should note the potential for bias caused by indeterminate evaluation policies and standards. Leventhal's (1980) theory of procedural justice specifies that fair allocations require that ground rules be set—

procedures for determining how potential rewards may be attained. The rewards in the case of performance appraisal—the evaluation judgment and any promotions or pay raises resulting from it—need to be based on consistently applied standards (Leventhal et al., 1980). Employees may be expected to resist the administration of appraisal methods that employ standards that vary through time and between ratees. It appears to be with this principle of justice in mind that legally defensible performance appraisal systems have been described as requiring the use of *predetermined, written criteria* as the basis for personnel decisions (Klasson et al., 1980)

SUMMARY AND CONCLUSIONS

The evidence reviewed in this chapter suggests that procedural factors are important determinants of fair employee performance appraisals. In fact, research has shown that procedural variables may be more important than distributive (outcome) variables as determinants of the perceived fairness of performance appraisals. Perceptions of procedural justice may be enhanced by allowing employees to have input into their appraisals— in the gathering of performance-relevant information, the making of the evaluation, and/or the performance review interview. Research also suggests that perceived fair performance appraisals may be facilitated by the use of thorough record-keeping practices such as using diaries. Fair appraisals also demand the use of procedures that minimize various sources of rater bias, such as those caused by the use of incomplete and inaccurate information, the motives of various raters to bias their responses, and the use of indeterminate evaluation policies and standards.

Although some of the discussion in this chapter was based on research directly inspired by attempts to understand performance appraisal from the perspective of procedural justice theory and research, much of it was based on logical extrapolations from studies conducted for other purposes, and some was mere speculation. It is principally the newness of the ideas presented here that is primarily responsible for the incomplete and imperfect state of present knowledge. Clearly, more research is needed to realize the potential benefits of the ideas sketched in this chapter.

Probably the important question for the future research agenda is this: What are the consequences of following fair or unfair procedures? Unfortunately, the practice of measuring the consequences of fair and unfair performance appraisal procedures has been the exception in the existing research (e.g., Kanfer et al., 1987) rather than the rule. More attempts at measuring both behavioral reactions (job performance) and psychological reactions (job satisfaction) are needed in future research applying procedural justice to performance appraisal. In doing this research, however, it may be unreasonable to expect that feelings of unfair appraisals would adversely affect work performance. There are just too many determinants of performance operating in organizations to expect these negative feelings to have such profound behavioral effects. Employees unwilling to jeopardize their positions by lowering their job performance may prefer to express verbally their concern about the problem—a considerably less costly alternative.

This is not to say that behavioral expressions of dissatisfaction would not manifest themselves. Two forms of employee withdrawal behaviors may be particularly sensitive to perceived unfairness: absenteeism and turnover (Mowday, Porter, & Steers, 1982). Studies have found these forms of behavior to be sensitive to violations of distributive justice (see Greenberg, 1982) and may be just as sensitive to violations of procedural justice as well. Taking off a day or looking for a new job may be controlled ways of expressing dissatisfaction with unfair procedures.

This reasoning points to some of the untapped areas of research on procedural justice in organizations—specifically, the consequences side. Researchers have focused on the antecedents, but now, it appears, we need to be more sensitive to the consequences of procedural fairness violations. Does it matter in any significant ways? Moreover, we need to ask a related question, namely, just how consequential are the consequences? What forms of expression follow from what types of procedural fairness violations? These are just some of the questions that need to be looked at in the future.

The research presented in this chapter is just the tip of the iceberg with respect to what needs to be learned about procedural justice in organizations. It was only recently that researchers became aware of the topic. Now, we are turning the corner and looking at some more sophisticated questions—questions not only about antecedents and consequences but about mechanisms as well. I hope that research on this topic will lead us to uncover psychological mechanisms that are applicable to understanding the role of procedural justice in many different areas of organizational behavior—ones that go beyond performance evaluations.

REFERENCES

Alexander, S., & Ruderman, M. (1987). The role of procedural and distributive justice in organizational behavior. *Social Justice Research, 1,* 177-198.

Allen v. City of Mobile, 331 F. Supp. 1134 (1971).

Arvey, R. D. (1979). *Fairness in selecting employees.* Reading, MA: Addison-Wesley.

Bassett, G. A., & Meyer, H. H. (1968). Performance appraisal based on self-review. *Personnel Psychology, 21,* 421-430.

Bernardin, H. J., & Beatty, R. W. (1984). *Performance appraisal: Assessing human behavior at work.* Boston: Kent.

Bernardin, H. J., & Buckley, M. R. (1981). A consideration of strategies in rater training. *Academy of Management Review, 6,* 205-212.

Borman, W. C. (1978). Exploring upper limits of reliability and validity in job performance ratings. *Journal of Applied Psychology, 63,* 135-144.

Bradley, G. W. (1978). Self-serving biases in the attribution process: A reexamination of the fact or fiction question. *Journal of Personality and Social Psychology, 36,* 56-71.

Brito v. Zia, 478 F.2d 1200 (1973).

Carroll, S. J., & Schneier, C. E. (1982). *Performance appraisal and review systems.* Glenview, IL: Scott, Foresman.

Cascio, W. F., & Bardin, H. S. (1981). Implications of performance appraisal litigation for personnel decisions. *Personnel Psychology, 34,* 221-225.

Cooper, W. H. (1981). Ubiquitous halo. *Psychological Bulletin, 90,* 218-244.

Dipboye, R. L., & de Pontbraind, R. (1981). Correlates of employee reactions to performance appraisals and appraisal systems. *Journal of Applied Psychology, 66,* 248-251.

Folger, R., & Greenberg, J. (1985). Procedural justice: An interpretive analysis of personnel systems. In K. M. Rowland & G. R. Ferris (Eds.), *Research in personnel and human resources management* (Vol. 3, pp. 141-183). Greenwich, CT: JAI.

Freedman, S. M., & Montanari, J. R. (1980). An integrative model of managerial reward allocation. *Academy of Management Review, 5,* 381-390.

Fry, W. R., & Cheney, G. (1981, May). *Perceptions of procedural fairness as a function of distributive preference.* Paper presented at the meeting of the Midwestern Psychological Association, Detroit, MI.

Fry, W. R., & Leventhal, G. S. (1979, March). Cross-situational procedural preferences: A comparison of allocation preferences and equity across different social settings. In A. Lind (Chair), *The psychology of procedural justice.* Symposium conducted at the meeting of the Southwestern Psychological Association, Washington, DC.

Greenberg, J. (1982). Approaching equity and avoiding inequity in groups and organizations. In J. Greenberg & R. L. Cohen (Eds.), *Equity and justice in social behavior* (pp. 389-435). New York: Academic Press.

Greenberg, J. (1984, August). *Inflated performance evaluations as a self-serving bias.* Paper presented at the meeting of the Academy of Management, Boston.

Greenberg, J. (1985, August). *Explaining the self-serving bias in performance evaluations: Perceptual bias or response bias?* Paper presented at the meeting of the Academy of Management, San Diego, CA.

Greenberg, J. (1986). The distributive justice of organizational performance evaluations. In H. W. Bierhoff, R. L. Cohen, & J. Greenberg (Eds.), *Justice in social relations* (pp. 337-351). New York: Plenum. [Chapter 7, this volume.]

Greenberg, J. (1987). Using diaries to promote procedural justice in performance appraisals. *Social Justice Research, 1,* 219-234. [Chapter 9, this volume.]

Greenberg, J., & Folger, R. (1983). Procedural justice, participation, and the fair process effect in groups and organizations. In P. B. Paulus (Ed.), *Basic group processes* (pp. 235-256). New York: Springer-Verlag.

Homans, G. C. (1961). *Social behavior: Its elementary forms.* New York: Harcourt, Brace, & World.

Ilgen, D. R., & Barnes-Farrell, J. L. (1984). *Performance planning and evaluation.* Chicago: SRA.

Ilgen, D. R., & Feldman, J. M. (1983). Performance appraisal: A process focus. In B. M. Staw & L. L. Cummings (Eds.), *Research in organizational behavior* (Vol. 5, pp. 141-197). Greenwich, CT: JAI.

Kane, J. S., & Lawler, E. E. (1978). Methods of peer assessment. *Psychological Bulletin, 85,* 555-586.

Kanfer, R., Sawyer, J., Earley, P. C., & Lind, E. A. (1987). Information exchange in evaluation procedures: The effects of input and knowledge on performance and attitudes. *Social Justice Research, 1,* 235-249.

Klasson, C. R., Thompson, D. E., & Luben, G. L. (1980). How defensible is your performance appraisal system? *Personnel Administrator, 25,* 77-83.

Kleiman, L. S., & Durham, R. L. (1981). Performance appraisal, promotion, and the courts: A critical review. *Personnel Psychology, 34,* 103-121.

Landy, F. J., Barnes, J. L., & Murphy, K. R. (1978). Correlates of perceived fairness and accuracy of performance evaluation. *Journal of Applied Psychology, 63,* 751-754.

Landy, F. J., Barnes-Farrell, J., & Cleveland, J. N. (1980). Perceived fairness and accuracy of performance evaluation: A follow-up. *Journal of Applied Psychology, 65,* 355-356.

Landy, F., & Zedeck, S. (1983). Introduction. In F. Landy, S. Zedeck, & J. Cleveland (Eds.), *Performance measurement and theory* (pp. 1-7). Hillsdale, NJ: Lawrence Erlbaum.

Latham, G. P., & Wexley, K. N. (1981). *Increasing productivity through performance appraisal.* Reading, MA: Addison-Wesley.

LaTour, S. (1978). Determinants of participant and observer satisfaction with adversary and inquisitorial modes of adjudication. *Journal of Personality and Social Psychology, 36,* 1531-1545.

Leventhal, G. S. (1976). Fairness in social relationships. In J. W. Thibaut, J. T. Spence, & R. C. Carson (Eds.), *Contemporary topics in social psychology* (pp. 211-239). Morristown, NJ: General Learning Press.

Leventhal, G. S. (1980). What should be done with equity theory? In K. J. Gergen, M. S. Greenberg, & R. H. Willis (Eds.), *Social exchange: Advances in theory and research* (pp. 27-55). New York: Plenum.

Leventhal, G. S., Karuza, J., & Fry, W. R. (1980). Beyond fairness: A theory of allocation preferences. In G. Mikula (Ed.), *Justice and social interaction* (pp. 167-218). New York: Springer-Verlag.

Levine, M. J. (1975). *Comparative labor relations law.* Morristown, NJ: General Learning Press.

Lind, E. A. (1982, August). *The social psychology of procedural justice.* Paper presented at the University of North Carolina Alumni and Friends Conference, Chapel Hill.

Lind, E. A., Kurtz, S., Musante, L., Walker, L., & Thibaut, J. W. (1980). Procedure and outcome effects on reactions to adjudicated resolution of conflicts of interest. *Journal of Personality and Social Psychology, 39,* 643-653.

Lissak, R. I. (1983). *Procedural fairness: How employees evaluate procedures.* Unpublished doctoral dissertation, University of Illinois, Urbana-Champaign.

Mahoney, T. A. (1975). Justice and equity: A recurring theme in compensation. *Personnel, 52*(5), 60-66.

Maier, N. R. F. (1970). *Problem solving and creativity in individuals and groups.* Belmont, CA: Brooks/Cole.

Maier, N. R. F. (1976). *The appraisal interview: Three basic approaches.* La Jolla, CA: University Associates.

Meyer, H., Kay, E., & French, J. R. P. (1965). Split roles in performance appraisal. *Harvard Business Review, 43,* 123-129.

Miller, D. T. (1978). What constitutes a self-serving bias? A reply to Bradley. *Journal of Personality and Social Psychology, 36,* 1221-1223.

Mitchell, T. W., & Klimoski, R. J. (1984). *Accountability bias in performance appraisals.* Unpublished manuscript.

Mowday, R. T., Porter, L. W., & Steers, R. (1982). *Employee linkages: The psychology of commitment, absenteeism and turnover.* New York: Academic Press.

Nash, A. N., & Carroll, S. J., Jr. (1975). *The management of compensation.* Belmont, CA: Brooks/Cole.

Schneier, D. B. (1978). The impact of EEO legislation on performance appraisals. *Personnel, 55*(4), 24-34.

Sheppard, B. (1984). Third party conflict intervention: A procedural framework. In B. M. Staw & L. L. Cummings (Eds.), *Research in organizational behavior* (Vol. 6, pp. 141-190). Greenwich, CT: JAI.

Steers, R. M., & Lee, T. W. (1983). Facilitating effective performance appraisals: The role of employee commitment and organizational climate. In F. Landy, S. Zedeck, & J. Cleveland (Eds.), *Performance measurement and theory* (pp. 75-88). Hillsdale, NJ: Lawrence Erlbaum.

Teel, K. S. (1978). Self-appraisal revisited. *Personnel Journal, 57,* 364-367.

Thibaut, J., & Walker, L. (1975). *Procedural justice: A psychological analysis.* Hillsdale, NJ: Lawrence Erlbaum.

Tyler, T. R. (1986). When does procedural justice matter in organizational settings? In R. J. Lewicki, B. H. Sheppard, & M. H. Bazerman (Eds.), *Research on negotiation in organizations* (Vol. 1, pp. 7-23). Greenwich, CT: JAI.

Tyler, T. R., & Caine, A. (1981). The role of distributional and procedural fairness in the endorsement of formal leaders. *Journal of Personality and Social Psychology, 41,* 642-655.

Walker, L., Lind, E. A., & Thibaut, J. (1979). The relation between procedural justice and distributive justice. *Virginia Law Review, 65,* 1401-1420.

Walton, R. W., & McKersie, R. B. (1965). *A behavioral theory of labor negotiations.* New York: McGraw-Hill.

Watson, D. (1982). The actor and the observer: How are their perceptions of causality different? *Psychological Bulletin, 88,* 682-701.

9

Using Diaries to Promote
Fair Performance Appraisals

Despite the wealth of available information concerning ways of improving performance appraisal procedures (for a review, see Bernardin & Beatty, 1984), considerably less is known about employees' reactions to such procedures. Yet given the beneficial personal and organizational outcomes claimed to result from appropriately validated appraisal techniques (e.g., Latham & Wexley, 1981), a better understanding of the consequences of appraisal procedures appears to be of fundamental importance to the understanding of the performance appraisal process.

AUTHOR'S NOTE: This chapter was originally published in *Social Justice Research,* Vol. 1, No. 2, pp. 219-234, under the title "Using Diaries to Promote Procedural Justice in Performance Appraisals." Copyright © 1987 by Plenum Press. Reprinted by permission.

An approach toward gaining this understanding is suggested by work (reviewed by Folger & Greenberg, 1985) showing that reactions to performance appraisals are strongly related to the fairness of the procedures used in conducting them. One experiment, for example, has demonstrated that appraisal procedures that workers considered fair resulted in higher levels of satisfaction and performance than procedures they considered to be unfair (Kanfer, Sawyer, Earley, & Lind, 1987). Given the important consequences of perceived fair performance appraisals demonstrated by Kanfer et al., I attempt in this study to examine more closely some antecedent factors contributing to the perceived fairness of performance appraisals.

THE JUSTICE OF
PERFORMANCE APPRAISAL PROCEDURES

This study is further inspired by previous work suggesting that the perceived fairness of performance appraisals is related to the procedures used in conducting the appraisals. For example, in a study assessing the reactions of managerial and professional employees to their performance appraisal systems, Landy, Barnes, and Murphy (1978) found that *process variables,* such as the rater's familiarity with the ratee and the frequency of evaluation, were significantly correlated with ratings of the evaluation system's fairness. In a follow-up study, the same results were obtained even when the respondents' performance evaluation outcomes were controlled for (Landy, Barnes-Farrell, & Cleveland, 1980). These studies suggest that workers may be more sensitive to *how* their performance appraisals are conducted than to the *outcome* of those appraisals in judging its fairness.

This distinction between procedures and outcomes as the basis of fairness is basic to the distinction between procedural justice (Leventhal, 1980; Thibaut & Walker, 1975) and distributive justice (Adams, 1965; Homans, 1961) that recently has been applied to various organizational contexts (e.g., Folger & Greenberg, 1985; Greenberg & Folger, 1983; Sheppard, 1984). Briefly distinguished, distributive justice refers to the perceived fairness of a distribution of outcomes, whereas procedural justice refers to the fairness of the procedures used to determine those distributions (for more on this distinction, see Walker, Lind, & Thibaut, 1975). In these terms, the research of Landy et al. (1980) demonstrates the relative dominance of procedural justice over distributive justice in determining reactions to performance appraisals. Given that procedural justice has been found to have a greater effect than distributive justice on other variables, such as job satisfaction (Alexander & Ruderman, 1987) and leadership endorsement (Tyler & Caine, 1981), it is not surprising that Landy's work in the field of performance appraisal also reflects the figural qualities of procedural justice.

On the basis of this background, it seems reasonable to ask what factors may contribute to employees' assessments of a fair evaluation procedure (for a review, see Folger & Greenberg, 1985). For one, evaluation procedures in which workers' input is solicited appear to be recognized as procedurally just. Both laboratory research (e.g., Kanfer et al., 1987) and field research (e.g., Dipboye & de Pontbraind, 1981; Lissak, 1983, Field Study 1) have found that workers consider appraisal procedures to be fairer when they are allowed to contribute information on which the appraisal is based than when no such input is permitted. This finding supports theoretical statements on procedural justice (e.g., Leventhal, 1980; Thibaut & Walker, 1975) that emphasize the importance of providing control over decisions as a determinant of procedural justice.

Even if procedures are used in which workers are allowed direct input into their evaluation, these may be considered procedurally fair only to the extent that they are based on accurate information (Leventhal, 1980). Indeed, the use of incomplete and/or inaccurate performance information often has been cited as a problem inherent in supervisory ratings (e.g., DeCotiis & Petit, 1978). In an attempt to avoid this problem and to yield more accurate ratings, several techniques have been described that provide a common frame of reference for reporting job performance (Borman, 1979), one of which is diary keeping (for a review, see Bernardin & Buckley, 1981). The regular recording of observations of critical incidents or everyday work behavior in a diary has been found to result in supervisory ratings that are less biased (Bernardin & Walter, 1977) and more reliable (Buckley & Bernardin, 1980) than the ratings of supervisors who did not keep diaries. It is not known, however, how workers respond to evaluations derived from information recorded in their supervisors' diaries.

HYPOTHESES

On the basis of extrapolation from research and theory on procedural justice, it appears that the use of diaries enhances the perceived fairness of evaluation procedures relative to those procedures using a less thorough and systematic means of collecting information on which to base appraisals. This is directly suggested by Leventhal's (1980) conceptualization of procedural justice in which it is noted that the procedures used in gathering information serving as the basis for reward allocation decisions are a key determinant of procedural justice. A program of research on legal dispute resolution by Thibaut and Walker (1975) has consistently shown that courtroom procedures perceived by defendants as enhancing their opportunities for gathering evidence relevant to their cases were seen as more fair than procedures using less precise means of gathering evidence. In this same tradition, Tyler and Caine (1981) found that classroom grading procedures based on complete information enhanced students' perceptions of the overall fairness of the instructor. In the present study, diaries were conceived as thorough information-gathering procedures that were hypothesized to be perceived as a fairer basis for making performance appraisals than a control procedure in which no ostensible basis for the evaluation was provided. In addition to comparing a systematic, diary-keeping procedure with a seemingly random, control procedure, this study also included a condition in which appraisals were based on regular but nonrecorded observations. This enabled assessment of the degree to which the thoroughness of the information-gathering procedures affected perceptions of procedural fairness in a continuous rather than a discrete fashion.

To permit generalization of the effects of diary use on the perceived fairness of evaluation procedures, this study assessed these effects on a variety of evaluation outcomes. Inasmuch as Tyler and Caine (1981) have found that students' evaluations of the fairness of grading procedures were unaffected by the grades they received, however, there was no basis for predicting differential effects of evaluation procedure across levels of evaluation outcome in the present study. Moreover, the repeated failure to find significant interactions between procedures and outcomes in fairness ratings in other research (e.g., Lissak, 1983; Thibaut & Walker, 1975; Tyler & Caine, 1981) led to the prediction that the hypothesized main effect of evaluation procedure would not be qualified by an interaction involving evaluation outcomes.

A second set of hypotheses was concerned with participants' ratings of the fairness of the evaluations received (as opposed to the fairness of the procedures on which they were based). With respect to this measure, previous research suggests that people believe outcomes to be fair to the extent that they were benefited by them (i.e., the egocentric bias in perceived fairness; Greenberg, 1983a). Specifically, Thibaut and Walker (1975) reported that defendants in legal proceedings believe legal verdicts are more fair when they are found innocent than when found guilty. In an educational performance evaluation setting, students have been found to believe teachers act more fairly when they give them higher grades than when they give them lower grades (Tyler & Caine, 1981). On the basis of this evidence, I hypothesized a significant main effect of evaluation outcome on ratings of distributive justice for the present study. Specifically, favorable performance evaluations were expected to be rated as fairer than unfavorable performance evaluations.

The possibility that ratings of distributive justice would be differentially influenced by evaluation procedures is supported by Leventhal's (1976, 1980) assertion that fair procedures are required to create fair outcome distributions. Accordingly, unless the procedures leading to various outcomes are considered fair, the resulting outcomes will not be considered to be fair. This supposition is supported by Thibaut and Walker's (1975) consistent finding of significant procedural influences on distributive decisions. Accordingly, I hypothesized that participants whose performances were appraised by an evaluator using a diary would rate the evaluations they received as fairer than those in the control condition whose performances were appraised without any apparent basis. Following from previous research (e.g., Thibaut & Walker, 1975; Tyler & Caine, 1981), this effect was not expected to be qualified by finding a significant interaction between evaluation outcome and evaluation procedure for ratings of distributive justice.

In addition, on an exploratory basis, questions were included that assessed participants' liking for the task they performed and for the person doing the performance appraisal. Although the lack of attention to these variables in existing research and theory on procedural justice precluded the possibility of developing formal hypotheses with respect to them, items measuring these variables were included in the study to disclose information about the possibility of generalized reactions to evaluation procedures—reactions that extend beyond evaluation procedures and outcomes to the source of the evaluation and the work itself.

METHOD

The participants were 117 undergraduate students at a midwestern university who volunteered to participate in a study allegedly concerned with clerical task performance. This study included two participants who replaced two others whose responses were discarded because they did not indicate accurately on the manipulation check questionnaire the experimenter's behavior while he was in their workrooms.

Thirteen participants were assigned randomly to each cell of a 3 × 3 factorial design in which the independent variables were evaluation outcome (negative, neutral, and positive) and evaluation procedure (diary, observation, and control).

Procedure

The participants worked individually in each experimental session. They were told that the experiment was designed to develop performance norms for clerical workers and that they would perform a clerical task on which they would later be evaluated.

The experimenter then instructed the participants how to perform the clerical task. This task consisted of locating certain items in a department store catalog and copying their prices onto index cards on which the items were identified. Several features of this task made it suitable for use in this study. First, because performance on this task was readily quantifiable, participants were expected to accept the basis for their evaluation. Second, because performance was also easily observable, it was likely for participants to accept the possibility that performance information was recorded in the evaluator's diary. Finally, because performance standards on this task have been found to be ambiguous (Greenberg, 1983b), the possibility of nonacceptance of the evaluation was minimized. Participants were instructed to work as rapidly and as accurately as they could for 20 minutes and were told that their performance would then be evaluated. They were further instructed to continue working without stopping even if the experimenter entered the room while they were working.

The evaluation procedure was manipulated by leading participants to believe that their evaluation was based on one of three different methods. In the two experimental conditions, the diary condition and the observation condition, the experimenter entered participants' workrooms at approximately 5 minutes, 10 minutes, and 15 minutes into the work period and remained there for approximately 1 minute, ostensibly to evaluate participants' performance. In the diary condition, the experimenter stood in front of participants' desk, silently observed their performance, and with clipboard, paper and pencil in hand, acted as if he were taking notes on their performance. In the observation condition, the experimenter silently observed workers' performance but did not take any notes. In the control condition, the experimenter did not enter participants' workrooms until the end of the work session.

After 20 minutes, the experimenter entered the participants' workrooms and instructed them to stop working. Without ostensibly examining the cards, the experimenter put the stack into an envelope. (Pilot testing revealed that this procedure was necessary for participants in the control condition to believe that the experimenter had any basis at all for making his evaluation.) He then gave them one of the three levels of feedback that constituted the evaluation outcome manipulation. Participants in the positive evaluation condition were told that the experimenter believed them to be performing much better than average. He noted that the quantity and quality of their work was superior to most others. In the neutral evaluation condition, the experimenter told participants that the quantity and quality of their work was average, about as good as most others. In the negative evaluation condition, the experimenter told participants that they had performed at a level much lower than average and that the quantity and quality of their performance was inferior to most others. Except for these statements, no other performance evaluation information was provided.

After being evaluated, participants were asked to complete a six-item experimental questionnaire containing 9-point bipolar scales with verbal anchors at the end points. The questions required participants to indicate (a) their satisfaction with the evaluation procedure, (b) their satisfaction with the evaluation they received (for both items, 1 = *extremely dissatisfied*, 9 = *extremely satisfied*), (c) the fairness of the evaluation procedure, (d) the fairness of the evaluation they received (for both items, 1 = *extremely unfair*, 9 = *extremely fair*), (e) their liking for their experimenter-evaluator, and (f) their liking for the task (for both items, 1 = *dislike very much*, 9 = *like very much*).

To validate both manipulations, several additional questionnaire items were included. As a check on the evaluation outcome manipulation, participants were asked to indicate on a 9-point scale how positive or negative the evaluation was that they had received (1 = *extremely negative*, 9 = *extremely positive*). To check on the evaluation procedure manipulation, participants were given an open-ended questionnaire asking them to indicate how many times, if any, they had seen the experimenter enter their workroom while they performed the experimental task. Following this, participants in the diary condition and the observation condition were given an additional open-ended questionnaire asking them to describe what the experimenter did while he was there. After completing these questionnaires, participants were completely dehoaxed with respect to the deceptions and were debriefed about the actual purpose of the study.

RESULTS

Manipulation Checks

Before analyzing the experimental data, the questionnaire items designed to validate the manipulations were analyzed. Responses to the evaluation outcome manipulation check question were analyzed with a 3×3 factorial analysis of variance (ANOVA), which yielded as the only significant source of variance a significant main effect of evaluation outcome, $F(2, 108) = 316.42, p < .0001$. Post hoc tests using the Newman-Keuls procedure (all Newman-Keuls tests reported in this chapter use the 0.05 level of significance) revealed that the means for all three levels were significantly different from each other (negative $M = 1.89$, neutral $M = 5.07$, positive $M = 7.77$). The direction of these differences supports the success of the evaluation outcome manipulation in creating distinguishable evaluation outcomes.

The evaluation procedure manipulation was validated by analyzing responses to the open-ended questions. All participants in the diary and observation conditions accurately noted that the experimenter had entered their workrooms on three occasions while they worked on the task. Participants in the control condition also correctly reported that the experimenter had not entered their workrooms while they performed the task. Only two participants in the diary condition (whose responses were subsequently ignored in the data analyses) did not report that the experimenter appeared to be taking notes on their work performance. Correctly, no participants in the observation condition reported that the experimenter made any written record of their performance. Taken together, these findings suggest that the evaluation procedure manipulations were successfully recognized by participants.

Preliminary Analyses

A multivariate analysis of variance was performed using all six dependent measures to determine whether the univariate analyses necessary to test the hypotheses were warranted. On the basis of Wilks's criterion, the multivariate F ratios for both main effects and the interaction term were highly significant (the lowest multivariate F was 2.34, $p < .0005$), justifying the univariate analyses of variance.

Because some of the dependent measures were highly intercorrelated, however, a principal factors analysis with a varimax rotation was performed to determine which variables should be combined. Three factors accounted for 98.1% of the total variance. Two different measures loaded at least twice as highly as any of the others on each of the three factors, and these were combined to yield indexes (with a possible range of 2 to 18) named to reflect the theme of the questions from which they were composed. Specifically, ratings of satisfaction with the evaluation procedure and the fairness of the evaluation procedure loaded highly on the first factor (.94 and .93, respectively) and were combined to form a procedural justice index. Similarly, ratings of liking for the experimenter-evaluator and liking for the task loaded highly on the second factor (.93

TABLE 9.1 Mean Scores on the Procedural Justice Index and the Distributive Justice Index for Evaluation Outcomes and Evaluation Procedures

| | Evaluation Outcome | | | Evaluation Procedure | |
Condition	Procedural Justice Index	Distributive Justice Index	Condition	Procedural Justice Index	Distributive Justice Index
Positive	10.49a	11.92a	Diary	15.36a	12.36a
Neutral	10.92a	8.77b	Observation	10.64b	8.38b
Negative	9.15b	5.51c	Control	4.56c	5.46c

NOTE: Within each column, means not sharing a common subscript are significantly different at the .05 level or beyond according to the Newman-Keuls procedure. In each cell, $n = 39$.

and .91, respectively) and were combined to form a generalized liking index. Finally, ratings of satisfaction with the evaluation outcome and fairness of the evaluation outcome loaded highly on the third factor (.82 and .79, respectively) and were combined to form a distributive justice index.

Preliminary analyses of variance on all dependent measures initially included sex of participant as a between-participants factor. Because neither main effects nor interactions involving this factor were found to be significant, however, it was ignored in all subsequent data analyses.

Procedural Justice Scores

An ANOVA on the procedural justice index yielded significant main effects for evaluation outcome, $F(2, 108) = 8.78, p < .0003$, and evaluation procedure, $F(2, 108) = 302.57, p < .0001$, but no significant interaction between them, $F(4, 108) = 0.50$, ns. Although both main effects were statistically significant, the proportion of variance accounted for by the evaluation procedure manipulation ($\omega^2 = .82$) was much greater than the proportion of variance accounted for by the evaluation outcome manipulation ($\omega^2 = .02$).

The means corresponding to the significant main effects for the procedural justice index are shown in the first and third columns of Table 9.1. Comparisons across the different evaluation procedures (third column of means) revealed that all three conditions were significantly different from each other and that the direction of these differences was as hypothesized. Specifically, participants in the diary condition rated their evaluation procedure as fairer than participants in either of the other two conditions. Although the perceived procedural fairness of the observation procedure was lower than that in the diary condition, it was higher than that in the control condition, further supporting the idea that the more systematic an information-gathering procedure is, the more procedurally fair it is believed to be.

The significant main effect of evaluation outcome on the procedural justice index is contrary to expectations, although it accounted for only 2% of the overall variance. Newman-Keuls comparisons of the corresponding means (shown in the first column of Table 9.1) revealed that this effect resulted from participants in the negative outcome conditions giving lower ratings than participants in either the neutral outcome or positive outcome conditions, which were not significantly different from each other.

Distributive Justice Scores

An ANOVA on the distributive justice index yielded significant main effects for evaluation outcome, $F(2, 108) = 95.44$, $p < .0001$, and evaluation procedure, $F(2, 108) = 111.35$, $p < .0001$, but no significant interaction between them, $F(4, 108) = 1.86$, ns. A relatively high proportion of variance was accounted for by both the evaluation outcome manipulation ($\omega^2 = .36$) and the evaluation procedure manipulation ($\omega^2 = .42$).

The means corresponding to the significant main effects are displayed in the second and fourth columns of Table 9.1. The pattern of significant differences between means in the second column of Table 9.1, as assessed by Newman-Keuls tests, supports the hypothesis that more favorable outcomes would be rated as more fair. Specifically, the highest ratings of distributive justice were made in the positive outcome condition and the lowest ratings were made in the negative outcome condition. The hypothesis suggesting that fair procedures lead to perceived fair outcomes is supported by the pattern of significant differences between means, as assessed by Newman-Keuls tests, shown in the fourth column of Table 9.1. The evaluation outcomes were rated as most fair in the diary condition and least fair in the control condition.

Generalized Liking Scores

An ANOVA on the generalized liking index yielded significant effects for evaluation outcome, $F(2, 108) = 317.06$, $p < .0001$, and evaluation method, $F(2, 108) = 6.29$, $p < .0026$, that were qualified by the significant interaction between them, $F(4, 108) = 11.94$, $p < .0001$. The proportion of variance accounted for by the main effect of evaluation outcome ($\omega^2 = .79$) was much greater than either the proportion of variance accounted

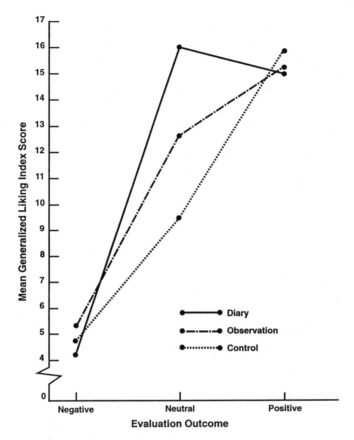

Figure 9.1. Mean Generalized Liking Index Scores as a Function of Evaluation Outcome and Evaluation Procedure

for by the evaluation procedure manipulation ($\omega^2 = .01$) or the interaction term ($\omega^2 = .05$). The means corresponding to the significant interaction are displayed graphically in Figure 9.1.

Tests of simple main effects were performed to compare the means constituting this interaction. Such tests revealed that the means across levels of evaluation procedure in both the negative evaluation condition and the positive evaluation condition did not differ significantly from each other, in both cases, $F(2, 36) < 1$, *ns*. The means, however, differed significantly across levels of evaluation procedure within the neutral evaluation condition, $F(2, 36) = 27.34$, $p < .0001$. Newman-Keuls post hoc tests revealed that there were significant differences between all three means. Specifically, within the neutral evaluation condition, the mean generalized liking score was higher in the diary condition ($M = 16.08$) than in either of the other two conditions and lower in the control condition ($M = 9.92$) than in either of the other two conditions. The mean in the observation condition ($M = 12.69$) was lower than the mean in the diary condition but higher than the mean in the control condition.

DISCUSSION

This study successfully demonstrates the effectiveness of using diaries to enhance the perceived fairness of performance evaluations. Persons whose work was appraised by an evaluator who regularly observed and recorded their performance in a diary believed both the evaluation procedure itself and the evaluations resulting from it to be more fair than those whose evaluations were based on observations not recorded in diaries and those whose evaluations were not based on any observations whatsoever. It is noteworthy that these individual beliefs in the perceived justice of using diaries are in keeping with broader legal perspectives on justice, such as those underlying the Civil Service Reform Act of 1978, emphasizing the need to base appraisal decisions on carefully documented information (Kleiman & Durham, 1981). Furthermore, these findings extend the benefits of using diaries as a tool for enhancing the validity of performance evaluations (Bernardin & Buckley, 1981) to a means of enhancing the acceptance of those evaluations. To the extent that well-accepted performance evaluations enhance worker motivation and performance (Kanfer et al., 1987; Latham & Wexley, 1981), the present study identifies a potentially important benefit of using diaries in the performance appraisal process.

Implications

In addition to this practical implication, these results support recent research and theorizing in the field of procedural justice. The findings that participants differentiated between procedural and distributive bases of perceived fairness and that the procedural manipulations consistently accounted for a greater proportion of the variance in perceived fairness than the outcome manipulation corroborates previous research (e.g., Alexander & Ruderman, 1987; Tyler & Caine, 1981) and theory (e.g., Leventhal, 1980) emphasizing the perceptual salience of procedural justice relative to distributive justice and their operational independence (see Folger & Greenberg, 1985). By providing a more thorough and systematic means of gathering performance information than mere observation—a crucial determinant of procedural justice according to Leventhal (1980)—diary use promoted the acceptance of appraisal outcomes independent of what those outcomes were. Similarly, Landy et al. (1980) also reported that various procedural variables are associated with the perceived fairness of a performance evaluation system independently of the evaluation outcomes. The present findings, however, not only establish a direct causal link between evaluation procedures and perceived fairness but do so with respect to a specific means of making performance evaluations.

The obtained support for the hypotheses regarding the significant main effects of evaluation procedures on measures of both procedural justice and distributive justice is consistent with Thibaut and Walker's (1975) findings obtained in courtroom simulation studies and Tyler and Caine's (1981) findings obtained in classroom settings. Apparently, the perceived fairness of performance evaluation procedures operates much as dispute resolution procedures used in courtrooms and the evaluation methods used in the classroom in that it is influenced by the amount of information gathered before making a decision. This appears to be the case for judgments of both the fairness of the procedures used and the fairness of the resulting evaluations.

Support was also found for the hypothesis regarding the egocentric bias in perceived outcome fairness (see Greenberg, 1983a). Like defendants in legal cases who believe the verdicts to be fairer when they are found innocent than when found guilty (Thibaut & Walker, 1975) and students in the classroom who believe their grades to be fairer when they are high than when they are low (Tyler & Caine, 1981), workers believed their performance evaluations were fairer when they were positive than when they were negative or neutral. Indicative of a linear relationship, neutral evaluations were also perceived as fairer than negative outcomes. In addition, although outcome factors have not been found to influence procedural justice judgments in previous research (Thibaut & Walker, 1975), such an effect was found in the present study, disconfirming one of the hypotheses. The significant main effect of evaluation outcome on procedural justice was the result of significantly lower ratings given in the negative evaluation condition than in the neutral and positive evaluation conditions. Although it may be tempting to interpret this result as a generalization of the egocentric bias effect to procedural justice ratings, the extremely small magnitude of the effect (outcome accounted for only 2% of the variance in ratings of procedural justice, compared with 82% accounted for by the procedure itself) dictates against doing so.

This study broke some new ground by the finding of a significant interaction between evaluation outcome and evaluation procedure on the generalized liking index, a measure of participants' affective reactions to the evaluator and the task. Regardless of the evaluation procedure used, negative evaluations led to low liking scores and positive evaluations led to high liking scores. Evaluation procedures were apparently unimportant determinants of participants' affective reactions when these were made extremely negative by negative evaluations or extremely positive by positive evaluations. When evaluations were neutral, however, the procedures used had a pronounced effect on the generalized liking index. In this case, diaries enhanced liking relative to evaluations made using mere observations, and observation enhanced liking relative to evaluations made on no apparent basis. Such an interaction effect was not paralleled in ratings of either procedural or distributive justice. In addition, the high proportion of variance accounted for by the procedural manipulation in fairness ratings was not approached in participants' affective reactions. Liking for the task and the evaluator was based mostly on the evaluation itself, with procedures making a difference only when the evaluation was neutral. This suggests that evaluation procedures and outcomes may cause different effects on different varieties of worker reactions, a possibility not recognized in previous studies of procedural or distributive justice.

This study takes its place among several other investigations highlighting the importance of understanding performance appraisal from the perspective of procedural justice. Most of these efforts have focused on the degree of input that evaluated workers are allowed into the evaluation process. Specifically, studies have found that appraisal systems in which appraised workers are given an opportunity to offer information about their performance are perceived more favorably (Dipboye & de Pontbraind, 1981) and are recognized as more fair (Kanfer et al., 1987; Lissak, 1983) than appraisal systems in which input into the appraisal process is not permitted. Although this chapter examines the thoroughness of the information-gathering mechanism as a procedural element, these previous studies focus on employees' voice into the evaluation procedure (Greenberg & Folger, 1983), both of which are recognized as determinants of procedural justice (Leventhal, 1980). As such, these findings may be recognized as painting part of a rapidly emerging picture of the importance of various performance appraisal procedures as determinants of reactions to the appraisal process.

Limitations and Future Research

Despite the strength of these findings, several limitations of the study suggest the need for future research. One obvious set of limitations is imposed by the laboratory methodology used. It is possible, for example, that the greater personal implications of the performance evaluations made in an organizational setting may have differentially affected the results. Beyond this possibility, extension of the present research into a field setting would enhance the generalizability of the findings and help identify potentially moderating influences of the observed effects.

A more specific limitation of this study concerns the compound nature of the evaluation procedure manipulation. Specifically, it remains unclear exactly what it is about diary use—the perceived differences in the *amount* of information, the systematic *recording* of that information, or both— that contributes to the perceived fairness of evaluations made using information recorded in diaries. Now that the effects of the compound evaluation manipulation have been demonstrated, it would be useful to isolate the individual procedural elements responsible for the obtained effects. Such efforts not only would extend the conceptual understanding of procedural justice but also would provide some useful practical assistance in identifying potentially effective appraisal techniques.

REFERENCES

Adams, J. S. (1965). Inequity in social exchange. In L. Berkowitz (Ed.), *Advances in experimental social psychology* (Vol. 2, pp. 267-299). New York: Academic Press.

Alexander, S., & Ruderman, M. (1987). The role of procedural and distributive justice in organizational behavior. *Social Justice Research, 1,* 177-198.

Bernardin, H. J., & Beatty, R. W. (1984). *Performance appraisal: Assessing human behavior at work.* Boston: Kent.

Bernardin, H. J., & Buckley, M. R. (1981). Strategies in rater training. *Academy of Management Review, 6,* 205-212.

Bernardin, H. J., & Walter, C. S. (1977). Effects of rater training and diary-keeping on psychometric error in ratings. *Journal of Applied Psychology, 62,* 64-69.

Borman, W. C. (1979). Format and training effects on rating accuracy and rater errors. *Journal of Applied Psychology, 64,* 410-421.

Buckley, M. R., & Bernardin, H. J. (1980, October). *An assessment of the components of a rater training program.* Paper presented at the meeting of the Southeastern Psychological Association, Washington, DC.

DeCotiis, T. A., & Petit, A. (1978). The performance appraisal process: A model and some testable propositions. *Academy of Management Review, 3,* 635-645.

Dipboye, R. L., & de Pontbraind, R. (1981). Correlates of employee reactions to performance appraisals and appraisal systems. *Journal of Applied Psychology, 66,* 248-251.

Folger, R., & Greenberg, J. (1985). Procedural justice: An interpretive analysis of personnel systems. In K. M. Rowland & G. R. Ferris (Eds.), *Research in personnel and human resources management* (Vol. 3, pp. 141-183). Greenwich, CT: JAI.

Greenberg, J. (1983a). Overcoming egocentric bias in perceived fairness through self-awareness. *Social Psychology Quarterly, 46,* 152-156.

Greenberg, J. (1983b). Self-image versus impression management in adherence to distributive justice standards: The influence of self-awareness and self-consciousness. *Journal of Personality and Social Psychology, 44,* 5-19.

Greenberg, J., & Folger, R. (1983). Procedural justice, participation and the fair process effect in groups and organizations. In P. B. Paulus (Ed.), *Basic group processes* (pp. 235-256). New York: Springer-Verlag.

Homans, G. C. (1961). *Social behavior: Its elementary forms.* New York: Harcourt, Brace, & World.

Kanfer, R., Sawyer, J., Earley, P. C., & Lind, E. A. (1987). Information exchange in evaluation procedures: The effects of input and knowledge on performance and attitudes. *Social Justice Research, 1,* 235-249.

Kleiman, L. S., & Durham, R. L. (1981). Performance appraisal, promotion, and the courts: A critical review. *Personnel Psychology, 34,* 103-121.

Landy, F. J., Barnes, J. L., & Murphy, K. R. (1978). Correlates of perceived fairness and accuracy of performance evaluation. *Journal of Applied Psychology, 63,* 751-754.

Landy, F. J., Barnes-Farrell, J., & Cleveland, J. N. (1980). Perceived fairness and accuracy of performance evaluation: A follow-up. *Journal of Applied Psychology, 65,* 355-356.

Latham, G. P., & Wexley, K. N. (1981). *Increasing productivity through performance appraisal.* Reading, MA: Addison-Wesley.

Leventhal, G. S. (1976). Fairness in social relationships. In J. W. Thibaut, J. T. Spence, & R. C. Carson (Eds.), *Contemporary topics in social psychology* (pp. 211-239). Morristown, NJ: General Learning Press.

Leventhal, G. S. (1980). What should be done with equity theory? In K. J. Gergen, M. S. Greenberg, & R. H. Willis (Eds.), *Social exchange: Advances in theory and research* (pp. 27-55). New York: Plenum.

Lissak, R. I. (1983). *Procedural fairness: How employees evaluate procedures.* Unpublished doctoral dissertation, University of Illinois, Urbana-Champaign.

Sheppard, B. H. (1984). Third-party conflict intervention: A procedural framework. In B. M. Staw & L. L. Cummings (Eds.), *Research in organizational behavior* (Vol. 6, pp. 141-190). Greenwich, CT: JAI.

Thibaut, J., & Walker, L. (1975). *Procedural justice: A psychological analysis.* Hillsdale, NJ: Lawrence Erlbaum.

Tyler, T. R., & Caine, A. (1981). The role of distributional and procedural fairness in the endorsement of formal leaders. *Journal of Personality and Social Psychology, 41,* 642-655.

Walker, L., Lind, E. A., & Thibaut, J. (1979). The relation between procedural and distributive justice. *Virginia Law Review, 65,* 1401-1420.

PART IV

Employee Theft and Acceptance of a Smoking Ban

WHILE teaching my students about equity theory some years ago, the question came up of how people might go about raising their outcomes in response to perceived underpayment. When a raise was not forthcoming, one direct way was for employees to help themselves to things of value—that is, to steal company property. Although interview studies linked employee theft and feelings of inequity, a direct causal link had not been established. So, one day when my phone rang and I found myself with an opportunity to study a company in which some employees were about to experience a temporary pay cut, I immediately recognized it as a chance to test this idea.

Chapter 10 describes this study, which can be viewed as a straightforward test of equity theory. Demonstrating that theft rates were higher among those whose pay was cut than among those whose pay was maintained was completely consistent with what equity theory predicts. In my opinion, however, a more interesting aspect of the research lies in the manipulation of the ways in which information about the pay cut was described to the employees. Because there were two different plants in which the company decided to institute the pay cut, it was possible to present the situation differently in each. On the basis of emerging research and theory on the interpersonal aspects of justice (reviewed in Chapter 3), I decided to give a thorough and interpersonally sensitive explanation in one plant and a more superficial and insensitive explanation in the other. The strong tendency for the thorough and sensitive explanation to help reduce employee theft reinforced my belief in the importance of interpersonal treatment as a moderator of reactions to inequity.

Shortly after this study, I conducted a follow-up experiment in the laboratory that not only replicated the field experiment but also allowed me to disentangle two key variables. This work is presented in Chapter 11. Specifically, I independently manipulated both the amount of information people had about the reason why they were underpaid and the amount of social sensitivity displayed while presenting this explanation. Each of these variables contributed independently to a reduction in theft induced by underpayment inequity. These findings confirmed in my mind the importance of two key aspects of interpersonal treatment identified in my conceptualization of justice presented in Chapter 3—information and social sensitivity.

To fully substantiate the importance of these variables, it was necessary to document their effect in another setting in which negative information is presented. Just as learning that one will be underpaid represents exposure to negative information, so too is the imposition of a corporate smoking ban among smokers. Both are highly threatening situations in which desired outcomes are cut back. Nevertheless, if carefully explaining negative outcomes and showing sensitivity to the harm they create reduces feelings of inequity, I reasoned, then doing these things should get smokers to accept a smoking ban. Indeed, the research reported in Chapter 12 did just that. Although the applied context of this field experiment is extremely different than that of my theft field experiment (Chapter 10), together they both hone in on the same basic conceptual issue: the role of interpersonal treatment on reactions to undesirable outcomes. To me, the opportunity to develop theoretical ideas in a variety of applied settings is the real joy of conducting research on organizational justice.

10

Employee Theft as a Reaction to Underpayment Inequity

Employee theft constitutes one of the most pervasive and serious problems in the field of human resources management. Although exact figures are difficult to come by, the American Management Association (1977) has estimated that employee theft cost American businesses from $5 billion to $10 billion in 1975, representing the single most expensive form of nonviolent crime against businesses.

AUTHOR'S NOTE: This chapter was originally published in the *Journal of Applied Psychology,* Vol. 75, No. 5, pp. 561-568, under the title "Employee Theft as a Reaction to Underpayment Inequity: The Hidden Cost of Pay Cuts." Copyright © 1990 by the American Psychological Association. Reprinted by permission.

Traditionally, social scientists have considered several plausible explanations for employee theft. Among the most popular are theories postulating that theft is the result of attempts to ease financial pressure (Merton, 1938), moral laxity among a younger workforce (Merriam, 1977), available opportunities (Astor, 1972), expressions of job dissatisfaction (Mangione & Quinn, 1975), and the existence of norms tolerating theft (Horning, 1970). More recently, Hollinger and Clark (1983) conducted a large-scale survey and interview study designed to explore these and other explanations of employee theft. They found that the best predictor was employee attitudes: "When employees felt exploited by the company . . . these workers were more involved in acts against the organizations as a mechanism to correct perceptions of inequity or injustice" (p. 142).

Hollinger and Clark's (1983) suggestion that employee theft is related to feelings of injustice is consistent with several schools of sociological and anthropological thought. For example, studies of hotel dining room employees (Mars, 1973) and maritime dockworkers (Mars, 1974) showed that employees viewed theft *not* as inappropriate but "as a morally justified addition to wages; indeed, as an entitlement due from exploiting employers" (Mars, 1974, p. 224). Similarly, Kemper (1966) argued that employee theft may be the result of "reciprocal deviance," that is, employees' perceptions that their employers defaulted on their obligations to them, thereby encouraging them to respond with similar acts of deviance. Fisher and Baron (1982) made a similar argument in presenting their equity-control model of vandalism. They claimed that vandalism is a form of inequity reduction in that an individual vandal's breaking the rules regarding property rights follows from the vandal's feelings of mistreatment by authorities. Recent evidence in support of this idea is found in a study by DeMore, Fisher, and Baron (1988). In that study, university students claimed to engage in more vandalism the less fairly they felt they had been treated by their university and the less control they believed they had over such treatment.

Such conceptualizations are in keeping with current theoretical positions in the field of organizational justice (Greenberg, 1987[1]). These formulations allow more precise hypotheses to be developed regarding when employee theft is likely to occur. For example, consider equity theory's (Adams, 1965) claim that workers who feel inequitably underpaid (i.e., those who believe that the rewards they are receiving relative to the contributions they are making are less than they should be) may respond by attempting to raise their outcomes (i.e., raise the level of rewards received). Although research has supported this claim (for a review, see Greenberg, 1982), studies have been limited to situations in which persons paid on a piecework basis produce more goods of poorer quality to raise their outcomes without effectively raising their inputs. Given earlier conceptual claims and supporting evidence associating student vandalism with inequitable treatment (DeMore et al., 1988), it may be reasoned analogously that employee theft is a specific reaction to underpayment inequity and constitutes an attempt to bring outcomes into line with prevailing standards of fair pay.

Later research in the area of procedural justice (Lind & Tyler, 1988) has shown that perceptions of fair treatment and outcomes depend not only on the relative level of one's outcomes but also on the explanations given for those outcomes (for a review, see Folger & Bies, 1989). For example, researchers have found that decision outcomes and procedures were better accepted when (a) people were assured that higher authorities were sensitive to their viewpoints (Tyler, 1988), (b) the decision was made without bias (Lind & Lissak, 1985), (c) the decision was applied consistently (Greenberg, 1986[6]), (d) the decision was carefully justified on the basis of adequate information (Shapiro & Buttner, 1988), (e) the decision makers communicated their ideas honestly (Bies, 1986), and (f) persons influenced by the decision were treated in a courteous and civil manner (Bies & Moag, 1986). Such findings suggest that interpersonal treatment is an important determinant of reactions to potentially unfair situations (Tyler & Bies, 1990).

Perceptions of inequity (and corresponding attempts to redress inequities) may be reduced when explanations meeting the criteria presented in the preceding paragraph are offered to account for inequitable states. This notion was tested in the present study by capitalizing on a naturalistic manipulation—temporary pay reduction for employees of selected manufacturing plants. Data were available for 30 consecutive weeks: 10 weeks before a pay reduction occurred, 10 weeks during the pay reduction period, and 10 weeks after normal pay was reinstated. Following from equity theory, it was hypothesized that ratings of payment fairness would be lower during the pay reduction period than during periods of normal payment (i.e., before and after the pay reduction). It was similarly hypothesized that rates of employee theft would be higher during the reduced-pay period than during periods of normal payment. Such actions would be consistent with equity theory's claim that one likely way of responding to underpayment inequity is by attempting to raise the level of rewards received. Although not previously studied in this connection, employee theft is a plausible mechanism for redressing states of inequity (Hollinger & Clark, 1983).

Additional hypotheses were derived from research (e.g., Cropanzano & Folger, 1989; Folger & Martin, 1986; Shapiro & Buttner, 1988; Weiner, Amirkhan, Folkes, & Varette, 1987) showing that explanations for negative outcomes mitigate people's reactions to those outcomes (for a review, see Folger & Bies, 1989; Tyler & Bies, 1990). In general, in these studies the use of adequate explanations (i.e., ones that relied on complete, accurate information presented in a socially sensitive manner) tended to reduce the negative reactions that resulted from such outcomes and facilitated acceptance of the outcomes. From the perspective of Folger's (1986) referent cognitions theory, adequate explanations help victimized parties place their undercompensation in perspective by getting them to understand that things could have been worse. As such, in the present study, adequate explanations were expected to lessen the feelings of inequity that accompanied the pay cut. Thus, I reasoned that employees' feelings of payment inequity and attempts to reduce that inequity (such as by pilfering) would be reduced when adequate explanations were given to account for the pay reduction. Specifically, I hypothesized that the magnitude of the expressed inequity—and the rate of employee theft—would be lower when pay reductions were adequately explained than when they were inadequately explained.

METHOD

Participants

Participants in the study were nonunion employees working for 30 consecutive weeks in three manufacturing plants owned by the same parent company. The plants were located in different sections of the midwestern United States and manufactured small mechanical parts mostly for the aerospace and automotive industries. The employees' average age ($M = 28.5$ years), level of education ($M = 11.2$ years), and tenure with the company ($M = 3.2$ years) did not significantly differ among the three plants, $F < 1.00$, in all cases. The local unemployment rates in the communities surrounding the three plants were not significantly different from each other (overall $M = 6.4\%$), $F < 1.00$. It is important to establish this equivalence of characteristics across research sites because the assignment of individuals to conditions was not random across sites, thereby precluding the assumption of equivalence afforded by random assignment (Cook & Campbell, 1976).

As the study began, Plant A employed 64 workers in the following jobs: 5 salaried low-level managerial employees (4 men, 1 woman); 47 hourly wage semiskilled and unskilled production workers (38 men, 9 women); and 12 hourly wage clerical workers (all women). Almost identical proportions with respect to job type (and sex of employees within job type)

TABLE 10.1 Distribution of Attrition and Turnover Across Conditions

			Resignations			
Condition	Starting n	Missing Data	Before Pay Cut	During Pay Cut	After Pay Cut	Final n
Adequate explanation						
(Plant A)	64	6	1	1	1	55
Inadequate explanation						
(Plant B)	53	8	1	12	2	30
Control (Plant C)	66	5	1	0	2	58

existed in Plant B ($n = 53$) and Plant C ($n = 66$). Because some employees did not complete questionnaires during some weeks and because some employees voluntarily left their jobs during the study, complete sets of questionnaires were available from 55 employees of Plant A, 30 employees of Plant B, and 58 employees of Plant C. This constituted a total sample of 143 employees, distributed to conditions as summarized in Table 10.1. The demographic characteristics of the 40 workers who were not included in the study did not differ significantly from the characteristics of the 143 who remained in the study (in all cases, $F < 2.00$), minimizing the possibility that those who remained in the study were a select group.

Procedure

Because of the loss of two large manufacturing contracts, the host company was forced to reduce its payroll by temporarily cutting wages by 15% across-the-board in two of its manufacturing plants (Plants A and B). This was done in lieu of laying off any employees. After this decision was made, I was asked to help assess the effect of the wage cuts in several key areas, including employee theft. Each of the payment group manipulations was carried out in a separate plant. The assignment of Plant A to one experimental condition and Plant B to another experimental condition was determined at random. Assignment to the control group was determined by the host company's decision that pay cuts were not necessary in Plant C.[1]

The *adequate explanation* condition was created in Plant A. To effect this, a meeting (lasting approximately 90 minutes) was called at the end of a workweek. At that meeting, all employees were told by the company president that their pay was going to be reduced by 15%, effective the following week, for a period expected to last 10 weeks. During this meeting, several types of explanations were provided. On the basis of recent research

(Folger & Bies, 1989; Tyler & Bies, 1990), I hypothesized that these explanations would mitigate reactions to the pay cut. The workers were told that company management seriously regretted having to reduce their pay but that doing so would preclude the need for any layoffs. They were further assured that all plant employees would share in the pay cuts and that no favoritism would be shown.[2] A relevant verbatim passage follows.

> Something we hate to do here at [company name] is lay off any of our employees. But as you probably know, we've lost our key contracts with [company names], which will make things pretty lean around here for a little while. As a result, we need to cut somewhere, and we've come up with a plan that will get us through these tough times. I've been working on it with [name of person] in accounting, and we're sure it will work. The plan is simple: Starting Monday, we will each get a 15% cut in pay. This applies to you, to me, to everyone who works here at [name of plant]. If we do it this way, there'll be no cut in benefits and no layoffs—just a 15% pay reduction. So, either your hourly wages or your salary will be reduced by 15%. Will it hurt? Of course! But it will hurt us all alike. We're all in it together. Let me just add that it really hurts me to do this, and the decision didn't come easily. We considered all possible avenues, but nothing was feasible. I think of you all as family, and it hurts me to take away what you've worked so hard for. But for the next 10 weeks, we'll just have to tough it out.

In addition to these remarks, the basis for the decision was clearly explained and justified by presenting charts and graphs detailing the temporary effects of the lost contracts on cash-flow revenues. Projections verified that the cash-flow problem dictating the need for the pay cuts was only temporary, and this was clearly explained. All employees were assured that the pay cut was designed to last only 10 weeks.[3] Specifically, the employees were told the following:

> The reason I'm sharing all this information with you is that I want you to understand what is happening here. It's just a temporary problem we're facing, and one that I hope will never happen again. At least the best course of action from our accounting department is clear: The pay cuts will work, and they will not have to last longer than 10 weeks. The new jobs we'll be picking up from [name of company] will really help get us back on our feet. Hopefully, by then we'll be stronger than ever. Of course, I know we're no stronger than our people, and I personally thank each and every one of you for your strength.

The tone of the presentation was such that a great deal of respect was shown for the workers, and all questions were answered with sensitivity. The president spent approximately 1 hour answering all questions. Each response brought an expression of remorse at having to take such action (e.g., "Again, I really wish this weren't necessary."). The good intent of this message was reinforced by the president's issuing the message in person.

Plant B was the site of the *inadequate explanation* condition. Here, a meeting lasting approximately 15 minutes was called at the end of a workweek. All employees were told by a company vice president that their pay was going to be reduced by 15%, effective the following week, for a period expected to last 10 weeks. The only additional information that was provided indicated that the lost contracts dictated the need for the pay cut. No expressions of apology or remorse were shared, and the basis for the decision was not clearly described. The following verbatim remarks characterize this condition:

> It is inevitable in a business like ours that cost-cutting measures are often necessary to make ends meet. Unfortunately, the time has come for us to take such measures here at [company name]. I know it won't be easy on anyone, but [name of company president] has decided that a 15% across-the-board pay cut will be instituted effective Monday. This is largely the result of the fact that we've lost our contracts with [name of companies]. However, soon we'll be picking up jobs with [name of company], so we're sure the pay cuts will last only 10 weeks. I realize this isn't easy, but such reductions are an unfortunate fact of life in the manufacturing business. On behalf of [company president's name] and myself, we thank you for bearing with us over these rough times. I'll answer one or two questions, but then I have to catch a plane for another meeting.

Because the parts manufactured at Plant C were unaffected by the lost contracts, no pay cuts were mandated there. Plant C constituted the *control* condition for the study.

Measures

Two categories of dependent measures were used: actuarial data on employee theft and self-report measures tapping some of the processes assumed to be underlying the theft behavior.

Employee theft rates. The measure of employee theft used for this study was the company accounting department's standard formula for computing "shrinkage." The formula yielded the percentage of inventory (e.g., tools, supplies, etc.) unaccounted for by known waste, sales, use in the conduct of business, or normal depreciation. (For a discussion of the difficulties attendant to deriving such measures, see Hollinger & Clark, 1983.) These measures were obtained unobtrusively (during nonwork hours) by representatives of the company's headquarters on a weekly basis during the study. The persons taking inventory were aware of any legitimate factors that contributed to accounted-for changes in inventory levels (such as shipments received, supplies used during projects, etc.) but were blind to the experimental hypotheses.[4]

Because no single standard for computing shrinkage is uniformly used (Hollinger & Clark, 1983), it was not possible to compare the base rates of employee theft in the present sample with any industrywide average. Evidence that the employee theft rate studied here was not atypical, however, was provided by showing that the mean theft rate for the 10-week period before the pay cut was not significantly different from the overall theft rate for all three plants for the prior year, $F < 1.00$. These data are important in that they provide some assurance that the changes in theft rates observed were not simply deviations from unusual patterns that later merely regressed to the mean.[5]

Questionnaire measures. Two types of questionnaire measures were needed to establish the validity of the study and to facilitate interpretation of the theft data: one group of questions to verify differences in familiarity with the basis for establishing pay (the manipulation check) and another group of questions to establish differences in perceived payment equity. The questionnaires were administered biweekly (during odd-numbered weeks in the study) at the plant sites during nonworking hours. Because a larger, unrelated study had been going on for several months, the workers were used to completing questionnaires, making it unlikely that any suspicions were aroused by the questions inserted for this study. Participants were assured of the anonymity of their responses.

The "pay basis" measure was designed to provide a check on the validity of the payment-group variable. Participants answered four items on a 5-point scale ranging from 1 (*not at all*), to 2 (*slightly*), to 3 (*moderately*), to 4 (*highly*), to 5 (*extremely*). The questions were (a) "How adequate was your employer's explanation regarding the basis of your current pay?" (b) "How familiar are you with the way your employer determines your pay?" (c) "How thoroughly did your employer communicate the basis for your current pay to you?" and (d) "How much concern did your employer show about your feelings when communicating your pay?" A high degree of internal consistency was found for these items (coefficient alpha = .89).

The "pay equity" measure consisted of four items, three of which were anchored with the same scale points as the pay basis items. Specifically, participants responded to the following items: (a) "To what extent do you believe your current pay reflects your actual contributions to the job?" (b) "How fairly paid do you feel you currently are on your job?" and (c) "How satisfied are you with your current overall pay level?" The fourth item asked, "Relative to what you feel you should be paid, do you believe your current pay is: _____ much too low, _____ a little too low, _____ about right, _____ a little too high, _____ much too high?" Because only the first 3 points of this bidirectional scale were actually used, responses to this 3-point scale were combined with the 5-point unidirectional scales for the other items. Coefficient alpha was high (.84), justifying combining the individual items. The option of using existing standardized scales tapping reactions to pay (e.g., the Pay Satisfaction Questionnaire; Heneman & Schwab, 1985) was rejected in favor of ad hoc measures because these were judged to be much more sensitive to the measurement objectives of this study (cf. Heneman, 1985).

RESULTS

Preliminary Analyses

Prior to the principal data analyses, preliminary analyses were conducted to determine whether to separate the 15 biweekly questionnaire responses into three equal groups, reflecting responses before, during, and after the pay cut. The five 2-week response periods were treated as a repeated measure in mixed-design analyses of variance (ANOVAs) in which the payment group was the between-participants factor (adequate explanation, inadequate explanation, no pay cut). Separate analyses were conducted for each of the three groups. Because no significant main effects or interactions involving the response periods were obtained in analyses for either questionnaire measure (all $Fs < 1.00$), the decision was made to combine the observations into three groups composed of more reliable observations (before, during, or after the pay cut).

Because only one employee theft rate figure was reported for each week (the figure was aggregate, as opposed to individual, data), it was not possible to conduct a parallel set of ANOVAs for this measure. Separate tests, however, were performed within each payment group to compare each week's theft rate with the mean for all 10 weeks. This process was repeated separately for each of the three response periods (i.e., before, during, and after the pay cut). Because no significant effects emerged in any of these analyses (all values of $t < .50$, $df = 9$), the decision was made (paralleling that for the questionnaire measures) to group the weekly scores into three 10-week response periods.

Employee Theft Rate

Analyses of theft rates were based on a 3×3 mixed-design ANOVA in which payment group was the between-participants variable, response period was the within-participants variable, and the 10 weekly theft rates

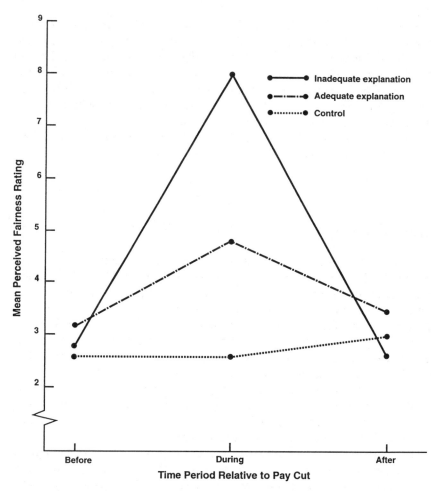

Figure 10.1. Mean Percentage of Employee Theft as a Function of Time Relative to Pay Cut

within each cell constituted the data. A significant Payment Period × Response Period interaction was found, $F(4, 56) = 9.66$, $p < .001$. Figure 10.1 summarizes the means contributing to this interaction.

For each payment group, simple effects tests were performed to determine whether the means differed significantly across response periods. Any significant effects were followed up with the Tukey honestly significant difference (HSD) procedure (with alpha set at .05). In addition, tests for quadratic trend components were performed using orthogonal polynomials (Hays, 1963). This analysis was performed to note trends in the data through time in a situation in which the number of available data points was too small to use time series analyses (Zuwaylif, 1970).

A simple effects test within the inadequate explanation condition was significant, $F(2, 27) = 9.15$, $p < .001$. Post hoc tests revealed that significantly higher levels of theft were observed during the pay reduction than before or after the pay reduction. Consistent with this configuration, the quadratic trend was highly significant, $F(1, 27) = 12.18$, $p < .001$.

Within the adequate explanation condition, the overall simple effects test was weaker but still significant, $F(2, 52) = 3.76$, $p < .05$. This effect was the result of a similar, though less pronounced, pattern of means showing theft to be higher during the pay cut than either before or after the pay cut. Tests for a quadratic trend component failed to reach conventional levels of significance, $F(2, 52) = 2.10$, $p < .15$. Finally, within the control group, simple effects tests revealed that the means did not differ from each other significantly across the three response periods, $F(2, 55) < 1.00$.

To establish pre- and postmanipulation equivalence, it was useful to compare means between payment groups (adequate explanation, inadequate explanation, no pay cut) within response periods. Simple effects tests showed no significant simple main effects of payment group before or after the pay cut, $F < 1.00$ in both cases. The effect of payment group, however, was highly significant during the pay cut, $F(2, 27) = 10.71$, $p < .001$. Tukey HSD tests revealed that the three means were significantly different from each other. In other words, within the pay reduction period, the theft rate in the inadequate explanation condition ($M = 8.9$) was significantly higher than that in the adequate explanation condition ($M = 5.7$), which was in turn higher than that in the control condition ($M = 3.7$).

Questionnaire Responses

Responses to the pay basis and pay equity questionnaires were analyzed with ANOVA designs identical to that used for the employee-theft measure. For these dependent variables, however, the data consisted of individual responses to the summed items constituting each questionnaire within each cell. The two questionnaire measures were not significantly correlated, $r = .07$.

For the pay basis measure, a significant Payment Group × Response Period interaction was obtained, $F(4, 280) = 256.10$, $p < .0001$. The corresponding means and standard deviations are summarized at the top of Table 10.2. As shown, post hoc tests revealed that employees in the adequate explanation condition demonstrated greater understanding of

TABLE 10.2 Data Summaries for Questionnaire Measures

Measure/ Payment Group	n	Before M	Before SD	During M	During SD	After M	After SD
Pay basis[a]							
Inadequate explanation	30	40.70$_a$	4.38	42.39	3.40	43.74$_a$	4.93
Adequate explanation	55	43.22$_a$	5.58	76.10$_b$	6.48	73.73$_b$	5.70
Control	58	42.36$_a$	6.49	40.72$_a$	3.83	41.90$_a$	4.46
Pay equity[b]							
Inadequate explanation	30	56.87$_a$	5.54	40.20$_b$	7.56	57.43$_a$	6.70
Adequate explanation	55	61.22$_a$	9.57	59.56$_a$	9.52	56.03$_a$	9.37
Control	58	61.29$_a$	8.67	60.98$_a$	9.18	58.02$_a$	8.57

NOTE: Within each row and each column, means not sharing a common subscript are significantly different from each other beyond the .05 level on the basis of the Tukey honestly significant difference technique corrected for confounded comparisons with the Cicchetti (1972) approximation.
[a] Mean scores for the pay basis measure could range from 20 to 100. Higher scores reflect greater degrees of familiarity with the basis for establishing pay.
[b] Mean scores for the pay equity measure could range from 20 to 90. Higher scores reflect greater degrees of perceived payment equity.

the basis for pay determination than employees in the other two conditions once the explanation occurred (i.e., during and after the pay cut). The adequate explanation manipulation successfully enhanced employees' understanding of the basis for pay determination.

A significant interaction effect also was obtained for the pay equity measure, $F(4, 280) = 29.05$, $p < .001$. The corresponding means and standard deviations are summarized at the bottom of Table 10.2. As shown, post hoc tests revealed that during the pay cut, employees in the inadequate explanation condition expressed the greatest perceptions of pay inequity. Workers whose pay reductions were adequately explained to them did not express heightened payment inequity while their pay was reduced.

Turnover

A summary of missing data and data lost because of voluntary turnover appears in Table 10.1. Not surprisingly, the majority of the turnover occurred among employees experiencing inadequately explained pay reductions (12 of the 52 workers, or 23.1% of those still on the job at that time).

Resignations in other conditions were uniformly 5% or less. Consistent with this, the distribution of resignations across conditions during the pay cut was highly significant, $\chi^2(2, N = 13) = 20.48$, $p < .001$, a result of 12 of the 13 resignations occurring in the inadequate explanation group. By contrast, the distribution of resignations across conditions was equal before the pay cut, $\chi^2(2, N = 3) < 0.5$, and after the pay cut, $\chi^2(2, N = 5) < 0.5$.

DISCUSSION

The data support the hypothesis derived from equity theory (Adams, 1965) that workers experiencing underpayment inequity would attempt to redress that inequity by raising their inputs—in this case, by pilfering from their employer. Indeed, while workers experienced a 15% pay reduction, they reported feeling underpaid and stole more than twice as much as they did when they felt equitably paid. Two distinct interpretations of these theft data may be offered, both of which are consistent with equity theory (Adams, 1965). First, it is possible that the pay reduction led to feelings of frustration and resentment, which motivated the aggressive acts of theft. This possibility is in keeping with research findings demonstrating that pay cuts are associated with negative affective reactions to organizational authorities (Greenberg, 1989[16]) and that increases in vandalism correlate positively with perceptions of mistreatment by authorities (DeMore et al., 1988). Such an interpretation follows from a reciprocal deviance orientation to inequity reduction, which suggests that employees' acts of deviance are encouraged by their beliefs that their employers defaulted on their obligations to them by reducing their pay (Kemper, 1966). From this perspective, acts of theft may be understood as a manifestation of feelings of mistreatment.

It is also possible to interpret the thefts as direct attempts to correct underpayment inequity by adjusting the balance of valued resources between the worker and the specific source of that inequity. As such, acts of theft may be interpreted as unofficial transfers of outcomes from the employer to the employee. Because no direct evidence is available suggesting that the stolen items had any positive valence to the employees, it is impossible to claim unambiguously that the theft rates represented employees' attempts to increase their own outcomes. Although such an interpretation is consistent with a considerable amount of evidence on the distribution of rewards and resources (for reviews, see Freedman & Montanari, 1980; Leventhal, 1976), it is also possible that disgruntled employees may have been content to reduce the valued resources available to the agent of their discontent. They may have been motivated to reduce the employer's worth whether or not doing so directly benefited themselves. Unfortunately, the questionnaire items that would have been necessary to provide more refined interpretations of the present data might also have aroused participants' suspiciousness that theft was being studied, thereby creating the potential for participant reactance (Webb, Campbell, Schwartz, Sechrest, & Grove, 1981). As a result, no such self-report data were collected. Nevertheless, the results are clearly in keeping with equity theory.

The data also reveal a critical moderator of the tendency to pilfer to restore equity with one's employer, namely, the use of an adequate explanation for the pay cut. Pay cuts that were explained in an honest and caring manner were not seen by employees as unfair as pay cuts that were not explained carefully. Accordingly, reactions to carefully explained underpayment also were less severe (i.e., the pilferage rates were lower). These findings add to the recently developing research showing that the use of adequately reasoned explanations offered with interpersonal sensitivity tends to mitigate the negative effects associated with the information itself (for reviews, see Folger & Bies, 1989; Tyler & Bies, 1990). The explanations used in the present study were obviously quite successful in reducing costs, both to employees (inequity distress) and employers (pilferage and turnover).

A sizeable portion of the participants in the inadequate explanation condition voluntarily left their jobs during the pay reduction period; in fact, a much larger proportion resigned than did so in any other condition (or within the same condition at other times). It is tempting to take this finding as support for the idea that quitting one's job is an extreme form of reaction to underpayment inequity (Finn & Lee, 1972) and that the voluntary turnover found here was another form of reaction to inequity. Because of the nonrandom design of the study, however, it is not possible to rule out factors other than the experimental manipulation—a difficulty common to quasi-experimental studies (Cook & Campbell, 1976). Despite this problem, several facts lend support to the inequity interpretation. First, the finding that the theft rate immediately before the manipulations did not differ significantly from the previous year's theft rate suggests that nothing out of the ordinary was happening that may have been responsible for the results. Second, because the theft rate was highest precisely under the only conditions in which feelings of inequity were high (i.e., during the pay cut period following an inadequate explanation), feelings of inequity and theft rate probably are related, both resulting from the manipulated variable exactly as predicted by equity theory (Adams, 1965) and referent cognitions theory (Folger, 1986).

Because this interpretation is theoretically supported, its position is strengthened relative to alternatives that may be raised in the absence of random assignment.

Generalizing from these findings, it appears that adequately explaining inequitable conditions may be an effective means of reducing potentially costly reactions to feelings of underpayment inequity. To be effective, however, such explanations must be perceived as honest, genuine, and not manipulative (Tyler, 1988). Still, to the extent that underpayment conditions are acknowledged and justified by employers (as opposed to ignored or minimized by them), it appears that both workers and their organizations may stand to benefit. On the basis of the high costs of employee theft (American Management Association, 1977), it appears that explaining the basis for inequities may be an effective (and totally free) mechanism for reducing the costs of employee theft.

Practical implications notwithstanding, the findings raise some important questions for equity theory (Adams, 1965) about the use of various modes of inequity reduction. Although the focus of the present study was on pilferage, turnover was another type of response that occurred. Unfortunately, the nature of the data makes it impossible to determine the trade-offs between various modes of inequity reduction. Did some employees resign in response to underpayment, whereas others (perhaps those with fewer options for alternative employment) stayed on and expressed their negative feelings by stealing? Or did the most aggrieved employees steal company property before leaving, whereas others simply lowered their inputs? Because the theft rates were aggregate, actuarial data could not be traced to particular employees, and because performance data were not collected, it was not possible to determine when and how different forms of inequity reduction behavior are likely to occur. As a result, serious questions remain regarding how different inequity resolution tactics may be used in conjunction with each other.

Confidence in interpretations of these findings is limited because actuarial-level dependent measures (theft and turnover) were collected in conjunction with an individual-level variable (perceived payment equity), thereby making it impossible to conduct mediational analyses of the results. Exacerbating this problem is the use of a quasi-experimental design that does not allow the discounting of alternative explanations (as noted earlier). Thus, although it is plausible that inequity leads to stealing unless mitigated by an adequate explanation, it is impossible to statistically discount the alternative possibility that unknown preexisting differences between the plants constituting the payment groups (e.g., different norms against stealing or differential acceptance of management's promise that the pay cut would be temporary) may have been responsible for the results. In support of the findings, however, it is important to note that such limitations are inherent to some degree in all quasi-experimental research designs (Cook & Campbell, 1976).

Although nonrandom assignment precludes the discounting of alternative explanations, support for the present interpretation of the data may be derived from converging sources of theoretically based data. In this case, several lines of analogous research converge with my claim that adequate explanations enhanced the acceptance of undesired outcomes. For example, Folger and his associates (e.g., Folger & Martin, 1986; Folger, Rosenfield, & Robinson, 1983) measured laboratory participants' feelings of discontent in reaction to procedural changes that created unfavorable conditions for them. Consistent with referent cognitions theory (Folger, 1986), Folger and his colleagues found that these feelings of discontent were reduced only when the need to make procedural changes was adequately explained. Similarly, in another investigation, Weiner et al. (1987) found that persons victimized by another's harm doing expressed less anger toward the harm doer when claims of mitigating circumstances were offered for the harm doer's actions. Both areas of investigation show that negative affective reactions are reduced by the presentation of adequate explanatory information. As such, they provide good convergent evidence for my claim that adequately explained pay cuts mitigated feelings of inequity and reactions to underpayment inequity.

In addition, an important question may be raised about the compound nature of the explanation manipulation used in this study. Because the adequate explanation condition and the inadequate explanation condition differed along several dimensions (postulated a priori to contribute to mitigation of the effects of the inequity), it was not possible to determine the individual effects of the various contributing factors. Specifically, the explanations differed regarding several factors. Some of these, such as the quality of the information and the interpersonal sincerity of its presentation, have been recognized as mitigating reactions to undesirable outcomes (Shapiro & Buttner, 1988). Other differences between conditions, such as possible differences in the credibility of the source (the president versus the vice president) have not yet been studied. Clearly, the unique effects of these factors are prime candidates for future research efforts.

In conclusion, the results of this study shed new light on employee theft —one of the most important problems in the field of human resources management. The evidence confirms that employee theft is a predictable response to underpayment inequity and reveals that such reactions can be substantially reduced by the inexpensive tactic of explaining the basis for the inequity in clear, honest, and sensitive terms.

NOTES

1. Admittedly, conducting the study in this manner meant that the two randomly assigned groups may have been nonequivalent with respect to some unknown variables that might have otherwise affected the results (Cook & Campbell, 1976). Some reassurance of between-group similarity, however, is provided by the demonstrated equivalence between worker characteristics, economic conditions, and job duties for both plants. Moreover, the deliberate assignment of Plant C to the control condition raises the possibility that something besides the lack of manipulation may have been responsible for the results (Cook & Campbell, 1976). Informal postexperiment interviews with plant officials and employees, however, confirmed that no unusual "local history" events occurred during the study. Further assurance that this was not a problem is provided because before and after the pay cut, the control group's responses were identical to the other groups' responses for all measures used in the study.

2. Before the meetings scheduled in each plant, the individuals involved (i.e., company president in Plant A and a vice president in Plant B) met with me to develop outlines of their presentations. Several carefully crafted sentences conveying salient aspects of the manipulation were prepared for inclusion in the speaker's notes. Because local company norms dictated using informal meetings instead of formal presentations, complete scripts for the entire sessions could not be prepared in advance. As a result, it was necessary to establish that key differences in the manipulated variables were actually communicated in the meetings. With this in mind, each session was videotaped, and the videotapes were played back to a group of 112 undergraduate students after all identifying information was deleted. The students were asked to indicate in which of the two tapes (Tape A for Plant A; Tape B for Plant B) the speaker (a) presented more information about the pay cuts and (b) expressed greater remorse about the pay cuts. The order of presentation of the tapes was randomized. Virtually all of the students agreed that the speaker on Tape A presented more information and expressed greater remorse. Taken together with my in-person confirmation that the manipulations were conducted as desired, these findings suggest that differentially adequate explanations were given to the two groups. Unfortunately, it was not possible to conduct further analyses on these tapes because the host company insisted that they be destroyed to prevent the unwanted dissemination of sensitive company information.

3. Because of the sensitive and privileged nature of the internal accounting information, I was not permitted to divulge these data. Indeed, although I helped company officials present this information in understandable form, these charts and graphs were never made part of my file.

4. Although the theft rate figures (i.e., percentage of inventory loss unaccounted for) were used internally to compute dollar-loss figures, data substantiating a specific dollar-loss amount caused by the thefts were not made available to me. Again, this decision was prompted by the company's desire to avoid potential embarrassment.

5. Unfortunately, week-by-week theft rate data were not available prior to the study. As a result, it was impossible to compare the weekly theft rates during the study with earlier weekly theft rates. Thus, it was not possible to rule out the possibility raised by one reviewer that the results may reflect some seasonal fluctuations in theft that coincided with the manipulation period.

REFERENCES

Adams, J. S. (1965). Inequity in social exchange. In L. Berkowitz (Ed.), *Advances in experimental social psychology* (Vol. 2, pp. 267-299). San Diego, CA: Academic Press.

American Management Association. (1977, March). *Summary overview of the "state of the art" regarding information gathering techniques and level of knowledge in three areas concerning crimes against business: Draft report.* Washington, DC: National Institute of Law Enforcement and Criminal Justice, Law Enforcement Assistance Administration.

Astor, S. D. (1972). Twenty steps to preventing theft in business. *Management Review, 61*(3), 34-35.

Bies, R. J. (1986, August). *Identifying principles of interactional justice: The case of corporate recruiting.* Symposium conducted at the annual meeting of the Academy of Management, Chicago.

Bies, R. J., & Moag, J. S. (1986). Interactional justice: Communication criteria of fairness. In R. J. Lewicki, B. H. Sheppard, & M. H. Bazerman (Eds.), *Research on negotiation in organizations* (Vol. 1, pp. 43-55). Greenwich, CT: JAI.

Cicchetti, D. V. (1972). Extension of multiple-range tests to interaction tables in the analysis of variance: A rapid approximate solution. *Psychological Bulletin, 77,* 405-408.

Cook, T. D., & Campbell, D. T. (1976). The design and conduct of quasi-experiments and true experiments in field settings. In M. D. Dunnette (Ed.), *Handbook of industrial and organizational psychology* (pp. 223-326). Chicago: Rand McNally.

Cropanzano, R., & Folger, R. (1989). Referent cognitions and task decision autonomy: Beyond equity theory. *Journal of Applied Psychology, 74,* 293-299.

DeMore, S. W., Fisher, J. D., & Baron, R. M. (1988). The equity-control model as a predictor of vandalism among college students. *Journal of Applied Social Psychology, 18,* 80-91.

Finn, R. H., & Lee, S. M. (1972). Salary equity: Its determination, analysis and correlates. *Journal of Applied Psychology, 56,* 283-292.

Fisher, J. D., & Baron, R. M. (1982). An equity-based model of vandalism. *Population and Environment, 5,* 182-200.

Folger, R. (1986). Rethinking equity theory: A referent cognitions model. In H. W. Bierhoff, R. L. Cohen, & J. Greenberg (Eds.), *Justice in social relations* (pp. 145-162). New York: Plenum.

Folger, R., & Bies, R. J. (1989). Managerial responsibilities and procedural justice. *Employee Responsibilities and Rights Journal, 2,* 79-90.

Folger, R., & Martin, C. (1986). Relative deprivation and referent cognitions: Distributive and procedural justice effects. *Journal of Applied Psychology, 22,* 531-546.

Folger, R., Rosenfield, D., & Robinson, T. (1983). Relative deprivation and procedural justification. *Journal of Personality and Social Psychology, 45,* 268-273.

Freedman, S. M., & Montanari, J. R. (1980). An integrative model of managerial reward allocation. *Academy of Management Review, 5,* 381-390.

Greenberg, J. (1982). Approaching equity and avoiding inequity in groups and organizations. In J. Greenberg & R. L. Cohen (Eds.), *Equity and justice in social behavior* (pp. 389-435). San Diego, CA: Academic Press.

Greenberg, J. (1986). Determinants of perceived fairness of performance evaluations. *Journal of Applied Psychology, 71,* 340-342. [Chapter 6, this volume.]

Greenberg, J. (1987). A taxonomy of organizational justice theories. *Academy of Management Review, 12,* 9-22. [Chapter 1, this volume.]

Greenberg, J. (1989). Cognitive re-evaluation of outcomes in response to underpayment inequity. *Academy of Management Journal, 32,* 174-184. [Chapter 16, this volume.]

Hays, W. L. (1963). *Statistics.* New York: Holt, Rinehart, & Winston.

Heneman, H. G., III. (1985). Pay satisfaction. In K. M. Rowland & G. R. Ferris (Eds.), *Research in personnel and human resources management* (Vol. 3, pp. 115-139). Greenwich, CT: JAI.

Heneman, H. G., III, & Schwab, D. P. (1985). Pay satisfaction: Its multidimensional nature and measurement. *International Journal of Psychology, 20,* 129-141.

Hollinger, R. D., & Clark, J. P. (1983). *Theft by employees.* Lexington, MA: Lexington Books.

Horning, D. (1970). Blue collar theft: Conceptions of property, attitudes toward pilfering, and work group norms in a modern industrial plant. In E. O. Smigel & H. L. Ross (Eds.), *Crimes against bureaucracy* (pp. 46-64). New York: Van Nostrand Reinhold.

Kemper, T. D. (1966). Representative roles and the legitimization of deviance. *Social Problems, 13,* 288-298.

Leventhal, G. S. (1976). The distribution of rewards and resources in groups and organizations. In L. Berkowitz & E. Walster (Eds.), *Advances in experimental social psychology* (Vol. 9, pp. 91-131). San Diego, CA: Academic Press.

Lind, E. A., & Lissak, R. (1985). Apparent impropriety and procedural fairness judgments. *Journal of Experimental Social Psychology, 21,* 19-29.

Lind, E. A., & Tyler, T. (1988). *The social psychology of procedural justice.* New York: Plenum.

Mangione, T. W., & Quinn, R. P. (1975). Job satisfaction, counter-productive behavior, and drug use at work. *Journal of Applied Psychology, 11,* 114-116.

Mars, G. (1973). Chance, punters, and the fiddle: Institutionalized pilferage in a hotel dining room. In M. Warner (Ed.), *The sociology of the workplace* (pp. 200-210). New York: Halsted.

Mars, G. (1974). Dock pilferage: A case study in occupational theft. In P. Rock & M. McIntosh (Eds.), *Deviance and social control* (pp. 209-228). London: Tavistock.

Merriam, D. (1977). Employee theft. *Criminal Justice Abstracts, 9,* 380-386.

Merton, R. T. (1938). Social structure and anomie. *American Sociological Review, 3,* 672-682.

Shapiro, D. L., & Buttner, E. H. (1988, August). *Adequate explanations: What are they, and do they enhance procedural justice under severe outcome circumstances?* Paper presented at the annual meeting of the Academy of Management, Anaheim, CA.

Tyler, T. R. (1988). What is procedural justice? *Law and Society Review, 22,* 301-335.

Tyler, T. R., & Bies, R. J. (1990). Beyond formal procedures: The interpersonal context of procedural justice. In J. Carroll (Ed.), *Applied social psychology and organizational settings* (pp. 77-98). Hillsdale, NJ: Lawrence Erlbaum.

Webb, E. J., Campbell, D. T., Schwartz, R. D., Sechrest, L., & Grove, J. B. (1981). *Nonreactive measures in the social sciences* (2nd ed.). Boston: Houghton Mifflin.

Weiner, B., Amirkhan, J., Folkes, V. S., & Varette, J. A. (1987). An attributional analysis of excuse giving: Studies of a naive theory of emotion. *Journal of Personality and Social Psychology, 52,* 316-324.

Zuwaylif, F. H. (1970). *General applied statistics.* Reading, MA: Addison-Wesley.

11

Interpersonal Deterrents to Employee Theft

How do people respond to being inequitably underpaid? Most of the current knowledge regarding this question is derived from Adams's (1965) theory of inequity, which postulates that individuals who are underpaid are likely to respond by lowering their inputs (i.e., their work contributions) or by attempting to raise their outcomes (i.e., job-related rewards, such as pay). Considerable research has supported equity theory's claim that underpayment inequity leads to lowered job performance (e.g., Lord & Hohenfeld, 1979; Pritchard, Dunnette, & Jorgenson, 1972). Also in

AUTHOR'S NOTE: This chapter was originally published in *Organizational Behavior and Human Decision Processes*, Vol. 54, No. 1, pp. 81-103, under the title "Stealing in the Name of Justice: Informational and Interpersonal Moderators of Theft Reactions to Underpayment Inequity." Copyright © 1993 by Academic Press. Reprinted by permission.

support of equity theory is the finding that underpaid workers paid on a piecework basis produce more goods of lower quality—a means of raising their outcomes without also raising their inputs (for a review, see Pritchard, 1969). Such reactions effectively redress states of underpayment inequity by restoring an equitable balance between one's outcome/input ratio and that of a comparison standard (Greenberg, 1982).

THEFT AS A REACTION TO INEQUITY

Another form of reaction to underpayment inequity that has been recognized by social scientists is disruptive, deviant behavior, such as vandalism and theft (Hollinger & Clark, 1983). For example, anthropological accounts of pilferage among employees have been based on workers' expressed beliefs that theft is "a morally justified addition to wages . . . an entitlement due from exploiting employers" (Mars, 1974, p. 224). According to equity theory, acts of employee theft may be an effective means of increasing one's outcomes to reduce feelings of underpayment inequity. In fact, a recent study (Greenberg, 1990a[10]) has shown that in manufacturing plants in which a temporary 15% pay cut was introduced, the workers felt highly underpaid and employee theft rates were as much as 250% higher than occurred under normal pay conditions. Given the costly impact of employee theft on companies—from $5 billion to $10 billion annually according to estimates by the American Management Association (1977)—the need to understand the conditions affecting underpayment-induced employee theft is paramount.

Some insight into the processes underlying inequity-induced theft is suggested by research and theory demonstrating that perceptions of fair treatment and outcomes depend not only on the level of one's outcomes but also on the explanations given for those outcomes (for reviews, see Bies, 1987; Folger & Bies, 1989; Greenberg, 1990b[5]; Greenberg, Bies, & Eskew, 1991; Tyler & Bies, 1990). In general, research has found that negative outcomes perceived as unfair when they were not adequately explained were perceived as fairer when they were accompanied by thorough and informative explanations (e.g., Bies & Shapiro, 1988; Bies, Shapiro, & Cummings, 1988; Greenberg, 1991). In my study (Greenberg (1990a[10]) regarding the issue of employee theft, I found that the theft rate in a plant of underpaid workers was considerably lower when the basis for their underpayment was thoroughly and sensitively explained to them ($M = 5.7\%$) than when limited information was given in an insensitive manner ($M = 8.9\%$). (The base rate of theft was 3.7%.)

Although such findings (Greenberg, 1990a[10]) clearly illustrate the mitigating effect of explanations on costly reactions to inequity, they suffer from several limitations. For one, because the investigation was conducted in a field setting, it lacked the degree of random assignment to conditions and high degree of experimental control needed to unambiguously establish causality. Another limitation of the study that dictates the need for a follow-up laboratory study is the compound nature of the explanation variable. The explanation given for the pay cut was administered in a manner that intentionally combined two potentially distinct contributors—the quality of the information given and the interpersonal sensitivity demonstrated in the interaction. By basing my explanation manipulation on past research showing that people tend to associate these variables (Bies et al., 1988), my field findings (Greenberg, 1990a[10]) are limited by a built-in naturalistic confounding in need of disentangling in laboratory research. In other words, understanding how explanations act to reduce inequity-induced theft requires that a clear experimental distinction be made with respect to *what* is said and *how* the message is communicated.

INFORMATIONAL AND INTERPERSONAL MODERATORS OF INEQUITY REACTIONS

If one carefully examines the many variables that have been found to influence perceptions of fairness, it becomes clear that both interpersonal and informational factors are implicated—specifically, the *validity of the information* provided as the basis for decision making (i.e., information that is verifiably correct and thus worthy of use in decision making) and the *interpersonal sensitivity* shown regarding the personal affects of the decision (i.e., displays of empathy and concern for the individual). Indeed, these factors are closely related to several rules of procedural fairness identified by Leventhal (1980). To illustrate the prevalence of both informational and interpersonal elements of justice perceptions, I will consider some of the variables identified in recent literature reviews highlighting the importance of explanations on perceptions of fairness (e.g., Folger & Bies, 1989; Greenberg et al., 1991; Tyler & Bies, 1990).

A good example of the confusion within this literature may be seen in evidence showing that perceptions of fairness are enhanced when attention is paid to employees' viewpoints. In support of this idea, survey evidence by Reutter (1977) suggests that the perceived fairness of employee suggestion systems is related to the degree to which all suggestions are carefully considered and decisions about them are communicated in a tactful manner (for a review, see Folger & Greenberg, 1985). Clearly, both the nature of the information considered (careful evaluation of the suggestion) and the communicator's interpersonal concern (providing a tactful review of the suggestion) are involved in assessments of the system's fairness.

The same can be said about subsequent research on the adequacy of accounts given for decisions. In this connection, Bies and Shapiro (1987, 1988) found that when bosses provided an explanation why it was necessary to refuse employees' requests, employees felt less disapproval toward the bosses and perceived greater fairness of the decision-making process than when no explanations were given. Thus, claims of mitigating circumstances (e.g., financial constraints) may enhance the acceptance of negative outcomes (e.g., rejection of budget proposals). Further research by the same investigators (Bies et al., 1988) has revealed that explanations for rejection may enhance perceptions of fairness only when the reasoning in support of the explanation was judged to be adequate and when it was communicated sincerely (Bies et al., 1988). Thus, both the appropriateness of the information used and the interpersonal sensitivity shown are involved in perceptions of fairness.

A final example of this phenomenon may be seen in Bies's (1986) findings that honest messages were perceived as fairer than dishonest ones. Even here, both interpersonal and informational factors appear to be involved. To wit, a truthful message not only imparts more valid information but also reflects the communicator's willingness to treat recipients in a moral and ethical manner. In conclusion, the enhanced fairness found to result from explanations and other procedural variables may well be because of the interpersonal and informational elements underlying those procedures.

HYPOTHESES

As this review of the literature suggests, it appears that reactions to potentially unfair situations are mitigated in part by the validity of the information provided and in part by the interpersonal sensitivity shown. Considerations of fairness appear to involve the use of valid decision-making criteria (e.g., careful consideration of relevant facts and reliance on accurate information) as well as sensitive interpersonal treatment (e.g., tactful communication of outcomes and expressions of sincerity). The explicit role of these variables on reactions to an underpayment inequity is considered in this investigation.

Operationally, this study confronted some participants with a situation in which underpayment was manipulated by telling them that they were supposed to be paid $3 instead of the $5 they originally were promised (the underpaid group). No change in the promised pay rate was manipulated in the equitably paid, control group. Participants were then allowed to take their own pay in a situation in which it appeared that the actual amount of money they took could not be detected. Because they were encouraged to take the amount of pay they expected (and which was established as the going rate), equitably paid participants were expected to refrain from stealing—that is, taking more than the $5 promised them. Specifically, I hypothesized the following:

> *Hypothesis 1:* Equitably paid participants will not take significantly more than the amount promised them ($5).

Moreover, because the situation confronted by equitably paid participants already discouraged stealing, there was no reason to believe that the amount of money they took would be differentially influenced by either the validity of the information presented to them or the interpersonal sensitivity of their treatment. Although such procedural and interpersonal factors may mitigate reactions to unfair outcomes (Bies & Shapiro, 1987, 1988), they may have little incremental effect on reactions to already fair outcomes (Greenberg, 1987[14]). Thus, I hypothesized as follows:

> *Hypothesis 2a:* The amount of pay taken by equitably paid participants will not differ significantly as a function of information validity.
> *Hypothesis 2b:* The amount of pay taken by equitably paid participants will not differ significantly as a function of interpersonal sensitivity.

By contrast, it was expected that participants asked to take less than the initially promised amount (underpaid group) would redress the inequity by taking more than they were supposed to (i.e., they would steal additional money to reduce the inequity). Thus, I hypothesized as follows:

> *Hypothesis 3:* Participants whose pay rate is unfairly reduced (underpaid group) will take more money than the $3 they were permitted to take. (Thus, in general, underpaid participants will be expected to steal.)

Further complicating this effect is the tendency for inequities to be mitigated by the use of valid information and sensitive interpersonal treatment (Bies et al., 1988; Greenberg, 1990a[10]). Applying these variables to the present experiment, it was expected that the tendency for underpaid participants to take more than $3 would be reduced by the imparting of thorough and accurate information about the reduced pay in an interpersonally sensitive manner. Thus, I hypothesized as follows:

Hypothesis 4a: Underpaid participants will take significantly less pay (i.e., they will steal less) when they are given high valid information about how their pay rate is determined than when they are given low valid information.

Hypothesis 4b: Underpaid participants will take significantly less pay (i.e., they will steal less) when they are treated with high interpersonal sensitivity than when treated with low interpersonal sensitivity.

Because there is no evidence to suggest that information validity and interpersonal sensitivity qualify each other in any way, no significant interactions were expected between these two variables. On the basis of evidence suggesting that each factor alone influences perceptions of fairness (Bies et al., 1988), however, their effects were expected to be additive. As such, the combined effect of both variables was expected to be greater than their individual effects. Consistent with this reasoning, I hypothesized as follows:

Hypothesis 5a: Underpaid participants given high valid information about how their pay was determined who are also treated in a high interpersonally sensitive manner will take lower pay (i.e., steal less) than underpaid participants in the other conditions. (In other words, their mean theft rate will be lowest.)

Hypothesis 5b: Underpaid participants given low valid information about how their pay was determined who are also treated in a low interpersonally sensitive manner will take higher pay (i.e., steal more) than underpaid participants in the other conditions. (In other words, their mean theft rate will be highest.)

METHOD

Participants and Design

The final pool of participants in the study consisted of 102 undergraduate students at a midwestern university who volunteered to participate in a study allegedly concerned with consumers' use of sales catalogs, requiring them to look up and record the prices of items appearing in catalogs. As part of the recruitment procedure, they were promised $5 for a session described as lasting approximately 1 hour. (Pilot testing revealed that people from the same population from which the participants were drawn believed this constituted fair compensation.) There were 58 men and 44 women; their mean age was 20.5 years. Ten additional participants were scheduled to participate but did not complete the experiment either because they did not agree to participate in the study after the task was described to them ($n = 2$) or because they were unable to stay for the allotted time ($n = 8$).

A 2 × 2 × 2 complete factorial design was used in which the independent variables were *payment* (equitably paid or underpaid), *interpersonal sensitivity* (high or low), and *information validity* (high or low). Approximately equal numbers of participants (ranging from 11 to 14) were assigned to each cell of the design. The unequal cell counts resulted from the 10 dropouts noted above. In no case was a participant's responses excluded from the study after any data were collected.

Procedure

Participants were scheduled individually to appear at a room on a university campus. On arrival, they were told that they would be participating in a study designed to measure how quickly and accurately people could find items in a department store catalog. The task described to participants required them to go through a list of items appearing on a printed sheet, find their prices in a department store catalog, and record those prices in blank spaces provided on the sheet. The rationale was given that the experimenter was interested in seeing how the design of catalogs affected people's ability to use them. They were reminded that they would be paid $5 at the end of the 1-hour session for performing the task and completing some questionnaire items. This task was used because of its high degree of acceptance among participants demonstrated in earlier studies and because it has been found that participants have no preconceived ideas regarding what constitutes equitable payment for this task, thereby making it a suitable platform for launching inequity manipulations (e.g., Greenberg, 1983, 1987[14]).

After the task was described and participants consented to participate, they were taken to a nearby room and seated at a desk equipped with the materials needed to perform the task: item pricing sheets, a department store catalog, and pencils. After allowing 45 minutes for participants to perform the task, the experimenter entered their workrooms and asked them to stop working. At this point, the various experimental manipulations were carried out.

Payment. The payment manipulation was affected by telling the participants either that they would be paid the $5 promised for participating (equitable payment) or that they would be paid a lower amount, $3 (underpayment). Because additional information about the payment manipulation was incorporated into the other manipulations, further description of the manner in which this factor was manipulated follows below.

Informational validity. The informational validity variable manipulated the amount and quality of information used as the basis for determining payment. Specifically, the high valid information conditions were consistently characterized by (a) the use of directly acquired information (b) from an expert source (c) that is publicly revealed and (d) double-checked with an independent source. By contrast, the low valid manipulations relied on (a) the use of hearsay information (b) from a person of undisclosed expertise (c) that is kept private and (d) not independently verified. These elements of the informational validity variable follow from research in the field of attitude change in which similar factors have been found to contribute to the acceptance of messages as valid sources of information contributing to the changing of attitudes (McGuire, 1985).[1] Moreover, pilot research has independently verified that each of these elements contributes to assessments of informational validity.[2]

To enhance realism, statements regarding the payment and information about its determination were incorporated with each other.[3] Thus, *underpaid-high valid information* participants were instructed that they would be paid less than the promised amount and were given a considerable amount of information in support of that decision. Specifically, they were told,

> While you were working, I found out from my supervisor that our research sponsor is really only paying $3 instead of the $5 you were promised. As you can see from this document [experimenter shows participant fake budget figures], this is the amount that was planned in the original budget proposal. To make sure, I also called the project's budget officer and was reassured of this figure. Because of a typographical error, some participants did get $5, but this was a mistake. Starting now, you can get only $3.

In the *equitable-high valid information* condition, participants were instructed that they would be paid exactly the stated amount and were given a considerable amount of information in support of that decision. Specifically, they were told,

> While you were working, I verified with my supervisor that our research sponsor is paying the $5 you were promised. As you can see from this document [experimenter shows participant fake budget figures], this is the amount that was planned in the original budget proposal. To make sure, I also called the project's budget officer and was reassured of this figure. Everyone who participates is getting paid $5.

In the low valid information conditions, participants received much less assurance regarding the appropriateness of the stated pay rates.

Specifically, in the *underpayment-low valid information* condition, participants were told,

> While you were working, I heard from someone in the hall that our research sponsor is really only supposed to be paying $3, instead of the $5 you were promised. As a result, that's what I'll be paying you.

In the *equitable-low valid information* condition, participants were told, "As I told you, our research sponsor is paying $5 for this study, so that's what I'll be paying you."

Interpersonal sensitivity. Following the administration of the payment information, additional comments were made that helped create the interpersonal sensitivity manipulation (abbreviated as sensitivity). These remarks varied in the degree of caring and sensitivity shown the participants with respect to their pay rate. Specifically, the high sensitivity conditions were characterized by (a) repeated expressions of remorse (or satisfaction) and (b) attempts to dissociate from (or associate with) the outcome. Low sensitivity conditions were characterized by (a) expressions of disinterest with the participants' outcomes and (b) claims of greater concern with one's own personal outcomes. Such operational guidelines are in keeping with suggestions from the literature describing interpersonally sensitive behavior in social contexts (Hornstein, 1976). They are also justified by the results of pilot tests (analogous to those described for the informational validity variable in note 2) showing that participants perceive these dimensions to be differentially suggestive of interpersonal sensitivity.

As in the case of the information validity variable, these remarks were tailored slightly to the payment condition.

In the *high sensitivity-underpayment* condition, the experimenter expressed considerable regret about the underpayment. Specifically, he said,

> You really got a bad deal and I feel very sorry for you. I know it's only a $2 difference, but I feel awful for misleading you. Please recognize that it's not my fault, and that I would pay you more if I could. You seem like such a nice person, I really hate to have to do this to you. I don't want to upset you. It's probably not much consolation, but I feel very badly about this myself.

In the *high sensitivity-equitable payment* condition, the experimenter expressed considerable satisfaction about the participant's fair payment. Specifically, he said:

You really got a fair deal, and I feel good for you. I'm glad you were able to get paid $5 for this job; you deserve it. You seem like such a nice person. I'm really glad that this all worked out all right for you.

By contrast to the highly sensitive treatment accorded participants in these conditions, much less sensitivity was shown in the low interpersonal sensitivity conditions. Specifically, in both the *low sensitivity-underpayment* condition and the *low sensitivity-equitable payment* condition, participants were told,

That's the way it is; I don't make the rules around here. I really don't care how much you get paid. I don't care too much about how much others get; I'm more concerned about how much I get paid myself.

Payment procedure/theft measure. After the final interpersonal sensitivity remarks were made, the experimenter announced that he would have to go down the hall to begin another experimental session. At this point, he reached into his hip pocket and removed a handful of money, some $1 bills, as well as some quarters, nickels, dimes, and pennies, and placed it on a nearby desk. The experimenter's seemingly disorganized state helped create the impression that he was unaware of the exact amount of money he put on the table. Reinforcing this image, he said,

I have to go down the hall now to begin another session, so [reaching into his pocket] I'll just have to leave you some money to pay yourself with. I don't know how much is here, but it looks like there's more than enough for you. Just take the $5 ($3) you are supposed to be paid and leave the rest on the table.

This procedure made it possible for participants to take as much money as they wanted without believing that the experimenter would be able to tell how much was actually taken. In actuality, a total of $10.42 was available: 7 $1 bills, 6 quarters, 11 dimes, 12 nickels, and 22 pennies, making it possible for the experimenter to determine exactly how much participants took.

As he was leaving, the experimenter handed the participants a questionnaire in a large manila envelope and asked them to complete it and return it to the envelope before putting it into a large stack of other envelopes on a table in the corner of the room. This procedure was used to lead participants to believe that their responses could not be identified (although, of course, they could, because of coding marks surreptitiously placed on the envelope). It was necessary to promote the belief of anonymity to minimize the threat of a social desirability bias that could have been activated had participants believed that the experimenter could identify their responses. I have used a similar procedure successfully in earlier research (e.g., Greenberg, 1983, 1987[14]).

Questionnaire measures. In support of the cover story, participants were asked to complete several questionnaire items focusing on their reactions to the task at hand. Among these were 16 items that were relevant to the present study. These tapped justice perceptions (9 items), manipulation checks (4 items), and supplementary measures (3 items). Unless otherwise noted, the questions were completed using a scale ranging from 1 (*not at all*) to 7 (*extremely*).

The nine *justice perception* items were written in a manner that made them both sensitive to the concerns of this study and consistent with various conceptual perspectives regarding the forms of justice assessed— distributive (Deutsch, 1985; Leventhal, 1976), procedural (Greenberg, 1986b; Lind & Tyler, 1988), and interactional (Bies & Moag, 1986). Thus, although the measures were ad hoc, they were carefully connected to established conceptual bases (see Greenberg, 1990c[2]).

Three items measured perceptions of *distributive justice:* (a) "How fair is the amount of pay you were given to perform this task?" (b) "To what extent was the amount of the payment you received appropriate for the task performed?" and (c) "To what extent was your pay in keeping with prevailing pay standards?" Coefficient α was .93.

Three items measured perceptions of *procedural justice:* (a) "How fair was the method used to determine your pay?" (b) "To what extent were proper rules and procedures used to determine your pay?" and (c) "How consistent and unbiased was the method used for establishing your pay?" Coefficient α was .84.

Three items measured perceptions of *interactional justice:* (a) "To what extent was the experimenter concerned about your fair treatment during the study?" (b) "How fair was the experimenter in considering your needs and well-being?" and (c) "To what degree did the experimenter give fair consideration to your personal feelings?" Coefficient α was .88.

Four items were included as *manipulation checks.* To assess the validity of the payment manipulation, participants were asked, "How much money did the experimenter say you should be paid for this study?" A scale ranging from $1 to $7 in $1 increments was used to record the responses. A follow-up question asked, "Is this: _____ less than, _____ equal to, or _____ more than (check one) the amount you expected when you first showed up?" To assess the validity of the information validity manipulation, participants were asked, "How much information were you given about the rate of pay you were supposed to receive?"[4] Last, to assess the validity of the interpersonal sensitivity manipulation participants were asked, "How much personal concern did the experimenter show for you?"

Three *supplementary measures* were included to gain insight into participants' feelings about their self-payment behavior. The first question asked, "To what extent do you believe you were acting honestly or dishonestly in taking the pay you did?" The response scale ranged from 1 (*very dishonestly*) to 7 (*very honestly*) with the midpoint labeled *neither honestly nor dishonestly*.

A second question asked, "How justified or unjustified were you in taking the amount of pay that you did?" The response scale ranged from 1 (*completely unjustified*) to 7 (*completely justified*). A third question asked, "How fair or unfair was it for you to take the amount of pay you took?" The response scale ranged from 1 (*completely unfair*) to 7 (*completely fair*). Because the responses to these two questions were highly correlated ($r = .91$), they were combined to form a single *perceived justification* measure.

Debriefing. On leaving their workrooms, the participants were intercepted by the experimenter, who then dehoaxed and debriefed them about the true purpose of the experiment. The discussion continued until such time as the participants appeared to fully understand and accept the nature of the study and the need to use deception (Greenberg & Folger, 1988). During the debriefing, no participants expressed any suspicions about the true purpose of the study. The pay of all participants who took less than the $5 promised was supplemented so that their actual final pay totaled $5. Effectively, then, no participants were really underpaid.

RESULTS

Manipulation Checks

All manipulation check questionnaires (except the checklist item) were based on $2 \times 2 \times 2$ factorial univariate analyses of variance (ANOVAs). For the payment manipulation check, the only significant source of variance was a significant payment effect, $F(1, 94) = 126.88$, $p < .0001$, revealing that underpaid participants reported that they were supposed to be paid less than the equitably paid participants ($Ms = 3.06$ vs. 5.00, respectively). Moreover, these means did not differ significantly from the $3 and $5 manipulated values, in both cases, $t < 1.00$, *ns*. The follow-up question revealed that (a) all participants in the underpaid group acknowledged that the amount they were told to take was less than they

TABLE 11.1 Summary of Analysis of Variance for Amount of Pay Taken

Source	df	MS	F	p	ω^2
Payment (A)	1	33.35	114.68	.0001	.39
Interpersonal sensitivity (B)	1	2.51	8.14	.0053	.10
Informational validity (C)	1	1.64	5.33	.0232	.08
A × B	1	2.63	8.52	.0044	.11
A × C	1	1.43	4.64	.0338	.04
B × C	1	0.06	0.18	.6688	.00
A × B × C	1	0.13	0.44	.5105	.00
Residual	94	0.31			

expected and (b) all participants in the equitably paid group acknowledged that the amount they were told to take was equal to what they expected. Together, these data reveal that the payment manipulation was unequivocally successful in differentiating payment conditions as desired.

For the informational validity item, the only significant source of variance was the significant main effect of the informational validity manipulation, $F(1, 94) = 96.80$, $p < .0001$. This effect reflected the tendency for more information to be perceived as given in the high information condition than in the low information condition ($Ms = 5.41$ vs. 3.02, respectively). Thus, the informational validity manipulation was successful in creating conditions in which different amounts of information were recognized as imparted.

For the sensitivity item, the only significant source of variance was the significant main effect of the sensitivity manipulation, $F(1, 94) = 186.46$, $p < .0001$. This effect reflected the tendency for greater sensitivity to be recognized as given in the high sensitivity condition than in the low sensitivity condition ($Ms = 5.70$ vs. 2.66, respectively). Thus, the sensitivity manipulation was successful in creating conditions in which different amounts of sensitivity were recognized as used in communicating with participants.

Tests of Hypotheses

Because the hypotheses were based on the amount of money taken as a function of payment, validity, and sensitivity, a 2 × 2 × 2 factorial ANOVA was performed on these data. A summary of this analysis appears in Table 11.1, and a summary of all the various cell means appears in Figure 11.1.

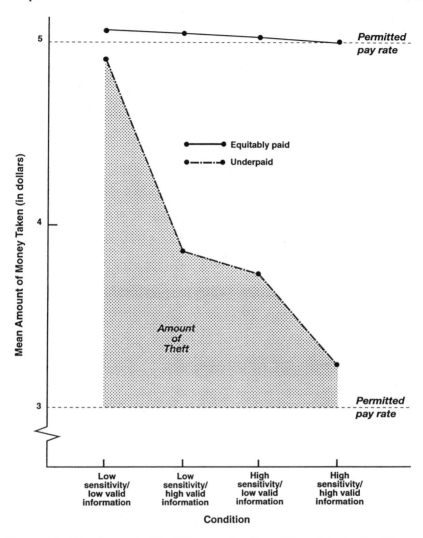

Figure 11.1. Mean Amount of Pay Taken as a Function of Experimental Conditions

Hypothesis 1. Hypothesis 1 claimed that equitably paid workers would not take more than the $5 promised them. Inspection of the means constituting the almost flat line for the equitable condition at the $5 level across the top of Figure 11.1 visually confirms the hypothesis. More formally, a simple effects test revealed that the four means were not significantly different from each other, $F < 1.00$, *ns,* nor were any of them

TABLE 11.2 Mean Amount of Pay Taken as a Function of Payment and
Informational Validity

Payment	Low Valid Information	High Valid Information	Comparison (two-tailed)
Equitable payment	$M = 5.02$ $SD = 0.07$ $n = 23$	$M = 5.00$ $SD = 0.17$ $n = 27$	$t(48) = 0.62$, ns
Underpayment	$M = 4.07$ $SD = 0.89$ $n = 28$	$M = 3.58$ $SD = 0.74$ $n = 24$	$t(50) = 2.19$, $p < .05$

TABLE 11.3 Mean Amount of Pay Taken as a Function of Payment and Interpersonal Sensitivity

Payment	Low Interpersonal Sensitivity	High Interpersonal Sensitivity	Comparison (two-tailed)
Equitable payment	$M = 5.00$ $SD = 0.17$ $n = 25$	$M = 5.00$ $SD = 0.10$ $n = 25$	$t(48) = 0.10$, ns
Underpayment	$M = 4.17$ $SD = 0.85$ $n = 26$	$M = 3.52$ $SD = 0.73$ $n = 26$	$t(50) = 2.99$, $p < .01$

significantly different than \$5, t values < 1.00. Thus, Hypothesis 1 was supported.

Hypothesis 2. Hypothesis 2a claimed that informational validity would not influence the amount of money taken by equitably paid participants. A subset of the means in the Significant Payment × Informational Validity interaction (identified in Table 11.1) bears on this interaction. These means are shown in Table 11.2. As I hypothesized, Table 11.2 shows that equitably paid participants took relatively equal amounts of payment regardless of whether they received high valid information or low valid information.

Hypothesis 2b claimed that sensitivity would not influence the amount of money taken by equitably paid participants. A subset of the means in the Significant Payment × Sensitivity interaction (identified in Table 11.1) bears on this interaction. These means are shown in Table 11.3. As I hypothesized, Table 11.3 shows that equitably paid participants took relatively equal amounts of payment regardless of whether they were treated with high or low interpersonal sensitivity.

Hypothesis 3. Hypothesis 3 claimed that underpaid participants would take significantly more than the $3 they were asked to pay themselves. The overall amount of pay taken by underpaid workers was $3.84, an amount significantly higher than $3, $t(51) = 7.49$, $p < .001$, thus confirming Hypothesis 3. Cell-by-cell comparisons of the means in the underpaid condition (see lower line on Figure 11.1) to $3 revealed that significantly higher pay was taken by participants in the low sensitivity-low information condition, $t(13) = 6.78$, $p < .005$, the low sensitivity-high information condition, $t(11) = 3.55$, $p < .005$, and the high sensitivity-low information condition, $t(13) = 3.14$, $p < .005$, but not in the high sensitivity-high information condition, $t(11) = 1.41$, *ns*. Thus, only when sensitivity and information were both high did participants refrain from stealing.

Hypothesis 4. Hypothesis 4a claimed that the use of high valid information would reduce the amount of money taken by underpaid participants. A subset of the means in the Significant Payment × Informational Validity interaction (identified in Table 11.1) bears on this interaction. These means are shown in Table 11.2. As I hypothesized, Table 11.2 shows that underpaid participants took significantly less pay when they were given high valid information than when they were given low valid information.

Hypothesis 4b claimed that sensitivity would reduce the amount of money taken by underpaid participants. A subset of the means in the Significant Payment × Sensitivity interaction (identified in Table 11.1) bears on this interaction. These means are shown in Table 11.3. As hypothesized, Table 11.3 shows that underpaid participants took significantly less pay when they were treated with high sensitivity than when they were treated with low sensitivity.

Hypothesis 5. As Table 11.1 reveals, the interaction between informational validity and interpersonal sensitivity was not significant. The individual effects of these variables were significant, however. A simple effects test determined that the underpaid participants differed in their theft rate across all levels of information and sensitivity, $F(3, 94) = 64.20$, $p < .0001$. The line shown at the bottom of Figure 11.1 shows the means associated with this simple main effect, revealing that for underpaid participants, the effects of sensitivity and validity were additive. Each contributed some to the overall tendency to reduce theft. When both were high, theft was least; when both were low, theft was greatest. Specifically, for underpaid participants, the overall pattern of significant differences in theft rates (using Newman-Keuls tests with $\alpha = .05$) was as follows: low sensitivity, low validity > low sensitivity, high validity = high sensitivity, low validity > high sensitivity, high validity.

Consistent with Hypothesis 5a was the finding that the lowest amount of theft occurred when both informational validity and interpersonal sensitivity were high. Newman-Keuls tests revealed that the mean in this condition ($M = 3.32$) was significantly lower than the mean for any of the other three conditions. Moreover, as noted in conjunction with Hypothesis 3, the mean pay taken in this condition was not significantly higher than the required pay rate of $3 (the only condition in which this occurred).

Consistent with Hypothesis 5b was the finding that the highest amount of theft occurred when both informational validity and interpersonal sensitivity were low. Newman-Keuls tests revealed that the mean in this condition ($M = 4.45$) was significantly higher than the mean of any of the other three conditions.

Justice Perception Measures

Responses to all justice perception items were analyzed using $2 \times 2 \times 2$ factorial univariate ANOVAs. These analyses were justified in view of the high degree of statistical independence between the measures (mean $r = .04$). For each of the three measures, the only significant source of variance found was for the variable most closely associated with that measure.

Specifically, for the distributive justice measure, a significant main effect was found for payment, $F(1, 94) = 485.59$, $p < .0001$, reflecting the greater perceived fairness of pay provided in the equitable condition than in the underpaid condition ($Ms = 5.91$ vs. 2.22, respectively). For the procedural justice measure, a significant main effect was found for informational validity, $F(1, 94) = 444.17$, $p < .0001$, such that procedures were recognized as procedurally fairer when high valid information about pay determination was provided than when low valid information was provided ($Ms = 5.53$ vs. 2.64, respectively). Finally, for the interactional justice variable, a main effect was found for sensitivity, $F(1, 94) = 254.85$, $p < .0001$, reflecting the tendency for participants to recognize the greater degree of interactional justice shown by an individual demonstrating high degrees of interpersonal sensitivity than by one demonstrating low degrees of interpersonal sensitivity ($Ms = 5.46$ vs. 2.71, respectively).

Supplementary Questionnaire Measures

The questionnaire tapping participants' self-perceived honesty-dishonesty of their pay-taking behavior revealed a significant main effect for the payment variable, $F(1, 94) = 6.92$, $p < .01$. Participants reported being more honest ($M = 5.11$) in the equitably paid condition than in the overpaid condition ($M = 3.31$). Because these means were on opposite sides of the scale midpoint, it appears that participants distinguished between the honesty and the dishonesty of their actions (as opposed to simply a difference between degrees of either pole alone).

No significant sources of variance were found for the perceived justification measure. This was the result of the tendency for participants to report that their pay-taking behavior was uniformly fair and justified (overall $M = 6.01$).

DISCUSSION

These findings support equity theory's (Adams, 1965) claim that people who are inequitably underrewarded will respond by increasing their outcomes. In the present study, they did so by taking rewards in excess of the amount they were permitted—that is, by stealing. Such deviant behavior is consistent with Kemper's (1966) notion of reciprocal deviance, according to which theft may result when employees believe that their employers defaulted on their role obligations to them, thereby encouraging further deviant acts. That is precisely what appears to have happened in this study. Not surprisingly, underpaid participants perceived their stealing as honest but also completely fair and justifiable. Indeed, earlier research has also found that unfairly paid workers believe that acts of stealing are morally justified as sources of outcome to which they are entitled (Mars, 1973, 1974). Although earlier field studies of employee theft behavior (e.g., Greenberg, 1990a[10]; Hollinger & Clark, 1983) provide aggregate data suggesting that theft is associated with feelings of underpayment, the present laboratory findings clearly demonstrate that stealing is a direct causal effect of the use of an underpayment procedure.

The incidence of theft behavior was reduced independently by each of two variables: the validity of the information provided about the underpayment and the interpersonal sensitivity shown the underpaid victim. Previous research has shown that these factors make people more willing to accept undesirable outcomes and the individuals responsible for them (Bies & Shapiro, 1987, 1988; Bies et al., 1988). The present findings extend this research by demonstrating that valid information and high sensitivity also moderate reactions to unfair outcomes. Thus, each of these factors lessened the degree to which redressing inequity was attempted. High levels of both factors led to no significant attempts to redress underpayment inequity, whereas low levels of both factors led to extreme attempts to redress the inequity. As such, it may be said that informational validity and interpersonal sensitivity work individually and together to facilitate acceptance of inequities, thereby moderating efforts at redressing them.

Implications

Several aspects of these findings are noteworthy. First, by disentangling the informational and interpersonal contributions of explanations that are frequently intercorrelated in naturalistic settings (Bies et al., 1988), it is now possible to understand more precisely what makes explanations so effective as mechanisms facilitating the acceptance of fairness judgments (Bies, 1987; Greenberg, 1990b[5]). Such information can raise questions about existing research. For example, in several studies, Tyler (1984, 1988, 1990) has found that people are more likely to accept authority figures' judgments as fair when they believe those authorities considered their own viewpoints. Why? Both informational validity and interpersonal sensitivity may be involved. Hearing another's viewpoint may improve the validity of the information used, and/or it may demonstrate concern for that individual's feelings. Thus, it is unclear to what degree each underlying variable is responsible for the demonstrated effects. By revealing the separate and combined effects of these elements, the present study paves the road for future researchers to more precisely examine this issue.

Beyond the obvious scientific benefits of explaining why an effect occurs, these findings may also have practical significance. Specifically, learning what factors encourage acceptance of undesirable outcomes may be useful for designing techniques for facilitating judgment acceptance (e.g., impression management techniques; Greenberg, 1990b[5]). In fact, simply knowing that explaining underpayment situations in a highly informative and interpersonally sensitive manner may reduce employee theft is itself a valuable piece of information that can be used for combating this extremely disruptive form of inequity reduction.

Another aspect of the findings is that the different degrees of inequity redress shown were not linked to concomitant beliefs in distributive fairness. Indeed, equity theory claims that the differential effects at reducing an underpayment would be associated with differential perceptions about the strength of the inequity (Greenberg, 1984). Greater perceived inequities would be associated with greater attempts to redress them. In the present study, this occurred only at the extremes—that is, distributive justice was seen as violated in the underpayment condition (in which the stealing occurred) but not in the equitable payment condition (in which no stealing occurred). It was *not* found, however, that perceptions of distributive justice were associated with the differential attempts to redress inequities caused by the information and sensitivity variables. Redress behavior continued although no less distributive justice was perceived. Instead, when a lack of information raised redress efforts, procedural justice was perceived as violated, and when low interpersonal sensitivity raised redress efforts, interactional justice was perceived as violated. As such, it appears that differential willingness to redress underpayment is motivated by perceptions of procedural justice and interactional justice, as well as by distributive justice (as traditionally established).

An important implication of these findings is that it extends equity theory's (Adams, 1965) claims regarding the mediational effects of inequity perceptions on inequity redress behavior (see Greenberg, 1984). Apparently, attempts to redress inequity may be motivated by the belief not only that the outcomes are distributively unfair but also that the procedures used and the interpersonal treatment received were unfair. Such a theoretical extension is an intriguing possibility in need of investigation in future research. For now, however, showing that people discriminate between informational and interpersonal aspects of justice perceptions argues against the recent trend toward incorporating the two together as different aspects of procedural justice (Folger & Bies, 1989; Tyler & Bies, 1990). At least until the interpersonal aspects of justice are better understood, attempts to fold interactional justice into procedural justice may be seen as a premature move toward parsimony (Greenberg, 1990c[2]).

Limitations and Qualifications

Various aspects of the present laboratory study may have encouraged theft behavior. Specifically, it may be claimed that participants in this study were provided ample opportunities to steal (excess money was left in front of them) and that the experimenter implicitly condoned stealing by providing this opportunity. It is in fact true that opportunities for theft to occur were necessary for the experiment to be conducted and that sanctions against stealing were not implemented. Both factors have been shown to influence employee theft (Astor, 1972; Horning, 1970). Moreover, the circumstances encouraging theft as a behavioral act were strong. Specifically, participants had only a limited, transient relationship with their victims, the effects of the theft were assumed to be focused on an impersonal source, and participants did not expect to be subject to retaliation. Given that such factors have been shown to encourage inequitable acts under certain conditions (Greenberg, 1978, 1986a[6]), it is easy to appreciate how the present study facilitated the possibility of theft as a reaction to underpayment inequity.

Although this study may have paved the way for theft reactions to occur, this is a limitation only insofar as one is interested in comparing different possible reactions to inequity. It is important to keep in mind, however, that one common purpose of a laboratory study (including this one) is to see what people *would do* in certain circumstances (Greenberg & Folger, 1988). Previous field research has already established that people *actually do* steal in response to feelings of underpayment (Greenberg, 1990a[10]; Hollinger & Clark, 1983). The value of the present study comes not from attempts to generalize what might happen in the field but from understanding what processes might be operating in that context. It is precisely because the field is an impossible place to gain control of the many variables that make theft more or less likely to occur that the need to isolate variables of interest in the laboratory is warranted. Indeed, it was the need to isolate variables of interest that often covary in naturalistic settings that stimulated the study.

This justification for the use of the laboratory is not to imply that this study is without limitations. The most important limitation is based on the idea that the relative strength of the interpersonal sensitivity and informational validity variables was a function of the script used to manipulate levels of these variables. Although the experimental scripts used gave both factors prominence in this study (demonstrating that they *can* be involved), it would be misleading to conclude that informational validity and interpersonal sensitivity are always relatively equal determinants of reactions to unfairness. In fact, an interesting possibility is that in certain contexts, only one factor or the other may be involved, or both factors may be involved interactively. For example, if an individual's interpersonal sensitivity can be attributed to strong normative pressures ("he had to behave that way"), people may be unwilling to use that factor as an element in judging the fairness of that person's behavior (Jones & Davis, 1965). Thus, although the present study demonstrates that interpersonal sensitivity and information integrity may moderate reactions to inequity, it should not be implied that these factors always operate as demonstrated here.

Although the present research represents an advance over previous studies in which informational and interpersonal variables have been confounded (e.g., Bies & Shapiro, 1987; Greenberg, 1990a[10]), it underscores the need for further refinement of these variables. As noted earlier, the manipulations of interpersonal sensitivity and informational validity were, of necessity, complex and composed of many different elements. As a result, it is not possible to identify the relative contributions of the individual elements from which the manipulations were composed. For this reason, readers should exercise caution in generalizing beyond the present results. Moreover, follow-up research should be directed at refining these variables if their unique effects are to be ultimately identified. This caution is raised in recognition of the possibility that identifying a complex set of variables with a single condition name might fail to reflect the unique effect of its component parts. Given the possibility that specific elements of the manipulations used may be differentially involved in producing the present results, future research is needed to more precisely pinpoint the most potent elements of the informational and interpersonal variables studied.

In addition, this study was designed so that participants would express their feelings of underpayment by stealing. As equity theory (Adams, 1965) notes, however, it is also possible for underpaid workers to react in other ways, such as by cognitively reevaluating their outcomes (Greenberg, 1989[16]) or by lowering their work contributions (Pritchard, et al., 1972)—options that were not viable in the present context. Moral and ethical constraints against stealing may make it a relatively less preferable form of expression (Shull, Delbecq, & Cummings, 1970)—but apparently, a relatively common reaction to inequity in certain circumstances (Greenberg, 1990a[10]). As such, it appears to be worthwhile for future researchers to consider the conditions under which responses to underpayment inequity may take the form of theft as opposed to other, more socially acceptable options. Indeed, the more general questions of when various reactions to inequity will occur and how they are interrelated remain one of the most serious limitations of equity theory (Greenberg, 1989[16], 1990c[2]).

NOTES

1. Although the term *informational validity* is used as the name of the variable that appears to capture the essence of the complex manipulation used, it is prudent to caution that the phrase fails to reflect all possible shadings of interpretation suggested by the verbal phrases used as the basis of the operationalization. For example, as one reviewer has noted, it is possible that the manipulation may have caused differences in the perceived characteristics of the person presenting the information as well as differences in the quality of the information itself. Such possibilities, however, are an inevitable consequence of *any* complex manipulations based on differing verbal content. The major implication of this point is that care should be exercised in interpreting the manipulation solely on the basis of the label used to define it.

2. A pilot study was conducted requiring participants (drawn from the same population as the main study) to judge the perceived validity of information gained through the use of (a) directly acquired versus hearsay information, (b) statements by experts versus statements by persons of undisclosed expertise, (c) data that are willingly shared versus data that are not shared, and (d) data that are double-checked with an independent source versus data that are not double-checked with an independent source. It was found that the perceived level of informational validity was significantly higher for the first element of each pair, thereby empirically justifying the use of each of these subcriteria as the basis for deriving the manipulation.

3. Although manipulations of the information communicated and the interpersonal sensitivity used to communicate it were made independently, one reviewer has noted the possibility that participants might draw inferences about the communicator's sensitivity on the basis of the information itself. As such, readers are cautioned that there may be an inherent potential confounding between the variables at the phenomenological level. It also should be noted that differences in the phrasing of manipulations were required to incorporate both manipulations together in a logical way. For this reason, it is prudent to advise that some combinations of conditions are potentially confounded by the inclusion of slightly different types of information. The risk of doing so, however, was judged to be less serious than combining potentially "purer" combinations of manipulations that appeared unnatural. Indeed, the results of manipulation check data (disclosed later) provide no support for the possibility that the manipulations had any effects other than those intended.

4. Because low valid information may be readily discounted, it follows that differences in the sheer amount of information received would be perceived if the informational validity variable were successful. In hindsight, however, a more direct measure tapping the overall perceived validity of the information (or its subcomponents: see note 1) would have been more appropriate.

REFERENCES

Adams, J. S. (1965). Inequity in social exchange. In L. Berkowitz (Ed.), *Advances in experimental social psychology* (Vol. 2, pp. 267-299). New York: Academic Press.

American Management Association. (1977, March). *Summary overview of the "state of the art" regarding information gathering techniques and level of knowledge in three areas concerning crimes against business: Draft report.* Washington, DC: National Institute of Law Enforcement and Criminal Justice, Law Enforcement Assistance Administration.

Astor, S. D. (1972). Who's doing the stealing? *Management Review, 61,* 34-35.

Bies, R. J. (1986, August). *Identifying principles of interactional justice: The case of corporate recruiting.* Paper presented at the meeting of the Academy of Management, Chicago.

Bies, R. J. (1987). The predicament of injustice: The management of moral outrage. In L. L. Cummings & B. M. Staw (Eds.), *Research in organizational behavior* (Vol. 9, pp. 289-319). Greenwich, CT: JAI.

Bies, R. J., & Moag, J. S. (1986). Interactional justice: Communication criteria of fairness. In R. J. Lewicki, B. H. Sheppard, & M. H. Bazerman (Eds.), *Research on negotiation in organizations* (Vol. 1, pp. 43-55). Greenwich, CT: JAI.

Bies, R. J., & Shapiro, D. L. (1987). Interactional fairness judgments: The influence of causal accounts. *Social Justice Research, 1,* 199-218.

Bies, R. J., & Shapiro, D. L. (1988). Voice and justification: The influence on procedural fairness judgments. *Academy of Management Journal, 31,* 676-685.

Bies, R. J., Shapiro, D. L., & Cummings, L. L. (1988). Causal accounts and managing organizational conflict: Is it enough to say it's not my fault? *Communication Research, 15,* 381-399.

Deutsch, M. (1985). *Distributive justice.* New Haven, CT: Yale University Press.

Folger, R., & Bies, R. J. (1989). Managerial responsibilities and procedural justice. *Employee Responsibilities and Rights Journal, 2,* 79-90.

Folger, R., & Greenberg, J. (1985). Procedural justice: An interpretive analysis of personnel systems. In K. M. Rowland & G. R. Ferris (Eds.), *Research in personnel and human resources management* (Vol. 3, pp. 141-183). Greenwich, CT: JAI.

Greenberg, J. (1978). Effects of reward value and retaliative power on allocation decisions: Justice, generosity, or greed? *Journal of Personality and Social Psychology, 36,* 367-379.

Greenberg, J. (1982). Approaching equity and avoiding inequity in groups and organizations. In J. Greenberg & R. L. Cohen (Eds.), *Equity and justice in social behavior* (pp. 389-435). New York: Academic Press.

Greenberg, J. (1984). On the apocryphal nature of inequity distress. In R. Folger (Ed.), *The sense of injustice* (pp. 167-188). New York: Plenum.

Greenberg, J. (1986a). Determinants of perceived fairness of performance evaluations. *Journal of Applied Psychology, 71,* 340-342. [Chapter 6, this volume.]

Greenberg, J. (1986b). Differential intolerance for inequity from organizational and individual agents. *Journal of Applied Social Psychology, 16,* 191-196.

Greenberg, J. (1987). Reactions to procedural injustice in payment distributions: Do the means justify the ends? *Journal of Applied Psychology, 72,* 55-61. [Chapter 14, this volume.]

Greenberg, J. (1989). Cognitive re-evaluation of outcomes in response to underpayment inequity. *Academy of Management Journal, 32,* 174-184. [Chapter 16, this volume.]

Greenberg, J. (1990a). Employee theft as a reaction to underpayment inequity: The hidden costs of pay cuts. *Journal of Applied Psychology, 75,* 561-568. [Chapter 10, this volume.]

Greenberg, J. (1990b). Looking fair vs. being fair: Managing impressions of organizational justice. In B. M. Staw & L. L. Cummings (Eds.), *Research in organizational behavior* (Vol. 12, pp. 111-157). Greenwich, CT: JAI. [Chapter 5, this volume.]

Greenberg, J. (1990c). Organizational justice: Yesterday, today, and tomorrow. *Journal of Management, 16,* 401-434. [Chapter 2, this volume.]

Greenberg, J. (1991). Using social accounts to manage impressions of performance appraisal fairness. *Employee Responsibilities and Rights Journal, 4,* 51-60.

Greenberg, J., Bies, R. J., & Eskew, D. E. (1991). Establishing fairness in the eye of the beholder: Managing impressions of organizational justice. In R. Giacalone & P. Rosenfeld (Eds.), *Applied impression management: How image making affects managerial decisions* (pp. 111-132). Newbury Park, CA: Sage.

Greenberg, J., & Folger, R. (1988). *Controversial issues in social research methods.* New York: Springer-Verlag.

Hollinger, R. D., & Clark, J. P. (1983). *Theft by employees.* Lexington, MA: Lexington Books.

Horning, D. (1970). Blue collar theft: Conceptions of property, attitudes toward pilfering and work group norms in a modern industrial plant. In E. O. Smigel & H. L. Ross (Eds.), *Crimes against bureaucracy* (pp. 46-64). New York: Van Nostrand Reinhold.

Hornstein, H. A. (1976). *Cruelty & kindness.* Englewood Cliffs, NJ: Prentice Hall.

Jones, E. E., & Davis, K. E. (1965). From acts to dispositions: The attribution process in person perception. In L. Berkowitz (Ed.), *Advances in experimental social psychology* (Vol. 2, pp. 45-68). New York: Academic Press.

Kemper, T. D. (1966). Representative roles and the legitimization of deviance. *Social Problems, 13,* 288-298.

Leventhal, G. S. (1976). The distribution of rewards and resources in groups and organizations. In L. Berkowitz & E. Walster (Eds.), *Advances in experimental social psychology* (Vol. 9, pp. 91-131). New York: Academic Press.

Leventhal, G. S. (1980). What should be done with equity theory? In K. J. Gergen, M. S. Greenberg, & R. H. Willis (Eds.), *Social exchange: Advances in theory and research* (pp. 27-55). New York: Plenum.

Lind, E. A., & Tyler, T. (1988). *The social psychology of procedural justice.* New York: Plenum.

Lord, R. G., & Hohenfeld, J. A. (1979). A longitudinal field assessment of equity effects on the performance of major league baseball players. *Journal of Applied Psychology, 64,* 19-26.

Mars, G. (1973). Chance, punters, and the fiddle: Institutionalized pilferage in a hotel dining room. In M. Warner (Ed.), *The sociology of the workplace* (pp. 200-210). New York: Halsted.

Mars, G. (1974). Dock pilferage: A case study in occupational theft. In P. Rock & M. McIntosh (Eds.), *Deviance and control* (pp. 209-228). London: Tavistock.

McGuire, W. J. (1985). Attitudes and attitude change. In G. Lindzey & E. Aronson (Eds.), *Handbook of social psychology* (3rd ed., Vol. 2, pp. 233-346). New York: Random House.

Pritchard, R. A. (1969). Equity theory: A review and critique. *Organizational Behavior and Human Performance, 4,* 75-94.

Pritchard, R. D., Dunnette, M. D., & Jorgenson, D. O. (1972). Effects of perceptions of equity and inequity on worker performance and satisfaction. *Journal of Applied Psychology, 56,* 75-94.

Reutter, V. G. (1977). Suggestion systems: Utilization, evaluation, and implementation. *California Management Review, 19,* 78-89.

Shull, F. A., Delbecq, A. L., & Cummings, L. L. (1970). *Organizational decision making.* New York: McGraw-Hill.

Tyler, T. R. (1984). The role of perceived injustice in defendants' evaluation of their courtroom experience. *Law and Society Review, 18,* 51-74.

Tyler, T. R. (1988). What is procedural justice: *Law and Society Review, 22,* 301-335.

Tyler, T. R. (1990). *Why people follow the law: Procedural justice, legitimacy, and compliance.* New Haven, CT: Yale University Press.

Tyler, T. R., & Bies, R. J. (1990). Beyond formal procedures: The interpersonal context of procedural justice. In J. Carroll (Ed.), *Applied social psychology and organizational settings* (pp. 77-98). Hillsdale, NJ: Lawrence Erlbaum.

12

Promoting Acceptance of
a Work Site Smoking Ban

Voluminous evidence attests to the adverse effects of tobacco smoking on both the health of employees and the efficient functioning of the organizations in which they work (Aronow, 1978; Ockene, 1984). Linked to ailments such as cardiovascular disease, lung cancer, strokes, and emphysema, tobacco smoking costs U.S. companies approximately $95 billion per year—an estimated $2,000 to $5,000 annually per employee (Colosi, 1988). This expense comes not only from illnesses caused by the

AUTHOR'S NOTE: This chapter was originally published in the *Journal of Applied Psychology,* Vol. 79, No. 2, pp. 288-297, under the title "Using Socially Fair Treatment to Promote Acceptance of a Work Site Smoking Ban." Copyright © 1994 by the American Psychological Association. Reprinted by permission.

direct inhalation of smoke but also from secondary, or sidestream, smoke: the smoke from burning tobacco that pollutes the air (for a review, see Martin, 1990). Indeed, nonsmokers exposed to sidestream cigarette smoke on a regular basis suffer physical damage equivalent to that suffered by someone who smokes 10 cigarettes a day (Wynder & Stellman, 1977).

Because evidence of the adverse effects of sidestream cigarette smoke has become well publicized in the popular press (e.g., Manning, 1990), it is not surprising that many nonsmokers have come to favor a policy that restricts cigarette smoking on the job (Fielding, 1986; Sorensen & Pechacek, 1989). Following such public opinion, some laws—generally known as clean indoor air acts (Schein, 1987)—have been enacted that protect employees from working in environments containing cigarette smoke and hold employers responsible for providing a smoke-free workplace (for reviews, see American Lung Association, 1983; Martin, 1990). These movements have been responsible, to a great extent, for the growing trend for companies to institute some form of restrictive smoking policy (Levin-Epstein, 1986). In fact, one survey reported that as many as half of the companies responding imposed some type of restrictions on smoking (Verespej, 1988). These range from written policies requiring compliance with local laws outlawing smoking to policies prohibiting the hiring of smokers.

Despite this negative publicity and the overall decline of smoking in the general population (Gonzales & Edmonson, 1988; Pierce, Fiore, Novotny, Hatziandreu, & Davis, 1989b), acceptance of smoking bans is far from universal (Gibbs, 1988). Indeed, the potential violation of smokers' rights has made the introduction of work site smoking bans a highly controversial issue (Ludington, 1991). Specifically, it has been argued by several sources, including the American Civil Liberties Union, that smokers constitute an oppressed minority and that smoking restrictions in the workplace constitute a form of heavy-handed, Big Brother oppression ("Marietta Board OKs," 1988). Moreover, banning smoking at work runs the risk of lowering employees' morale (particularly if it segregates smokers from nonsmokers) and encouraging turnover among those who find it difficult to stop smoking (Martin, 1990). Thus, existing pressures for and against work site smoking bans make their introduction controversial, that is, they constitute a critical organizational policy change requiring workers' acceptance.

Given this, it is potentially valuable to identify ways of promoting workers' beliefs that a work site smoking ban is a fair and acceptable policy. Considerable insight into this issue has been provided by research and theory on the social determinants of justice (Bies, 1987; Greenberg, 1990a[10], 1990b[5], 1990c[2], 1993a[3], 1993b[11]; Greenberg, Bies, & Eskew, 1991; Greenberg & McCarty, 1990). Such work, focusing on the interpersonal treatment received during the process of explaining how decisions are made, represents a social complement to the more structural determinants of procedural justice traditionally studied (e.g., Leventhal, 1980). Specifically, it has been found that subordinates perceive superiors as fair when those superiors provide adequate explanations of decisions affecting them and when the superiors treat them with respect and dignity (Folger & Bies, 1989; Greenberg et al., 1991; Tyler & Bies, 1990).

In a recent review and conceptual analysis of this burgeoning literature, I distinguished between two different classes of justice that focus on socially fair treatment (Greenberg, 1993b[11]). *Informational justice* refers to the adequacy of the information used to explain how decisions are made and the thoroughness of the accounts provided. *Interpersonal justice* refers to the degree of concern and social sensitivity demonstrated about the outcomes received. (These concepts expand on the concept of interactional justice, which has neglected to distinguish between the adequacy of information imparted about procedures used and the sensitivity displayed about the outcomes received; Bies & Moag, 1986.) Several studies have demonstrated that high amounts of informational justice, interpersonal justice, or both mitigate people's reactions to negative outcomes. For example, in a field experiment, I found that rates of employee theft among underpaid workers were dramatically reduced when they were given a thorough explanation for the underpayment they faced that was presented in an interpersonally sensitive manner (i.e., by expressing sympathy and concern over forthcoming pay cuts; Greenberg, 1990a[10]). Following up these findings in a laboratory experiment (Greenberg, 1993b[11]), I independently manipulated both the interpersonal sensitivity shown to people who were underpaid and the amount of information given about reasons for the underpayment. I found that each factor alone reduced levels of theft and feelings of inequity somewhat but that together these factors combined additively to yield even greater beneficial effects. In summary, this evidence suggested that people's acceptance of negative outcomes is facilitated by using socially fair treatment, that is, by thoroughly explaining the reasons why negative outcomes occur and doing so in a manner that shows considerable interpersonal sensitivity.

The present study was an attempt to extend the generalizability of this conclusion to a context in which the negative outcome in question is a total prohibition on smoking at a work site. Following from my earlier work (Greenberg, 1990a[10], 1993b[11]), I expected that giving a thorough account of the reasons for a smoking ban and showing interpersonal sensitivity regarding the distress such a ban might cause would each independently contribute to the acceptance of the smoking ban. Specifically, I hypothesized the following:

Hypothesis 1a: A smoking ban will be better accepted when employees receive high amounts of information about the ban than when they receive low amounts of information about the ban.

Hypothesis 1b: A smoking ban will be better accepted when it is announced in a manner demonstrating a high amount of social sensitivity than when it is announced in a manner demonstrating a low amount of social sensitivity.

Moreover, on the basis of previous research (e.g., Greenberg, 1993b[11]), I did not expect these effects to qualify each other but to combine additively:

Hypothesis 1c: The lowest degree of acceptance will occur when levels of both information and social sensitivity are low, and the highest degree of acceptance will occur when levels of both information and social sensitivity are high.

It is important to note that the introduction of a work site smoking prohibition does not necessarily represent a negative outcome for everyone. Indeed, for nonsmokers, such a policy may be viewed quite positively. Because employees differ in their smoking habits, the introduction of a smoking ban provided an opportunity to study the degree to which acceptance of a ban was affected by the sacrifices it demands. In other words, because some employees smoke more than others, a smoking ban represents a differentially severe outcome. To what extent does an outcome's severity influence people's reactions to it?

Fortunately, literature exists that sheds light on this question. Notably, previous research has disclosed a general tendency for people to perceive as fairest those outcomes that most benefit themselves and as least fair those outcomes that are most costly to themselves. This so-called self-serving bias in perceptions of fairness is manifested by the general tendency for people to perceive as fairest those outcomes that best serve their interests (e.g., Greenberg, 1983, 1987a[14]). This effect has been demonstrated in many different contexts. For example, in an earlier study, I found that motorists believed that the fairest gasoline allocation plans were ones that provided the largest allotments to themselves, given their automobile's performance and their individual driving habits (Greenberg, 1981). In a conceptually similar manner, Grover (1991) found that the perceived fairness of corporate parental leave policies was positively related to the employees' own plans to bear children (hence to subsequently benefit from the plan themselves). Extending these findings, I predicted that employees' acceptance of a work site smoking ban would be perceived as beneficial or harmful to themselves:

Hypothesis 2a: Nonsmokers (i.e., those benefiting most from the ban) will perceive the ban as more acceptable than will smokers.

Hypothesis 2b: Among smokers, heavy smokers (i.e., those most adversely affected by the ban) will perceive the ban as less acceptable than will light smokers.

Research has revealed that the acceptance of negative outcomes depends not only on the severity of those outcomes and the nature of the explanation given to account for them independently but also on the combined effect of these factors. Notably, several recent studies have found that socially fair treatment statistically interacted with the severity, or negativity, of outcomes such that outcomes were perceived as most unfair and least accepted when they were highly severe and when socially fair treatment was low, whereas less consequential outcomes were less influenced by socially fair treatment. For example, Shapiro, Buttner, and Barry (1994; see Study 1) found that MBA students seeking jobs perceived employment decisions to be especially unfair when they were denied a highly desirable job in the absence of an adequate explanation for being rejected. In the case of less desired jobs, however, the absence of an explanation had significantly less effect on perceptions of fairness. An identical interaction pattern was obtained in several studies of reactions to layoffs conducted by Brockner et al. (1994). Specifically, these researchers examined levels of organizational commitment among layoff survivors as a function of interpersonal justice (defined as the use of clear explanations delivered in a "nice" manner) and the severity of the outcomes experienced (the percentage of coworkers laid off). They found that the greatest self-reported drops in job commitment occurred among people receiving highly limited explanations that were presented in an unkind manner when the outcomes were most severe. Although completely different variables were studied in both investigations, the results of Brockner et al.'s study are conceptually similar to those of Shapiro et al.'s (1994). Both found that socially fair treatment had a greater effect on acceptance of negative outcomes when the outcomes were more severe than when they were less severe.

This pattern of findings is consistent with Folger's (1986; Cropanzano & Folger, 1989) referent cognitions theory. According to that theory, people's feelings of resentment are triggered by the receipt of negative outcomes whenever they believe that they would have received more favorable outcomes had the decision makers implemented the procedure that they should have implemented. From this perspective, thorough explanations of outcomes may aid acceptance of negative outcomes insofar as they are likely to provide justifiable grounds for the undesirable outcomes. Indeed, several laboratory tests of referent cognitions theory (e.g., Cropanzano & Folger, 1989; Folger & Martin, 1986) have confirmed that the introduction of various interpersonal justice variables promotes the acceptance of negative outcomes, minimizing perceptions of unfairness and feelings of resentment (see also Bies, 1987; Brockner et al., 1994).

Extrapolating from this body of research and theory, I derived a third research hypothesis. Namely, I expected that informational justice and interpersonal justice would each interact with outcome severity. Specifically, the thoroughness of information presented and the amount of sensitivity shown were each expected to have a greater effect on promoting acceptance among those who were most adversely affected by the smoking ban (i.e., heavy smokers) than on those who were least adversely (or most positively) affected by the smoking ban (i.e., nonsmokers).

Hypothesis 3a: Nonsmokers will perceive the ban as acceptable regardless of the thoroughness of the information imparted and the interpersonal treatment received when it is explained.

Hypothesis 3b: Heavy smokers will perceive the ban as more acceptable when informational justice is high (i.e., when high amounts of information are presented) than when it is low.

Hypothesis 3c: Heavy smokers will perceive the ban as more acceptable when interpersonal justice is high (i.e., when high amounts of social sensitivity about the effects of the smoking ban are shown) than when it is low.

METHOD

Sample

Participants were 732 nonunion clerical employees (291 men and 441 women) who worked in the credit and data-processing facility of a large financial services corporation. These individuals voluntarily attended a meeting held during normal working hours in which they expected to hear important announcements as part of an ongoing corporate-training session. Their mean age was 31.44 years, and their mean tenure with this company was 3.82 years. The racial composition of the sample was 63.25% white, 29.78% black, and 5.33% Hispanic. The remaining participants either labeled themselves as "other" or did not answer the question. Most of the employees (82.24%) had no managerial responsibilities; the remaining employees held some type of supervisory position. With respect to education, 53.96% reported that they had graduated from high school (or had an equivalency degree), 20.68% had some college training (including 2-year degrees), and 19.13% had graduated from college (or had some amount of postgraduate training). The remaining participants (6.15%) did not complete the question.

Employees who currently smoked made up 28.96% of the sample, and those who did not smoke made up 71.04% of the sample. These figures are comparable with those reported in a national survey (Pierce et al., 1989b), suggesting that the incidence of smoking in the present sample is not atypical. The sample was consistent with the profile of smokers in other respects as well; for example, those who smoked had done so for a mean period of 11.53 years. The median number of cigarettes smoked per day was 23.50 ($M = 18.48$), a volume comparable with that reported in other research (e.g., Peterson et al., 1988). The sample was also representative of national trends with respect to smoking in that smoking prevalence was greater among men than women and greater among blacks than whites (Fiore et al., 1989) as well as greater among those with less formal educations (Pierce, Fiore, Novotny, Hatziandreu, & Davis, 1989a). In short, the overall smoking-behavior profile of the present sample closely matched that obtained in other samples.

Design

A $2 \times 2 \times 3$ complete factorial design was used. The variables (and their levels) were as follows: information thoroughness (low information and high information), social sensitivity (low sensitivity and high sensitivity), and outcome severity (nonsmoking, light smoking, and heavy smoking). Assignment to the information thoroughness and social sensitivity conditions was made at random after the procedures described next, with approximately one quarter of participants in each condition. Levels of the outcome severity variable were created on the basis of the participants' responses to a questionnaire addressing their smoking habits.

Procedure

The study was conducted in four adjacent rooms created by positioning floor-to-ceiling partitions in the host company's large assembly hall. Employees participating in the study were assigned at random to each of the four rooms as part of a companywide training program. Because the employees recently had met in these same rooms for other purposes, it would not have seemed peculiar to them to assemble in separate rooms for this study. On the day of the study, all employees were invited to return to the rooms in which they last met (thereby re-creating the initial random assignment), allegedly to hear some announcements and to follow up on recent training sessions.

After the participants arrived in their separate rooms, they were greeted by a high-ranking company official who told them that an announcement by the company president was about to be made. It was explained that because the president was at the corporate headquarters (located in a distant city), his message was going to be broadcast live from his office through the company's closed-circuit television system and shown on large-screen television monitors. (Because the company had used this technology in the past, participants had no reason to question this explanation.) In reality, the participants were shown a videotaped presentation in which the president announced the company's new smoking ban. Four versions of the announcement were prepared, one reflecting each combination of the information thoroughness and the social sensitivity manipulations.

In all conditions, the presentation began with a greeting from the president of the company, who expressed his regrets about not being able to be there in person. He then announced what he called "a crucial new policy" for the company. He said,

> Effective Monday, there will be a total ban on smoking of any kind on any company property. [This announcement was made the Wednesday before the ban was to begin.] This means that no cigars, pipes, or cigarettes of any kind may be smoked anywhere. The ban includes all offices, warehouses, rest rooms, and cafeterias.

Independent Variables

The thoroughness of the information presented to support this decision (informational justice) and the degree of social sensitivity shown while making the announcement (interpersonal justice) were systematically varied by having the president record on videotape four different versions of the announcement. These announcements crosscut the information thoroughness and social sensitivity variables and were prepared in consultation with the investigator. During the sessions, one of these recordings was played back in each room. The assignment of each of the four messages to each of the rooms was made randomly.

Information thoroughness. In two of the messages, the president presented a great deal of detailed information about the reason for the smoking ban (high-information condition). In the other two messages, he presented only the most cursory information about the reason for the smoking ban (low-information condition). Specifically, in the high-information condition, the president presented charts and graphs detailing the hazards of smoking. His remarks focused both on the health risks to smokers and their coworkers and on the costs to the company. The salient portion of his presentation was as follows:

> As you all know, smoking is hazardous to your health. What you may not know is that it is also very hazardous to the health of your nonsmoking coworkers and to the financial health of this entire company. Don't take my word for it, just look at the facts and figures [show chart]. Medical researchers have clearly linked smoking to such serious ailments as cardiovascular disease, lung cancer, strokes, and emphysema. In fact, tobacco smoking is the most prevalent cause of premature death among Americans. This knowledge has scared many people into breaking their smoking habits. Still, there are many who continue to smoke, including some of us here at [company name]. Sadly, smokers are not only harming themselves, but they are also endangering those who live and work around them. As you know, smokers not only inhale dangerous chemicals, but the smoke given off from their cigarettes is very dangerous too. Such secondary, or sidestream, smoke, as it is called, is a great concern. Nonsmokers exposed to sidestream smoke often suffer the same diseases as smokers themselves. In fact, regular exposure to sidestream smoke causes the same amount of physical harm as smoking a half pack of cigarettes a day! If you don't think this matters, you're wrong [show chart]. Each year as many as 5,000 nonsmokers die from lung cancer caused by exposure to sidestream smoke. Maybe you remember the comedian Andy Kaufman from the old TV shows *Taxi* and *Saturday Night Live* [show photo]. Sadly, he was one such victim. We here at [company name] think that all of this is plenty good reason for you to stop smoking. But there's more behind our smoking ban than just the health risks! There are also several important statistics about the effects of smoking on the job that cannot be ignored [show charts]. For example, did you know that compared to nonsmokers, smokers are 50% more likely to be hospitalized and also 50% more likely to take off sick days? Smokers also cause twice as many job-related accidents, and an unsafe workforce endangers us all. For example, cigarette smoking is a frequent source of fires on the job. Other kinds of accidents are also caused by smoking on the job as workers fumbling with cigarettes often divert their attention from what they're supposed to be doing. Our insurance company estimated that last year alone, we lost over $300,000 due to smoking-related accidents. We lost about the same amount from computer terminals that went down due to smoke in the air. No matter how you look at it, smoking costs us money.

By contrast, in the low-information condition, the president gave a cursory explanation of the reasons for the smoking ban. The salient portion of his presentation was as follows:

As you all know, smoking is hazardous to your health; it leads to many serious, often deadly, diseases. Not only is smoking dangerous to those who smoke but also to those exposed to smoke from others' cigarettes. In addition to the health effects, we must consider the costs of smoking to our company. Between increased insurance expenses and workplace dangers, smoking costs us all a great deal.

Social sensitivity. After the information manipulation, the president expressed either a high or a low degree of social sensitivity toward the employees affected by the ban. In the high-sensitivity condition, a great deal of concern was expressed, whereas in the low-sensitivity condition, limited concern was expressed. Specifically, the salient portion of the president's remarks in the high-sensitivity condition was as follows:

It is very important to the management here at [company name], and to me personally, for you to understand that we did not decide to implement a smoking ban without giving the matter very serious consideration. We realize that this new policy will be very hard on those of you who smoke. Smoking is an addiction, and it's very tough to stop. We are quite aware of this, and we do not want you to suffer. Sure, it will be tough, but we have your long-term interest at heart in implementing this policy. We are all affected by cigarette smoke, so we are all in this together. That's why the plan will be implemented for all employees at all levels in all departments. This prohibition will cover everyone, without exception. Although some of you may not find it too difficult to refrain from smoking on the job, others may find it very tough to go for any time at all without a cigarette. Please understand that we don't want you to suffer or to resign. To the contrary, we do want you here, healthy and productive for a long time. To show you that we mean it, and that we really care, we are prepared to help you. We have investigated some of the most effective smoking-cessation programs and have selected one to use here at [company name]. We'll tell you more about this program later in this session. But, for now, let me assure you that you can participate in the program absolutely free of charge, during your regular working hours, and, of course, at your regular full pay. As you can see, we really do care. Although I cannot be with you in person now, for which I apologize, I will be visiting [name of facility] on Friday to answer any questions you may have in person. Your acceptance of our no-smoking policy is just too important for me to not discuss it with you directly. Our goal is to keep you both happy and healthy while working here at [name of company].

By contrast, in the low-sensitivity condition, the president's remarks showed less personal concern, emphasizing instead the business-related aspect of the decision. Specifically, the salient portion of his remarks in this condition was as follows:

I realize that it's tough to stop smoking, but it's in the best interest of our business to implement the smoking ban. And, of course, business must come first. To help you continue to work effectively while adjusting to the new policy, we will be making a smoking-cessation program available to you. It will be free of charge to you and conducted during your regular working hours while you are receiving full pay. We'll be giving you more information about this program later on. For now, though, we want you to understand that our goal is to minimize disruption of the work flow while you adjust to this new policy.

Outcome severity. The severity of outcomes faced was operationally defined in self-reports of the number of cigarettes smoked. Participants reporting that they currently did not smoke were recorded as in the nonsmoking condition; the smoking ban was expected to have the least severe (most beneficial) impact on them. Those who reported smoking more than the median number of cigarettes were recorded as in the heavy-smoking condition; the smoking ban was expected to have the most adverse impact on them. Those who reported smoking less than the median number of cigarettes were recorded as in the light-smoking condition; the smoking ban was expected to have a moderate impact on them.

Dependent Variables

Immediately after the president's announcement, participants were administered a questionnaire designed to tap their reactions to the smoking ban and to assess the validity of the manipulations. The questions dealing with reactions to the ban distinguished between acceptance of the ban itself and the perceived fairness of the process used to decide on the ban. This distinction follows from conceptualizations of organizational justice (Greenberg, 1987b[1]) that differentiate between the fairness of outcome distributions (distributive justice) and the fairness of the procedures leading to those outcomes (procedural justice). Responses were made on 7-point scales anchored by *not at all* (1) and *to a great extent* (7). No identifying marks were made on the questionnaire booklets, and participants were assured of the anonymity of their responses.

Acceptance of the smoking ban. It was conceived that acceptance of the smoking ban would be reflected by three different components that roughly corresponded to the classical distinction among the cognitive, affective, and conative (behavioral intention) components of attitudes (McGuire, 1969). These were perceived fairness of the smoking ban, affective commitment toward the job, and behavioral intentions toward the job and the ban—each of which was measured with a separate subscale.

Perceptions of the fairness of the ban (a specific application of distributive, or outcome, justice; Greenberg, 1987b[1]) were assessed with four questions. These tapped the extent to which participants (a) "believe it is fair for the company to impose a smoking ban," (b) "find the smoking ban acceptable," (c) "believe the company did the right thing by imposing a smoking ban," and (d) "support the company's smoking ban." The coefficient alpha estimate of internal consistency for these items was .87. Accordingly, responses to these items were combined to form a subscale.

I created a second subscale by using Meyer and Allen's (1984) eight-item Affective Commitment Scale, an instrument whose validity has been thoroughly established (e.g., McGee & Ford, 1987). To maintain consistency with the other scales, I reworded all items, using "to what extent" as the lead-in for each. To facilitate interpretation of the responses in a uniform direction, I reverse scored negatively worded items before analyzing the data. The internal consistency estimate for this subscale was .85, a figure comparable with that obtained by Meyer and Allen (1984).

Finally, behavioral intentions were measured with four items. Two items were similar to those used to assess turnover intentions in earlier research (e.g., Mobley, Horner, & Hollingsworth, 1978; Mowday, Koberg, & McArthur, 1984). Specifically, participants were asked to indicate the extent to which they (a) were "thinking of quitting your job" and (b) "intend to quit your job." Before data analysis, these items were reverse scored. The other two items tapped intentions to comply with the ban and were completed only by smokers. Specifically, smokers were asked to indicate how likely they were "to go along with the ban" and "to stop smoking completely while at work." The behavioral intention items demonstrated a high degree of internal consistency ($\alpha = .85$).

Because the scores on the three subscales were highly intercorrelated (mean $r = .78$, range $= .66$ to .93), they were combined to create a single index of acceptance of the smoking ban, formed as an average of all the items. Accordingly, scores could range from 1 to 7, with higher scores reflecting greater acceptance of the smoking ban. The overall index had a high level of internal consistency ($\alpha = .79$).

Procedural justice: Fairness of the procedure used to implement the ban. Although it was not the subject of any experimental hypotheses, I considered it potentially useful to explore the possibility that perceptions of procedural justice might be influenced by the manipulations. Toward this end, I included a group of four items that tapped perceived fairness of the procedure used to implement the smoking ban. These were adaptations of items used to assess the fairness of procedures for making other types of decisions (Greenberg, 1993b[11]). Specifically, participants indicated the extent to which they believed (a) "the company's decision to implement a smoking ban was made in a fair manner," (b) "the way the company decided to implement the smoking ban was fair and aboveboard," (c) "the procedure used to decide on a smoking ban shows that [company name] treats its employees fairly," and (d) "the smoking ban was determined in a manner that is morally and ethically proper." The coefficient alpha estimate of internal consistency for these items was extremely high (.91), so the items were combined to form a single scale.

Manipulation checks. As a check on the validity of the information thoroughness and social sensitivity manipulations, I asked participants to indicate the extent to which they believed that they (a) "received sufficiently thorough information about the reason for the smoking ban" and (b) "were treated in a manner which showed that [name of the company president] really cares about you as a person."

It also was necessary to establish the extent to which the outcome severity variable was recognized as differentially severe. This was done in two ways. First, participants were asked to indicate the degree to which they believed they would be "personally harmed or inconvenienced by the smoking ban" and the extent to which they believed they would "personally benefit and be helped by the smoking ban" (this item was reverse scored to maintain consistency). Second, they were asked to report the degree to which they responded negatively to tobacco smoke on the job. They did this by completing questionnaire items indicating the extent to which they (a) "are annoyed by tobacco smoke on the job," (b) "become uncomfortable or ill because of tobacco smoke on the job," and (c) "find that tobacco smoke interferes with your ability to perform on the job." The five items had a high degree of internal consistency ($\alpha = .79$) and were thus combined.

Debriefing

Immediately after the questionnaires were collected, the participants were given a thorough explanation of the study. An important part of this process involved giving participants any missing information and showing any social sensitivity they did not receive during the study. Specifically, in conditions in which low amounts of information were given or low amounts of social sensitivity were shown, it was explained that, for experimental purposes, some randomly selected employees were purposely not given enough information about the smoking ban or were not

TABLE 12.1 Intercorrelations Between Dependent Variables ($N = 732$)

Dependent variable	1	2	3	4	5
1. Acceptance of smoking ban	—	.84*	.89*	.82*	.04
2. Fairness of the ban		—	.75*	.66*	.07
3. Affective commitment			—	.93*	.02
4. Behavioral intentions				—	.03
5. Procedural fairness					—

*$p < .001$.

treated with sufficient social sensitivity by the president. Special debriefing tapes in which the president of the company provided the high amounts of information or social sensitivity were prepared and played back to those groups that did not initially hear messages with high amounts of these variables. Thus, all participants were exposed to the conditions expected to yield the most positive reactions before they were dismissed. The president of the company then explained that these messages were prepared as part of an experimental study dealing with people's reactions to smoking bans. After this, the experimenter discussed the nature and purpose of the study with the entire group. High-ranking company officials were on hand to provide information about the program that was to be used to help employees quit smoking and to answer additional questions about the smoking ban itself.

RESULTS

Table 12.1 shows the intercorrelations between the dependent measures. The pattern of correlations obtained reveals that the three subscales making up the acceptance index were significantly correlated with each other and with the overall index. Moreover, the procedural fairness measure was not significantly correlated with either the acceptance index or any of its subscales. These data support the decision to combine the three subscales into a single unified scale and to analyze this measure separately from the procedural fairness measure.

Manipulation Checks

To check on the validity of the manipulations, I analyzed responses to each of the three manipulation check scales by using a $2 \times 2 \times 3$ factorial analysis of variance (ANOVA). With respect to the thoroughness of the information presented, the only significant source of variance was the main effect of information thoroughness, $F(1, 720) = 312.31$, $p < .001$, $\omega^2 = .38$. As expected, participants in the high-information condition ($M = 5.62$, $SD = 1.22$) believed that they received more thorough information than did those in the low-information condition ($M = 2.85$, $SD = 1.06$), suggesting that the manipulation was successful. Analogously, the ANOVA on judgments of the social sensitivity shown revealed that the only significant source of variance was for the social sensitivity variable, $F(1, 720) = 382.44$, $p < .001$, $\omega^2 = .40$. As expected, participants in the high-sensitivity condition ($M = 5.81$, $SD = 1.24$) perceived that the company president showed more concern about them than did those in the low-sensitivity condition ($M = 3.01$, $SD = 1.02$), suggesting that this manipulation also was successful.

The final manipulation check item was designed to determine the degree to which participants either believed they were harmed by or felt negatively toward the smoking ban. As expected, a main effect obtained was for outcome severity, $F(2, 720) = 228.30$, $p < .001$, $\omega^2 = .33$. Tukey honestly significant difference (HSD) tests (with alpha set at .05) revealed that heavy smokers believed that the smoking ban was more harmful to themselves and felt more negatively about it ($M = 5.91$, $SD = 1.02$) than did light smokers ($M = 4.84$, $SD = 1.11$). Nonsmokers ($M = 3.02$, $SD = 0.92$) believed the ban was more beneficial to themselves than did either light or heavy smokers. These data confirm that nonsmokers believed they were not harmed by the smoking ban but that smokers believed that they were harmed by it (with heavy smokers harmed more than light smokers). These findings support the decision to use smoking behavior as an indicator of outcome severity. Also found were significant main effects for information thoroughness $F(1, 720) = 18.40$, $p < .001$, $\omega^2 = .12$ (high-information $M = 5.83$, $SD = 0.97$; low-information $M = 3.81$, $SD = 0.91$)—and social sensitivity—$F(1, 720) = 15.63$, $p < .001$, $\omega^2 = .09$ (high-sensitivity $M = 5.02$, $SD = 0.93$; low-sensitivity $M = 3.22$, $SD = 1.08$)—neither of which threatened the validity of the measure.

Acceptance of the Smoking Ban

Responses to the index tapping acceptance of the smoking ban were analyzed by using a $2 \times 2 \times 3$ factorial ANOVA. For exploratory purposes, separate analyses also were performed for each of the subscales from which the acceptance measure was composed. Because these analyses yielded results that were identical to each other and were identical to the results for the aggregated scale, only the overall acceptance measure is reported. A summary of the ANOVA for this measure is shown in Table 12.2.

TABLE 12.2 Summary of Analysis of Variance for Acceptance Index

Source	df	MS	F	ω^2
Information thoroughness (I)	1	25.42	39.06*	.06
Outcome severity (O)	2	256.20	393.70*	.17
Social sensitivity (S)	1	69.97	107.52*	.12
I × O	2	5.39	8.20*	.06
I × S	1	1.77	2.71	.00
O × S	2	33.27	51.12*	.13
I × O × S	2	0.84	1.29	.00
Residual	720	0.65		

*$p < .001$.

Consistent with Hypothesis 1a, this analysis yielded a significant main effect for information thoroughness, revealing that the smoking ban was better accepted when it was explained by using a high amount of information ($M = 5.38$, $SD = 1.08$) than a low amount of information ($M = 5.04$, $SD = 1.36$). Consistent with Hypothesis 1b, a significant main effect was found for sensitivity, reflecting the tendency for participants in the high-sensitivity condition ($M = 5.42$, $SD = 0.96$) to express greater acceptance of the smoking ban than those in the low-sensitivity condition ($M = 5.00$, $SD = 1.41$). As expected, these effects did not significantly interact with each other. Supporting Hypothesis 1c, the effects of social sensitivity and information thoroughness were additive: Greatest acceptance was found when both social sensitivity and information thoroughness were high ($M = 5.52$, $SD = 0.94$), and the lowest amount of acceptance was found when both were low ($M = 4.77$, $SD = 1.57$). In addition, immediate levels of acceptance were observed when information thoroughness was high and sensitivity was low ($M = 5.24$, $SD = 1.19$) and when information thoroughness was low and sensitivity was high ($M = 5.32$, $SD = 1.04$). Planned contrasts confirmed that in comparison with the means of the high-low and the low-high conditions (which were not significantly different from each other), acceptance was significantly greater when both factors were high, $t(364) = 2.29$, $p < .05$, and significantly less when both factors were low, $t(364) = 3.64$, $p < .05$.

The second set of hypotheses addressed the self-serving bias in acceptance of the smoking ban. Support for the hypothesized effect was provided by a significant main effect for outcome severity. Tukey HSD tests ($\alpha = .05$) revealed that this effect resulted from the tendency for nonsmokers ($M = 5.71$, $SD = 0.78$) to perceive the ban as fairer than did smokers ($M = 3.98$, $SD = 1.14$), thereby supporting Hypothesis 2a. Also, among smokers, heavy smokers ($M = 3.40$, $SD = 1.39$) accepted the ban significantly less than did light smokers ($M = 4.56$, $SD = 0.89$), thereby supporting Hypothesis 2b. Taken together, insofar as lower degrees of acceptance were associated with higher degrees of outcome severity, evidence for the self-serving bias was provided.

The three main effects described thus far are qualified by two different significant interactions: one for Information Thoroughness × Outcome Severity and one for Interpersonal Sensitivity × Outcome Severity. The means and standard deviations corresponding to these interactions are displayed in Figure 12.1.

Both interactions took identical forms. Consistent with Hypothesis 3a, findings showed that among nonsmokers, neither the level of information thoroughness nor the level of social sensitivity demonstrated had an incremental effect on acceptance; in both cases, the level of acceptance was uniformly high, $t < 1.00$, ns. By contrast, these variables had a profound effect on heavy smokers. Specifically, consistent with Hypothesis 3b, the smoking ban was better accepted when high amounts of information were given than when low amounts were given, $t(102) = 3.63$, $p < .01$. Analogously, and consistent with Hypothesis 3c, findings showed that the smoking ban was better accepted when social sensitivity was high than when it was low, $t(103) = 9.51$, $p < .001$.

With respect to both variables, less pronounced—but still significant—differences were observed in the case of light smokers. Specifically, light smokers better accepted the smoking ban when it was presented by using high information in comparison with low information, $t(105) = 2.59$. $p < .05$, and when it was presented in a manner demonstrating a high amount of social sensitivity in comparison with a low amount of social sensitivity, $t(105) = 2.71$, $p < .05$. Taken together, these data reveal that the greatest gains resulting from treating others in socially fair ways were obtained when the outcomes faced were most severe. By contrast, socially fair treatment had virtually no effects on the acceptance of positive outcomes.

Procedural Fairness

The perceived fairness of the procedures used to decide on a smoking ban was analyzed by using a 2 × 2 × 3 factorial ANOVA. A significant main effect was found for information thoroughness, $F(1, 720) = 103.67$, $p < .001$, $\omega^2 = .09$. When the smoking ban was explained by using a high amount of information ($M = 4.77$, $SD = 1.24$), the procedure used was believed to be fairer than when it was explained by using a low amount

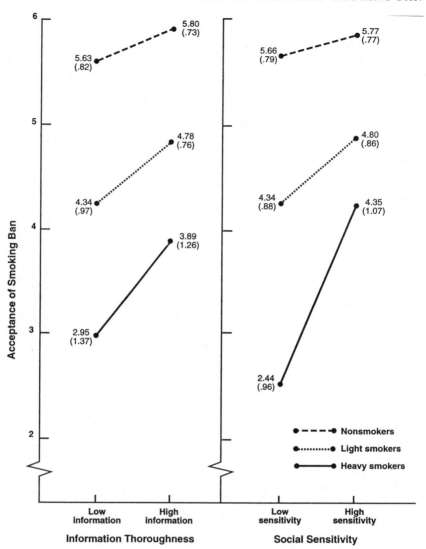

Figure 12.1. Mean Acceptance of Smoking Ban (With Standard Deviations Shown in Parentheses) for Interactions Between Information Thoroughness and Outcome Severity (Left Panel) and Social Sensitivity and Outcome Severity (Right Panel)

of information ($M = 3.73$, $SD = 1.60$). The only other significant source of variance was a significant main effect for social sensitivity, $F(1, 720)$ = 435.19, $p < .001$, $\omega^2 = .27$. When the smoking ban was explained by using a high amount of sensitivity ($M = 5.32$, $SD = 0.99$), the procedure used was believed to be fairer than when it was explained by using a low amount of sensitivity ($M = 3.20$, $SD = 1.19$).

DISCUSSION

These findings suggest that acceptance of a work site smoking ban is facilitated by using socially fair treatment. Specifically, providing a great deal of information about a ban's necessity (i.e., informational justice) and announcing it in a manner that shows considerable awareness of the inconvenience it is likely to cause (i.e., interpersonal justice) were found to enhance the degree to which employees embraced such a potentially threatening policy. These findings are important insofar as they identify an effective technique for reducing immediate negative reactions to the introduction of a type of organizational policy that is becoming increasingly common (Verespej, 1988). Indeed, a potential problem caused by work site smoking prohibitions is that they may encourage turnover among employees who smoke (Martin, 1990). Announcing smoking bans in a socially fair manner may be an effective way of mitigating the negative reactions likely to be responsible for this form of undesirable employee withdrawal (e.g., Hulin, 1991). In addition, as employees come to accept the legitimacy of smoking bans, these policies are less likely to be recognized as unwarranted restrictions of personal rights (Ludington, 1991), a reaction that may be expected to improve employees' morale greatly (Martin, 1990).

Implications

The potential benefits of using socially fair treatment to promote acceptance of a smoking ban are especially great when one recalls that it was the heaviest smokers who were most positively affected by socially fair treatment, that is, the heaviest smokers showed the greatest incremental rise in acceptance. Although as a whole, heavy smokers were less accepting of the smoking ban than were nonsmokers, the socially fair treatment raised their acceptance to levels approximating (but not reaching) those of light smokers. By contrast, for nonsmokers, the smoking ban was a highly beneficial outcome that was readily accepted regardless of the manner in which it was presented. This finding is consistent with findings in the procedural justice literature (e.g., Greenberg, 1987a[14], 1990b[5], 1990c[2]) showing that fair procedures have little incremental impact on perceptions of fair outcomes when these outcomes are high (and are already perceived as fair).

Although as expected, socially fair treatment did not raise nonsmokers' acceptance of the smoking ban beyond their already high levels, it would be misleading to suggest that nonsmokers (the majority of the participants) were completely unaffected by the messages they heard. Indeed, their perceptions of procedural fairness, the fairness of the way the smoking ban was implemented, were greatly affected. With respect to this type of reaction, nonsmokers were no different than smokers in recognizing that the company acted fairly when giving information and when demonstrating social sensitivity. Consistent with previous research and theorizing (e.g., Greenberg, 1987b[1], 1993b[11], these data suggest that in judging fairness, people distinguish between the way decisions are made and the outcomes resulting from those decisions. These findings also underscore the value of announcing a smoking ban in a socially fair manner. Although nonsmokers' acceptance of the ban itself was unaffected by the way it was announced, socially fair treatment had profound effects on their perceptions of how fair the organization was in making an important decision.

From a conceptual standpoint, it is important to note that the present findings support my earlier suggestion to distinguish between the interpersonal and informational classes of justice (Greenberg, 1993a[3]). These factors—separately and together—not only moderate theft reactions to underpayment inequity (as found previously; Greenberg, 1990a[10], 1993b[11]) but also moderate acceptance of a smoking ban (as demonstrated here). By demonstrating the impact of informational justice and interpersonal justice in a new context, the current findings provide valuable evidence of the generalizability of the effects of these variables. This evidence substantiates the value of conceptually distinguishing between the distributive and procedural aspects of the social determinants of justice (i.e., interpersonal justice and informational justice).

This study also complements the existing research on the social determinants of justice by introducing a methodological improvement. Specifically, much of what is currently known about the benefits of socially fair treatment comes from studies (e.g., Bies & Shapiro, 1988, Study 2; Bies, Shapiro, & Cummings, 1988) in which participants were asked to recount an unfair event that occurred earlier in their lives (for a review, see Greenberg, 1993b[11]). Given the potential for people to rationalize their reactions to past events in retrospective accounts (and to recall them only selectively in the first place), such findings are potentially biased (Greenberg & Folger, 1988). By measuring immediate reactions to an event, however, the present findings are not participant to this criticism. It may be speculated that because perceptions of procedural justice were assessed immediately after procedures were implemented, participants in this study did not have a chance to rationalize their reactions by forming consistent cognitions between their assessment of these procedures and other attitudes (cf. Wicklund & Brehm, 1976). This reasoning may be used to account for the absence of a significant correlation between procedural justice and affective commitment in the present study in comparison with the positive correlations between these variables found in other studies in which participants focused on previously established procedures (e.g., Konovsky & Cropanzano, 1991).

The results of the present study are consistent with previous research (e.g., Greenberg, 1981, 1983, 1987a[14]; Grover, 1991) demonstrating a self-serving bias in the acceptance of outcomes: Those outcomes that are more beneficial to oneself (e.g., a smoking ban to a nonsmoker) are perceived to be fairer and more acceptable than those that are costly to oneself (e.g., a smoking ban to a smoker). In this case, the more heavily participants smoked, the less they were in favor of smoking bans in general and the less they accepted the smoking ban that confronted them. At first, these findings seem inconsistent with previous research (e.g., Sorensen & Pechacek, 1989) showing that acceptance of smoking bans tends to be quite high, even among smokers. Participants in these other studies, however, responded long after a smoking ban was in place (e.g., 12 months to 18 months afterward, in Sorensen & Pechacek, 1989). In such cases, it may be expected that those who kept their jobs despite the smoking ban resolved cognitive dissonance by justifying that the ban was acceptable. In the present study, by contrast, acceptance judgments were made immediately after the ban was announced but before it was experienced. Although it may be claimed that these reactions are transient and may not be meaningful, it may be countered that even short-lived affective reactions can have a serious effect on organizational behavior (e.g., Isen & Baron, 1991), such as employee withdrawal (Hulin, 1991). Still, I caution that the duration of the attitudinal effects of the manipulations used in the present study cannot be determined in the absence of a follow-up investigation that extends the latency period between the manipulations and the measurement of their effect.

One may consider why the observed effects were obtained. What is it about providing information about an outcome or showing concern about its potential effect that promotes its acceptance? Writing elsewhere (Greenberg, 1993a[3]), I speculated that high doses of information and social sensitivity may make negative outcomes appear less negative. They may take away some of the sting encountered, much as a topical anesthetic helps reduce the pain from a wound. This may occur because feelings of resentment are reduced by learning that there is a justifiable basis for the negative outcome, a suggestion derived from referent cognitions theory

(Folger, 1986). Evidence consistent with this possibility is provided by the two unexpected effects observed in analyses of the outcome severity manipulation check scale. Individuals receiving high amounts of information about the smoking ban perceived it less negatively than did those receiving low amounts of information. Similarly, those shown high sensitivity perceived the ban less negatively than did those shown low sensitivity. Assuming that an outcome is better accepted when its impact is less adverse, it follows that the observed effect may have been, at least in part, because of the tendency for socially fair treatment to attenuate negative reactions to the smoking ban. This suggestion is not definitive, and there are likely to be additional explanations (e.g., see Greenberg, 1993a[3]). Clearly, systematic attempts at identifying the underlying processes responsible for the beneficial effects of socially fair treatment appear warranted.

Limitations

An important limitation of this study is that only attitudinal measures were used and that no behavioral measures were collected (e.g., compliance with the ban). Admittedly, it would have been ideal to gather such evidence to determine the longer-term behavioral effects of the interpersonal and informational justice manipulations. Doing so, however, would have necessitated delaying exposure to the socially fair treatments, an ethically dubious procedure. Because previous research (e.g., Greenberg, 1990a[10], 1993b[11]) suggested that the manipulations of socially fair treatment would have positive effects on workers' attitudes, it would have been unethical to withhold these anticipated benefits by dismissing the participants before exposing them to these manipulations (for a general discussion of this practice, see Greenberg & Folger, 1988). This was done in postexperimental sessions held immediately after the data were collected, thereby precluding the opportunity to interpret any subsequent behavioral differences as responses to differential exposure to socially fair treatment and obviating the need to collect follow-up behavioral data. Still, it would be ideal in future research to compare the long-term reactions to smoking bans imposed in sites in which differing degrees of interpersonal and informational justice are used in the process of announcing smoking bans.

A possible problem associated with manipulating high amounts of information in a highly socially sensitive manner is that it takes longer to do so than to present low amounts of these variables. As a result, a confounding exists between these variables and the length of the messages themselves: High amounts of information, sensitivity, or both covary with greater message length. Indeed, although more sensitive and thorough messages take more time to impart, it may be argued that such a confounding merely reflects the natural richness of a compound manipulation, a point also made in connection with similar studies conducted in naturalistic settings (e.g., Greenberg, 1990a[10]). Although one would be hard-pressed to reinterpret the present findings in possible confoundings with message length per se, it would still be wise to attempt to disentangle these variables in future investigations. Doing so would be in keeping with the need to isolate the factors responsible for the interpersonal aspects of justice in organizations (Greenberg, 1993a[3]).

Another limitation of the present study is that the lower number of smokers relative to nonsmokers in the sample caused subsample sizes to be lower in conditions involving smokers than those involving nonsmokers. Although this state of affairs limits the stability of the findings, it is the inevitable result of studying a behavior with a relatively low base rate. Nevertheless, confidence in the present pattern of results may be bolstered because smokers and nonsmokers were evenly distributed across each of the various interpersonal justice conditions and because the smoking profile of the sample closely matched that of other samples. Still, the need to replicate these findings must be stressed. Despite these limitations and the need for additional research, it is safe to conclude that the present work provides useful preliminary guidance as to how work site smoking bans can be implemented in a way that promotes their acceptance.

REFERENCES

American Lung Association. (1983). *More facts and figures for nonsmokers and smokers.* New York: Author.

Aronow, W. S. (1978). Effect of passive smoking on angina pectoris. *New England Journal of Medicine, 299*(1), 21-30.

Bies, R. J. (1987). The predicament of injustice: The management of moral outrage. In L. L. Cummings & B. M. Staw (Eds.), *Research in organizational behavior* (Vol. 9, pp. 289-319). Greenwich, CT: JAI.

Bies, R. J., & Moag, J. S. (1986). Interactional justice: Communication criteria of fairness. In R. J. Lewicki, B. H. Sheppard, & M. H. Bazerman (Eds.), *Research on negotiation in organizations* (Vol. 1, pp. 43-55). Greenwich, CT: JAI.

Bies, R. J., & Shapiro, D. L. (1988). Voice and justification: Their influence on procedural fairness judgments. *Academy of Management Journal, 31,* 676-685.

Bies, R. J., Shapiro, D. L., & Cummings, L. L. (1988). Causal accounts and managing organizational conflict: Is it enough to say it's not my fault? *Communication Research, 15,* 381-399.

Brockner, J., Konovsky, M., Cooper-Schneider, R., Folger, R., Martin, C., & Bies, R. J. (1994). The interactive effects of interactional justice and outcome negativity on victims and survivors of job loss. *Academy of Management Journal, 37,* 397-409.

Colosi, M. (1988, April). Do employees have the right to smoke? *Personnel Journal*, pp. 72-79.

Cropanzano, R., & Folger, R. (1989). Referent cognitions and task decision autonomy: Beyond equity theory. *Journal of Applied Psychology, 74*, 293-299.

Fielding, J. E. (1986). Banning work site smoking. *American Journal of Public Health, 76*, 857-862.

Fiore, M. C., Novotny, T. E., Pierce, J. P., Hatziandreu, E. J., Patel, S., & Davis, R. M. (1989). Trends in cigarette smoking in the United States: The changing influence of gender and race. *Journal of the American Medical Association, 261*, 49-55.

Folger, R. (1986). Rethinking equity theory: A referent cognitions model. In H. W. Bierhoff, R. L. Cohen, & J. Greenberg (Eds.), *Justice in social relations* (pp. 145-162). New York: Plenum.

Folger, R., & Bies, R. J. (1989). Managerial responsibilities and procedural justice. *Employee Responsibilities and Rights Journal, 2*, 79-90.

Folger, R., & Martin, C. (1986). Relative deprivation and referent cognitions: Distributive and procedural justice effects. *Journal of Experimental Social Psychology, 22*, 531-546.

Gibbs, N. (1988, April 18). All fired up over smoking. *Time*, pp. 64-71.

Gonzales, M., & Edmonson, B. (1988). The smoking class. *American Demographics, 27*, 34-59.

Greenberg, J. (1981). The justice of distributing scarce and abundant resources. In M. J. Lerner & S. C. Lerner (Eds.), *The justice motive in social behavior* (pp. 289-316). New York: Plenum.

Greenberg, J. (1983). Overcoming egocentric bias in perceived fairness through self-awareness. *Social Psychology Quarterly, 46*, 152-156.

Greenberg, J. (1987a). Reactions to procedural injustice in payment allocations: Do the ends justify the means? *Journal of Applied Psychology, 72*, 55-61. [Chapter 14, this volume.]

Greenberg, J. (1987b). A taxonomy of organizational justice theories. *Academy of Management Review, 12*, 9-22. [Chapter 1, this volume.]

Greenberg, J. (1990a). Employee theft as a reaction to underpayment inequity: The hidden cost of pay cuts. *Journal of Applied Psychology, 75*, 561-568. [Chapter 10, this volume.]

Greenberg, J. (1990b). Looking fair vs. being fair: Managing impressions of organizational justice. In B. M. Staw & L. L. Cummings (Eds.), *Research in organizational behavior* (Vol. 12, pp. 111-157). Greenwich, CT: JAI. [Chapter 5, this volume.]

Greenberg, J. (1990c). Organizational justice: Yesterday, today, and tomorrow. *Journal of Management, 16*, 399-432. [Chapter 2, this volume.]

Greenberg, J. (1993a). The social side of fairness: Interpersonal and informational classes of organizational justice. In R. Cropanzano (Ed.), *Justice in the workplace: Approaching fairness in human resource management* (pp. 79-103). Hillsdale, NJ: Lawrence Erlbaum. [Chapter 3, this volume.]

Greenberg, J. (1993b). Stealing in the name of justice: Informational and interpersonal moderators of theft reactions to underpayment inequity. *Organizational Behavior and Human Decision Processes, 54*, 81-103. [Chapter 11, this volume.]

Greenberg, J., Bies, R. J., & Eskew, D. E. (1991). Establishing fairness in the eye of the beholder: Managing impressions of organizational justice. In R. Giacalone & P. Rosenfeld (Eds.), *Applied impression management: How image making affects managerial decisions* (pp. 111-132). Newbury Park, CA: Sage.

Greenberg, J., & Folger, R. (1988). *Controversial issues in social research methods.* New York: Springer-Verlag.

Greenberg, J., & McCarty, C. (1990). The interpersonal aspects of procedural justice: A new perspective on pay fairness. *Labor Law Journal, 41*, 580-586.

Grover, S. L. (1991). Predicting the perceived fairness of parental leave policies. *Journal of Applied Psychology, 76*, 247-255.

Hulin, C. (1991). Adaptation, persistence, and commitment in organizations. In M. D. Dunnette & L. M. Hough (Eds.), *Handbook of industrial and organizational psychology* (2nd ed., Vol. 2, pp. 445-505). Palo Alto, CA: Consulting Psychologists Press.

Isen, A. M., & Baron, R. A. (1991). Positive affect as a factor in organizational behavior. In L. L. Cummings & B. M. Staw (Eds.), *Research in organizational behavior* (Vol. 13, pp. 1-53). Greenwich, CT: JAI.

Konovsky, M. A., & Cropanzano, R. (1991). Perceived fairness of employee drug testing as a predictor of employee attitudes and job performance. *Journal of Applied Psychology, 76,* 698-707.

Leventhal, G. S. (1980). What should be done with equity theory? In K. J. Gergen, M. S. Greenberg, & R. H. Willis (Eds.), *Social exchange: Advances in theory and research* (pp. 27-55). New York: Plenum.

Levin-Epstein, S. (1986). *Where there's smoke: Problems and policies concerning smoking in the workplace: Special report.* Rockville, MD: Bureau of National Affairs.

Ludington, D. M. (1991). Smoking in public: A moral imperative for the most toxic of environmental wastes. *Journal of Business Ethics, 10,* 23-27.

Manning, A. (1990, December 6). Passive smoke "class A" threat, says EPA panel. *USA Today,* p. A1.

Marietta board OKs policy banning use of tobacco in school. (1988, August 16). *Atlanta Constitution,* p. A4.

Martin, C. (1990). *An analysis of workplace smoking policy: A strategy for effective implementation.* Unpublished manuscript, Louisiana State University, Shreveport.

McGee, G. W., & Ford, R. C. (1987). Two (or more?) dimensions of organizational commitment: Reexamination of the affective and continuance commitment scales. *Journal of Applied Psychology, 72,* 638-642.

McGuire, W. J. (1969). The nature of attitudes and attitude change. In G. Lindzey & E. Aronson (Eds.), *The handbook of social psychology* (2nd ed., Vol. 3, pp. 136-314). Reading, MA: Addison-Wesley.

Meyer, J. P., & Allen, N. J. (1984). Testing the "side-bet theory" of organizational commitment: Some methodological considerations. *Journal of Applied Psychology, 69,* 372-378.

Mobley, W. H., Horner, S. O., & Hollingsworth, A. T. (1978). An evaluation of precursors of hospital employee turnover. *Journal of Applied Psychology, 63,* 408-414.

Mowday, R. T., Koberg, C. S., & McArthur, A. W. (1984). The psychology of the withdrawal process: A cross-validational test of Mobley's immediate linkages model of turnover in two samples. *Academy of Management Journal, 27,* 79-94.

Ockene, J. (1984). Toward a smoke-free society. *American Journal of Public Health, 74,* 1198-1217.

Peterson, L. R., Helgerson, S. D., Gibbons, C. M., Calhoun, C. R., Ciacco, K. H., & Pitchford, K. C. (1988). Employee smoking behavior changes and attitudes following a restrictive policy on work site smoking in a large company. *Public Health Reports, 103*(2), 115-120.

Pierce, J. P., Fiore, M. C., Novotny, T. E., Hatziandreu, E. J., & Davis, R. M. (1989a). Trends in cigarette smoking in the United States: Educational differences are increasing. *Journal of the American Medical Association, 261,* 56-60.

Pierce, J. P., Fiore, M. C., Novotny, T. E., Hatziandreu, E. J., & Davis, R. M. (1989a). Trends in cigarette smoking in the United States: Projections to the year 2000. *Journal of the American Medical Association, 261,* 61-65.

Schein, D. (1987). Should employers restrict smoking in the workplace? *Labor Law Journal, 38,* 173-188.

Shapiro, D. L., Buttner, E. H., & Barry, B. (1994). Explanations for rejection decisions: What factors enhance their perceived adequacy and moderate their enhancement of justice perception? *Organizational Behavior and Human Decision Processes, 58,* 346-368.

Sorensen, G., & Pechacek, T. F. (1989). Implementing nonsmoking policies in the private sector and assessing their effects. *New York State Journal of Medicine, 89,* 11-15.

Tyler, T. R., & Bies, R. J. (1990). Beyond formal procedures: The interpersonal context of procedural justice. In J. Carroll (Ed.), *Applied social psychology and organizational settings* (pp. 77-98). Hillsdale, NJ: Lawrence Erlbaum.

Verespej, M. (1988). Controlling smoking in the workplace. *Labor Law Journal, 38,* 743-750.

Wicklund, R. A., & Brehm, J. W. (1976). *Perspectives on cognitive dissonance.* Hillsdale, NJ: Lawrence Erlbaum.

Wynder, E. L., & Stellman, S. D. (1977). Comparative epidemiology of tobacco-related cancers. *Cancer Research, 37,* 4608-4619.

PART V

Monetary Rewards
PAY FAIRNESS

WHEN most people think of fairness on the job, I am sure the first thing that comes to mind is money. How fairly are they paid? No one studying organizational justice for long could possibly ignore the issue of pay equity. Indeed, many of my colleagues in the field of human resources management have found that conceptualizations of distributive justice and procedural justice are valuable tools for analyzing reactions to pay. The two chapters in this part of the book deal with different aspects of pay.

In Chapter 13, I analyze the highly charged issue of comparable worth from the perspective of both distributive justice and procedural justice. Research is reviewed suggesting that gender is sometimes perceived as a relevant criterion of entitlement, men and women employ different comparison standards in assessing outcome fairness, and norms discourage the expression of inequity distress. Furthermore, conceptualizations of procedural justice suggest that pay satisfaction may be influenced by the use of participatory and open pay plans, grievance resolution procedures, job evaluation techniques, and pay communication practices. These analyses highlight the great difficulties involved in getting people to agree on what constitutes fair pay. Although we all agree on the importance of fair pay, agreement on exactly how to achieve pay equity for all is not so easily found.

One reason why it is so difficult to find payment that all can agree is fair is the existence of a self-serving (or egocentric) bias—the tendency for people to perceive as fair those outcomes that most benefit themselves. This perspective, however, ignores the possibility that even less-than-desirable outcomes may be perceived as fair to the extent that they result from procedures that are themselves fair. Can fair procedures enhance the perceived fairness of undesirable outcomes (e.g., low levels of pay)? The experiment reported in Chapter 14 addresses this question. Participants in this laboratory study were given either high, medium, or low levels of pay following performance on the basis of either a fair procedure (how well they performed) or an unfair, highly capricious, procedure. I found that participants perceived high and medium levels of pay to be fair regardless of the pay they received but perceived low levels of pay as fair only when they followed from fair procedures. Perceived as most unfair were low outcomes based on a highly capricious procedure. In fact, participants in this condition were most inclined to express their dissatisfaction behaviorally, by taking the phone number of an agency alleged to be responsible for the fair treatment of research participants. Although this behavioral intention measure proved not to be highly sensitive to all levels of the independent variables, it was a unique feature of this study.

13

Comparable Worth

Is It Fair?

Compensation specialists have witnessed few livelier debates during the past decade than that concerning the quest for comparable worth or pay equity—the doctrine establishing that equal pay should be given to persons performing jobs of comparable (e.g., equal) worth (Lorber, 1985; Mahoney, 1987).[1] For example, economists have disagreed about the extent to which wage rates are freely determined by supply and demand forces operating within the labor market or constrained by sociopolitical

AUTHOR'S NOTE: This chapter was originally published in *Research in Personnel and Human Resources Management* (G. R. Ferris & K. M. Rowland, Eds.), Vol. 8, pp. 265-301, under the title "Comparable Worth: A Matter of Justice" by J. Greenberg and C. L. McCarty. Copyright © 1990 by JAI Press. Reprinted by permission.

forces that impose barriers to career entry among certain groups—notably, women (England, 1984; Rynes & Milkovich, 1986). Wage and salary practitioners have disagreed about the value of wage surveys and job evaluation plans as tools for effectively abolishing payment inequities (Madigan, 1985; Mahoney, Rosen, & Rynes, 1984). Not surprisingly, politicians also have expressed widely differing opinions about comparable worth. Although former U.S. Representative Geraldine A. Ferraro (1984) referred to pay equity as "an issue of human dignity" (p. 1166) that "holds great promise" (p. 1170), former President Ronald Reagan called comparable worth a "cockamamie idea," and the late chairman of the U.S. Commission on Civil Rights, Clarence M. Pendleton Jr., referred to it as "the looniest idea since Looney Tunes" (cited in Patten, 1988, p. 15). Given these various disagreements about comparable worth along so many fronts, it is not surprising to find it described as "currently the most controversial equity issue regarding . . . pay structures" (Heneman, Schwab, Fossum, & Dyer, 1989, p. 482), and the "top labor issue in the 1980s" (Newman, 1982, p. 49).

Given the many excellent reviews of these various positions that have appeared (e.g., Aaron & Lougy, 1986; Mahoney, 1987; Patten, 1988), this chapter does not recapitulate the economic, administrative, or political aspects of the comparable worth controversy. Instead, it focuses on yet another perspective—what Mahoney (1983) has identified as the "social philosophy" approach to payment equity. This approach, derived from social-psychological theories of equity and distributive justice (e.g., Adams, 1965; Homans, 1961; Walster, Walster, & Berscheid, 1978), emphasizes that job earnings should be proportional to one's work contributions (as determined, for example, by one's education, skill, and experience). As such, it claims that "persons or groups expending equal work capabilities ought to be paid equally, and pay differentials should be proportional to the expenditure of work capabilities" (Mahoney, 1983, p. 16).

Although such an approach is clearly relevant to understanding comparable worth, it merely skims the surface of the broad array of social justice perspectives that have been imported into organizational use in recent years (for a review, see Greenberg, 1987b[1]). Indeed, as conceptualizations of organizational justice have begun to focus on the fairness of the procedures used to determine organizational outcomes (i.e., *procedural justice;* Folger & Greenberg, 1985; Greenberg & Tyler, 1987), it has become clear that conceptualizations of fairness based only on the relative distributions of outcomes (i.e., *distributive justice;* Homans, 1961) fail to completely account for perceptions of the fairness of social phenomena (Brockner & Greenberg, 1990). Such limitations are inherent in Mahoney's (1983, 1987) repeated claims regarding the explanatory value of the social philosophy approach to comparable worth. In fact, not only have broader conceptualizations of social justice been ignored in attempts to explain comparable worth, but even the full value of the more popularly cited distributive justice concept has not been carefully examined. To focus only on fairness in pay proportionate to contributions and to label this as the primary contribution of a social philosophy approach to comparable worth systematically ignores the wealth of insight provided by various theories of organizational justice (Greenberg, 1987b[1]).

Despite the seemingly obvious link between the pay equity concept and theories of organizational justice, there have been few attempts to apply social justice theorizing to comparable worth research and even fewer attempts to use comparable worth as a social issue within which to study social justice concepts. With these voids in mind, this chapter identifies areas of potential conceptual overlap between the bodies of research and theory on social justice and comparable worth. Specifically, this chapter distinguishes between distributive justice and procedural justice by reviewing and analyzing theoretical ideas and empirical findings within each approach that shed conceptual light onto the construct of comparable worth. In so doing, the objectives are not only to expand the applied potential of these social justice constructs but also to take a step toward bringing to fruition the virtues of a social justice orientation to comparable worth. Considering recent analyses of comparable worth as a social and political issue (Mahoney, 1987), an expanded social justice analysis of comparable worth appears to have considerable value.

DISTRIBUTIVE JUSTICE:
THE FAIRNESS OF PAY DISTRIBUTIONS

Traditionally, the principle of distributive justice (Homans, 1961) is cited as a justice-oriented approach among theorists recognizing the value of a social-psychological orientation toward comparable worth (e.g., Mahoney, 1983, 1987). The distributive justice principle recognizes that fair distributions of reward are ones that reflect people's relative contributions to any social exchange. It is this axiom that formed the conceptual basis for the more formal derivative—equity theory (Adams, 1965; Walster et al., 1978). Specifically, equity theory asserts that employees compare the ratios of their own perceived outcomes (i.e., work rewards) to their own perceived inputs (i.e., work contributions) relative to the corresponding ratios of some comparison standard (e.g., a coworker or a prevailing wage rate). Resulting imbalances are considered states of inequity, which people are motivated to redress (Greenberg, 1984). In support of the theory, research has shown that workers psychologically and/or behaviorally adjust their perceived outcomes and inputs to convert inequitable states to ones that are equitable (for reviews, see Greenberg, 1982, 1987b[1]).

Three key aspects of equity theory prove to be especially central to this analysis of comparable worth. First, perceptions of equity and inequity are subjective. Thus, reactions to imbalances between outcomes and inputs are based on people's perceptions about what those rewards and contributions are, rather than on any objective measures. Second, these subjective assessments are based on social comparison processes. In other words, assessment of equitable treatment depends on the nature of the referent comparisons employed. Third, reactions to inequity may take many different forms. Because attempts to redress inequities may occur either behaviorally or psychologically, no universal criterion can be employed to gauge inequity resolution efforts. These aspects of equity theory (reviewed in more detail by Walster et al., 1978) deserve to be highlighted in view of their key role in this application of the theory to comparable worth. As described in this section, equity theory provides insight into the construct of comparable worth primarily with respect to three basic issues: (a) the status of gender as a work input, (b) the choice of a comparison standard, and (c) reactions to inequitable conditions.

Gender as a Work Input:
Is the Wage Gap Fair?

If comparable worth requires that employees are paid in equal proportion to their relative work contributions, it is imperative to discern what constitutes those contributions. The Equal Pay Act of 1963 specifies that four factors may be used as the basis for assessing workers' contributions—skill, effort, responsibilities, and working conditions—and that exceptions may be made for differences in seniority, merit, or factors other than sex (Williams & McDowell, 1980).

Despite the law's admonition against using sex as the basis for determining one's job contributions, there appears to be a tradition of recognizing gender as a determinant of worth. Equity theory is specific in this regard. In defining inputs in the equity equation, Adams (1965) cited several examples, including "education, intelligence, training, skill, seniority, age, *sex,* ethnic background, social status, and . . . effort" (pp. 276-277; emphasis added). These are the work contributions, or investments, for which workers expect a just return. Adams admits that disagreements about equity will arise when persons hold different opinions about the relevance of various input factors. Certainly, the inclusion of sex and ethnic background on the list of inputs is likely to raise questions of sexism and racism as they may be applied. The point is not that these should constitute relevant inputs in the normative sense but that they are often used in practice to define a person's worth. In recasting this matter in terms relevant to comparable worth, a key question arises: Is being a man a more valuable work contribution than being a woman? Insight into this question is provided by several areas of research.

Human capital theory (Becker, 1964; Polachek, 1981) emphasizes that men are often paid more than women because they possess greater education, skill, and experience. Because wage differentials are often based directly on these highly valued characteristics, which themselves tend to covary with gender in the workforce (Mahoney, 1987), what might appear to be gender-based pay discrimination may be an artifact of historical differences in the distribution of valued human capital. For example, analyzing the earnings of women and men, Smith and Ward (1984) found women's lower wages to be based on their lower levels of education and fewer years of work experience. Indeed, the tendency for women to work intermittently (such as because of pregnancy leaves) depreciates the value of their skills and tends to perpetuate the earnings gap between the sexes (Mincer & Ofek, 1982; Polachek, 1975). Contrary to human capital theory, sizeable increases in skill-related variables among women have failed to be followed by proportionate reductions in the pay differential (Milkovich, 1988). These and other failures of human capital theory to account for wage discrimination (e.g., Corcoran, 1979; England, 1982) refocus attention to the possibility that sex differences in wages are more likely to reflect a true pattern of discriminatory perceptions rather than the by-product of statistical covariation.

Curiously, an integration between human capital theory and equity theory has been recommended on the grounds that both approaches agree that workers should be paid the same amount for making equivalent work contributions (Mahoney, 1987). Although such an integration may have some value, one should be careful to note the differences between these approaches. Essentially, human capital theory assumes that a worker's sex may have value only insofar as it is related to a profit-producing skill. In contrast, equity theory recognizes that people may believe that men should be paid more than women simply because they are men, that is, being a man is an independent contribution worthy of reward. Equity theory, thus, raises the possibility that the wage differential between men and women may be the result of beliefs about the relative worth of men and women directly because of their sex, as opposed to factors that covary with sex.

The idea that sex operates as an input factor in the equity equation—
that is, as a determinant of one's worth—raises questions about the
relative value society places on the work of men and women. Why might
women's job contributions be perceived as less valuable than men's?
According to Lawler (1981) and Blumrosen (1980), the answer lies, in
great part, on the long-standing patterns of sex discrimination that reflect
an undervaluing of "women's work."[2] Specifically, the history of wage
discrimination against women appears to have lowered their own expectations of how much pay they deserve (Major & Deaux, 1982). Such a
possibility is consistent with several independent research findings:

1. Callahan-Levy and Messé (1979) found that when asked to pay themselves fairly
   for doing the same work, women paid themselves significantly less than men.
2. When asked to work as long as necessary to fairly earn a certain amount of pay,
   Major, McFarlin, and Gagnon (1984) found that women worked significantly
   longer than men and also performed at a higher level of quality.
3. In an experiment in which participants played the role of job evaluators, McArthur
   and Obrant (1986) found that people regarded the work performed by female
   job incumbents to have less financial worth than the same jobs performed
   by males.
4. Finally, when asked to recommend fair payment to persons in moderate-status
   occupations, participants in Jackson and Grabski's (1988) study gave lower pay
   to female employees than to those whose gender was unspecified.

Taken together, these findings suggest that people (including women
themselves) believe that women are less deserving of the same pay as men
performing the same jobs. Not surprisingly, wage differentials reflecting
this bias may be perceived as fair. The perception that the wage gap is
justified on the basis of women's relatively lower levels of deservingness
tends to be self-perpetuating. Paying women less for their work than men
serves to consensually reinforce the belief that they are worth less, thereby
maintaining the perception that fairness demands paying women less
than men (Donnerstein, 1988). Such beliefs appear to manifest themselves through mechanisms that institutionalize discriminatory practices.
For example, it has been argued that allowing the labor market to determine wages is unfair because it is itself a discriminatory transmitter of
wage information (Grune, 1984). The same may be said about allegedly
more objective mechanisms for determining fair wages, such as job evaluations. These also have been found to be highly subject to the discriminatory
beliefs of those whose evaluations of job worth are solicited (Grams &
Schwab, 1985; Schwab & Grams, 1985). Bias in perceptions of the deservingness of men and women is insidious: The very mechanisms that seek

to eliminate discriminatory practices (e.g., free labor markets and job evaluations) merely serve to promulgate wage differentiation on the basis of well-entrenched stereotypes that make the wage gap appear fair.

As discriminatory beliefs about women's work contributions proliferate, it is not surprising to find that occupational segregation occurs—that is, for men and women to work in different occupations and for those dominated by women to be paid less than those dominated by men (Treiman & Hartmann, 1981). Traditionally, segregation into "occupational ghettos" has been explained by (a) the "crowding" of women into occupations, which relieves pressure to pay high wages to the abundant supply of workers (Bergmann, 1974), and (b) the tendency for the labor market to discriminate by denying women access to higher-paid occupations (Berger, 1984).

Equity theory's recognition that sex bias may manifest itself in perceptions of pay fairness (Donnerstein, 1988) suggests yet another explanation. Given that women believe they are less deserving of high-paying jobs than men, it is not surprising that they continue to gravitate toward lower-paying jobs (Gethman, 1987) and report less dissatisfaction with their lower pay than men (Steel & Lovrich, 1987). Moreover, to the extent that women purposely seek entry into professions that offer valued rewards other than pay (e.g., flexible working hours and more pleasant working conditions) (Hollenbeck, Ilgen, Ostroff, & Vancouver, 1987)—often at the expense of higher pay (Marini & Brinton, 1984)—they inadvertently may be reinforcing the stereotype that they are not worthy of working in higher-paying jobs. After all, some may wish to interpret such occupational segregation as the result of a lack of fit, rather than a conscious choice. As one management consultant put it, "although the law has mandated equal opportunity, women have continued to pursue gender-stereotyped education and employment opportunities—and have unwittingly perpetuated sexual segregation in the workplace" (Cuddy, 1984, p. 33). Assuming that being female represents a lower set of work contributions than being male (Dipboye, Arvey, & Terpstra, 1977), equity theory recognizes that women may gravitate toward the lower echelons of their chosen professions, thereby accounting for occupational segregation (Treiman & Hartmann, 1981).

Although the preceding analyses have rested primarily on differential perceptions on the basis of societal stereotypes, it is also possible to explain the devaluing of women's contributions from an attributional perspective (Deaux, 1984; Major & Deaux, 1982). Two sets of attributions appear to be involved. First, people are more inclined to attribute women's than men's successful job performance to external causes (such as luck; Hansen & O'Leary, 1985). Likewise, women themselves are more likely than men to attribute their success to external causes and their failures to internal causes (such as skill; e.g., Deaux & Farris, 1977). This externalization of performance credit is critical because people are generally unwilling to reward themselves for outcomes on the basis of externally determined factors (i.e., those over which they have no control). They not only believe that it is unfair to accept rewards on the basis of such determinants (Greenberg, 1979) but also fail to allocate outcomes (e.g., monetary rewards) in proportion to inputs for which they are not responsible (Greenberg, 1980). In combining both sets of findings, it appears reasonable to conclude that women may be unlikely to accept as much reward as men for doing the same work because they are prone to externalize the credit for their contributions.

Evidence suggests that a second attributional dynamic may be involved. Namely, people tend to discount the amount of effort and ability it takes to succeed at tasks associated with women than similar tasks associated with men (McArthur & Obrant, 1986; Taynor & Deaux, 1973). To the extent that the gender-associated nature of a task somehow qualifies the nature of one's contributions (i.e., augmenting them for men but discounting them for women), it follows that the application of those contributions to judgments of fairness of entitlement will reflect this (Deaux, 1976). According to equity theory, perceptions of various input factors interact such that the perceived value of one's contributions is qualified by attributional biases regarding the sex of the person making those contributions. Such reasoning is consistent with recent evidence (Greenberg, 1989) and theoretical speculation concerning the possible interdependence between various input variables in equity theory (Adams, 1965).

Gender continues to operate in many ways as an input in the assessment of pay equity despite the introduction of laws explicitly prohibiting payment on the basis of one's sex. Yet to the extent that employers pay higher wages to employees with characteristics that covary with sex and the work performed by women is valued less than the work performed by men, it is clear that Adams (1965) was correct in noting that sex functions as an input in assessing payment equity.

The Choice of a Comparison Standard

According to equity theory, the perceived fairness of one's treatment depends on whom one uses as a basis of comparison (Goodman, 1974; Masters & Keil, 1987). Whether one selects referents from other organizations (external equity), the same organization (internal equity), or oneself at another time (individual equity), different conclusions about the fairness of one's treatment will be reached by persons comparing themselves with different reference standards. Such multiple comparison possibilities provide serious challenges to personnel managers attempting to establish feelings of pay equity within their employees (Schwab, 1985).

Theoretical insight into the effect of comparing one's outcomes with another's is provided by research on the concept of relative deprivation (Crosby, 1984; Martin, 1981).[3] The earliest research derived from this framework explained the relative satisfaction of black soldiers stationed in the South during World War II by their tendency to compare themselves with their less privileged southern civilian counterparts rather than to their more privileged northern military counterparts (Stouffer, Suchman, DeVinney, Star, & Williams, 1949). They were deprived relative to northern soldiers, but they were not deprived relative to the southern civilians against whom they compared themselves. Simply put, the concept of relative deprivation (like equity theory, although it is not as specific in this regard) recognizes that one's feelings of satisfaction and discontent are likely to depend on whom one uses as a basis of comparison (i.e., the choice of a comparison, or referent, standard).

Recently, the concept of relative deprivation has been used to explain the high levels of satisfaction among female employees (who report levels of job and pay satisfaction equal to male employees), despite being objectively underpaid relative to their male counterparts (Steel & Lovrich, 1987). Specifically, Crosby (1982) compared the job satisfaction of 345 full-time employees of both sexes who were matched with respect to the prestige of their occupations. In keeping with other salary surveys (e.g., Dreher, 1981), Crosby found that women were paid less than men holding jobs of similar prestige. She found that although the women were aware of their own underpayment—and the underpayment of women in general—they reported no feelings of personal deprivation or dissatisfaction with their own jobs or the pay they received. Crosby referred to this as the "paradox of the contented female worker" (p. 160). This evidence is consistent with findings showing that women expect to be paid less than men—16.5% less at career entry and 46% less at career peak, according to one study (Major & Konar, 1984)—thereby fulfilling their lower expectations with lower pay.

Writing extensively on this topic, Major and her associates (e.g., Major, 1989; Major & Forcey, 1985; Major & Konar, 1984; Major & Testa, 1989) have explained such lowered expectations by differences in the comparison standards used by men and women. Several explanatory mechanisms have been proposed. One explanation is based on the established finding that people are more likely to compare themselves with similar others (such as those of the same sex or those performing the same jobs) than with dissimilar others (Goodman, 1974; Oldham et al., 1982; Suls & Miller, 1977). Because labor markets tend to be segregated by sex (Bielby & Baron, 1984), it is likely that women and men will be more knowledgeable about the established pay rates in their own different segments of the market. Given that the pay for the female-dominated jobs tends to be lower than that for male-dominated jobs (Treiman & Hartmann, 1981), it follows that women develop lower pay expectations than men. Thus, as Major (1989) explained, a "proximity" explanation may account for the tendency for women to compare themselves with disadvantaged others.

Borrowing from theories of social comparison (e.g., Goethals & Darley, 1977), Major (1989) also proposed a less passive, more proactive explanation for this bias in comparison standards—the "similarity principle." This principle claims that women may seek comparisons with other women working in similar jobs because they may be assumed to be similar with respect to pay-related dimensions (e.g., job qualifications) and are therefore perceived to be most appropriate for use in gauging the fairness of work outcomes. In support of this idea, Major and Forcey (1985) found that male and female college students allowed to compare their own wages with those paid to others strongly preferred obtaining information about the wages of the most similar others (i.e., those of the same sex performing the same job) over obtaining any other equally available wage information.

The tendency to prefer comparing oneself with similar others, Major (1989) noted, may serve a useful self-protective function. For example, to the extent that comparing themselves with men may reveal information that makes salient women's disadvantaged position, such frustration-arousing comparisons may be avoided (Brickman & Bulman, 1977). Indeed, research has found that women who compare their jobs with men's jobs were less satisfied than those who compared their jobs with those held by other women (Zanna, Crosby, & Lowenstein, 1987). The consistency of such findings with existing formulations of social comparison (e.g., Willis, 1981) suggests that self-protection may be a key determinant of the choice of a referent comparison. Such a dynamic may lead men and women to seek different comparison others—both selecting persons of their own sex.

It is important to caution that even if men and women compare themselves with the same others, they still may develop different expectations about pay. The reason is that they expose themselves to different information when making social comparisons. For example, men place greater importance on pay and women place greater importance on the intrinsic interest of the job when judging the value of work-related rewards (Hollenbeck et al., 1987; Major & Konar, 1984). This evidence may account for the finding that women make less accurate judgments than men with respect to the amount of pay others receive (Major & Konar, 1984). Given that women may be more interested in factors other than pay, it follows that their selective attention to these factors would interfere with the accuracy of their judgments about pay. Such differences in attention may foster the development of different pay expectations.

As explained earlier, equity theory recognizes that assessments of payment equity greatly depend on who is chosen as a comparison other. As just noted, people tend to compare themselves with similar others because they tend to be readily available and nonthreatening. It is also important to point out that a potentially even more salient comparison standard may exist—the self.[4] In this regard, Major (1989) claimed that low pay expectations may be the result of repeated life experiences that tend to undervalue women's work contributions (Deaux, 1976). Such differential socialization, coupled with the tendency for discriminatory pay practices to legitimize lower pay for women (Treiman & Hartmann, 1981), cannot help lowering women's pay expectations on the basis of self-comparisons. Thus, when comparing their low earnings with their internalized standards for low pay developed through time, it is not surprising that women do not feel relatively deprived.

A related dynamic that may depress the comparison standards of women relative to men lies in differences in prevailing social norms (Major, 1989). Indeed, as norms governing a social situation become internalized, they tend to serve as referents against which claims of entitlement may be made (Willis, 1981). In the case of payment for jobs, Kessler-Harris (1982) notes that the passage of the Equal Pay Act of 1963 and the Civil Rights Act of 1964 marked a period before which it was considered acceptable to pay women less than men because women were not recognized as needing the pay to support their families. Although such norms may be less prevalent now than they were a quarter century ago when landmark legislation sought to end sex discrimination in pay, evidence suggests that people still undervalue the work performed by women. For example, Major and Forcey (1985) found that people performing jobs characterized as women's work expected to get paid less than those performing the same jobs characterized as men's work. Similarly, in a simulation study, Buttner and Rosen (1987) found that people were more likely to recommend using salary raises to retain employees in male sex-typed jobs than those in female sex-stereotyped jobs. Together, these and other findings (e.g., McArthur & Obrant, 1986) support the idea that despite legislation to the contrary, norms undervaluing the job contributions of women still remain. To the extent that such norms dictate socially acceptable behavior, it is not surprising that women expect lower pay than men.

Because Major (e.g., 1989; Major & Konar, 1984) has made the primary contributions to the understanding of sex differences in comparison standards, it is only fitting to conclude this section of the chapter with a summary quotation directly from her.

> To summarize, there is substantial evidence that women's comparison standards for pay for work generally are lower than men's. These lower comparison standards are a byproduct of cognitive and affective preferences for comparing with similar or ingroup others, a sex-segregated labor market, and the lower pay to women and women's jobs than to men and men's jobs. (Major, 1989, p. 108)

Reactions to Inequitable Conditions

Having established that the earnings differential between women and men may be perceived as fair, it is tempting to conclude that women would be unlikely to recognize—hence, respond to—payment inequities. In general, whenever sex differences in reactions to inequities have been reported in the literature, men are likely to respond more strongly than women (for a review, see Major & Deaux, 1982). One possible reason for this is simply that men experience a greater degree of felt inequity (as explained earlier). Consistent with this, research has shown that although both sexes were dissatisfied with inequitable exchanges, women displayed less dissatisfaction than men (Brockner & Adsit, 1986). Accordingly, less inequity experienced may lead to weaker attempts to alter the inequitable state. Indeed, equity theory recognizes that the magnitude of inequity resolution efforts is proportional to the magnitude of the inequity experienced (Adams, 1965; Walster et al., 1978). Analogously, Graham (1986) has claimed that the more strongly people feel they have been victimized by an organizational wrongdoing, the more extremely they will respond.

Despite this rationale, it is quite naive to argue that women do not respond to payment inequities encountered on their jobs. Of course they do. Indeed, social movements, such as the women's rights movement (Haftner, 1979) and the feminist movement (Chafe, 1977), may be recognized as responses to payment inequities. How is the development of such movements reconciled with the wealth of evidence reported earlier suggesting that women do not feel dissatisfied with their lower pay? The answer is based on a key distinction originally made by Runciman (1966) and later clarified by relative deprivation theorists (e.g., Crosby, 1984; Martin, 1981) between egoistic deprivation (feelings of deprivation for oneself) and fraternal deprivation (feelings of deprivation for one's group). Crosby's (1982) seminal research on relative deprivation in working women found that women experienced deprivation fraternally—recognizing that they were deprived as a group relative to men—but not egoistically—feeling no personal discontent. In a consistent manner, several other theorists have recognized this distinction, noting that it is quite possible to experience deprivation at a group level without feeling any deprivation as an individual (Vanneman & Pettigrew, 1972). In fact, several studies have found that it is group-level, rather than individual-level, deprivation that instigates social protest as a response to experienced deprivation (e.g., Dion, 1986; Dube & Guimond, 1986).

As women become increasingly aware of their inferior treatment regarding pay distributions (e.g., via reports in the popular press; Bergmann, 1985), they are likely to develop shared perceptions of injustice that legitimize the basis for their opposition. One manifestation of this is the formation of groups that provide an ideological vehicle for their solidarity (Blau, 1964). As Lawler (1975) put it:

> It is not only dissatisfaction that is important to coalitional responses to inequity, but the fact that the subordinates expect others to share their disenchantment and to be receptive to mobilizing insurgent action. Inequity probably increases subordinates' sense of "common position" vis-a-vis a leader and engenders a "class consciousness" that is reflected in mutual expectations of support. (p. 177)

This is, in fact, one of the stated reasons behind various women's movements (Chafe, 1977; Haftner, 1979). Indeed, research has shown that groups often form for the expressed purpose of mobilizing resources against, and attempting to redress, unfair resource distributions (Lawler, 1975; Webster & Smith, 1978). For such movements to be effective, they must overcome obstacles such as multiple subgroups with different goals and lack of social contact (Cook & Hegtvedt, 1986). Although such barriers may have limited the effectiveness of many organized group efforts at promoting the Equal Rights Amendment to the U.S. Constitution and systematically eliminating wage discrimination in litigated cases (LaVan, Katz, Malloy, & Stonebraker, 1987), such groups have been extremely effective in bringing the relevant issues to public awareness. Indeed, cultivating such awareness may be of critical importance in triggering other types of responses.

What other reactions, besides social mobilization, may be likely in response to perceived inequitable payment? Martin (1981) suggested several possibilities. If people are optimistic about the chances of reducing payment inequities, they may respond by attempting to improve themselves (e.g., by seeking training and education) or their organization (e.g., by making suggestions). If they feel frustrated and pessimistic about redressing inequitable conditions, they may exhibit symptoms of stress (e.g., depression and substance abuse) and display their feelings of alienation destructively (e.g., through sabotage and vandalism). Despite considerable research demonstrating these responses (e.g., Crosby, 1984; Martin, 1981), no clear pattern of sex differences in type of reaction has emerged. These, of course, represent individual reactions to payment inequity, responses that are not likely to occur in the face of fraternal deprivation. Accordingly, the failure to find sex differences in individual responses to group-level inequities is not surprising.

It may be argued, however, that not all women know or care about social movements but instead focus on more immediate, proximal concerns: their own underpayment relative to men—a state that may be made salient to them through situational factors (e.g., a woman might find out that her equally qualified male counterpart doing the same job is more highly paid.) Again, in such instances, the data reveal a general reluctance for women to take action (Major & Deaux, 1982). Some insight into the underlying reasons why is provided by Cohen's (1986) analysis of power differences between parties in a social exchange. Specifically, he claimed that victims of inequity, because of their relatively lower resources, have little recourse but to succumb to the wishes of more powerful others, thereby perpetuating inequitable conditions. In these terms, men might be expected to attempt to convince women that existing wage discrimination conditions are actually quite reasonable. As Hogan and Emler (1981) explained, powerful parties are typically more concerned about defending their own advantaged position while keeping peace with the less powerful than they are about establishing justice. In their own highly paternalistic words, they "must keep peace among the flock they tend" (p. 129). Because one repeatedly hears claims that raising women's wages to establish payment equity would bring economic chaos that would actually harm women (e.g., Killingsworth, 1985), it is difficult to dismiss the possibility that such attempts by the more powerful to legitimize the status quo in the name of justice (disguised here as economic rationality) may be precisely the type of enforcement mechanism to which Hogan and Emler are referring.

Extending this reasoning, Cohen (1986) suggested that the power differences between people (such as the historical sex discrimination against women in organizations; Blau, 1984) may make the weaker parties (women, in this case) unwilling to take action in response to inequitable conditions. Specifically, he argued that implicit norms discourage disadvantaged persons from publicly expressing their anger, fearing that such a display would be misperceived as an improper and undue expression of self-interest. Moreover, disadvantaged parties may fear, on the basis of their past experiences, that their attempts to rectify injustices perpetrated by more powerful parties will be unsuccessful (Mikula, 1986). Similarly, Major (1989) also has claimed that women may refrain from attempting to redress inequities because they may fear that their chances of actually raising their pay are poor. It is possible that the tendency for women to be more concerned than men about others' feelings about them (Sampson, 1975; Watts, Messé, & Vallacher, 1982) and their history of being less powerful in social exchange settings (Major & Deaux, 1982) may combine to make women less publicly responsive to inequities than men. This, of course, serves to maintain the status quo, thereby tacitly legitimizing the inequities perpetrated by the more powerful. In short, women might fear that attempting to correct past wage inequities may be like trying to "fight city hall" (or at least, so may more powerful men attempt to convince them). Assuming the futility of such efforts, they may remain frustrated in silence, thereby only exacerbating an already inequitable condition. Responses to inequity that only serve to remind victimized parties of their plight without effectively redressing the underlying inequities are unlikely to occur (Walster et al., 1978).

To summarize, women may be unlikely to respond to payment inequities for several reasons. Most directly, their tendency to not feel deprived despite their objectively underpaid status may fail to prompt attempts to redress inequities. Pay inequities may be felt, however, especially at the group level. Such fraternal deprivation may be recognized for instigating group-level mobilization, as witnessed by the women's rights movement. Even individually experienced inequities, if perceived, may fail to elicit direct attempts at redress. This is primarily because of women's perceived powerlessness at being able to change the status quo. Thus far, comparable worth has been analyzed from a distributive justice perspective. As such, the focus has been on the perceived fairness of pay distributions between the sexes. Now, however, attention will be focused on the analysis of comparable worth from a procedural justice perspective, revealing that perceptions of pay equity extend beyond considerations of what pay distributions emerge to how such distributions are determined.

PROCEDURAL JUSTICE:
THE FAIRNESS OF PAY DETERMINATION POLICIES

The idea that justice requires consideration of how outcomes are determined independent of what those outcomes are is basic to the idea of procedural justice, defined as "the perceived fairness of the procedures used in making decisions" (Folger & Greenberg, 1985, p. 143). Procedural justice was introduced initially as a concept differentiating the degree of control disputants had in various dispute resolution procedures—termed *process control* (Thibaut & Walker, 1975). Research has shown that procedures granting disputants control over the process by which their cases were heard (e.g., opportunities to select the evidence to be presented) were believed to be fairer than those offering lower degrees of process control (for a review, see Lind & Tyler, 1988). Later research and theorizing broadened the conceptual base of procedural justice as well as its domains of application. In general social interaction, Leventhal and his associates (1980; Leventhal, Karuza, & Fry, 1980) have postulated that fair procedures for distributing rewards are ones that (a) apply allocation practices consistently, (b) minimize opportunities for self-interested decisions, (c) ensure the use of accurate information in decision making, (d) provide opportunities for decisions to be appealed and modified, (e) represent the concerns of all parties, and (f) are based on prevailing moral and ethical practices. Subsequent research has validated the existence of these elements of procedural justice as determinants of fairness in organizational settings (e.g., Greenberg, 1986a[6], 1986b[8]; Sheppard & Lewicki, 1987).

Given the growing interest in applying the concept of procedural justice to the field of human resources management (e.g., Dyer, 1989; Folger & Greenberg, 1985; Greenberg & Tyler, 1987; Newman & Milkovich, 1989), it is likely to become less accurate in the future to claim that the social justice approach to comparable worth "emphasize[s] exogenous criteria of worth rather than the process of wage determination" (Mahoney, 1983, p. 17). Indeed, Heneman (1985) has called for future research into how the design and administration of pay systems influences pay satisfaction. Expanding one's approach to social justice to include procedural justice is likely to provide insight into the concept of comparable worth. Questions of how payment distributions are derived are likely to have a profound effect on perceived fair payment independent of what those distributions are. Five particular organizational procedures—open pay systems, participatory pay plans, grievance resolution procedures, job evaluation techniques, and pay communication practices—hold especially interesting implications for the understanding of comparable worth.

Open Pay Systems

Open pay systems are compensation plans that provide employees with information about other employees' pay. Varying degrees of information about pay may be provided by different systems. These range along a continuum from those plans in which no information is shared, through those in which pay ranges and median pay levels are announced and those in which only the size of employees' pay raises are given, to those in which the pay of specific employees is provided (Burroughs, 1982).

Research has shown that openly sharing information about others' pay enhances pay satisfaction. Lawler (1965) found that managers in an organization that kept pay secret overestimated the salaries of their immediate subordinates and were more dissatisfied with their pay the more closely they believed their subordinates' pay approached their own. Employees of companies in which pay information was openly shared were found to be just as inaccurate in their judgments about others' pay as those employed in companies maintaining pay secrecy (Lawler, 1986). This same research, however, revealed that individuals working under open pay systems were more satisfied with their pay and their companies' pay systems than employees working under secretive pay systems. Supplementing this cross-sectional research is analogous longitudinal evidence. Specifically, a field experiment by Futrell (1978) compared the satisfaction levels of managers whose organizational units changed from a secret pay system to an open pay system. After 1 year in the open pay system, workers reported higher levels of pay satisfaction than they did before the change and also higher satisfaction than control group workers who encountered no change in their pay system. These studies clearly demonstrate workers' positive reactions to open pay systems.

Such findings are readily explainable from conceptualizations of procedural justice. Open pay systems give workers information about how others' pay decisions are made and reassure workers that the procedures are not being violated (Folger & Greenberg, 1985). Open pay systems assure workers of the existence of safeguards against abuses of power by decision makers, thereby increasing confidence that payment decisions will be consistent across cases and unbiased in implementation (Leventhal, 1980). It is almost as if a certain degree of assurance is provided that a management that "lives in a glass house" will refrain from "throwing stones." Survey research on pay satisfaction has implicitly supported this notion in reporting that satisfaction with pay is attributed to the inherent fairness of open compensation systems as least as much as it is to the pay distributions that result from those systems (Milkovich & Anderson, 1972). As such, it is not surprising to find increasing recognition of the idea that "perceptions about how pay is administered do appear to have a bearing on people's perceptions of pay satisfaction" (Heneman, 1985, p. 132).

It is not difficult to imagine how open pay systems might enhance the perceived fairness of pay from a comparable worth perspective. By making wages known to all, organizations may be inviting inspection of the wage differential between male and female employees. Being secretive about wages may lead women to suspect that they are being unfairly disadvantaged (Lawler, 1965). In contrast, open pay systems may be used to highlight an organization's efforts at promoting comparable worth. Whenever wage structures are altered, openly reporting salary information may be used to showcase evidence of reduced pay differentials—movement toward establishing comparable worth. In fact, the policy of ostensibly displaying wages may be itself understood as a gesture that the company has "nothing to hide." Secret pay structures may lead to questions regarding why the company is being secretive, questions that might sensitize employees to the possibility of unfair wage discrimination.

In addition to publicizing wages, it also may be a good idea for companies to share information about market surveys or job evaluation surveys that are used as the basis for justifying wage differentials. Openly shared information that explains the rationale for an organizational decision, showing that it was not made capriciously or maliciously, is likely to enhance perceptions of the fairness of the decision, hence its acceptance (Greenberg & Folger, 1983). As will be detailed later, explanations regarding how outcomes were determined may help ameliorate reactions to undesirable outcomes (Bies, 1987; Greenberg, 1990[5]).

In concluding this section, I suggest that open pay systems may be a useful way of subverting the disenchantment likely to arise from perceptions of unfavorable wage differentials (Ronan & Organt, 1973). Open pay systems may discourage persons inclined to administer discriminatory wages from doing so. As a result, employees may feel more confident that their pay is not discriminatory, thereby promoting pay satisfaction.

Participatory Pay Plans

In addition to compensation systems that openly share information about others' pay, plans that give workers input into determining their pay represent another class of procedures that may enhance perceptions of pay equity. Traditionally, employees believe that they exercise little influence in pay determination, although they desire to have greater control in this area (Renwick & Lawler, 1978).

Research has shown that the effectiveness of pay incentive plans is enhanced when workers help determine the way the plan is implemented. For example, Lawler and Hackman (1969) compared the attendance rates of three work groups that developed their own incentive plans for rewarding high performance with those of two similar work groups that had identical plans imposed on them. After 16 weeks of implementing the plans, they found a significant increase in the attendance rates only among groups for which the plans were participatively developed. One year later, in a follow-up study, Scheflen, Lawler, and Hackman (1971) found that the attendance rate remained high for the one participatory group in which the plan was continued but that it dropped below pretreatment levels in the two other participatory groups in which the plan was discontinued. Additional evidence by Jenkins and Lawler (1981) corroborates this finding. This study made post hoc comparisons of the job performance of two work groups—one whose members actively participated in the setting of their wage rates (i.e., they voted on the incentive plan to be used) and another whose members worked under a plan that was unilaterally imposed on them by management. Those employees who helped set their own wages were consistently more productive than those who had no such voice. The effectiveness of participation in pay determination (reviewed by Lawler, 1981) has been explained by the tendency for "members of the participative groups . . . to become more trusting of management's intentions to administer the plans fairly" (Lawler & Hackman, 1969, p. 471).

These studies illustrate a basic tenet of procedural justice: Voice in the development of an outcome (a pay plan, in this case) enhances the perceived fairness of that outcome independent of the effects of its implementation (for a review, see Lind & Tyler, 1988). In the case of the Lawler and Hackman studies, attendance rates appear to have improved because workers were involved in determining how the incentives were to be paid regardless of what those incentives were. Analogously, research in dispute resolution settings has shown that disputants are more satisfied with decisions they had a hand in making than identical decisions imposed on them by a third party (Musante, Gilbert, & Thibaut, 1983). The reason for such findings goes beyond that participation enhances opportunities to receive desired outcomes (which, of course, would not explain Lawler and Hackman's findings). Another analysis of similar evidence (Greenberg & Folger, 1983) argued that the selection of one's outcomes enhances commitment to those outcomes in an attempt to justify the choice made. Moreover, there is likely to be a spillover effect such that satisfaction with outcomes generalizes to satisfaction with a system (e.g., management) that allows and encourages such participatory practices. After all, as Jenkins and Lawler (1981) explained, such participation promotes trust between superiors and subordinates, furthering an atmosphere of cooperation that encourages employees to perform at a high level. It is not difficult to imagine that claims of payment inequity and unfair wage differentials between men and women may be reduced in systems that give workers a voice in determining their own pay. Indeed, Lawler (1981) cited several anecdotal examples of companies in which workers in participatory pay plans reported that such plans yielded perceptions of fair pay. Workers who are involved in the setting of their own wages are not only unlikely to settle for unfavorable wage differentials but also likely to have a better understanding and acceptance of any differentials that do result. Unfortunately, the absence of available evidence precludes a hypothesis of any sex differences in reactions to participatory pay plans. In fact, assuming that both men and women may be equally likely to benefit psychologically from such plans, there is hope—albeit as of yet undocumented—that such procedures may effectively promote perceptions of comparable worth.

A practical caveat to these remarks is that many companies may be unwilling to relinquish or even share control over pay determination decisions. Yet there may be several ways of approximating the expected beneficial effects of participatory pay plans. One way would be to involve employees in the process of evaluating the worth of jobs used to determine wages (Carey, 1977). In this connection, Milkovich and Newman (1987) noted that in some companies, "employees may be asked to sign off on the analyses of their jobs, they may serve on compensation task forces that select compensable factors, and they may indicate which employees they feel should be included in pay surveys" (pp. 551-552). Such practices may represent an indirect, secondary form of participation that provides employees with opportunities to safeguard against unfair wage differentials.

Second, even companies that may be reluctant to give employees any voice in pay determination may be willing to give them a choice of desired fringe benefits. Programs that do so, known as cafeteria-style benefit plans, have been recognized for their value in promoting procedural justice (Folger & Greenberg, 1985; Greenberg & Folger, 1983). In particular, the process of allowing employees to select their own fringe benefits gives them such a direct opportunity to control their outcomes that it may be viewed as a particularly fair procedure. Indeed, research has shown that procedures that enhance opportunities to avoid undesirable outcomes are perceived to be fair and enhance job satisfaction (Greenberg, 1987a[14]). In assessments of comparable worth, procedures allowing even limited choice over outcomes may effectively reduce perceptions of payment inequities by allowing employees to tailor their total outcomes so that they are positively valent to themselves (Hollenbeck et al., 1987).

In summary, allowing employees to participate in the setting of their own wages may be an effective means of promoting their belief in the fairness of those wages. Such participation not only may enhance the chances of receiving desired outcomes (particularly in the case of procedures providing direct choice, such as cafeteria-style benefit plans) but also may promote a highly cooperative and trusting atmosphere that enhances overall job satisfaction.

Grievance Resolution Procedures

As noted earlier, one of Leventhal's (1980; Leventhal et al., 1980) criteria for procedural justice is that the procedure used provides opportunities for decisions to be appealed and modified. An open-ended questionnaire study (Greenberg, 1986a[6]) found that employees cited this factor as one determinant of what constituted a fair performance appraisal. Research on formal dispute resolution procedures also has recognized the importance of opportunities to appeal judicial decisions that are believed to be unfair (Lind & Tyler, 1988). Similarly, in industry, collective bargaining agreements between unions and management typically provide some opportunity for the redress of grievances (Aram & Salipante, 1981; Boisseau & Caras, 1983). Together, such mechanisms have been recognized with respect to their enhancement of procedural justice (Folger & Greenberg, 1985; Milkovich & Newman, 1987); procedures that allow wrongs to be corrected are perceived as fair.

How may formal procedures for resolving grievances in organizations help safeguard against wage discrimination on the basis of sex (or race, or any other factor)? One suggestion is that the availability of such mechanisms may help ensure that existing organizational policies for pay determination will be applied equally to all employees (i.e., Leventhal's consistent application of standards criterion). Thus, unless the practice of discriminating against women is formally incorporated into organizational policies, employees who feel they have been victims of discrimination may use their companies' due process mechanisms to seek redress. Of course, such procedures are more likely to be useful in instances of individualized violation of corporate fair pay practices (e.g., discrimination by one particular manager) than they are for normatively institutionalized discrimination (e.g., veiled corporate policies undervaluing the work of women). The availability of mechanisms for hearing charges of pay inequities may remove psychological barriers against responding to inequities predicated on the belief that such resolution attempts will be ineffective (Cohen, 1986). This is especially applicable whenever local norms encourage rather than discourage the use of such vehicles. In this regard, merely having formal grievance resolution mechanisms in place and having a culture that supports their use are two distinct things. In fact, believing that one is discouraged from actually using formal grievance procedures that are in place (such as local norms that label grievants as troublemakers) might do more harm than good when taking into account the frustration that is likely to be created by dashing hopes of effectively being able to eliminate pay discrimination (Greenberg & Folger, 1983).

In a related manner, the availability of grievance resolution procedures may dissuade individuals tempted to discriminate against women in determining wages. As such, they may be recognized as mechanisms of equity enforcement. Knowing that wage decisions perceived as discriminatory may be appealed may discourage individuals from promoting discriminatory ends. In fact, managers repeatedly charged with attempting to discriminate against women in corporate grievance resolution procedures may pay the high price of gaining a reputation as unfair (Greenberg, 1990[5]). Given the potential costs of such an unfavorable attributional label, individuals predisposed to promote discriminatory wages may refrain from doing so to the extent that avenues for correcting these decisions exist as a viable option for aggrieved parties. Of course, in the absence of direct evidence regarding the deterrent value of fears of developing a reputation for unfairness (Greenberg, 1990[5]), such a possibility must be considered tentative.

Job Evaluation Techniques

By synthesizing previous definitions, Milkovich and Newman (1987) have defined a job evaluation as "a systematic procedure designed to aid in establishing pay differentials among jobs within a single employer" (p. 106). Among the several long-recognized purposes of this practice is that of establishing a standard of pay equity (Gombert, 1955). Indeed, Remick (1984) has argued that attempts to operationally define comparable worth are closely linked to the nature of the job evaluation systems used. This chapter previously noted that attempts to establish comparable worth by relying on job evaluation techniques are likely to be flawed because the techniques simply may reflect society's biases about the lower value of women's work compared with men's (Grams & Schwab, 1985). This is not to deny that some elements of the job evaluation process might be useful in enhancing the perceived fairness of the pay systems to which they are applied. In fact, several features of the job evaluation process may be recognized for their incorporation of procedurally fair properties.

Most basic is merely that job evaluation techniques represent an attempt to establish wages on the basis of some a priori, standardized set of criteria (for an overview of such techniques, see Milkovich & Newman, 1987). From the perspective of procedural justice, the existence of standardized procedures for determining outcomes (be they legal regulations governing courtroom procedures or organizational policies dictating the use of certain job evaluation techniques) is necessary to promote the belief that the resulting outcome is unbiased. Thus, just as a legal system whose rules of jurisprudence change from case to case may be considered unfair (Lind & Tyler, 1988; Thibaut & Walker 1975), so too may an organization whose pay system appears to be inconsistent and capricious. The mere existence of a standardized procedure contributes to the attainment of procedural justice—albeit as a necessary, but not a sufficient, criterion. Obviously, more is involved than the mere consistent application of standards.

A widely recognized desideratum of job evaluation plans is that they are acceptable to all parties involved (Nash & Carroll, 1975). One mechanism for achieving this is simply polling employees at all organizational levels with respect to what they believe are the factors worthy of compensation—a technique often used in conjunction with the point system of job evaluation (Belcher, 1974). A more elaborate variant of this technique is the practice of forming compensation committees that include incumbent employees from a variety of different organizational positions, in addition to managers and compensation professionals (Carey, 1977). Including female employees on these panels, especially those performing jobs held primarily by women, may reduce bias in job evaluation plans (Thomsen, 1978). The decisions made by these panels may range from being merely advisory to central decision-making power to being required before change can be made. Such employee participation in the making of compensation decisions has been recognized by Lawler (1986) as a prime determinant of organizational trust, commitment, and perceived fair pay.

The rationale for involving employees in the process of pay determination is also supported by research and theory on procedural justice. Specifically, one of the best-established findings of this literature is that outcomes—even undesirable ones—are more likely to be accepted as fair when those affected by them have had a voice in bringing them about than when identical outcomes result from nonvoice procedures (for a review, see Greenberg & Folger, 1983; Lind & Tyler, 1988). Such an effect—dubbed the "fair process effect" (Greenberg & Folger, 1983)—has been found to occur in contexts as widespread as leadership endorsement (Tyler & Caine, 1981), performance appraisal (Greenberg, 1986a[6], 1986b[8]), and encounters with the court system (Tyler, 1984), among others (Lind & Tyler, 1988). With relevance to the focus of this chapter, Lawler and Hackman (1969) reported significant improvements in turnover and job satisfaction among workers whose pay was determined by a committee of employees and managers compared with those who had no such voice in determining their own pay.

Several processes appear to account for the fair process effect (see Greenberg & Folger, 1983), thereby explaining the benefits likely to arise from involving employees in job evaluation. For one, participation is likely to expose employees to a broader range of information than they would be likely to encounter had they not been involved in decision making. Providing such information (i.e., giving employees "the big picture") might alter one's perspective on fairness by discouraging the self-serving perceptions that are likely to arise whenever highly limited information (e.g., information about oneself) is available (Greenberg, 1990[5]). Second, people have a tendency to rationalize as acceptable those outcomes they receive as a result of their considerable investment in attaining (e.g., such as by publicly demonstrating their support for them) (Greenberg & Folger, 1983). Third, the opportunity to express voice in a system may be recognized by employees as a display of faith and trust in them. In turn, employees may experience satisfaction with organizations that communicate such goodwill, attributing fairness to them (Greenberg, 1990[5]). Together, these theoretical possibilities support one of Lind and Tyler's (1988) key conclusions from the procedural justice literature: "The opportunity to express one's views enhances procedural justice judgments in and of itself" (p. 215). As such, employee participation in job evaluation techniques is expected to promote positive reactions to the resulting pay plans and the organizations using them.

Yet another aspect of job evaluation plans may be understood from the perspective of procedural justice, that is, opportunities to appeal or review decisions. As Milkovich and Newman (1987) advise, "a procedure for review should be developed and included in the [job evaluation] manual to help ensure that employees can voice their questions and disagreements" (p. 158). Such procedures are consistent with Leventhal's (1980) claim that procedural fairness requires that opportunities exist for decisions to be appealed and modified. In the context of performance appraisal, I found that workers reported opportunities to review and correct the evaluations they received as an important determinant of the fairness of their evaluation (Greenberg, 1986a[6]). Because no analogous evidence is available in the context of job evaluation plans, it can be hypothesized only by extrapolation that opportunities to revise and/or correct job evaluation information will enhance perceptions of pay fairness.

Two important aspects of such appeals procedures deserve mention. First, their very existence may preclude their use. Thus, to the extent that making such mechanisms available raises employees' pay satisfaction, the use of mechanisms that may alter these outcomes is unlikely (Greenberg, 1987a[14]). Second, whenever such mechanisms are employed, a potential cost is involved: They raise the expectations of employees who use them, thereby exacerbating the dissatisfaction of those whose appeals are rejected (adding insult to injury). In fact, research has shown that raising and then dashing the hopes of people seeking redress from perceived unfair procedures may lower their satisfaction below the low levels that initially inspired their attempts at redress—a phenomenon called the "frustration effect" (Greenberg & Folger, 1983). Such frustration may be avoided by providing assurances that the appeals were carefully and impartially considered and not merely rejected capriciously. (Folger & Greenberg, 1985, have recommended similar practices in other human resources management contexts.) With this concern in mind, Milkovich and Newman (1987) have cautioned as follows:

> Employers who open the appeals process to all employees theorize that jobholders are the ones most familiar with the work performed and the most sensitive to significant changes or misrepresentations. No matter what the outcome from the appeal, the results need to be explained in detail to anyone who requests reevaluation. (p. 165)

In sum, theory and research on procedural justice support the practices of involving workers from a variety of different organizational positions into the job evaluation process and providing opportunities to appeal and review job evaluations. In fact, although little available evi-dence directly assesses reactions to these practices, extrapolations from procedural jus-tice evidence collected in other domains (for a review, see Lind & Tyler, 1988) strongly underscore the likely benefits to be derived from these practices. Thus, once again, the procedural justice literature provides some compelling hypotheses in need of future research.

Pay Communication Practices

Thus far, this chapter has discussed formal organizational procedures that influence perceptions of pay fairness—a perspective in keeping with current trends in human resources management (e.g., Dyer, 1989; Newman & Milkovich, 1989). It would be misleading, however, to con-clude that only formal organizational procedures influence reactions to pay. Recent research and theorizing (Bies, 1987; Greenberg, 1990[5]) suggest that informal interpersonal communication also may be quite important in determining perceptions of fairness.[5] In fact, it may be argued that the way information about pay is communicated from supe-riors to their subordinates greatly influences assessments of pay fairness. What information is given about how pay is determined? What explana-tions are given about the procedures used to arrive at pay decisions? The way a superior completes the phrase, "Your pay will be $X because . . ." may greatly influence subordinates' reactions to their pay of $X. Moreover, such explanations may be critical to perceptions of comparable worth. Little has been written about the effects of explanations about pay on reactions to pay. Although some practitioners (e.g., Chauran, 1989; McMillan & Williams, 1982) have encouraged supervisors to explain the basis of pay determination to their subordinates, no direct research support for this advice can be found in the literature. Compensation texts (e.g., Milkovich & Newman, 1987) discuss the merits of openly describing what others' pay wages are but say little if anything about the idea of communicating how and why pay was determined. The closest appears to be management by objectives (MBO) programs, in which employees learn that the pay they receive is based on the extent to which they achieved mutually agreed-on performance goals (Mali, 1972). In such cases, pay expectations take the general form, "You will get paid $X because you achieved the established performance goal." As such, the explanations given are simply contractual in nature: "We agreed, and so by giving you this amount, I am meeting my obligation." Outside MBO programs, however, the rationale for pay determination may not be made explicit (see also Heneman, 1990).

This is likely to be the case because typically no formal organizational vehicles are available to structure interactions between superiors and subordinates in a manner that prompts such explanations. In contrast, explanations underlying performance appraisal ratings are often prompted by lines on rating forms asking for explanations. A previous study (Greenberg, 1988b) found that 90% of the explanations given for job performance fell into four categories: performance-based (how well the person performed), ideological (appeals to superordinate goals), referent (comparisons with others), and apology (expressions of remorse). This study found that giving an explanation for performance enhanced recipients' perceptions of the fairness of the ratings they received. Thus, evaluations that were explained (by any means) were recognized as fairer than those that were not explained.

Might explanations for pay determination similarly enhance acceptance of pay? Despite the lack of evidence bearing directly on this question, extrapolating from recent research and theorizing provides some important insight into this question. Notably, in a recent conceptual paper (Greenberg, 1990[5]), I have argued that it is beneficial to conceive of fairness as the result of an impression management process. In the face of ambiguity regarding any objective standards of justice, what appears to be fair is often what is presented to one as such. Indeed, managers have been found to express interest in convincing their subordinates of the fairness of their actions (Greenberg, 1988a[4]). Applying this perspective to comparable worth results in a most intriguing possibility: By virtue of the information that is selectively presented to employees, they may come to believe that their organizations' wage policies are fair. As previously detailed (Greenberg, 1990[5]), the mechanisms for cultivating such impressions of fairness are both defensive and assertive in nature. People are interested in both eliminating others' impressions that they behaved unfairly (e.g., in this case, that they really did not follow discriminatory pay policies) and creating the impression that they behaved fairly (e.g., in this case, that they distributed pay in an unbiased fashion). Some of the research inspired by this approach may be fruitfully applied to the understanding of comparable worth.

To defend against claims that one has acted unfairly, it is possible to rely on two types of social accounts—excuses (attempts to minimize the apparent unfairness of a situation) and justifications (attempts to minimize the apparent harm caused by an injustice) (Schlenker, 1980). Research by Bies and his associates (reviewed by Bies, 1987) has shown that excuses in the form of mitigating circumstances (i.e., events that lessen one's responsibility for an undesirable outcome) are frequently used to eliminate the negative impact of one's actions. In particular, in content analyzing workers' retrospective accounts of various requests denied by their bosses, Bies, Shapiro, and Cummings (1988) found that six types of mitigating circumstances were used. In order from most frequently cited to least frequently cited, these were workers' own behavior (e.g., incompetence), budgetary constraints, controls imposed by higher management, political limitations, restrictions due to formal company policies, and inconsistencies with company norms. In a series of laboratory studies, Bies and Shapiro (1987, Studies 1 and 2; 1988, Study 1) examined how claims of mitigating circumstances (e.g., an economic depression) influenced reactions to unfavorable organizational events (e.g., budget cutbacks). They repeatedly found that such accounts reduced people's feelings of unfair treatment relative to those encountering the same outcomes without any accompanying account. Follow-up research also has found that claims of mitigating circumstances enhanced perceptions of the fairness of a variety of other organizational outcomes, including rejection of employment applications (Bies & Moag, 1986), rejection of proposals for funding (Bies & Shapiro, 1987, Study 3; 1988, Study 2), and layoffs (Brockner & Greenberg, 1990). To elaborate on this, further evidence suggests that not all explanations are believed to ameliorate reactions to negative outcomes. Excuses that are most effective are ones that are perceived as logical (i.e., based on relevant information) and sincere (Bies et al., 1988; Shapiro & Buttner, 1988). Indeed, explanations for organizational events that are believed to be ingenuine and manipulative in intent may backfire, leading to hostile reactions (Greenberg & Ornstein, 1983[17]; Liden & Mitchell, 1988). Together, such evidence suggests that accounts of mitigating circumstances believed to be genuine discourage persons disappointed by managerial actions from attributing malevolent motives to the actor, thereby facilitating acceptance of the outcomes.

In regard to comparable worth, it may be expected that accounts of mitigating circumstances may be used to excuse wage discrimination in organizations. For example, managers may claim that they were required to enforce their companies' policies of paying certain wages for certain jobs: "I agree that it may be unfair for you to not get paid more, but my hands are tied by company policy." Given that most managers probably cannot completely determine their subordinates' pay, such claims of mitigating circumstances may be accepted, thereby excusing them, separating themselves from the harm caused by their actions. So long as employees understand that managers who make payment decisions may have to act within a set of guidelines that precludes their redressing an institutionalized pattern of wage discrimination, explanations to this effect may be perceived as sincere, thereby excusing their managers' actions. This tactic may be used effectively by managers to combat beliefs that they acted improperly, beliefs that could eventually erode their power base (Greenberg, 1990[5]). Such a defensive act may be politically astute because it discourages others from attributing illegitimate motives to the actor (Moberg, 1977). Of course, such claims may be made effectively only by persons who are actually innocent of the undesirable discriminatory attribution. Although those who are actually responsible for perpetuating discriminatory actions may attempt to introduce their own claims of mitigating circumstances (e.g., "industrywide market conditions force us to pay these wages"), these will fail to be effective if victims believe that they were ingenuine (Greenberg & Ornstein, 1983[17]).

Another way of attempting to defend against claims of unfair discrimination is by offering justifications—explanations that "things are not so bad." Schlenker (1980) noted that one way of doing this is by attempting to change the basis of one's social comparisons. In this regard, Bies (1986) found that people who had proposals rejected by their bosses were more likely to accept these actions as fair to the extent that they had some hope of having them accepted in the future. Similarly, Folger (1986) has shown that persons who believe the negative outcomes they are experiencing could have been worse were more accepting of the procedural changes that brought about those outcomes than others who were not led to have such beliefs. In the context of comparable worth, these findings suggest that persons responsible for explaining others' pay may attempt to explain that things could be worse but that they might improve in the future. Indeed, managers who point to improvement trends (noting that things were worse in the past than they are now and are projected to continue improving in the future) may be recognized as employing such a strategy.

Justification of undesirable outcomes also may be accomplished by appealing to superordinate goals, such as higher authorities, ideologies, and the like (Bies, 1987; Greenberg, 1990[5]; Schlenker, 1980). For example, I (Greenberg, 1988b) found that appeals to ideology were used among managers explaining their subordinates' low performance ratings (e.g., "this rating is good for you; it'll show you there's room for improvement"). Managers also may make some appropriate appeal to superordinate goals when attempting to justify discriminatory wage practices. For example, low wages may be justified as an economic necessity, a move that may discourage other undesirable outcomes, such as laying off workers (Brockner & Greenberg, 1990). By reframing such undesirable outcomes with loftier considerations, superiors may be attempting to ameliorate their subordinates' discontent.

In addition to attempting to excuse and/or justify undesirable outcomes, it is also possible to defend against them by apologizing. Indeed, I found that apologies were the most frequently used category of explanation given to accompany poor performance ratings (Greenberg, 1988b). Although research has shown that expressions of remorse might discourage victims from seeking retaliation against their apologetic harm doers (O'Malley & Greenberg, 1983), it is suspected that apologies alone may be ineffective to ameliorate negative reactions to discriminatory wage practices. In fact, because expressions of apology require acknowledgments of guilt (Goffman, 1959), they actually may exacerbate feelings of injustice. Whether or not this occurs is likely to depend in great part on the harm doer's expressed intent to undo the harm. Thus, if a company president were to accompany his or her expression of remorse with an acceptable plan for remedying past misdeeds, the apology would likely be well accepted. An expression of remorse alone, however, without a viable plan for improving existing unfair conditions, would probably be seen as adding insult to injury, aggravating existing conditions. In fact, one must wonder whether the perceived "hollow apologies" of insincere politicians may be taken as an example of such a tactic in action (Greenberg, 1990[5]).

Although thus far the focus has been on actions that may be taken to defend against perceptions of unfair behavior, it is critical to note that people also may proactively ensure that others are aware of their fair actions. Although several techniques may be used in this regard (Greenberg, 1990[5]), most relevant to the current theme is the technique known as enhancements—attempts to augment the positive impressions created by one's actions (Schlenker, 1980). I have argued that managers may attempt to promote themselves as fair by taking advantage of inherently ambiguous conditions regarding what constitutes fair actions (Greenberg, 1990[5]). Hence, they may attempt to "negotiate" an identify of themselves as fair by selectively presenting information about themselves that supports their desired image—a popularly used technique among organizational politicians (Allen, Madison, Porter, Renwick, & Mayes, 1979). The idea that this technique is also used at the organizational level is suggested by Thompson (1967) in his discussion of prospective rationality: "Organizations act rationally to increase their evaluations or ratings by others on whom they are dependent" (p. 65). With respect to the dissemination of pay information, anecdotal evidence exists that some organizations demonstrate such rationality by attempting to position themselves as fair with respect to their pay policies (Greenberg, 1990[5]). In fact, claims that a company is an equal opportunity employer (appearing in corporate literature such as advertisements, letterheads, etc.) may be interpreted as an effort in this regard. To the extent that they are supported by information accepted by the affected parties, such self-promoted claims of fairness may be an effective means of employee recruitment (Greenberg, 1990[5])—attracting good employees with socially responsible behavior (Etzioni, 1988). Having a reputation as an equal opportunity employer also may help retain current employees by discouraging them from interpreting the pay they receive as unfairly discriminatory. Of course, such self-labeling as fair by an organization may sensitize its employees, raising their expectations of fair treatment with respect to wages. Should employees suspect that such claims are not well-founded, they may arouse considerably more inequity distress than would likely have resulted had expectations of fair treatment not been elevated by enhancing corporate tactics (Greenberg, 1990[5]). Thus, enhancing activities may be recognized as a double-edged sword: To the extent that they are accepted, they may effectively enhance an organization's reputation as a fair employer; to the extent that they are challenged, they may do more harm than good.

At this point, it may be useful to comment on the seemingly manipulative nature of the activities described in the preceding paragraphs. Although it cannot be denied that some efforts at defending oneself against claims of perceived unfair actions may be deceitful, it would be erroneous to think of all such efforts as consciously duplicitous. Some justifications and excuses may be quite sincere, and the information presented may accurately represent the world as the speaker perceives it (Greenberg, 1990[5]). Because different persons have different information about exactly what is going on in an organization (thus, different ideas about what may constitute fair treatment), verbal claims about what is fair might not necessarily represent intentional dishonesty. Thus, claims by many managers with respect to their helplessness in affecting change in response to discriminatory wage structures may be in principle just as likely true as false. The present description of how people may defend against claims of unfair discrimination or how they may ensure credit for their fair wage policies makes it clear that more research is needed on this topic. What defensive or assertive tactics are used in connection with explaining wages? When, and by whom, are defensive or assertive mechanisms used? These are just a few of the most basic, and extremely important, questions that arise from considering comparable worth from the perspective outlined here.

In summary, an important consideration in assessing the fairness of a pay plan is information presented about that plan. Social accounts (excuses and justifications) and apologies may be used to defend against claims of unfair wage discrimination. In contrast, attempts to enhance the perceived fairness of an organization's fair wage policies may take the form of assertively self-promoting the company as a fair place to work. Together, these communicative techniques may be recognized as informal procedures for promoting perceptions of fair payment. Such practices are likely to operate in conjunction with more formal mechanisms, such as open pay systems, participatory pay plans, grievance resolution procedures, and pay evaluation techniques, to enhance the perceived fairness of pay.

CONCLUSION

The ideas advanced in this chapter represent the skeleton of a framework that uses social justice research and theory (for a review, see Greenberg, 1987b[1]) to examine the construct of comparable worth. Such analyses have implications both for the theoretical status of comparable worth and for the constructs of social justice applied to it.

Notably, the intrapsychic nature of equity theory underscores the point that an understanding of comparable worth requires greater attention to individual perceptions of fairness than has been seen to date. So long as people believe it is fair to compensate employees more generously just for being men (whether or not they admit it), it may be difficult to achieve comparable worth through legal channels. Indeed, one may interpret difficulties in enforcing and enacting comparable worth laws (LaVan et al., 1987; Williams & McDowell, 1980) with traditions of prevailing attitudes regarding the worth of men's work relative to women's work. As such, the time may have come for social scientists to expand and refocus their interest in comparable worth from an economic and a legal issue to a social-psychological issue.

Such a reorientation also may help stimulate a resurgence of interest in equity theory by introducing a rich new domain to which it may be applied. The issue of comparable worth represents a potentially fertile field for studying relevant theoretical issues, such as the likely nonindependence of inputs and impediments to ostensibly displaying reactions to perceived inequities, among others. Recent waning interest in equity theory has been attributed to the limited contexts to which it has been applied (Greenberg, 1987b[1]). On the basis of this chapter's analyses, it is plausible that research testing equity theory predictions regarding perceptions of and reactions to comparable worth may help revitalize the heuristic power of this well-known theory of social justice.

The present analysis also brings to awareness the need to examine the perceived fairness of payment distribution procedures independent of the effects of the resulting distributions themselves. This remains an underresearched topic but one with great importance to the field of pay satisfaction (Heneman, 1985). As researchers begin to expand the domain of procedural justice research to a vast majority of organizational phenomena (e.g., see Folger & Greenberg, 1985; Greenberg, 1986b[8]; Greenberg & Tyler, 1987), the stage is set for an understanding of this issue to emerge. Such efforts would not only qualify knowledge of the effect of payment distribution systems themselves but also allow procedural justice theorists to assess the generalizability of their theoretical constructs in a valuable, yet previously untested, domain. Moreover, the concept of procedural justice provides the most promising approach to date toward understanding the role of how payments are determined and communicated to employees and their reactions to those payments. Such an issue is critical to understanding the concept of comparable worth. In conclusion, as Mahoney (1987) observed, "What makes comparable worth such a fascinating topic is that it truly lies at the intersection of so many related disciplines" (p. 211). The field of social justice is one discipline that provides a particularly rich opportunity for insight into the topic of comparable worth. It is hoped that this chapter has also convinced others of its benefit as an approach worthy of future consideration.

NOTES

1. As noted by Mahoney (1983, 1987), the terms *comparable worth* and *pay equity* tend to be used interchangeably. Although both terms are used in this chapter, the term *comparable worth*

is favored to avoid confusing the term *pay equity* with more specific concepts, such as equity theory (Adams, 1965) and the equity norm of reward allocation (Deutsch, 1985; Leventhal, 1976). Elsewhere, shifts have occurred in the relative popularity of the terms, with *comparable worth* giving way to *pay equity* in recent years. Such changes reflect attempts (a) to refocus attention from comparable worth as an "issue of the '80s" to pay equity as "the solution of the '90s" (Patten, 1988, p. 15) and (b) to gain popular support for comparable worth by giving it a new name—after all, "Who could be against pay equity?" (Milkovich & Newman, 1987, p. 510). Because this chapter is not motivated by such marketing concerns, the use of the term *equity* is more narrowly limited to avoid the common tendency to call on equity theory as the only explanatory mechanism of social justice suitable for analyzing comparable worth (Greenberg, 1987b[1]).

2. Some, in fact, trace the earnings gap between the sexes to the following quote from the Bible: "And the Lord spoke to Moses. . . . Thy valuation for the male from twenty years old even unto sixty years old . . . shall be fifty shekels of silver. . . . And if it be a female, then thy valuation shall be thirty shekels" (Leviticus 27:1-4).

3. Relative deprivation theory has been categorized as similar to equity theory in its emphasis on reactions to outcome distributions (Greenberg, 1987b[1]). Because of its more explicit focus on the choice of a comparison standard, however, relative deprivation theory will be used as the primary theoretical vehicle for examining the issues addressed here. (For summary comparisons of both approaches, see Crosby & Gonzalez-Intal, 1984; Martin & Murray, 1983.)

4. For a review and analysis of the role of the self as a standard in making equity judgments, the reader is referred to treatments of this topic by Wegner (1982) and by me (Greenberg, 1990[5]).

5. Bies (1987; Bies & Moag, 1986) has referred to such an approach as interactional justice—the fairness of the interpersonal treatment received in connection with outcome distributions. Because informal communication about outcomes may be recognized as procedures themselves (i.e., what is said regarding a payment distribution, as opposed to the distribution itself), however, treatment of this topic has been incorporated into the section on procedural justice.

REFERENCES

Aaron, H. J., & Lougy, C. M. (1986). *The comparable worth controversy*. Washington, DC: Brookings Institution.

Adams, J. S. (1965). Inequity in social exchange. In L. Berkowitz (Ed.), *Advances in experimental social psychology* (Vol. 2, pp. 267-299). New York: Academic Press.

Allen, R. W., Madison, D. L., Porter, L. W., Renwick, P. A., & Mayes, B. T. (1979). Organizational politics: Tactics and characteristics of its actors. *California Management Review, 22,* 77-83.

Aram, J. D., & Salipante, P. F., Jr. (1981). An evaluation of organizational due process in the resolution of employee/employer conflict. *Academy of Management Review, 6,* 197-204.

Becker, G. S. (1964). *Human capital*. New York: National Bureau of Economic Research.

Belcher, D. W. (1974). *Compensation administration*. Englewood Cliffs, NJ: Prentice Hall.

Berger, B. (1984). Statement to U.S. Commission on Civil Rights. In *U.S. Commission on Civil Rights: Comparable worth issues for the '80s* (Vol. 2, pp. 26-28). Washington, DC: U.S. Commission on Civil Rights.

Bergmann, B. R. (1974, April-July). Occupational segregation, wages and profits when employees discriminate by race or sex. *Eastern Economic Journal, 1,* 103-110.

Bergmann, B. R. (1985, November). Pay equity: How to argue back. *Ms.*, p. 112.

Bielby, W. T., & Baron, J. N. (1984). A woman's place is with other women: Sex segregation within organizations. In B. F. Reskin (Ed.), *Sex segregation in the workplace: Trends, explanations, remedies* (pp. 27-55). Washington, DC: National Academy Press.

Bies, R. J. (1986). *The delivery of bad news in organizations: Strategies and tactics.* Unpublished manuscript, Northwestern University, Evanston, IL.

Bies, R. J. (1987). The predicament of injustice: The management of moral outrage. In L. L. Cummings & B. M. Staw (Eds.), *Research in organizational behavior* (Vol. 9, pp. 289-319). Greenwich, CT: JAI.

Bies, R. J., & Moag, J. S. (1986). Interactional justice: Communications criteria of fairness. In R. J. Lewicki, B. H. Sheppard, & M. H. Bazerman (Eds.), *Research on negotiation in organizations* (Vol. 1, pp. 43-55). Greenwich, CT: JAI.

Bies, R. J., & Shapiro, D. L. (1987). Interactional fairness judgments: The influence of causal accounts. *Social Justice Research, 1,* 199-218.

Bies, R. J., & Shapiro, D. L. (1988). Voice and justification: Their influence on procedural fairness judgments. *Academy of Management Journal, 31,* 676-685.

Bies, R. J., Shapiro, D. L., & Cummings, L. L. (1988). Causal accounts and managing organizational conflict: Is it enough to say it's not my fault? *Communication Research, 15,* 381-399.

Blau, F. D. (1984). Occupational segregation and labor market discrimination. In B. F. Reskin (Ed.), *Sex segregation in the workplace: Trends, explanations, remedies* (pp. 117-143). Washington, DC: National Academy Press.

Blumrosen, R. G. (1980). Wage discrimination, job segregation, and women workers. *Employee Relations Law Journal, 6,* 77-136.

Boisseau, R. T., & Caras, H. (1983, October). A radical experiment cuts deep into the attractiveness of unions. *Personnel Administrator,* 76-79.

Brickman, P., & Bulman, R. J. (1977). Pleasure and pain in social comparison. In J. M. Suls & R. L. Miller (Eds.), *Social comparison processes: Theoretical and empirical perspectives* (pp. 149-186). Washington, DC: Hemisphere.

Brockner, J., & Adsit, L. (1986). The moderating impact of sex on the equity-satisfaction relationship: A field study. *Journal of Applied Psychology, 71,* 585-590.

Brockner, J., & Greenberg, J. (1990). The impact of layoffs on survivors: Insights from procedural and distributive justice. In J. Carroll (Ed.), *Applied social psychology and organizational settings* (pp. 45-75). Hillsdale, NJ: Lawrence Erlbaum.

Burroughs, J. D. (1982). Pay secrecy and performance: The psychological research. *Compensation and Benefits Review, 14,* 44-54.

Buttner, E. H., & Rosen, B. (1987). The effects of labor shortages on starting salaries for sex-typed jobs. *Sex Roles, 17,* 59-71.

Callahan-Levy, C. M., & Messé, L. A. (1979). Sex differences in the allocation of pay. *Journal of Personality and Social Psychology, 37,* 433-446.

Carey, J. F. (1977). Participative job evaluation. *Compensation and Benefits Review, 9,* 29-38.

Chafe, W. H. (1977). *Women and equality: Changing patterns in American culture.* New York: Oxford University Press.

Chauran, T. (1989, January). Benefits communication. *Personnel Journal,* pp. 70-77.

Cohen, R. L. (1986). Power and justice in intergroup relations. In H. W. Bierhoff, R. L. Cohen, & J. Greenberg (Eds.), *Justice in social relations* (pp. 65-84). New York: Plenum.

Cook, K. S., & Hegtvedt, K. A. (1986). Justice and power: An exchange analysis. In H. W. Bierhoff, R. L. Cohen, & J. Greenberg (Eds.), *Justice in social relations* (pp. 19-41). New York: Plenum.

Corcoran, M. (1979). Work experience, labor force withdrawals, and women's earnings: Empirical results using the 1976 panel study of income dynamics. In C. B. Lloyd, E. Andrews, & C. L. Gilroy (Eds.), *Women in the labor market* (pp. 57-83). New York: Columbia University Press.

Crosby, F. (1982). *Relative deprivation and working women.* New York: Oxford University Press.

Crosby, F. (1984). Relative deprivation in organizational settings. In B. M. Staw & L. L. Cummings (Eds.), *Research in organizational behavior* (Vol. 6, pp. 51-93). Greenwich, CT: JAI.

Crosby, F., & Gonzalez-Intal, M. (1984). Relative deprivation and equity theories: Felt injustice and undeserved benefits of others. In R. Folger (Ed.), *The sense of injustice* (pp. 141-166). New York: Plenum.

Cuddy, R. W. (1984, January/February). Worthy adversaries. *Management Focus*, pp. 31-38.

Deaux, K. (1976). *The behavior of women and men.* Monterey, CA: Brooks/Cole.

Deaux, K. (1984). From individual differences to social categories: Analysis of a decade's research on gender. *American Psychologist, 39,* 105-116.

Deaux, K., & Farris, E. (1977). Attributing causes for one's own performance: The effects of sex, norms and outcome. *Journal of Research in Personality, 11,* 59-72.

Deutsch, M. (1985). *Distributive justice: A social-psychological perspective.* New Haven, CT: Yale University Press.

Dion, K. L. (1986). Responses to perceived discrimination and relative deprivation. In J. M. Olsen, C. P. Herman, & M. P. Zanna (Eds.), *Relative deprivation and social comparison: The Ontario Symposium* (Vol. 4, pp. 159-180). Hillsdale, NJ: Lawrence Erlbaum.

Dipboye, R. L., Arvey, R. D., & Terpstra, D. E. (1977). Sex and physical attractiveness of raters and applicants as determinants of resume evaluations. *Journal of Applied Psychology, 62,* 288-294.

Donnerstein, M. (1988). Pay equity evaluations of occupations and their bases. *Journal of Applied Social Psychology, 18,* 905-924.

Dreher, G. F. (1981). Predicting the pay satisfaction of exempt employees. *Personnel Psychology, 34,* 579-589.

Dube, L., & Guimond, S. (1986). Relative deprivation and social protest: The personal group issue. In J. M. Olsen, C. P. Herman, & M. P. Zanna (Eds.), *Relative deprivation and social comparison: The Ontario Symposium* (Vol. 4, pp. 201-216). Hillsdale, NJ: Lawrence Erlbaum.

Dyer, L. (1989, August). Procedural fairness in employee relations: Theory and research. In C. Martin (Chair), *Procedural fairness theory and research: Applications to human resource management.* Symposium presented at the meeting of the Academy of Management, Washington, DC.

England, P. (1982). The failure of human capital theory to explain occupational sex segregation. *Journal of Human Resources, 17,* 358-370.

England, P. (1984). Socioeconomic explanations of job segregation. In H. Remick (Ed.), *Comparable worth and wage discrimination* (pp. 107-132). Philadelphia: Temple University Press.

Etzioni, A. (1988). *The moral dimension: Toward a new economics.* New York: Free Press.

Ferraro, G. A. (1984). Bridging the wage gap: Pay equity and job evaluations. *American Psychologist, 39,* 1166-1170.

Folger, R. (1986). Rethinking equity theory: A referent cognitions model. In H. W. Bierhoff, R. L. Cohen, & J. Greenberg (Eds.), *Justice in social relations* (pp. 145-162). New York: Plenum.

Folger, R., & Greenberg, J. (1985). Procedural justice: An interpretive analysis of personnel systems. In K. M. Rowland & G. R. Ferris (Eds.), *Research in personnel and human resources management* (Vol. 3, pp. 141-183). Greenwich, CT: JAI.

Futrell, C. M. (1978). Effects of pay disclosure on pay satisfaction for sales managers: A longitudinal study. *Academy of Management Journal, 21,* 140-144.

Gethman, B. R. (1987). The job market, sex bias, and comparable worth. *Public Personnel Management, 16,* 173-180.

Goethals, G. R., & Darley, J. (1977). Social comparison theory: An attributional approach. In J. M. Suls & R. L. Miller (Eds.), *Social comparison processes: Theoretical and empirical perspectives* (pp. 259-278). Washington, DC: Hemisphere.

Goffman, E. (1959). *The presentation of self in everyday life.* Garden City, NY: Anchor Doubleday.

Gombert, W. (1955). *A trade union analysis of time study* (2nd ed.). Englewood Cliffs, NJ: Prentice Hall.

Goodman, P. S. (1974). An examination of the referents used in the evaluation of pay. *Organizational Behavior and Human Performance, 12,* 170-195.

Graham, J. W. (1986). Principled organizational dissent: A theoretical essay. In B. M. Staw & L. L. Cummings (Eds.), *Research in organizational behavior* (Vol. 8, pp. 1-52). Greenwich, CT: JAI.

Grams, R., & Schwab, D. P. (1985). An investigation of systematic gender-related error in job evaluation. *Academy of Management Journal, 28,* 279-290.

Greenberg, J. (1979). Protestant ethic endorsement and the fairness of equity inputs. *Journal of Research In Personality, 13,* 579-588.

Greenberg, J. (1980). Attentional focus and locus of performance causality as determinants of equity behavior. *Journal of Personality and Social Psychology, 38,* 579-588.

Greenberg, J. (1982). Approaching equity and avoiding inequity in groups and organizations. In J. Greenberg & R. L. Cohen (Eds.), *Equity and justice in social behavior* (pp. 389-435). New York: Academic Press.

Greenberg, J. (1984). On the apocryphal nature of inequity distress. In R. Folger (Ed.), *The sense of injustice: Social psychological perspectives* (pp. 167-186). New York: Plenum.

Greenberg, J. (1986a). Determinants of the perceived fairness of performance evaluations. *Journal of Applied Psychology, 71,* 340-342. [Chapter 6, this volume.]

Greenberg, J. (1986b). Organizational performance appraisal procedures: What makes them fair? In R. J. Lewicki, B. H. Sheppard, & M. H. Bazerman (Eds.), *Research on negotiation in organizations* (Vol. 1, pp. 25-41). Greenwich, CT: JAI. [Chapter 8, this volume.]

Greenberg, J. (1987a). Reactions to procedural injustice in payment distributions: Do the means justify the ends? *Journal of Applied Psychology, 72,* 55-61. [Chapter 14, this volume.]

Greenberg, J. (1987b). A taxonomy of organizational justice theory. *Academy of Management Review, 12,* 9-22. [Chapter 1, this volume.]

Greenberg, J. (1988a). Cultivating an image of justice: Looking fair on the job. *Academy of Management Executive, 2,* 155-158. [Chapter 4, this volume.]

Greenberg, J. (1988b, August). Using social accounts to manage impressions of performance appraisal fairness. In J. Greenberg & R. J. Bies (Cochairs), *Communicating fairness in organizations.* Symposium presented at the meeting of the Academy of Management, Anaheim, CA.

Greenberg, J. (1989). Cognitive reevaluation of outcomes in response to underpayment inequity. *Academy of Management Journal, 32,* 174-184. [Chapter 16, this volume.]

Greenberg, J. (1990). Looking fair vs. being fair: Managing impressions of organizational justice. In B. M. Staw & L. L. Cummings (Eds.), *Research in organizational behavior* (Vol. 12, pp. 111-157). Greenwich, CT: JAI. [Chapter 5, this volume.]

Greenberg, J., & Folger, R. (1983). Procedural justice, participation, and the fair process effect in groups and organizations. In P. B. Paulus (Ed.), *Basic group processes* (pp. 235-256). New York: Springer-Verlag.

Greenberg, J., & Ornstein, S. (1983). High status job title as compensation for underpayment: A test of equity theory. *Journal of Applied Psychology, 68,* 285-297. [Chapter 17, this volume.]

Greenberg, J., & Tyler, T. (1987). Why procedural justice in organizations? *Social Justice Research, 1,* 127-142.

Grune, J. A. (1984). Pay equity as a necessary remedy for wage discrimination. In *Comparable worth: Issues for the 1980s* (pp. 167-176). Washington, DC: U.S. Civil Rights Commission.

Haftner, D. M. (1979). An overview of women's history. In M. Richmond-Abbott (Ed.), *The American woman* (pp. 1-27). New York: Holt, Rinehart, & Winston.

Hansen, R. D., & O'Leary, V. E. (1985). Sex-determined attributions. In V. E. O'Leary, R. K. Unger, & B. S. Wallston (Eds.), *Women, gender, and social psychology* (pp. 67-100). Hillsdale, NJ: Lawrence Erlbaum.

Heneman, H. G., III. (1985). Pay satisfaction. In K. M. Rowland & G. R. Ferris (Eds.), *Research in personnel and human resources management* (Vol. 3, pp. 115-139). Greenwich, CT: JAI.

Heneman, H. G., III, Schwab, D. P., Fossum, J. A., & Dyer, L. D. (1989). *Personnel/human resource management* (4th ed.). Homewood, IL: Irwin.

Heneman, R. L. (1990). Merit pay research. In G. R. Ferris & K. M. Rowland (Eds.), *Research in personnel and human resources management* (Vol. 8, pp. 203-263). Greenwich, CT: JAI.

Hogan, R., & Emler, N. P. (1981). Retributive justice. In M. Lerner & S. C. Lerner (Eds.), *The justice motive in social behavior: Adapting to times of scarcity and change* (pp. 125-143). New York: Plenum.

Hollenbeck, J. R., Ilgen, D. R., Ostroff, C., & Vancouver, J. B. (1987). Sex differences in occupational choice, pay, and worth: A supply-side approach to understanding the male-female wage gap. *Personnel Psychology, 40,* 715-743.

Homans, G. C. (1961). *Social behavior: Its elementary forms.* New York: Harcourt, Brace, & World.

Jackson, L. A., & Grabski, S. V. (1988). Perceptions of fair pay and the gender wage gap. *Journal of Applied Social Psychology, 18,* 606-625.

Jenkins, G. D., Jr., & Lawler, E. E. (1981). Impact of employee participation in pay plan development. *Organizational Behavior and Human Performance, 28,* 111-128.

Kessler-Harris, A. (1982). *Out to work: A history of wage-earning women in the United States.* New York: Oxford University Press.

Killingsworth, M. R. (1985). The economics of comparable worth: Analytical, empirical, and policy questions. In H. I. Hartmann (Ed.), *Comparable worth* (pp. 86-115). Washington, DC: National Academy Press.

LaVan, H., Katz, M., Malloy, M. S., & Stonebraker, P. (1987). Comparable worth: A comparison of litigated cases in the public and private sectors. *Public Personnel Management, 16,* 281-293.

Lawler, E. E. (1965). Managers' perceptions of their subordinates' pay and their superiors' pay. *Personnel Psychology, 18,* 413-422.

Lawler, E. E. (1981). *Pay and organization development.* Reading, MA: Addison-Wesley.

Lawler, E. E. (1986). The new pay. In S. L. Rynes & G. T. Milkovich (Eds.), *Current issues in human resource management* (pp. 404-412). Plano, TX: Business Publications.

Lawler, E. E., & Hackman, J. R. (1969). Impact of employee participation in the development of pay incentive plans: A field experiment. *Journal of Applied Psychology, 53,* 467-471.

Lawler, E. J. (1975). An experimental study of factors affecting the mobilization of revolutionary coalitions. *Sociometry, 38,* 163-179.

Leventhal, G. S. (1976). The distribution of rewards and resources in groups and organizations. In L. Berkowitz (Ed.), *Advances in experimental social psychology* (Vol. 9, pp. 91-131). New York: Academic Press.

Leventhal, G. S. (1980). What should be done with equity theory? In K. J. Gergen, M. S. Greenberg, & R. H. Willis (Eds.), *Social exchange: Advances in theory and research* (pp. 27-55). New York: Plenum.

Leventhal, G. S., Karuza, J., & Fry, W. R. (1980). Beyond fairness: A theory of allocation preferences. In G. Mikula (Ed.), *Justice and social interaction* (pp. 167-218). New York: Springer-Verlag.

Liden, R. C., & Mitchell, T. R. (1988). Ingratiatory behaviors in organizational settings. *Academy of Management Review, 13,* 572-587.

Lind, E. A., & Tyler, T. (1988). *The social psychology of procedural justice.* New York: Plenum.

Lorber, L. A. (1985). *Sex and salary: A legal and personnel analysis of comparable worth.* Alexandria, VA: ASPA Foundation.

Madigan, R. M. (1985). Comparable worth judgments: A measurement properties analysis. *Journal of Applied Psychology, 70,* 137-147.

Mahoney, T. A. (1983). Approaches to the definition of comparable worth. *Academy of Management Review, 8,* 14-22.

Mahoney, T. A. (1987). Understanding comparable worth: A societal and political perspective. In L. L. Cummings & B. M. Staw (Eds.), *Research in organizational behavior* (Vol. 9, pp. 209-245). Greenwich, CT: JAI.

Mahoney, T. A., Rosen, B., & Rynes, S. (1984). Where do compensation specialists stand on comparable worth? *Compensation and Benefits Review, 16,* 27-40.

Major, B. (1989). Gender differences in comparisons and entitlement: Implications for comparable worth. *Journal of Social Issues, 45,* 99-116.

Major, B., & Deaux, K. (1982). Individual differences in justice behavior. In J. Greenberg & R. L. Cohen (Eds.), *Equity and justice in social behavior* (pp. 43-76). New York: Academic Press.

Major, B., & Forcey, B. (1985). Social comparisons and pay evaluations: Preferences for same-sex and same-job wage comparisons. *Journal of Experimental Social Psychology, 21,* 393-405.

Major, B., & Konar, E. (1984). An investigation of sex differences in pay expectations and their possible causes. *Academy of Management Journal, 27,* 777-792.

Major, B., McFarlin, D. B., & Gagnon, D. (1984). Overworked and underpaid: On the nature of gender differences in personal entitlement. *Journal of Personality and Social Psychology, 47,* 1399-1412.

Major, B., & Testa, M. (1989). Social comparison processes and judgments of entitlement and satisfaction. *Journal of Experimental Social Psychology, 25,* 101-120.

Mali, P. (1972). *Managing by objectives.* New York: John Wiley-Interscience.

Marini, M. M., & Brinton, M. C. (1984). Sex-typing in occupational socialization. In B. F. Reskin (Ed.), *Sex segregation in the workplace: Trends, explanations, remedies* (pp. 192-232). Washington, DC: National Academy Press.

Martin, J. (1981). Relative deprivation: A theory of distributive injustice for an era of shrinking resources. In L. L. Cummings & B. M. Staw (Eds.), *Research in organizational behavior* (Vol. 3, pp. 53-107). Greenwich, CT: JAI.

Martin, J., & Murray, A. (1983). Distributive injustice and unfair exchange. In D. M. Messick & K. S. Cook (Eds.), *Equity theory: Psychological and sociological perspectives* (pp. 169-205). New York: Praeger.

Masters, J. C., & Keil, L. J. (1987). Generic comparison processes in human judgment and behavior. In J. C. Masters & W. P. Smith (Eds.), *Social comparison, social justice, and relative deprivation* (pp. 11-54). Hillsdale, NJ: Lawrence Erlbaum.

McArthur, L. Z., & Obrant, S. W. (1986). Sex biases in comparable worth analyses. *Journal of Applied Social Psychology, 16,* 757-770.

McMillan, J. D., & Williams, V. C. (1982). The elements of effective salary administration programs. *Personnel Journal,* pp. 832-838.

Mikula, G. (1986). The experience of injustice: Toward a better understanding of its phenomenology. In H. W. Bierhoff, R. L. Cohen, & J. Greenberg (Eds.), *Justice in social relations* (pp. 103-123). New York: Plenum.

Milkovich, G. T. (1988). The nature of the earnings gap. In D. E. Friedman (Ed.), *Pay equity* (pp. 8-10). New York: Conference Board.

Milkovich, G. T., & Anderson, P. H. (1972). Management compensation and secrecy. *Personnel Psychology, 25,* 293-302.

Milkovich, G. T., & Newman, J. M. (1987). *Compensation* (2nd ed.). Plano, TX: Business Publications.

Mincer, J., & Ofek, H. (1982). Interrupted work careers: Depreciation and restoration of human capital. *Journal of Human Resources, 17,* 3-24.

Moberg, D. J. (1977, April). *Organizational politics: Perspectives from attribution theory.* Paper presented at the meeting of the American Institute for Decision Sciences, Chicago.

Musante, L., Gilbert, M., & Thibaut, J. (1983). Effects of control on perceived fairness of procedures and outcomes. *Journal of Experimental Social Psychology, 19,* 223-238.

Nash, A. N., & Carroll, S. J., Jr. (1975). *The management of compensation.* Belmont, CA: Wadsworth.

Newman, J. M., & Milkovich, G. T. (1989, August). Procedural justice: Applications and hypothesis in compensation administration. In C. Martin (Chair), *Procedural fairness theory and research: Applications to human resource management.* Symposium presented at the meeting of the Academy of Management, Washington, DC.

Newman, W. (1982, April). Pay equity emerges as a top labor issue in the 1980s. *Monthly Labor Review,* 49-51.

Oldham, G. R., Nottenburg, G., Kassner, M. W., Ferris, G., Fedor, D., & Masters, M. (1982). The selection and consequences of job comparisons. *Organizational Behavior and Human Performance, 29,* 84-111.

O'Malley, M. N., & Greenberg, J. (1983). Sex differences in restoring justice: The down payment effect. *Journal of Research in Personality, 17,* 174-185.

Patten, T. H., Jr. (1988). *Fair pay: The managerial challenge of comparable job worth and job evaluation.* San Francisco: Jossey-Bass.

Polachek, S. W. (1975). Differences in expected post-school investments as a determinant of market wage differences. *International Economic Review, 16*(2), 451-490.

Polachek, S. W. (1981). Occupational self-selection: A human capital approach to sex differences in occupational structure. *Review of Economics and Statistics, 63,* 60-69.

Remick, H. (1984). *Comparable worth and wage discrimination.* Philadelphia: Temple University Press.

Renwick, P. A., & Lawler, E. E. (1978, December). What do you really want from your job? *Psychology Today,* pp. 53-66.

Ronan, W. W., & Organt, G. J. (1973). Determinants of pay and pay satisfaction. *Personnel Psychology, 26,* 503-520.

Runciman, W. G. (1966). *Relative deprivation and social justice.* Berkeley: University of California Press.

Rynes, S. L., & Milkovich, G. T. (1986). Wage surveys: Dispelling some myths about the "market wage." *Personnel Psychology, 39,* 71-90.

Sampson, E. E. (1975). Justice as equality. *Journal of Social Issues, 31,* 45-61.

Scheflen, K. C., Lawler, E. E., & Hackman, J. R. (1971). Long-term impact of employee participation in the development of pay incentive plans: A field experiment revisited. *Journal of Applied Psychology, 55,* 182-186.

Schlenker, B. R. (1980). *Impression management: The self-concept, social identity, and interpersonal relations.* Belmont, CA: Brooks/Cole.

Schwab, D. P. (1985). Determining the worth of work. *Society, 22*(5), 61-67.

Schwab, D. P., & Grams, R. (1985). Sex-related errors in job evaluation: A real world test. *Journal of Applied Psychology, 70,* 533-539.

Shapiro, D. L., & Buttner, E. H. (1988, August). *Adequate explanations: What are they, and do they enhance procedural justice under severe outcome circumstances?* Paper presented at the meeting of the Academy of Management, Anaheim, CA.

Sheppard, B. H., & Lewicki, R. J. (1987). Toward general principles of managerial fairness. *Social Justice Research, 1,* 161-176.

Smith, J. P., & Ward, M. P. (1984). *Women's wages and work in the twentieth century.* Santa Monica, CA: RAND.

Steel, B. S., & Lovrich, N. P., Jr. (1987, May). Comparable worth: The problematic politicization of a public personnel issue. *Public Personnel Management,* pp. 23-36.

Stouffer, S. A., Suchman, E. A., DeVinney, L. C., Star, S. A., & Williams, R. M., Jr. (1949). *The American soldier: Vol. 1. Adjustment during Army life.* Princeton, NJ: Princeton University Press.

Suls, J., & Miller, R. L. (1977). *Social comparison processes: Theoretical and empirical perspectives.* Washington, DC: Hemisphere.

Taynor, J., & Deaux, K. (1973). When women are more deserving than men: Equality, attribution, and perceived sex differences. *Journal of Personality and Social Psychology, 28,* 360-367.

Thibaut, J., & Walker, L. (1975). *Procedural justice: A psychological analysis.* Hillsdale, NJ: Lawrence Erlbaum.

Thompson, J. D. (1967). *Organizations in action.* New York: McGraw-Hill.

Thomsen, D. J. (1978, September-October). Eliminating pay discrimination caused by job evaluation. *Personnel,* pp. 11-22.

Treiman, D. J., & Hartmann, H. I. (1981). *Women, work, and wages: Equal pay for jobs of equal value.* Washington, DC: National Academy Press.

Tyler, T. R. (1984). The role of perceived injustice in defendants' evaluations of their courtroom experience. *Law and Society Review, 18,* 51-74.

Tyler, T. R., & Caine, A. (1981). The influence of outcomes and procedures on satisfaction with formal leaders. *Journal of Personality and Social Psychology, 41,* 642-655.

Vanneman, R. D., & Pettigrew, T. G. (1972). Race and relative deprivation in the urban United States. *Race, 13,* 461-486.

Walster, E., Walster, G. W., & Berscheid, E. (1978). *Equity: Theory and research.* Boston: Allyn & Bacon.

Watts, B. L., Messé, L. A., & Vallacher, R. R. (1982). Toward understanding sex differences in pay allocation: Agency, communion, and reward distribution behavior. *Sex Roles, 8,* 1175-1187.

Webster, M., & Smith, L. R. (1978). Justice and revolutionary coalitions: A test of two theories. *American Journal of Sociology, 84,* 267-292.

Wegner, D. M. (1982). Justice and the awareness of social entities. In J. Greenberg & R. L. Cohen (Eds.), *Equity and justice in social behavior* (pp. 77-117). New York: Academic Press.

Williams, R. E., & McDowell, D. S. (1980). The legal framework. In R. E. Livernash (Ed.), *Comparable worth: Issues and alternatives* (pp. 197-249). Washington, DC: Equal Employment Advisory Council.

Willis, T. A. (1981). Downward comparison principles in social psychology. *Psychological Bulletin, 90,* 245-271.

Zanna, M. P., Crosby, F., & Lowenstein, G. (1987). Male reference groups and discontent among female professionals. In B. Gutek & L. Larwood (Eds.), *Women's career development* (pp. 28-41). Newbury Park, CA: Sage.

14

Reactions to Procedurally Unfair Payment

It is well established that distributions of organizational rewards (such as pay raises, promotions, job status, and the like) influence, in some manner, the attitudes and behavior of employees (Lawler, 1977). Indeed, several theoretical conceptualizations of justice in organizations, most notably, equity theory (Adams, 1965; Walster, Walster, & Berscheid, 1978), have focused extensively on how distributions of organizational rewards (also referred to as *outcomes*) affect job satisfaction and performance (for a review, see Greenberg, 1982). This legacy of theory and research, although

AUTHOR'S NOTE: This chapter was originally published in the *Journal of Applied Psychology,* Vol. 72, No. 1, pp. 55-61, under the title "Reactions to Procedural Injustice in Payment Distributions: Do the Means Justify the Ends?" Copyright © 1987 by the American Psychological Association. Reprinted by permission.

it reveals a great deal about reactions to the nature and level of organizational rewards, provides little insight into possible effects caused by the manner in which these rewards are established. As a result, questions remain about whether (and if so, how) the *way* organizational rewards are determined influences reactions to them.

A reorientation in emphasis from *what* the rewards are to *how* they are determined follows from theoretical conceptualizations of *procedural justice* (e.g., Thibaut & Walker, 1975), offering a broader, more procedurally oriented conceptualization of justice than the traditionally outcome-oriented, *distributive justice* perspective of equity theory (see Thibaut & Walker, 1978). Although distributive justice focuses on the fairness of a distribution of resources, procedural justice focuses on the fairness of the procedures used to make those distributive decisions. Research on procedural justice has highlighted the importance of resource distribution procedures as determinants of fairness in organizations (for reviews, see Folger & Greenberg, 1985; Greenberg, 1986c[8]; Greenberg & Folger, 1983). Alexander and Ruderman (1987), for example, surveying more than 2,800 federal employees, found that employees' concerns about how their salaries were determined accounted for more variance in job satisfaction than the level of those salaries. Similarly, with respect to another organizational outcome, performance evaluations, Landy, Barnes-Farrell, and Cleveland (1980) found that the process by which workers' performance appraisals were determined was related to the perceived fairness of their evaluations, regardless of how positive or negative they were. More generally, in a survey of executives, Sheppard and Lewicki (1987) found that procedural factors (the way outcomes were determined) were reported as more critical than specific outcome variables themselves as determinants of fair and unfair treatment in their organizations. Taken together, such evidence highlights the importance of procedural aspects of justice in the context of organizational reward distributions.

What makes a reward distribution procedure unfair? In his theory of procedural fairness, Leventhal (1976, 1980; Leventhal, Karuza, & Fry, 1980) posited that fair allocation procedures are characterized by resource distributions that are consistent across persons and through time, free from bias, based on accurate information, correctable, representative of all recipients' concerns, and based on prevailing moral and ethical standards. Recent survey studies have shown that workers report extreme dissatisfaction with resource distribution procedures that violate these standards and believe them to be unfair. For example, in their survey study, Sheppard and Lewicki (1987) found that accounts of unfair incidents frequently alluded to elements in Leventhal's conceptualization (such as inconsistency and bias in reward allocations). Similarly, I found that workers reported that performance evaluations made without keeping accurate performance records were unfair (Greenberg, 1987[9]). Finally, Barrett-Howard and Tyler (1986) have shown that role-playing participants responded negatively to violations of Leventhal's procedural justice standards in imagined work settings. Together, this body of work suggests that criteria for stipulating procedurally fair and unfair practices exist that recently have begun to receive empirical validation.

With increasing awareness of the importance of procedural justice in organizations and preliminary demonstrations of adverse reactions to procedural justice violations comes the need to know how reactions to outcome distributions and the procedures from which they are derived are related. The primary question of interest is how the fairness of the procedures used influences the perceived fairness of the resulting outcomes. Do fair procedures lead to fair outcomes? There is good reason to hypothesize a main effect of procedures on judgments of distributive fairness such that fair procedures lead to judgments of fairer outcomes than unfair procedures. Conceptual support for this hypothesis may be derived from several sources. For one, Leventhal (1976) claimed that unfair procedures cannot yield fair outcome distributions. Similarly, Thibaut and Walker (1975) suggested that a possible perceptual overlap between distributive justice and procedural justice such that the fairer the procedure used to determine outcomes, the more those outcomes are likely to be evaluated as distributively just. Indirect empirical support for the hypothesis can be found in studies simulating legal dispute resolution techniques in which the perceived fairness of the resulting verdicts was influenced by the procedures on which they were based; procedures promoting personal participation in adjudication were seen as fairest (Lind, Kurtz, Musante, Walker, & Thibaut, 1980; Walker, Lind, & Thibaut, 1979). Although these studies involve contexts and operational definition of procedural injustice that are quite different from the present study (and therefore only modest empirical justification for the hypothesis), they provide good insight into the question of interest.

A second major issue addressed in this chapter is the opposite question, namely, how do the outcomes received influence the perceived fairness of the procedures by which they were determined? It already has been established that higher outcomes are seen as fairer than lower outcomes—the so-called egocentric bias in perceptions of distributive justice (e.g., Greenberg, 1983a). Does this effect generalize to perceptions of procedural justice as well? The results of previous studies reveal a mixed answer to this question. Although several investigations have reported that beneficiaries of positive outcomes tend to view the procedures leading to them as fair (e.g., LaTour, 1978; Tyler & Caine, 1981, Studies 2 and

4), others have reported that outcome favorability does not influence perceptions of procedural justice (e.g., Lind et al., 1980). The evidence bearing on this question not only is contradictory but also is based on retrospective questionnaires or uninvolving role-playing techniques, which weakens confidence in its generalizability. Accordingly, the present study manipulated outcome level and measured its immediate impact on perceptions of procedural fairness. Corroboration of the egocentric bias would require finding a significant main effect of outcome level in ratings of outcome fairness such that higher outcomes are seen as fairer than lower outcomes. To the extent that this effect generalizes to perceptions of procedural fairness, a similar main effect of outcome level on procedural fairness ratings would be expected.

This study provided an opportunity to explore the possibility that reactions to procedural injustices are moderated by their underlying causal basis—either individual or organizational. This variable is suggested by research showing that reactions to distributive justice differ as a function of whether the inequity is caused by an individual or an organization (Greenberg, 1986b; Leventhal, Younts, & Lund, 1972). The following question was asked: Would individually based or organizationally based unfair procedures elicit greater reactions? A specific prediction is not immediately forthcoming because of recent evidence suggesting potentially opposite reactions. On one hand, Folger and Martin (1986) have shown that participants are likely to react more strongly against agents of injustice who are expected to be able to continue their unjust actions in the future. On the other hand, evidence also suggests that victims of injustice may refrain from striking back at causal agents when they believe their actions will have little impact (Martin, Brickman, & Murray, 1984). Combining these two findings makes it difficult to predict how individuals will respond when they believe the procedures they confront are based on organizational policies, which may be expected to be more enduring and serious sources of injustice but may also be more difficult to correct. The present study explored the possibility that attitudinal and behavioral reactions to procedural justice and injustice would be differentially influenced by the individual or organizational basis of their origin, although no specific hypotheses were tested.

METHOD

Participants and Design

The participants were 192 undergraduate students (96 men and 96 women) at a midwestern university who volunteered to participate in a study allegedly concerned about consumer use of sales catalogs. In exchange for taking part in the study, participants were promised a payment of "up to $8" for the 1-hour session. (This phrasing of the stated payment amount was revealed in pilot testing to result in a potential range of payments perceived to be fair compensation for participating in the study.) Five additional participants (3 men and 2 women), evenly distributed across the experimental conditions, also participated in the study, but their responses were not analyzed because they did not follow experimental instructions.

The overall design of the experiment was a $3 \times 2 \times 2 \times 2$ factorial in which the independent variables were outcome level (high, medium, or low), procedural fairness (fair or unfair), origin of procedure (individual or organizational), and sex of participant. An equal number of men and women were randomly assigned to each cell.

Procedure

Pairs of same-sex participants participated in each experimental session. They were told that they would be performing a catalog-searching task and then would complete a brief questionnaire assessing their reactions to the task.

Experimental task. The purpose of the experimental task was to provide an apparent basis for the experimentally manipulated payments that followed. To avoid arousing participants' suspicions about the experimental manipulations, a task was used that has been shown in previous research to be one for which participants have no preconceived standards of productivity (Greenberg, 1983b). The task consisted of locating specified items in a department store catalog and copying their prices onto index cards on which the items were identified. The rationale was given that this study was conducted to find out how the design of catalogs influences people's ability to use them. After the experimenter demonstrated the task and answered participants' questions about how to perform it, the participants were escorted to opposite ends of the same room and were seated at desks containing the index cards, pencils, and catalogs needed to perform the task. Because participants were seated facing opposite directions, they could not see each other's work.

After performing this task for 45 minutes, the experimenter entered the workroom and instructed participants to stop working. He then handed each participant a large manila envelope into which he instructed them to place all of their index cards, both the completed and incomplete ones. (This practice minimized participants' opportunities to assess their relative inputs.) The experimenter announced that he would get the participants started on the questionnaire and arrange for their payment but that first they would have to leave the workroom so that another group of participants could be brought in. Participants were then asked to go to any one of three nearby rooms, labeled "Room A," "Room B," and "Room C," to complete the study. The experimenter explained that because these rooms were small and contained only one desk, only one participant should enter a room and wait there for the experimenter to return. This procedure made it possible for the experimenter to independently manipulate the experimental conditions in each session.

Independent variable manipulations. Between 3 and 6 minutes later, the experimenter returned to each participant's experimental room and announced how the pay was determined. This information constituted the procedural fairness manipulation. In the *fair-procedure* condition, participants were told that their pay was based on how well they performed on the catalog-searching task relative to the other person. Better workers were said to receive a higher proportion of the $8 than poorer workers. In the *unfair-procedure* condition, participants were told that their pay was determined by the room that they selected. Each of the three rooms, it was explained, had a predetermined amount of money associated with it that constituted the payment of the person selecting it.[1] This manipulation of procedural injustice—a seemingly arbitrary procedure for determining pay—is justified by its inclusion of several procedural elements specified by Leventhal (1980), most notably that the procedure violates usual payment allocation practices and that it fails to base allocations on accurate performance information.

Following this, the experimenter commented on the origin of the allocation procedure he just explained. In the *individual* condition, the experimenter said that it was he who personally decided how the payment division decision was to be made. In the *organizational* condition, the experimenter explained that the decision to divide the pay this way was made by the large company that sponsored the research.

The experimenter explained that on the basis of the announced procedure, he would now pay participants their share of the $8. In particular, outcome level was manipulated by telling participants that they would be receiving either $7 (in the high-outcome condition), $4 (in the medium-outcome condition), or $1 (in the low-outcome condition). To enhance the salience of this manipulation, the experimenter took out eight $1 bills and handed the appropriate number to the participant.

Dependent measures. After participants took the money, the experimenter handed them each a booklet containing six questionnaire items.

Using 9-point bipolar scales, participants were asked to indicate the following: their perception of the fairness of the payment they received, the fairness of the procedure used to determine their payment (for both items, 1 = *extremely unfair*, 9 = *extremely fair*), their concern about the pay they received, their concern about how their pay was determined (for both items, 1 = *extremely unconcerned*, 9 = *extremely concerned*), their liking for the experimental task, and their liking for the experimenter (for both items, 1 = *extremely dislike*, 9 = *extremely like*). The four questions assessing concern and liking were considered supplementary measures designed to provide insight into the reasons underlying responses to the two fairness questions.

Participants were assured of the anonymity of their responses. In support of this claim, participants were given a letter-sized envelope into which they were to insert their completed questionnaires. These envelopes, it was explained, were to be inserted into a large folder tacked onto a bulletin board on the wall before leaving the room. The folder was labeled "Catalog Study—Completed Questionnaires" and contained some already-stuffed envelopes, thereby supporting the illusion of response anonymity.

On the bulletin board immediately to the left of the folder for depositing the completed questionnaires was a prominent notice on which was printed an octagonal-shaped sign containing the words STOP UNFAIR EXPERIMENTS. The remainder of the text read as follows: "Treated Unfairly in an Experiment? Call the Ethical Responsibility Board to Report any Unfair Treatment in Human Experimentation." At the bottom of the sign appeared the words "Take Our Number" immediately over a series of vertical cuts in the paper approximately 38 mm long. On each strip appeared a local telephone number that participants could easily take by tearing one strip off the sign. To invite participants to do so, four strips were already torn off the sign, leaving five phone number strips for participants. If one or more additional strips were missing after participants left the room, that was taken as the participant's behavioral intention to express dissatisfaction with the experiment, providing a behavioral measure of dissatisfaction to supplement the questionnaire responses.

Debriefing. As participants left their rooms, they were intercepted by the experimenter, who conducted the postexperimental debriefing. Participants were carefully debriefed and were given the difference between what they were already paid and the maximum stated payment, thereby leaving each participant with a total of $8. In postexperimental interviews, no participants expressed any suspicions about the actual purpose of the experiment or admitted having prior knowledge about it.

RESULTS

Preliminary Analyses

A 3 × 2 × 2 × 2 multivariate analysis of variance was performed, using as between-participants factors the three manipulated variables (outcome level, procedural fairness, and origin of procedure) and as an exploratory variable, sex of participant. The six questionnaire measures constituted the dependent variables. Statistically significant effects were obtained for outcome level, procedural fairness, and the interaction between them (all values of multivariate $F \geq 11.19$, $p < .001$). All other sources of variance were nonsignificant (all values of multivariate $F < 1.00$). Correlations between responses to the six questionnaire items were all nonsignificant; using Fisher's transformation, the mean of the 15 zero-order correlations in the matrix was .04, *ns*. Accordingly, none of the measures were combined prior to data analyses. On the basis of these findings, all analyses of the questionnaire results reported in this chapter are based on 3 × 2 (Outcome Level × Procedural Fairness) univariate analyses of variance.

Perceived Fairness Measures

Analyses of outcome fairness revealed a significant main effect of outcome level, $F(2, 186) = 6.06$, $p < .005$, $\omega^2 = .08$. Newman-Keuls tests ($\alpha = .05$) revealed that this effect resulted from the tendency for participants to report that low outcomes ($M = 4.45$) were less fair than medium outcomes ($M = 7.08$) or high outcomes ($M = 7.70$), which were not significantly different from each other. Also significant was the main effect of procedural fairness, $F(1, 186) = 12.18$, $p < .001$, $\omega^2 = .17$, such that fair procedures ($M = 7.55$) were believed to result in fairer outcomes than unfair procedures ($M = 5.27$). Both these effects, however, were qualified by a significant interaction between outcome level and procedural fairness, $F(2, 186) = 19.47$, $p < .001$, $\omega^2 = .27$. The means corresponding to this interaction are displayed in the left-hand panel of Figure 14.1.

Simple main effects tests across procedures revealed that a significant difference in the perceived fairness of outcomes occurred only at the low-outcome level, $F(1, 62) = 9.75$, $p < .001$, in which fair procedures were seen as responsible for fairer outcomes than unfair procedures. This is in contrast to medium- and high-outcome levels, in which the procedures

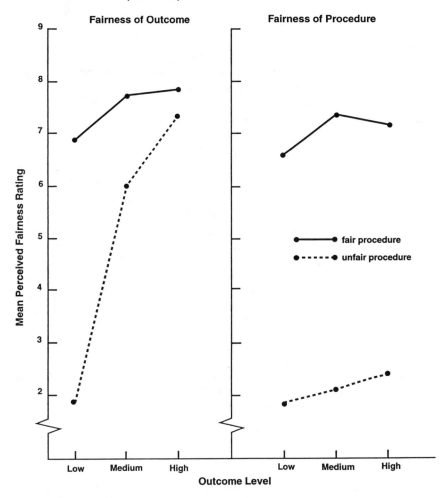

Figure 14.1. Mean Ratings of Outcome Fairness and Procedural Fairness as a Function of Outcome Level and Procedure

used were found to have no significant influence on the fairness of the resulting outcome: In both cases, $F < 2.00$, *ns*.

For ratings of the fairness of the procedures used, the only significant source of variance was the main effect of procedural fairness, $F(1, 186) = 20.69$, $p < .001$, $\omega^2 = .12$. As shown on the right side of Figure 14.1, the fair procedure was seen as fairer than the unfair procedure. Unlike ratings of outcome fairness, this effect was not qualified by outcome level; for the interaction, $F < 1.00$, *ns*.

Concern About
Outcomes and Procedures

Analyses of participants' ratings of amount of concern about the outcomes they received yielded as the only significant source of variance a main effect of outcome level, $F(2, 186) = 8.74$, $p < .005$, $\omega^2 = .19$. Newman-Keuls tests ($\alpha = .05$) revealed that this effect resulted from the tendency for participants in the low-outcome condition ($M = 7.40$) to express a significantly higher degree of concern about outcomes than either those in the medium-outcome condition ($M = 3.75$) or in the high-outcome condition ($M = 4.15$), which were not significantly different from each other.

Analyses of participants' concern about the procedures used resulted in a significant main effect of procedural fairness, $F(1, 186) = 4.12$, $p < .05$, $\omega^2 = .06$, such that higher concern was expressed under unfair conditions ($M = 5.62$) than fair conditions ($M = 3.10$). The meaning of this effect was qualified, however, by a significant Outcome Level × Procedural Fairness interaction, $F(2, 186) = 16.73$, $p < .001$, $\omega^2 = .26$. Simple main effects tests were used to compare responses across procedures at each level of outcome. When outcome levels were low, participants expressed significantly more concern about unfair procedures ($M = 8.05$) than fair procedures ($M = 2.80$), $F(1, 62) = 88.30$, $p < .001$. When outcome levels were either moderate ($M = 3.75$) or high ($M = 3.90$), however, there were no significant differences found between procedures; in both cases, $F < 1.00$, *ns.*

Liking for Task
and Experimenter

The only significant source of variance found for ratings of liking for the task was the main effect of outcome, $F(2, 186) = 9.40$, $p < .001$, $\omega^2 = .15$. Newman-Keuls tests ($\alpha = .05$) revealed that the means across all three levels of outcome (low $M = 3.75$, medium $M = 5.53$, high $M = 7.28$) were significantly different from each other. The higher the outcome, the more the task was liked.

For ratings of liking for the experimenter, the only significant source of variance was the main effect of procedural fairness, $F(1, 186) = 25.61$, $p < .001$, $\omega^2 = .11$. This effect was the result of the tendency for participants to be show greater liking for experimenters who treated them fairly ($M = 6.75$) than those who treated them unfairly ($M = 2.82$).

Behavioral Intention Measure

The final dependent measure was the number of participants who took the telephone number from the notice posted on the bulletin board—a measure of intention to complain about unfair treatment. Only participants in the unfair-procedure/low-outcome condition took the telephone number. Specifically, 14 of 32 participants in this condition (43.75%) took the number, whereas no participants in any of the other conditions did so.

Of the 14 participants who took the telephone number, 12 were in the condition in which they were told that the procedure was the result of an organizational policy, whereas only 2 were in the condition in which they were told that the procedure was the result of an individual decision. The difference between the proportion of participants in the two cells who took the telephone number (12 out of 14 [86%] vs. 2 out of 14 [14%]) was statistically significant ($z = 3.57$, $p = .0023$).

DISCUSSION

This research addresses two principal questions. One concerns the effects of procedures on outcomes; the complementary question is about the effects of outcomes on procedures.

The Influence of
Procedures on Outcomes

How do the procedures used affect the reactions to the outcomes received? By extrapolating from studies simulating legal dispute resolution contexts (e.g., Lind et al., 1980; Walker et al., 1979), I hypothesized that fair procedures would lead to outcomes believed to be fairer than would those resulting from unfair procedures. Although this hypothesis was strongly supported, the relative perceived fairness of the rewards based on fair procedures compared with unfair procedures only manifested itself when outcomes were low. In contrast, medium- and high-level outcomes were reported to be equally fair regardless of the fairness of the procedures used to bring them about. In other words, the means (procedures used) justified the ends (outcomes received) only when those ends were positive (medium- or high-outcome levels). This pattern of results partially supports but qualifies Leventhal's (1976) claim that "procedural fairness is a necessary precondition for the establishment and maintenance of distributive fairness" (p. 230). The present findings suggest that procedural justice may be a necessary precondition for distributive justice but only when the outcomes are low.

The way in which outcome level qualified the effects of procedure suggests that procedures may matter most to people when they result in negative outcomes. This possibility is supported by the finding that expressed concern about procedures was highest when unfair procedures resulted in low payments. Not surprisingly, it was precisely under these conditions that participants behaviorally expressed their concern about unfair treatment. Participants took action in response to the procedural impropriety only when their outcomes were low, despite that unfair procedures were seen as equally unfair across all outcome levels. Why didn't participants experiencing medium- and high-level outcomes react to the procedural injustice? Their perception of these higher outcomes as fair appears to have removed participants' justification for taking action in response to unfair procedures. This interpretation of the results is bolstered by evidence that segments of society benefiting from unfair procedures may express concern about the unfair situation but refrain from doing anything to jeopardize their privileged position (Cohen, 1986).

Victims of unfair procedures were more likely to take action directed at redressing the injustice when they believed the unfair procedure followed from an organizational policy than when it was an individual decision. An explanation for this difference is suggested by Folger and Martin's (1986) findings that reactions to procedural infractions are exaggerated when the infraction is especially serious and expected to continue in the future. To the extent that the organizationally based procedural injustices were seen as more serious and permanent than the individually based ones, these results are not surprising.[2]

Participants' positive reaction to their pay generalized to the task itself; participants liked tasks better for which they were highly paid than those for which they were poorly paid. Higher outcomes were believed to be fairer than lower outcomes, a finding that supports previous research (e.g., Greenberg, 1983a) showing that participants believed to be fair those outcomes that benefited themselves. This result is also consistent with Thibaut and Walker's (1975) finding that it is the losers of trials who are most likely to view the verdicts as unfair. Despite the corroborative nature of the present evidence, caution is needed in interpreting and generalizing from it because the meaning of apparent improprieties may be challenged in the context of a laboratory experiment. Similarly, limitations imposed by the single-item dependent measures used in this study (e.g., possible ambiguities) also restrict the potential generalizability of the findings.

The Influence of
Outcomes on Procedures

A complementary question of interest was how the outcomes received influenced reactions to the procedure used. The results showed that fair procedures were believed to be fairer than unfair procedures regardless of the resulting level of outcome. The egocentric bias found in ratings of outcome fairness (i.e., that higher outcomes are judged fairer than lower outcomes) did not generalize to ratings of procedural fairness. Of particular interest is the finding that even procedures leading to low outcomes were believed to be fair when they resulted from fair procedures. Analogous evidence has been obtained by Tyler (1984; Tyler & Folger, 1980), who found that citizens who were found guilty of a misdemeanor by a judge or who were cited for a traffic violation by a police officer believed they were treated fairly when the authority figure adhered to certain expected practices. Not surprisingly, such authority figures tended to be liked, as was the experimenter in the present study, when they followed a fair procedure.

Although outcome level did not influence judgments of the fairness of the procedure used, it did have other effects. For example, low outcomes aroused concern about outcomes and about the procedures by which they were obtained (especially when they resulted from unfair procedures) and diminished liking for the task. These findings clearly discount the possibility that outcome level failed to influence procedural fairness judgments because it was not made salient in the study. Instead, although the effects of outcome level were recognized, they did not influence perceptions of the fairness of the procedures used. The organizational ends received (monetary rewards) did not justify the means (procedures) by which they were attained.

A similar tendency for outcome favorability to have no influence on perceptions of procedural justice has also been found in a study by Lind et al. (1980), conducted in a legal dispute resolution context. Comparisons between the present findings and those of Lind et al. must be made cautiously because of the different experimental settings and operational definitions of procedural injustice used. Lind et al. operationally defined procedural injustice by limiting litigants' input into the decision-making process (inspired by Thibaut & Walker, 1975), whereas in the present study, unfair procedures were created by using a capriciously applied allocation rule (inspired by Leventhal, 1980). Both procedures were believed to be unfair, seemingly because both are counternormative in their respective settings. Yet it remains an untested possibility that different sources of procedural improprieties would have resulted in different reactions.

Implications

This study has important implications for research and theory on procedural justice. Primarily, it shows that many of the same reactions to the absence of control about the decision-making process demonstrated in studies of dispute resolution also manifest themselves in response to the capricious reward allocation procedure used in the present experiment. In particular, these results corroborated Lind et al.'s (1980) findings about the positive effects of outcome level on perceptions of distributive justice and the lack of effect of outcome level on perceptions of procedural justice. In addition, by showing the effects of manipulations of procedural fairness as suggested by Leventhal (1980), the present study supports and extends preliminary investigations (e.g., Sheppard & Lewicki, 1987) showing that such procedural concerns are expressed among workers by showing how these factors operate. Because a compound operationalization of an unfair procedure was used in the present study (violating prevailing standards and failing to use accurate performance information), however, it is unclear precisely which procedural characteristics accounted for the results. Implications for organizational behavior research also are suggested by this work. Notable in this regard is the suggestion that theoretical conceptualizations focusing on organizational rewards, such as equity theory (Adams, 1965) and expectancy theory (e.g., Porter & Lawler, 1968), may need to be expanded to incorporate considerations of *how* outcomes are determined as well as *what* they are. By focusing on relative outcome and input levels, equity theory is not equipped to interpret the observed differences in the perceived fairness of low-level rewards derived from fair and unfair procedures. To the extent that procedures qualify the meaning of outcomes (and reactions to them), as demonstrated, then it would be essential for conceptualizations of justice in organizations to incorporate procedural variables. Indeed, given that organizational procedures are more frequently cited than outcomes as causes of unfairness in organizations (Greenberg, 1986c[8]; Sheppard & Lewicki, 1987) and because procedures contribute more to job satisfaction than do outcomes (Alexander & Ruderman, 1987), the need to explore organizational procedures is further emphasized.

The results of the present study suggest several potentially fruitful new directions for future research. Among these is the important unaddressed issue of how workers' reactions to procedural injustice influence their job performance. Although equity theory (e.g., Adams, 1965) explains how workers are likely to react to unfair outcomes, it remains unclear how these reactions may be qualified by unfair organizational procedures. In a related vein, it appears useful for organizational researchers to assess the generalizability of these findings by examining the effects of a variety of potentially important procedural variables (such as those suggested by Folger & Greenberg, 1985; Sheppard & Lewicki, 1987). The restricted procedural improprieties examined in the present study, although responsible for interesting findings, may be of limited usefulness in permitting generalizations to be drawn about the general theoretical properties of procedural justice (Leventhal, 1980). A further potential limitation of the study rests in that the laboratory methodology used precludes the possibility of directly generalizing from the findings to field applications. As is the case in theoretically based research, however, the issue of generalizability applies to the phenomenon under investigation rather than to the research findings themselves. As future researchers begin to recognize the importance of distinguishing between the outcomes of managerial decisions and the procedures that led to these decisions in organizational contexts—as is just beginning to be done in the field of performance appraisal (Greenberg, 1986a[6])—it will become possible to assess the external validity of the concepts uncovered here.

NOTES

1. A preinquiry quasi-control group (Orne, 1969) of 28 participants from the same population as that used in the main study was used to assess the validity of this manipulation, without possible contamination created by knowledge of the outcomes. These participants were subjected to the same experimental procedure as the regular participants, but they did not receive information about their outcome level or the origin of the procedure. The participants (one half of the group) who received the fair-procedure manipulation ($M = 7.81$) reported that it was significantly fairer than did the other half who received the unfair-procedure manipulation ($M = 1.89$), $F(1, 26) = 89.76, p < .001$.

2. Indeed, the questionnaire responses of 127 pilot participants support the claim that injustices caused by organizational policy are more serious and more permanent than those caused by an individual decision. These participants read vignettes describing cases in which low outcomes resulted from an individually based or organizationally based procedure calling for outcomes to be based on an arbitrary decision rule—the choice of a room. It was found that ratings of seriousness of the infraction and permanence of the procedure (both on 9-point scales, with higher ratings reflecting greater degrees of seriousness and permanence) were significantly higher in the organizationally based condition (M for seriousness = 6.74 and M for permanence = 7.12) than in the individual-decision condition (M for seriousness = 3.82 and M for permanence = 4.02); values of $F(1, 126) = 12.73$ and 14.16, respectively, in both cases $p < .001$.

REFERENCES

Adams, J. S. (1965). Inequity in social exchange. In L. Berkowitz (Ed.), *Advances in experimental social psychology* (Vol. 2, pp. 267-299). New York: Academic Press.

Alexander, S., & Ruderman, M. (1987). The role of procedural and distributive justice in organizational behavior. *Social Justice Research, 1,* 177-198.

Barrett-Howard, E., & Tyler, T. R. (1986). Procedural justice as a criterion in allocation decisions. *Journal of Personality and Social Psychology, 50,* 296-304.

Cohen, R. L. (1986). Power and justice in intergroup relations. In H. W. Bierhoff, R. L. Cohen, & J. Greenberg (Eds.), *Justice in social relations* (pp. 65-84). New York: Plenum.

Folger, R., & Greenberg, J. (1985). Procedural justice: An interpretive analysis of personnel systems. In K. M. Rowland & G. R. Ferris (Eds.), *Research in personnel and human resources management* (Vol. 3, pp. 141-183). Greenwich, CT: JAI.

Folger, R., & Martin, C. (1986). Relative deprivation and referent cognitions: Distributive and procedural justice effects. *Journal of Experimental Social Psychology, 22,* 531-546.

Greenberg, J. (1982). Approaching equity and avoiding inequity in groups and organizations. In J. Greenberg & R. L. Cohen (Eds.), *Equity and justice in social behavior* (pp. 389-435). New York: Academic Press.

Greenberg, J. (1983a). Overcoming egocentric bias in perceived fairness through self-awareness. *Social Psychology Quarterly, 46,* 152-156.

Greenberg, J. (1983b). Self-image versus impression management in adherence to distributive justice standards: The influence of self-awareness and self-consciousness. *Journal of Personality and Social Psychology, 44,* 5-19.

Greenberg, J. (1986a). Determinants of perceived fairness of performance evaluations. *Journal of Applied Psychology, 71,* 340-342. [Chapter 6, this volume.]

Greenberg, J. (1986b). Differential intolerance for inequity from organizational and individual agents. *Journal of Applied Social Psychology, 16,* 191-196.

Greenberg, J. (1986c). Organizational performance appraisal procedures: What makes them fair? In R. J. Lewicki, B. H. Sheppard, & M. H. Bazerman (Eds.), *Research on negotiation in organizations* (Vol. 1, pp. 25-41). Greenwich, CT: JAI. [Chapter 8, this volume.]

Greenberg, J. (1987). Using diaries to promote procedural justice in performance appraisals. *Social Justice Research, 1,* 219-234. [Chapter 9, this volume.]

Greenberg, J., & Folger, R. (1983). Procedural justice, participation, and the fair process effect in groups and organizations. In P. B. Paulus (Ed.), *Basic group processes* (pp. 235-256). New York: Springer-Verlag.

Landy, F. J., Barnes-Farrell, J., & Cleveland, J. N. (1980). Perceived fairness and accuracy of performance evaluation: A follow-up. *Journal of Applied Psychology, 65,* 355-356.

LaTour, S. (1978). Determinants of participant and observer satisfaction with adversary and inquisitorial modes of adjudication. *Journal of Personality and Social Psychology, 36,* 1531-1545.

Lawler, E. E., III. (1977). Reward systems. In J. R. Hackman & J. L. Suttle (Eds.), *Improving life at work* (pp. 163-226). Santa Monica, CA: Goodyear.

Leventhal, G. S. (1976). Fairness in social relationships. In J. W. Thibaut, J. T. Spence, & R. C. Carson (Eds.), *Contemporary topics in social psychology* (pp. 211-239). Morristown, NJ: General Learning Press.

Leventhal, G. S. (1980). What should be done with equity theory? In K. J. Gergen, M. S. Greenberg, & R. H. Willis (Eds.), *Social exchange: Advances in theory and research* (pp. 27-55). New York: Plenum.

Leventhal, G. S., Karuza, J., & Fry, W. R. (1980). Beyond fairness: A theory of allocation preferences. In G. Mikula (Ed.), *Justice and social interaction* (pp. 167-218). New York: Springer-Verlag.

Leventhal, G. S., Younts, C. M., & Lund, A. K. (1972). Tolerance for inequity in buyer-seller relationships. *Journal of Applied Social Psychology, 2,* 308-318.

Lind, E. A., Kurtz, S., Musante, L., Walker, L., & Thibaut, J. W. (1980). Procedure and outcome effects on reactions to adjudicated resolution of conflicts of interest. *Journal of Personality and Social Psychology, 39*, 643-653.

Martin, J., Brickman, P., & Murray, A. (1984). Moral outrage and pragmatism: Explanations for collective action. *Journal of Experimental Social Psychology, 20*, 484-496.

Orne, M. T. (1969). Demand characteristics and the concept of quasi-controls. In R. Rosenthal & R. L. Rosnow (Eds.), *Artifact in behavioral research* (pp. 143-179). New York: Academic Press.

Porter, L. W., & Lawler, E. E., III. (1968). *Managerial attitudes and performance.* Homewood, IL: Richard D. Irwin.

Sheppard, B. H., & Lewicki, R. J. (1987). Toward general principles of managerial fairness. *Social Justice Research, 1*, 161-196.

Thibaut, J., & Walker, L. (1975). *Procedural justice: A psychological analysis.* Hillsdale, NJ: Lawrence Erlbaum.

Thibaut, J., & Walker, L. (1978). A theory of procedure. *California Law Review, 66*, 541-566.

Tyler, T. R. (1984). The role of perceived injustice in defendants' evaluations of their courtroom experience. *Law and Society Review, 18*, 386-401.

Tyler, T. R., & Caine, A. (1981). The role of distributional and procedural fairness in the endorsement of formal leaders. *Journal of Personality and Social Psychology, 41*, 642-655.

Tyler, T. R., & Folger, R. (1980). Distributional and procedural aspects of satisfaction with citizen-police encounters. *Basic and Applied Social Psychology, 1*, 281-292.

Walker, L., Lind, E. A., & Thibaut, J. (1979). The relation between procedural and distributive justice. *Virginia Law Review, 65*, 1401-1420.

Walster, E., Walster, G. W., & Berscheid, E. (1978). *Equity: Theory and research.* Boston: Allyn & Bacon.

PART VI

Nonmonetary Rewards
JOB TITLES AND THE WORK ENVIRONMENT

ALTHOUGH people usually think of monetary rewards on the job, it is obvious that various nonmonetary sources of payment are also important. Consider, for example, the rewards associated with working in lavishly decorated offices—or, for that matter, the punishment of working in surroundings that are less plush than those to which one is accustomed. Analogously, we may think of job titles as sources of compensation. By referring to someone as "director" of this or "head" of that, we are acknowledging the esteemed position that individual holds. There is little inherently rewarding about either fancy offices or job titles. Both, however, may be understood as mechanisms for bestowing status, itself an important organizational reward. To the extent that such status symbols are recognized as rewards, manipulating them may have a considerable effect on the balance of outcomes and inputs used to define equity.

This underlying reasoning formed the basis for the three chapters presented in this part of the book. For example, in Chapter 15, I describe an experiment in which employees at a large insurance company were temporarily reassigned to the offices of others of either higher, lower, or equal status while their own offices were being refurbished. As expected, those assigned to offices of higher-status associates responded in a manner reflecting their overpayment, by raising their inputs, whereas those assigned to offices of lower-status associates responded in a manner reflecting their underpayment, by lowering their inputs. It is interesting to see how inequity-based reactions may be triggered by such seemingly benign features of the work environment as office and desk size.

By the way, I am often asked how the opportunity to conduct this study came about. It was really quite fortuitous. One day, I was escorted down a corridor in an insurance company's corporate headquarters building while I was visiting to coordinate another project. In response to my inquiry about the construction materials lining the hallway, my host, a top executive, told me of the company's plans to spruce up the offices. I was pleased to help the company out by directing the manner in which the temporary assignments were made. The trick, in this case, was envisioning the study and seizing the opportunity. The actual study ran itself, without any subsequent involvement on my part. If you see the world as one gigantic laboratory, as I do, you find research opportunities where you least expect them.

The study presented in Chapter 16 follows up on the idea that workplace design can have reward value. Instead of manipulating the physical environment, this research assesses perceptions of the environment as a dependent variable. The idea is that people who are underpaid but remain on their jobs will need to highly evaluate the other sources of reward they receive to justify staying. To the extent that physical aspects of the workplace constitute a salient perceptual feature, it follows that they may be evaluated more positively by those who feel underpaid than those who feel equitably paid. Indeed, this was found to be the case.

Chapter 17 focuses on another nonmonetary reward that takes on value because of its status connotations: job titles. In two experiments, I gave laboratory participants a high-status job title that was either earned on the basis of their good performance or unearned, bestowed for no apparent reason. When extra work demands were imposed, the high-status job title proved to be adequate compensation, leading participants to feel equitably paid and to maintain steady levels of performance. This occurred, however, only when the job title was believed to be earned. When an unearned job title was bestowed, participants felt overpaid and temporarily raised their performance. These findings suggest that one type of work-related reward can compensate for another when judging equity. They are also among the earliest findings to reveal that people are sensitive to the perceived legitimacy of the rewards they receive: Only those bestowed on some legitimate basis have reward value. Together, these findings are consistent with equity theory but introduce complexities that go far beyond it.

15

Equity and Workplace Status

There can be little doubt about the existence of certain trappings of success in organizations—physical symbols (cf. Goodsell, 1977) reflecting the organizational status of job incumbents (Steele, 1973). Indeed, previous research has confirmed that certain indicators of status demarcation (cf. Konar & Sundstrom, 1985), such as large offices (Langdon, 1966), carpeting (Joiner, 1976), and proximity to windows (Halloran, 1978), are recognized as rewards symbolizing a person's high standing in an organizational status hierarchy. Although these environmental rewards typically are

AUTHOR'S NOTE: This chapter was originally published in the *Journal of Applied Psychology*, Vol. 73, No. 4, pp. 606-613, under the title "Equity and Workplace Status: A Field Experiment." Copyright © 1988 by the American Psychological Association. Reprinted by permission.

associated with relatively high-status individuals, thereby reinforcing the social order of organizations (Edelman, 1978), on some occasions the status of the job incumbent and the physical symbols associated with that status are not matched (Wineman, 1982). Such instances may be recognized as cases of status inconsistency (cf. Stryker & Macke, 1978), and as such, reactions to them may be explained by equity theory (e.g., Adams, 1965; Walster, Walster, & Berscheid, 1978).

According to equity theory, workers who receive levels of reward (i.e., outcomes) higher or lower than coworkers who make equivalent contributions to their jobs (i.e., inputs) are considered overpaid and underpaid, respectively. Such inequitable states have been shown to result in dissatisfaction and to bring about increases and decreases, respectively, in job performance (for a review, see Greenberg, 1982). As such, the present investigation addresses whether the characteristics of employees' work spaces influence their perceptions of equitable treatment on the job. If the characteristics of one's work space are perceived as constituting part of one's work-related rewards, then it follows that receiving work space-derived rewards greater or less than coworkers of equal status may create conditions of overpayment and underpayment inequity. The focal question of this investigation is whether equity theory explains the reactions of persons encountering consistencies and inconsistencies between their job status and the rewards offered by their work space.

Although little direct evidence bears on this question, managers have intuitively believed and long advocated the importance of basing office design decisions on employees' ranks in their organizations' status hierarchies to ensure equitable treatment (Robichaud, 1958). According to equity theory, employees' work space may be recognized as an element of equitable treatment insofar as it is perceived as a reward that reflects their organizational status. Indeed, previous research (e.g., Konar, Sundstrom, Brady, Mandel, & Rice, 1982) has shown that several elements of work space, such as the nature of the furnishings, amount of space, capacity for personalization, and the ability to control access by others, covary with workers' relative status rankings (for reviews, see Becker, 1981, 1982; Davis, 1984; Sundstrom, 1986).

Although previous researchers have not incorporated work space elements into equity theory-based predictions directly, extrapolations from existing research suggest that reactions to work space characteristics may be predictable from equity theory. For example, Burt and Sundstrom (1979) found in a field study that workers who were underpaid financially were less dissatisfied with their pay if they worked under conditions that were more environmentally desirable than those who did not receive additional work space-related benefits. These results suggest that the desirable working conditions constituted an additional reward that offset the dissatisfaction created by inadequate monetary payment. Such a finding is consistent with the possibility that workers' reactions to their work space may be explained by equity theory. In a previous study of inequities created by nonmonetary rewards (Greenberg & Ornstein, 1983[17]), experimental participants who were overpaid by receiving an inappropriately high job title responded by increasing their job performance, as predicted by equity theory. Thus, much as an inappropriately high job title resulted in attempts to redress overpayment inequity by raising inputs, similar reactions may result from overpayments created by the introduction of work space elements that are inappropriately lavish for one's organizational ranking.

On the basis of this logic, the present study tested hypotheses derived from equity theory in an organizational setting in which the refurbishing of offices required the reassignment of employees to temporary offices. Specifically, I hypothesized that employees reassigned to offices of higher-status workers (i.e., those who are overpaid in office status) would be more productive than those reassigned to offices of other equal-status workers. Similarly, employees reassigned to offices of lower-status workers (i.e., those who are underpaid in office status) would be expected to be less productive than those reassigned to offices of other equal-status workers.

In following equity theory's proposition that the magnitude of the inequity resolution efforts will be proportional to the magnitude of the inequity (Adams, 1965; Walster et al., 1978), I expected that improvements or decrements in performance would be greater the larger the over- or underpayments, respectively. Employees reassigned to offices of workers two levels above them would be expected to perform at a higher level than employees reassigned to offices of more modestly overpaid workers one level above them. Similarly, employees reassigned to offices of workers two levels below them would be expected to perform at a lower level than employees reassigned to offices of more modestly underpaid workers one level below them.

METHOD

Participants

The 198 participants in the study (123 men and 75 women) were drawn from three groups of salaried employees in the life insurance underwriting department of a large insurance company. There were 91 underwriter trainees (*Mdn* age = 24 years; *Mdn* job tenure = 8 months), 60 associate underwriters (*Mdn* age = 28 years; *Mdn* job tenure = 1 year, 9 months), and 47 underwriters (*Mdn* age = 31 years; *Mdn* job tenure = 3 years, 2 months). All these employees were charged with the responsibility for reviewing and either approving or disapproving applications for life insurance on the basis of the extent to which information uncovered in their investigations satisfied the company's criteria for risk. The primary difference in responsibility for the three groups was the monetary size of the policies they were permitted to approve.

Design

Because the offices of the underwriting department were being refurbished, an opportunity presented itself for studying the behavior of employees working temporarily (10 consecutive workdays) in offices regularly assigned to higher-, lower-, or equally ranked coworkers in the underwriting department. With the cooperation of the participating organization, assignment to temporary office conditions was made at random.[1] The reassignment made it possible to create conditions of potential overpayment (assignment to a higher-status office), underpayment (assignment to a lower-status office), or equitable payment (assignment to an equal-status office), as well as the degree of inequitable payment (office assignment either one or two levels above or below the worker's status). To create control groups, some workers in each employee group remained in their own permanent offices during the study. Table 15.1 summarizes the experimental design and reports the number of participants assigned to each condition.

In addition to these between-participants elements, the design of this study also included time as a within-participants element. Repeated measures of the dependent variables were taken at six intervals: the second week before reassignment to a temporary office, the first week before reassignment, the first week during the reassignment period, the second week during reassignment, the first week back in one's permanent office after reassignment, and the second week after reassignment.

Procedure

Office assignment procedure. Before the study began, workers (except those in the control groups) were informed that they would have to work for 2 consecutive 5-day workweeks in other offices while their own offices were refurbished.[2] To avoid disrupting performance but allow ample time for workers to gather their belongings, workers were informed of the

TABLE 15.1 Summary of Study Design

Worker Group/ Temporary Office	n	Payment Condition
Trainee		
Other trainee	42	Equitably paid
Associate	18	One-step overpaid
Underwriter	12	Two-steps overpaid
Own	19	Control
Associate		
Trainee	18	One-step underpaid
Other associate	18	Equitably paid
Underwriter	12	One-step overpaid
Own	12	Control
Underwriter		
Trainee	12	Two-steps underpaid
Associate	12	One-step underpaid
Other underwriter	12	Equitably paid
Own	11	Control

impending temporary move 2 workdays in advance. Workers drew lots to determine their temporary office assignments and were not permitted to switch these assignments. This procedure helped safeguard against the possibility that reactions to office assignments could be the result of perceived managerial favoritism or hostility resulting from an undisclosed (and potentially capricious) basis for the office assignments. The procedure also controlled against any possible self-selection bias in office reassignments.

Office characteristics. The offices used in the study were those regularly assigned to either underwriter trainees, associate underwriters, or underwriters. In the organization studied, as in others (e.g., Harris, 1977; Kleinschrod, 1987), the offices of workers of different status rankings differed along several predetermined, standardized dimensions. Consensual knowledge of such differences helped reinforce the status differences between the offices used in the study.[3] The key physical characteristics of the offices used in the experiment are described in Table 15.2. Although these dimensions were known within the host organization to reflect status differential, they are not idiosyncratic. Indeed, these dimensions are among those found in the survey study by Konar et al. (1982) to be associated with status differences among employees in other organizations.

As shown in Table 15.2, the offices of associate underwriters were shared by fewer office mates, allowed more space per person, and had larger desks

TABLE 15.2 Physical Characteristics of Offices

| | Offices | | |
Physical Characteristic	Underwriter Trainees (n = 15)	Associate Underwriters (n = 30)	Underwriters (n = 47)
No. of occupants per office	6[a]	2	1
Presence of door	No	No	Yes
Occupant space (m² per occupant)	21.34	29.87	44.81
Desk size (m²)	1.14	1.32	1.53

NOTE: Because the host company standardized office characteristics as a function of employee status, there was little or no variation in the values reported here.
[a] One of the 15 offices that was larger than the others housed seven underwriter trainees; the remaining 14 housed six.

than the offices of underwriter trainees. Underwriters' offices were always completely private (used by only one person), allowed the most space per person, and had the largest desks. In addition, the underwriters' offices had doors, whereas the offices of underwriter trainees and associate underwriters did not. The use of these status markers (cf. Konar & Sundstrom, 1985) is in keeping with previous studies showing that higher status is associated with the use of unshared, private offices (Sundstrom, Burt, & Kamp, 1980), greater floor space (Harris, 1977), larger desks (Wylie, 1958), and the option to limit access by the presence of doors (Geran, 1976).

Performance measure. The principal dependent measure was job performance in reviewing applications for life insurance. It was the practice of the company studied to derive corrected performance scores for all underwriters. (Such measures typically were used, in part, as the basis for performance evaluations and pay raises.) Raw performance measures were computed weekly on the basis of the number of cases completed. These were then adjusted by supervisory personnel for decision quality, the complexity of the cases considered (both of which were based on predetermined criteria), and the number of hours spent reviewing application files, resulting in a corrected performance score. As a basis of comparison for interpreting these scores, the mean corrected performance score of the workers studied in the 2 months prior to this investigation was 49.2. Because this score was not significantly different than the two prereassignment scores observed in this investigation, $F < 1.00$, ns, there is no reason to believe that the study period was in any way atypical.

Questionnaire measures. To help explain the performance measure, questionnaire data were collected as supplementary measures. These ques-

tionnaires were administered at three times: one week before reassignment, one week into the reassignment period, and one week after reassignment.

To measure job satisfaction, the 20-item general satisfaction scale of
the Minnesota Satisfaction Questionnaire (MSQ; Weiss, Dawis, England,
& Lofquist, 1967) was used. It requires participants to indicate whether
they are *very satisfied, satisfied, neither satisfied nor dissatisfied, dissatisfied,*
or *very dissatisfied* with respect to a broad range of job dimensions, such
as "the feeling of accomplishment I get from the job" and "the freedom
to use my own judgment." This scale was chosen because it has excellent
psychometric properties (Price & Mueller, 1986) and because its use
enhances comparability with other tests of equity theory using the same
measure (e.g., Pritchard, Dunnette, & Jorgenson, 1972). For this sample,
coefficient alpha was .88.

An additional set of questions was designed to determine the extent to
which workers recognized the outcome value of their office environments. As such, a measure of environmental satisfaction was derived by
asking participants, "How pleased or displeased are you with each of the
following aspects of your current work environment?: privacy, desk space,
floor space, noise level, lighting, furnishings, and overall atmosphere."
Scale values ranged from 1 (*extremely displeased*) to 7 (*extremely pleased*).
Coefficient alpha was computed to be .82.

Last, a separate item asked, "How would you characterize the overall
level of rewards you are now receiving from your job?" Scale values ranged
from 1 (*extremely low*) to 7 (*extremely high*).

Manipulation checks. As the basis for explaining performance differences relative to the inequities caused by status differences in office
assignments, it was necessary to establish that workers correctly perceived
the status differences of their temporary offices and also had unaided and
unimpaired opportunities to perform in their temporary offices. Accordingly, checklist questions addressing these matters were administered at
the end of the first week in the temporary offices (at the same time as the
second administration of the questionnaire measures). Because these
questions were not applicable to workers in the control group, the checklist was not administered to them.

Specifically, to determine whether participants recognized the status
differences between their regular offices and their temporary offices, they
were requested to respond to a checklist item that asked, "Is your temporary office usually assigned to a coworker of lower status than you,
equal status to you, or higher status than you?" An additional checklist
item asked participants, "Relative to your regular office, do the facilities

found in your temporary office help you do your job better, enable you to do your job equally well, or cause you to do your job more poorly?"

RESULTS

Manipulation Checks

Participants' responses to the questionnaire item asking them to identify the relative status attached to their temporary offices showed that they were, in fact, aware of the similarities or differences between their own offices and their temporary ones. Virtually all of the participants assigned to the offices of equal-status others recognized those offices as of equal status. All of the participants assigned to offices of higher- and lower-status others (whether one or two steps higher or lower) recognized the hierarchical level of those offices. This evidence supports the claim that participants were aware of the status similarities or differences they encountered during the study and that the manipulations of status were successful.

Another manipulation check sought to ensure that participants' performance differences could not be attributed to differential opportunities to perform their jobs while in the temporary offices. In response to a checklist item, virtually all 198 participants reported that the facilities in their temporary offices enabled them to perform their jobs as well as they did in their regularly assigned offices. These data discount the possibility that performance increases or decreases noted while in the temporary offices were the result of opportunities provided by or thwarted by office conditions.

Preliminary Analyses

Prior to testing hypotheses, analyses were conducted on the work performance data to determine whether combining the various cells that composed the identically defined payment conditions shown in Table 15.1 was justified. This was done by including the identically defined groups (as a between-participants factor) and the observation time (as a repeated measure) in mixed-design analyses of variance (ANOVAs). Justification for combining the responses of the identically defined groups required finding no significant differences between groups, either as main effects or in interactions with the observation time.

As shown in Table 15.1, four distinct payment conditions were identified by more than one group of workers. Specifically, three groups of workers (those reassigned to equal-status offices) were identified as equitably paid, three groups of workers (those who remained in their own offices) were identified as control participants, two groups of workers (those assigned to offices one status level higher) were identified as one-step overpaid, and two groups of workers (those assigned to offices one status level lower) were identified as one-step underpaid. Separate ANOVAs for the groups defining each of these four payment conditions revealed no significant main effects of group membership and no interaction of group membership with time, all values of $F < 1.00$, *ns*. Accordingly, distinct payment conditions were created by combining the data for the identically defined groups.

Performance Measure

To test hypotheses regarding the effects of payment equity on task performance, a $6 \times (6)$ mixed-design ANOVA was used, in which the six payment conditions composed the between-participants factor and the six observation periods composed the within-participants factor. A significant interaction effect between these two factors was obtained, $F(25, 950) = 8.41$, $p < .001$; the corresponding means are displayed in Figure 15.1.

Simple effects tests were performed to compare the six payment groups at each of the time periods. These tests revealed no significant differences between groups during each of the two weeks before reassignment, in both cases, $F < 1.00$, *ns*, and also during the second week after reassignment, $F < 1.00$, *ns*. Significant differences between groups were found, however, as workers readjusted to their permanent offices during the first week after reassignment, $F(5, 192) = 2.85$, $p < .025$. Newman-Keuls tests (this and all subsequent Newman-Keuls tests are based on an alpha level of .05) revealed that significant differences existed between workers in the one-step overpaid group and the one-step underpaid group, whereas those in the remaining groups were not significantly different from each other.

Significant differences emerged in simple effects tests comparing payment groups during the first week of reassignment, $F(5, 192) = 13.99$, $p < .001$. Newman-Keuls tests revealed that the performance of the equitably paid group and the control group did not differ significantly. Compared with this base level, however, the one-step overpaid group was significantly more productive and the one-step underpaid group was significantly less productive. Additional comparisons showed that those who were two-steps overpaid were significantly more productive than those who were one-step overpaid and that those who were two-steps

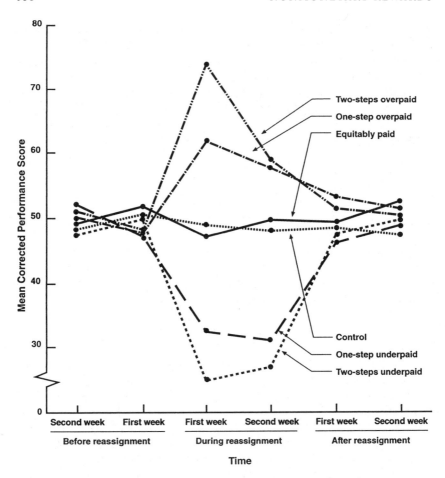

Figure 15.1. Mean Job Performance for Each Payment Group Through Time

underpaid were significantly less productive than those who were one-step underpaid. Thus, for the first week during reassignment, all hypotheses were supported.

During the second week of reassignment, a significant simple effect of payment group was found as well, $F(5, 192) = 11.60$, $p < .001$. As in the first week of reassignment, Newman-Keuls tests showed the equivalence of the control group and the equitably paid group. Also, as in the first week of reassignment, those who were one-step overpaid and underpaid performed significantly higher and lower than these base levels, respectively. The magnitude of inequity hypothesis was only partially supported during the second week of reassignment: Those who were two-steps underpaid were less productive than those who were one-step underpaid, but those who were two-steps overpaid did not perform at significantly higher levels than those who were one-step overpaid (although the difference between the means was in the predicted direction).

This finding is the result of a significant drop in performance from the first week during reassignment to the second week among those who were two-steps overpaid, $t(11) = 5.56, p < .001$ (this and subsequently reported t tests are two-tailed), indicating that the extreme initial reaction to gross overpayment was not sustained. By contrast, the failure to find significant differences between the first and second reassignment weeks for the one-step overpaid group, $t(29) = 1.98, ns,$ the one-step underpaid group, $t(29) = .76 \, ns,$ and the two-steps underpaid group, $t(11) = .88, ns,$ suggests that the effect of these inequities was relatively stable through time.

Questionnaire Measures

Correlations between the questionnaire measures were uniformly low. Specifically, the MSQ scores were not significantly correlated with either the environmental satisfaction measure $(r = .04)$ or the self-reports of overall reward $(r = .07)$. Likewise, the environmental satisfaction measure and the self-reports of overall reward were not significantly correlated with each other $(r = .03)$. The statistical independence of these measures justifies the use of separate univariate analyses.

As in the case of the performance measure, a set of preliminary analyses was performed for each questionnaire measure that showed nonsignificant differences between the various groups defining each payment condition, all values of $F < 1.00, ns.$ Accordingly, the same six payment conditions that were used for the performance measure were created in analyses of the questionnaire measures. Because there were three questionnaire administration periods (as opposed to six performance measurement periods), however, analyses of the questionnaire items were based on $6 \times (3)$ mixed-design ANOVAs.

A significant Payment $\times$ Time interaction was found for responses to the MSQ, $F(10, 389) = 3.01, p < .005.$ A simple effects test found this interaction to be the result of between-group differences during the reassignment period, $F(5, 192) = 2.59, p < .01,$ and no significant differences either before or after the reassignment, in both cases $F < 1.00, ns.$ Newman-Keuls comparisons of the means within the reassignment period revealed significantly lower levels of satisfaction reported by workers who were two-steps underpaid $(M = 44.15)$ compared with any of the other cells (combined $M = 75.50$), none of which were significantly different from each other.

Analyses of the environmental satisfaction questionnaire also revealed a significant interaction effect, $F(10, 389) = 3.65$, $p < .001$. Simple effects tests found that both the prereassignment and the postreassignment levels of satisfaction were not significantly different from each other, in both cases, $F < 1.00$, ns, although significant differences emerged during the reassignment period, $F(5, 192) = 3.18$, $p < .01$. Newman-Keuls tests showed that compared with the equitably paid group and the control group (which were not significantly different from each other; combined $M = 29.75$), the two overpaid groups were significantly higher (although not significantly different from each other; combined $M = 40.50$) and the two underpaid groups were significantly lower (although not significantly different from each other; combined $M = 18.10$).

Self-reports of overall reward received also revealed a significant Payment × Time interaction, $F(10, 389) = 3.74$, $p < .001$. Although perceived reward levels were not significantly different at the prereassignment and postreassignment sessions, in both cases, $F < 1.00$, ns, significant differences emerged during the reassignment period, $F(5, 192) = 3.61$, $p < .005$. Newman-Keuls tests comparing these means revealed that those who were two-steps overpaid ($M = 5.90$) reported significantly higher reward levels than either those who were only one-step overpaid, equitably paid, or in the control group (the means for which were not significantly different from each other; combined $M = 4.33$). The means for these groups, however, were significantly higher than the means for those who were either one- or two-steps underpaid (which were not significantly different from each other; combined $M = 2.75$).

DISCUSSION

The results of this study provide strong support for hypotheses concerning the status value of offices (Edelman, 1978; Konar & Sundstrom, 1985) as outcomes amenable to analysis by equity theory (e.g., Adams, 1965). The performance increases demonstrated by overpaid workers and the decreases demonstrated by underpaid workers in the present study take their place among many other studies that successfully support equity theory predictions (see reviews by Greenberg, 1982, 1987[1]). The unique contribution of this work, however, is the finding that conditions of overpayment and underpayment were able to be created by manipulating nonmonetary outcomes—elements of the work environment associated with organizational status.

Implications

As such, these findings support Adams's (1965) claim that "job status and status symbols" (p. 278) constitute outcomes in the equity equation, a notion that is just beginning to receive empirical support (e.g., Greenberg & Ornstein, 1983[17]). This is in contrast to the well-established impact of monetary outcomes demonstrated in the equity theory literature (Greenberg, 1982, 1987[1]). The specific vehicle of status examined in the present work, the physical environment of offices, although previously recognized by students of office design (e.g., Becker, 1981, 1982; Steele, 1973), heretofore has received scant attention as a possible determinant of workers' equity perceptions (e.g., Burt & Sundstrom, 1979). The present work extends the findings of research by Konar et al. (1982), which demonstrated that certain physical features of offices are related to organizational status by showing that these physical symbols of status demarcation operate as outcomes amenable to equity theory analysis. As such, these findings provide a useful complement to the accumulated literature on office design (e.g., Davis, 1984; Konar et al., 1982; Sundstrom, 1986) by providing an explanatory mechanism that may account for employees' reactions to their work environments (e.g., Wineman, 1982).

The present investigation also supports equity theory's prediction that the reaction to an inequity will be proportional to the magnitude of the inequity experienced (Adams, 1965). Specifically, underpaid workers were found to reduce their performance (i.e., lower their inputs) more when they were extremely underpaid (i.e., assigned offices of others two steps below them) than when they were more moderately underpaid (i.e., assigned offices of others one step below them). Likewise, workers who were more overpaid (i.e., assigned to offices of others two steps above them) raised their performance more than those who were more moderately overpaid (i.e., assigned to offices of others one step above them). This set of findings is particularly noteworthy in that it is one of only a few studies (e.g., Leventhal, Allen, & Kemelgor, 1969) that directly manipulate the magnitude of the inequity encountered. As such, it is notable in attempting to reverse a trend toward the "striking absence of attempts to quantify the magnitude of inputs and outcomes, and thus inequities in the research literature on equity" (Adams & Freedman, 1976, p. 52).

Of particular interest in the present research is the observed tendency for overpayment inequity to bring about overall lower levels of performance increments than did underpayments bring about performance decrements. Such a finding is in keeping with Adams's (1965) supposition that the threshold for experiencing overpayment inequity is higher than that for underpayment inequity. Similarly, several studies (see review by

Walster et al., 1978) have shown that reactions to underpayment are more pronounced than reactions to overpayment. The overall weaker effects of overpayment demonstrated in the present study appear to be the result of lower performance levels in the second week of overpayment than in the first week. Similar temporary effects of overpayment have been demonstrated in both laboratory (e.g., Greenberg & Ornstein, 1983[17]) and field (e.g., Pritchard et al., 1972) settings. Such findings are in keeping with theoretical assertions that reactions to inequity may be moderated by the passage of time (Cosier & Dalton, 1983). Knowing that their overpayment was going to be only temporary, workers may have had little motivation to redress the inequity they experienced by sustaining high levels of performance (Greenberg, 1984). In contrast to the sustained effects of underpayment, more precise explanations for the diminished effects of overpayment through time are lacking and should be recognized as a topic in need of future research.

Further evidence for the less potent effects of overpayment relative to underpayment are provided by the job satisfaction data. Significantly lower levels of satisfaction were found only for the most extremely underpaid workers but not for overpaid workers, thereby corroborating the weaker effects of overpayment demonstrated by Pritchard et al. (1972). In this regard, it is essential to note that the failure to find more pronounced differences on the job satisfaction measure does not weaken the equity theory-based interpretation of these findings. Although equity theory postulates that behavioral reactions to inequity are driven by attempts to alleviate feelings of dissatisfaction (Walster et al., 1978), it has been argued elsewhere (Greenberg, 1984) that such affective mediation has not been clearly demonstrated in previous research and may not be a necessary precondition for behavioral reactions to inequity.

Indeed, an equity theory analysis of the pattern of observed performance differences is supported by other questionnaire findings. Specifically, during the reassignment period, extremely overpaid workers reported receiving higher rewards and extremely underpaid workers reported receiving lower rewards than equitably paid workers. Apparently, the office assignment manipulation was successful in getting workers to perceive changes in their outcome levels. Specific evidence attesting to these overall rewards being the result of the work environment is provided by the findings of the environmental satisfaction questionnaire: During the reassignment period, overpaid workers reported greater satisfaction, and underpaid workers reported less satisfaction, compared with equitably paid workers (and compared with their reactions to their permanent offices). Such evidence shows not only that workers were aware of the differences in their work environments but also that changes in environmental satisfaction levels (outcomes) may account for the observed performance differences (inputs).[4]

Limitations and Future Research Directions

Prompted by the diminished effect of overpayment through time found in this study, one cannot help wonder how long the observed effects of status-based inequities would persist. Before managers can be advised to manipulate workplace elements as a tactic for improving subordinates' attitudes or job performance (cf. Goodsell, 1977; Ornstein, 1989), future longitudinal investigations need to be conducted to determine the persistence of the observed effects (or any reactions to inequity; Cosier & Dalton, 1983). Previous research suggesting that workers suspecting such manipulative intent might actually lower their performance (Greenberg & Ornstein, 1983[17]) dictates against intentional manipulations of inequity for instrumental purposes (Greenberg, 1982; Greenberg & Cohen, 1982). Clearly, future research is needed to determine the long-term reactions to inequities.

Additional research is also needed to help determine the relative contributions of the specific environmental elements manipulated in the present study. Indeed, the complex set of manipulations that defined relative status in this study makes it impossible to determine which specific features may have had the greatest effect on the results. For example, this study cannot determine whether the results were because of participants' knowledge of the status of the office's permanent resident or of the status value of any of the furnishings or design (cf. Davis, 1984; Sundstrom, 1986). Although the inherent confounding of these features was necessary to enhance the validity of this field experiment, it appears useful to isolate these factors in future laboratory experiments to determine their individual contributions (as outcomes) to inequity effects.

CONCLUSION

Given the importance of the workplace environment as a determinant of workers' job attitudes (Oldham & Fried, 1987; Sundstrom et al., 1980), it should not be surprising to find that workers' assignment to offices was related to their perceived level of job rewards and to their actual job performance. In this regard, equity theory proved to be a useful mechanism for explaining workers' reactions to temporarily encountered environmental conditions. As such, this work broadens the potential horizons of research and theory on organizational justice (Greenberg, 1987[1]), as well as those on workplace environments (Becker, 1981; Sundstrom, 1986). As the rapprochement between these areas of investigation develops, researchers may well begin to understand the potential of the work environment as a tool for use by practicing managers (cf. Goodsell, 1977; Ornstein, 1989; Steele, 1973).

NOTES

1. The number of employees within each worker group assigned to each condition was predetermined by the number of available offices and the number of desks per office. To maintain the characteristics of the permanent offices while they were used as temporary offices, the number of temporary residents assigned to an office was kept equal to the number of its permanent residents. Further stimulating the permanent characteristics of the offices, while also avoiding possible confoundings due to having mixed-status office mates, all multiple-employee offices were shared by equal-status coworkers.

2. To keep constant the amount of time that all of the workers spent in their temporary offices, none were allowed to return to their permanent offices in advance of the 2-week period, even if the work was completed ahead of schedule. The physical separation of the various offices and the placement of construction barriers made it unlikely that workers could learn of any possible early completions. Because the period allowed for completion of the offices was liberally budgeted, no delays in returning to permanent offices were needed.

3. A preexperimental questionnaire conducted among employees of the host organization indicated strong consensual agreement about the existence and nature of symbols of status demarcation in their organization. In responding to an open-ended question, 222 employees surveyed identified the four dimensions listed in Table 15.2 most frequently (from 75% to 88%) as reflective of status differences in their organization. Such findings are in keeping with those reported in more broad-based survey research (Louis Harris & Associates, 1978).

4. Unfortunately, however, because these questionnaires were administered only once during the reassignment, the responses cannot be used to gauge changes in affective reactions within this critical period.

REFERENCES

Adams, J. S. (1965). Inequity in social exchange. In L. Berkowitz (Ed.), *Advances in experimental social psychology* (Vol. 2, pp. 267-299). New York: Academic Press.

Adams, J. S., & Freedman, S. (1976). Equity theory revisited: Comments and annotated bibliography. In L. Berkowitz & E. Walster (Eds.), *Advances in experimental social psychology* (Vol. 9, pp. 43-90). New York: Academic Press.

Becker, F. D. (1981). *Workspace.* New York: Praeger.

Becker, F. D. (1982). *The successful office.* Reading, MA: Addison-Wesley.

Burt, R. E., & Sundstrom, E. (1979, September). Workspace and job satisfaction: Extending equity theory to the physical environment. In H. M. Parsons (Chair), *Physical environments at work.* Symposium presented at the meeting of the American Psychological Association, New York.

Cosier, R. A., & Dalton, D. R. (1983). Equity theory and time: A reformulation. *Academy of Management Review, 8,* 311-319.

Davis, T. R. V. (1984). The influence of the physical environment in offices. *Academy of Management Review, 9,* 271-283.

Edelman, M. (1978). *Space and social order.* Madison: University of Wisconsin, Institute for Research on Poverty.

Geran, M. (1976). Does it work? *Interior Design, 47*(2), 114-117.

Goodsell, C. T. (1977). Bureaucratic manipulation of physical symbols: An empirical study. *American Journal of Political Science, 21,* 79-91.

Greenberg, J. (1982). Approaching equity and avoiding inequity in groups and organizations. In J. Greenberg & R. L. Cohen (Eds.), *Equity and justice in social behavior* (pp. 389-435). New York: Academic Press.

Greenberg, J. (1984). On the apocryphal nature of inequity distress. In R. Folger (Ed.), *The sense of injustice: Social psychological perspectives* (pp. 167-186). New York: Plenum.

Greenberg, J. (1987). A taxonomy of organizational justice theories. *Academy of Management Review, 12,* 9-22. [Chapter 1, this volume.]

Greenberg, J., & Cohen, R. L. (1982). Why justice? Normative and instrumental interpretations. In J. Greenberg & R. L. Cohen (Eds.), *Equity and justice in social behavior* (pp. 437-469). New York: Academic Press.

Greenberg, J., & Ornstein, S. (1983). High status job title as compensation for underpayment: A test for equity theory. *Journal of Applied Psychology, 68,* 285-297. [Chapter 17, this volume.]

Halloran, J. (1978). *Applied human relations: An organizational approach.* Englewood Cliffs, NJ: Prentice Hall.

Harris, T. G. (1977, October 31). Psychology of the New York work space. *New York,* 51-54.

Joiner, D. (1976). Social ritual and architectural space. In H. Proshansky, W. Ittleson, & L. Rivlin (Eds.), *Environmental psychology: People and their physical settings* (2nd ed., pp. 224-241). New York: Holt, Rinehart & Winston.

Kleinschrod, W. A. (1987). A balance of forces. *Administrative Management, 48*(7), 18-23.

Konar, E., & Sundstrom, E. (1985). Status demarcation in the office. In J. Wineman (Ed.), *Behavioral issues in office design* (pp. 48-66). New York: Van Nostrand.

Konar, E., Sundstrom, E., Brady, C., Mandel, D., & Rice, R. W. (1982). Status demarcation in the office. *Environment and Behavior, 14,* 561-580.

Langdon, F. J. (1966). *Modern offices: A user survey* (National Building Studies Research Paper No. 41, Ministry of Technology, Building Research Station). London: HMSO.

Leventhal, G. S., Allen, J., & Kemelgor, B. (1969). Reducing inequity by reallocating rewards. *Psychonomic Science, 14,* 295-296.

Louis Harris & Associates, Inc. (1978). *The Steelcase national study of office environments: Do they work?* Grand Rapids, MI: Steelcase.

Oldham, G. R., & Fried, Y. (1987). Employee reactions to workspace characteristics. *Journal of Applied Psychology, 72,* 75-80.

Ornstein, S. (1989). Impression management through office design. In R. Giacalone & P. Rosenfeld (Eds.), *Impression management in organizations* (pp. 411-426). Hillsdale, NJ: Lawrence Erlbaum.

Price, J. L., & Mueller, C. W. (1986). *Handbook of organizational measurement.* Marshfield, MA: Pitman.

Pritchard, R. D., Dunnette, M. D., & Jorgenson, D. O. (1972). Effects of perceptions of equity and inequity on worker performance and satisfaction. *Journal of Applied Psychology, 56,* 75-94.

Robichaud, B. (1958). *Selecting, planning, and managing office space.* New York: McGraw-Hill.

Steele, F. (1973). *Physical settings and organizational development.* Reading, MA: Addison-Wesley.

Stryker, S., & Macke, A. S. (1978). Status inconsistency and role conflict. In R. H. Turner, J. Coleman, & R. C. Fox (Eds.), *Annual review of sociology* (Vol. 4, pp. 57-90). Palo Alto, CA: Annual Reviews.

Sundstrom, E. (1986). *Work places.* New York: Cambridge University Press.

Sundstrom, E., Burt, R., & Kamp, D. (1980). Privacy at work: Architectural correlates of job satisfaction and job performance. *Academy of Management Journal, 23,* 101-117.

Walster, E., Walster, G. W., & Berscheid, E. (1978). *Equity: Theory and research.* Boston: Allyn & Bacon.

Weiss, D. J., Dawis, R. V., England, G. W., & Lofquist, L. H. (1967). *Manual for the Minnesota Satisfaction Questionnaire.* Minneapolis: University of Minnesota, Industrial Relations Center.

Wineman, J. D. (1982). Office design and evaluation: An overview. *Environment and Behavior, 14,* 271-298.

Wylie, H. L. (1958). *Office management handbook* (2nd ed.). New York: Ronald Press.

16

Injustice and Cognitive
Reevaluation of the Work Environment

Equity theory (e.g., Adams, 1965; Walster, Walster, & Berscheid, 1978) postulates that workers who are inequitably paid—for whom the ratio of rewards (outcomes) to contributions (inputs) is unequal to the corresponding ratio of a comparison other—experience dissatisfaction and will be motivated to alleviate that condition by redressing the inequity. The most commonly studied responses to inequity are behavioral ones, including raising or lowering inputs such as job performance and, in

AUTHOR'S NOTE: This chapter was originally published in the *Academy of Management Journal*, Vol. 32, No. 1, pp. 174-184, under the title "Cognitive Re-evaluation of Outcomes in Response to Underpayment Inequity." Copyright © 1989 by the Academy of Management. Reprinted by permission.

extreme cases, quitting a job (Greenberg, 1982, 1987[1]). Equity theory, also acknowledges, however, that people can redress states of inequity cognitively, for instance, by altering their beliefs about the outcomes they receive from their jobs. For example, the theory asserts that workers who are underpaid financially may be able to reestablish overall levels of equity by convincing themselves that they are well compensated with respect to other outcomes. Despite this acknowledgment, research on equity theory has emphasized studying behavioral responses to inequity (for a review, see Mowday, 1987) and thus has revealed little about the cognitive strategies workers use to alter their perceptions of inequitable states.

This state of affairs is an important limitation on the understanding of reactions to inequities in organizations (Greenberg, 1987[1]). Although workers may raise or lower their outcomes in response to inequitable situations, the behaviors usually studied represent relatively extreme reactions. Research has ignored the more subtle and ubiquitous cognitive reactions that are likely to occur. For example, although workers may be reluctant to threaten their job security by lowering their inputs or to face chastisement from coworkers by raising their inputs, it may be simple for them to redress inequity by cognitively redefining a situation (Weick & Nesset, 1968). Indeed, a basic proposition of equity theory is that people will attempt to redress inequities in the least costly way (Walster et al., 1978). Cognitive redefinition of a situation represents one such strategy.

The little evidence available on the use of cognitive strategies to resolve inequity has followed from the tradition of research on cognitive dissonance (Festinger, 1957), focusing on people's perceptions of task characteristics. For example, Lawler and O'Gara (1967) and Weick (1964) found that underpaid people evaluated the jobs they were doing as more interesting than did people who were equitably paid. According to models of self-justification (Deci, 1975; Lepper & Greene, 1978), underpaid workers are motivated to perceive the tasks they perform as highly interesting to cognitively justify their performing them in exchange for low wages.

Although findings such as these suggest that workers' evaluations of job outcomes may depend on perceptions of outcomes, equity theory is admittedly extremely vague about the relationships among outcomes (Adams & Freedman, 1976). Equity theory treats outcomes as a unitary set although they are often manipulated independently in organizations. For example, the actual level of nonmonetary outcomes, such as job status or working conditions (Greenberg, 1988[15]), often does not change when a company implements a reduction in pay. It is likely, however, that the manipulation of monetary outcomes will affect workers' perceptions of outcomes that are not manipulated. Workers facing a pay reduction may seek an opportunity to redress the resulting underpayment inequity by cognitively augmenting the value of other outcomes they receive (Greenberg, 1982). In so doing, they may be effectively reducing the inequity they face in a low-risk manner.

The present investigation examined whether workers evaluated their nonmonetary rewards as higher during a period in which monetary rewards were reduced than they did when monetary rewards were increased to their previously established levels. The nonmonetary outcomes examined in this study were features of the physical work environment that previous research has shown to have reward value to employees (for a review, see Sundstrom, 1986). For example, opportunities to work in large, private offices or to have large desks have been recognized as valued organizational rewards (Konar, Sundstrom, Brady, Mandel, & Rice, 1982). Moreover, previous research has found such environmental rewards to be salient contributors to payment equity (Greenberg, 1988[15]), which justifies choosing the outcomes suitable for study as targets of cognitive reevaluation.

If features of a physical work environment have reward value to employees and if underpaid workers are motivated to redress inequitable conditions by highlighting the value of the environmental rewards they receive, it follows that workers will be more strongly motivated to cognitively augment the reward value of environmental features when they are underpaid than when they are equitably paid. Specifically, I expected workers to cognitively enhance the value of various nonmonetary, environmental rewards as determinants of their overall fair payment when they were financially underpaid. Such an effect is consistent with research on inadequate justification showing that people cognitively enhance the value of nonmonetary rewards when monetary rewards are reduced (for a review, see Lepper & Greene, 1978).

Hypothesis 1: The perceived importance of environmental features as determinants of overall fair payment will be greater during reduced pay than during reinstated pay.

A related hypothesis may be derived regarding the amount of non-monetary rewards people believe necessary to establish overall equitable payment. Research has shown that various features of office environments may function as rewards that can create states of equity or inequity (Burt & Sundstrom, 1979; Greenberg, 1988[15]). Thus, it follows that workers will believe that more environmental rewards are necessary to establish overall equitable payment when they are underpaid financially than when they are equitably paid.

Hypothesis 2: The perceived amounts of environmental features required to establish equitable payment will be greater during reduced pay than during reinstated pay.

Equity theory stipulates that inequitably paid workers will experience more job dissatisfaction than those who are equitably paid (Greenberg, 1984). If underpaid workers cognitively redefined outcomes as Hypotheses 1 and 2 predict, however, they would not be expected to experience dissatisfaction. The inequity they perceived would already have been redressed through cognitive reevaluation, and negative attitudinal responses to underpayment would thus be reduced.

Hypothesis 3: Workers' job satisfaction will not differ significantly during reduced pay and during reinstated pay.

METHODS

Respondents

The primary participants in the study were 114 salaried white-collar employees (68 men and 46 women) of a nonunionized manufacturing firm located in a large city. Among them were three subgroups representing different occupational classifications, including 34 secretaries, 36 clerical workers, and 44 lower-level managers. Their median age was 28 years, and their median job tenure with the organization was 3.5 years. An additional 18 employees completed the questionnaire initially but were no longer employed by the organization when the second questionnaire was administered.

Procedures

Because a slow sales period prompted a managerial decision to cut all employees' pay by 6%, an opportunity presented itself to study reactions to underpayment inequity in a naturalistic setting. Previous research has suggested that the reduction of an established pay level without any concomitant lowering of job responsibilities will lead workers to experience underpayment inequity (Greenberg, 1982). Employees were given no information about the circumstances leading to the pay reduction—although they knew that the company's sales were slow—and were merely told that an across-the-board cut was being implemented to avoid the layoff of any workers.

Data were collected twice: 6 months after institution of the pay cut and 14 months later, which was 6 months after the reinstatement of prereduction pay levels. The rationale for allowing workers to experience 6-month intervals at each pay level before administering the questionnaire was to ensure that their reactions were the result of relatively stable conditions. The 6-month delay also eliminated from the primary sample those who elected to respond to the inequity by leaving their jobs (Finn & Lee, 1972; Telly, French, & Scott, 1971). All participants completed the questionnaire voluntarily during nonwork periods and were assured of the anonymity of their responses. No employee approached by the investigator declined to participate.

The research questionnaire consisted of four parts. The first section contained an item designed as a check on the internal validity of the study—a question to establish that the workers studied felt more underpaid while working under the lower-salary conditions than they did after their previous pay level was reinstated. Specifically, respondents were asked, "Financially, how equitably or inequitably paid are you on your job?" Responses were made on a bidirectional scale ranging from 1 (*greatly underpaid*) to 9 (*greatly overpaid*), with the midpoint labeled *equitably paid.* Although the psychometric properties of this single-item measure may be suspect, its use was justified on the grounds that previous studies have successfully used similar items (Greenberg & Ornstein, 1983[17]).

The second part of the questionnaire consisted of a series of items asking workers "How important is each of the following features of your work environment as a determinant of your overall fair payment?" Responses could range from 1 (*not at all important*) to 15 (*extremely important*), with the midpoint labeled *moderately important.*[1] The features, derived from surveys probing what environmental characteristics are common sources of organizational reward among office workers (Konar et al., 1982; Sundstrom, 1986), were (a) amount of floor space, (b) amount of desk space, (c) amount of privacy, (d) number of coworkers sharing office, (e) amount of personal space, (f) capacity to personalize work environment, (g) number of work surfaces, (h) number of windows in work area, (i) opportunities to select decor and furnishings, and (j) amount of storage room. The 10 responses were averaged to form one scale ($\alpha = .93$).

A postexperimental questionnaire verified that each of the 10 environmental features constituted a potential source of reward for employees. Two months after the second administration of the questionnaire to the primary respondents, I contacted 38 new employees of the firm. The new employees, who were demographically similar to the study group, had

been hired after previous pay levels had been reinstated. Therefore, recol-
lections of the pay reduction could not bias their responses. They were
asked to indicate the perceived value as an organizational reward of each
of the 10 features on a response scale ranging from 1 (*not at all valuable
as a reward*) to 9 (*extremely valuable as a reward*), with the midpoint
labeled *moderately valuable as a reward*. All 10 features received high
ratings (vf$\bar{x}$ = 7.88) that did not differ significantly from each other ($F <$
1.00, *ns*), which verified that the features studied constituted potentially
valuable sources of reward to the employees. Preexperimental interviews
with supervisors from the host firm, who indicated that these features
were highly valued rewards in their organization, further supported the
selection of the 10 features.

The third part of the questionnaire was designed to tap perceptions of
the relative amounts of the 10 features workers believed they required to
be fairly paid. Workers were asked, "Compared to the amount you have
now, how much of each of the environmental features below do you
believe you should have to be equitably paid?" Scale values ranged from
1 (*much less*) to 15 (*much more*), with the midpoint labeled *same amount*.[2]
As with the previous question, I averaged responses to these items to form
a single scale (α = .90).

The final part of the questionnaire consisted of the 20-item version of
the Minnesota Satisfaction Questionnaire (MSQ) (Weiss, Dawis, England,
& Lofquist, 1967). Coefficient alpha was computed to be .89, a figure
comparable with other published internal consistency data for this scale
(Price & Mueller, 1986).

RESULTS

Exploratory analyses of the data revealed no significant differences
between the three subgroups of respondents used in the study on any of
the dependent measures. Accordingly, all subsequent analyses are based
on data from the three groups combined. In addition, to aid interpretation of the results, I computed Pearson product-moment correlations
between all pairings of measures taken at both pay periods. Table 16.1
shows the resulting intercorrelation matrix.

Perceived Payment Equity

The question assessing workers' perceptions of the equity or inequity
of their financial payment verified that they felt underpaid while their
pay was reduced. Specifically, during the reduced-pay period, the mean

TABLE 16.1 Intercorrelations Between Measures Within and Between Pay Periods[a]

Variables	1	2	3	4	5	6	7
Reduced-pay period							
1. Perceived payment equity[b]							
2. Importance of features	−.38***						
3. Amount of features	−.34***	.09					
4. MSQ score	.15	.06	.05				
Reinstated-pay period							
5. Perceived payment equity[b]	−.02	.00	.01	.03			
6. Importance of features	.04	.05	.02	.06	−.16		
7. Amount of features	.01	.07	.02	.04	−.18	.01	
8. MSQ score	.03	.03	.06	.07	.12	.00	−.03

[a] Unless otherwise noted, $N = 114$.
[b] Interpretation of correlations involving this bidirectional scale was facilitated by decomposing it into two unidirectional scales. Because 90.35% of the responses ranged from 1 (*greatly underpaid*) to 5 (the midpoint, *equitably paid*), however, I analyzed only one unidirectional scale ($N = 103$).
***$p < .001$.

response to the payment equity question (2.16) was significantly lower than it was during the reinstated-pay period (4.66, $t_{113} = 20.81$, $p < .001$).

Cognitive Reevaluation Questions

For the question assessing the perceived importance of the various status symbols, a MANOVA revealed significant differences between the responses during the reduced-pay and reinstated-pay periods ($F = 88.63$, $p < .001$). In support of Hypothesis 1, when they were underpaid financially, workers reported that the environmental rewards were more important determinants of overall fair pay than when they were equitably paid ($\bar{x} = 11.44$ vs. 9.42). In fact, as revealed by the statistically significant correlation of −.38 shown in Table 16.1, the more underpaid that workers felt, the more important the environmental features were to them during the reduced-pay period. A nonsignificant correlation of −.16 was obtained between the same variables during the reinstated-pay period. These two correlations differed from each other at a marginal level of statistical significance ($z = 1.70$, $p < .09$).

Individual comparisons between the pay periods revealed that workers placed greater importance on 8 of the 10 environmental features when their pay was reduced than they did when their pay was reinstated. Although the difference between the means for the remaining two environmental features failed to reach significance, they were in the predicted direction. The left side of Table 16.2 reports the corresponding means and standard deviations and the results of *t*-tests comparing the means.

For the question assessing the perceived amounts of the various environmental features workers believed they required to establish equitable payment, a MANOVA revealed significant differences between the responses during the reduced-pay and reinstated-pay periods ($F = 64.02$, $p < .001$). In support of Hypothesis 2, workers believed they required greater amounts of the various environmental rewards to be fairly paid when their pay was reduced than they did when their pay was reinstated ($\overline{x} = 11.14$ vs. 9.36). In fact, as revealed by the statistically significant correlation of $-.34$ shown in Table 16.1, the more underpaid that workers felt, the more of the features they reportedly needed to consider themselves fairly paid during the reduced-pay period. A nonsignificant correlation of $-.18$ was obtained between these same variables during the reinstated-pay period. These correlations were not significantly different from each other ($z = 1.13$, ns).

Individual comparisons between the pay periods revealed that workers reported requiring greater amounts of 9 of the 10 environmental features when their pay was reduced than they required when their pay was reinstated. Although the difference between the means for the "decor selection" feature failed to reach significance, it was in the predicted direction. The right side of Table 16.2 shows the corresponding means and standard deviations and the results of t-tests comparing these means.

Job Satisfaction

Analysis of the MSQ scores of workers during the reduced-pay period ($\overline{x} = 66.74$) and the reinstated-pay period ($\overline{x} = 67.81$) revealed a difference that was not statistically significant ($t < 1.00$, ns), thereby confirming Hypothesis 3. Moreover, although there was a positive trend in the relationship between satisfaction and perceived financial equity, the correlations between these variables, shown in Table 16.1, were not significant during either period.

DISCUSSION

These results highlight the operation of a process that equity theory has posited (Adams, 1965) but that previous research has not directly demonstrated. This process is the cognitive reevaluation of one set of outcomes in response to an inequitable state in another set of outcomes. Specifically, a pay cut, a reduction in monetary outcomes to below established levels, resulted in perceived financial underpayment among workers. Workers had concomitant tendencies (a) to enhance the perceived

TABLE 16.2 Means, Standard Deviations, and Comparisons Between Reduced-Pay and Reinstated-Pay Periods for Cognitive Reevaluation Questions[a]

Environmental Features	Importance of Feature[b]					Number of Features[c]				
	Reduced-Pay Period		Reinstated-Pay Period		t[d]	Reduced-Pay Period		Reinstated-Pay Period		t[d]
	Means	SD	Means	SD		Means	SD	Means	SD	
Floor space	11.64	3.66	8.14	2.28	9.72***	9.86	4.19	8.71	3.27	2.56**
Desk space	13.01	4.51	9.44	3.34	8.50***	10.75	3.80	9.06	2.12	4.83***
Privacy	11.86	4.56	10.51	2.63	3.46***	12.39	4.57	10.66	3.77	3.68***
Office mates	12.79	3.76	10.77	2.91	4.70***	11.67	4.20	9.45	2.88	5.69***
Personal space	12.19	4.20	9.65	4.36	4.79***	10.95	3.61	9.64	4.73	2.67**
Personalization	10.86	3.26	8.46	2.21	7.06***	12.48	4.39	9.81	2.69	5.93***
Work surfaces	8.54	4.55	7.98	3.42	1.08	9.61	3.74	8.59	3.90	2.17*
Windows	12.67	4.81	10.44	4.08	4.13***	12.51	4.86	10.42	3.41	3.87***
Decor selection	9.62	3.61	9.04	2.88	1.49	8.50	3.98	7.86	4.15	1.36
Storage room	11.18	4.71	9.81	3.98	2.54**	12.67	2.64	9.41	3.82	8.15***

[a] $N = 114$.
[b] Scores could range from 1 to 15, with higher scores reflecting greater perceived importance of the feature as a determinant of overall fair payment.
[c] Scores could range from 1 to 15, with higher scores reflecting greater amounts of the feature required to establish equitable payment, with the exception of "office mates," for which the scoring was reversed.
[d] $df = 113$.

*$p < .05$, one-tailed test.
**$p < .01$, one-tailed test.
***$p < .001$, one-tailed test.

importance of other outcomes—valued features of the work environment —as contributors to overall feelings of equitable payment and (b) to exaggerate the perceived level of these outcomes needed to establish equity. Although theorists have suggested that states of inequity reduce job satisfaction (Adams, 1965), in this study levels of job satisfaction were not lower during the period of underpayment. That finding may be taken as evidence that cognitive reevaluation responses effectively minimized the distressing effects of the inequity.

These results extend earlier findings showing that workers respond to underpayment inequity by enhancing the perceived interest value of work (Lawler & O'Gara, 1967; Weick, 1964). Apparently, an underpayment inequity may also facilitate cognitive enhancement of a work environment. Such cognitive reevaluation responses appear to represent relatively innocuous but effective ways of responding to an inequitable state, precisely the type of responses that equity theory proposes as desired mechanisms of inequity reduction (Walster et al., 1978). Specifically, workers may prefer to redress inequities by cognitively reevaluating outcomes than by engaging in the potentially riskier behavioral inequity resolution tactic of lowering their performance—especially when the latter may jeopardize their job security, as it would during an economic downturn such as the period studied here (Brockner & Greenberg, 1989). Because data were not available concerning workers' job performance, however, the present study does not provide insight into how workers may have used the cognitive inequity resolution strategies noted in conjunction with behavioral strategies. Accordingly, the generalizability of these results needs to be assessed in future research examining the relationships between multiple inequity resolution strategies (Adams & Freedman, 1976).

In this regard, the reader is cautioned that the focus on the cognitive reevaluation of environmental outcomes in the present study is not meant to imply that these are the only outcomes likely to be sensitive to the cognitive reevaluation process evidenced here. It would be premature to assume that these outcome variables have any special theoretical status other than that their selection for study made them salient to the participants. Accordingly, future research is needed to examine the conditions underlying workers' choice of an outcome variable (or set of variables) as the target of their cognitive enhancement efforts.

The generalizability of the process tapped in this study is also limited because self-comparisons appear to have been the referents used as the basis for making judgments about payment equity. Self-referents were salient in this study because all others in the same organization encountered an equivalent percentage pay cut. Thus, workers used themselves at an earlier time as referents (Austin, 1977). Although previous field research has found self-comparisons to be salient sources of inequity (e.g., Lord & Hohenfeld, 1979), it is possible that inequities prompted by comparisons with other referents would have triggered different reactions from those I observed (Goodman, 1974; Scholl, Cooper, & McKenna, 1987).

In addition, the present findings are limited because only reactions to underpayment inequities were studied. To test the symmetry of the phenomenon observed here, future research is needed that also examines workers' cognitive reactions to overpayment inequities. Because previous research has shown that the threshold for overpayment inequity is higher than that for underpayment inequity (Zedeck & Smith, 1968), there is reason to be cautious about premature generalization of these results in the opposite direction.

NOTES

1. For this and for the following question, I anticipated that respondents would use half the scale, the portion from *moderately important* to *extremely important*. Thus, 15-point bipolar scales were used to allow ample room for discrimination between responses while not biasing the potential range of responses with a unipolar scale.

2. Because both preexperimental interviews with supervisors and previous research (Konar et al., 1982) indicated that fewer office mates were more rewarding than more office mates, in contrast with the remaining nine features in which more constituted a greater reward level, I decided a priori to reverse-score the item "number of coworkers sharing office" to maintain consistency in scoring.

REFERENCES

Adams, J. S. (1965). Inequity in social exchange. In L. Berkowitz (Ed.), *Advances in experimental social psychology* (Vol. 2, 267-299). New York: Academic Press.

Adams, J. S., & Freedman, S. (1976). Equity theory revisited: Comments and annotated bibliography. In L. Berkowitz & E. Walster (Eds.), *Advances in experimental social psychology* (Vol. 9, pp. 43-90). New York: Academic Press.

Austin, W. (1977). Equity theory and social comparison processes. In J. M. Suls & R. M. Miller (Eds.), *Social comparison processes* (pp. 279-305). Washington, DC: Hemisphere.

Brockner, J., & Greenberg, J. (1989). The impact of layoffs on survivors: An organizational justice perspective. In J. Carroll (Ed.), *Applied social psychology and organizational settings* (pp. 45-75). Hillsdale, NJ: Lawrence Erlbaum.

Burt, R. E., & Sundstrom, E. (1979, September). Workspace and job satisfaction: Extending equity theory to the physical environment. In H. M. Parsons (Chair), *Physical environments at work*. Symposium presented at the meeting of the American Psychological Association, New York.

Deci, E. L. (1975). *Intrinsic motivation*. New York: Plenum.

Festinger, L. (1957). *A theory of cognitive dissonance*. Evanston, IL: Row, Peterson.

Finn, R. H., & Lee, S. M. (1972). Salary equity: Its determinants, analysis, and correlates. *Journal of Applied Psychology, 56*, 283-292.

Goodman, P. S. (1974). An examination of referents used in the evaluation of pay. *Organizational Behavior and Human Performance, 12,* 170-195.

Greenberg, J. (1982). Approaching equity and avoiding inequity in groups and organizations. In J. Greenberg & R. L. Cohen (Eds.), *Equity and justice in social behavior* (pp. 389-435). New York: Academic Press.

Greenberg, J. (1984). On the apocryphal nature of inequity distress. In R. Folger (Ed.), *The sense of injustice* (pp. 167-188). New York: Plenum.

Greenberg, J. (1987). A taxonomy of organizational justice theories. *Academy of Management Review, 12,* 9-22. [Chapter 1, this volume.]

Greenberg, J. (1988). Equity and workplace status: A field experiment. *Journal of Applied Psychology, 73,* 606-613. [Chapter 15, this volume.]

Greenberg, J., & Ornstein, S. (1983). High status job title as compensation for underpayment: A test of equity theory. *Journal of Applied Psychology, 68,* 285-297. [Chapter 17, this volume.]

Konar, E., Sundstrom, E., Brady, C., Mandel, D., & Rice, R. W. (1982). Status demarcation in the office. *Environment and Behavior, 14,* 561-580.

Lawler, E. E., III, & O'Gara, P. W. (1967). Effects of inequity produced by underpayment on work output, work quality, and attitudes toward the work. *Journal of Applied Psychology, 51,* 403-410.

Lepper, M. R., & Greene, D. (Eds.). (1978). *The hidden costs of reward.* Hillsdale, NJ: Lawrence Erlbaum.

Lord, R. G., & Hohenfeld, J. A. (1979). Longitudinal field assessment of equity effects on the performance of major league baseball players. *Journal of Applied Psychology, 64,* 19-26.

Mowday, R. T. (1987). Equity theory predictions of behavior in organizations. In R. M. Steers & L. W. Porter (Eds.), *Motivation and work behavior* (4th ed., pp. 89-110). New York: McGraw-Hill.

Price, J. L., & Mueller, C. W. (1986). *Handbook of organizational measurement.* Marshfield, MA: Pitman.

Scholl, R. W., Cooper, E. A., & McKenna, J. F. (1987). Referent selection in determining equity perceptions: Differential effects on behavioral and attitudinal outcomes. *Personnel Psychology, 40,* 113-124.

Sundstrom, E. (1986). *Work places.* New York: Cambridge University Press.

Telly, C. S., French, W. L., & Scott, W. G. (1971). The relationship of inequity to turnover among hourly workers. *Administrative Science Quarterly, 16,* 164-172.

Walster, E., Walster, G. W., & Berscheid, E. (1978). *Equity: Theory and research.* Boston: Allyn & Bacon.

Weick, K. E. (1964). Reduction of cognitive dissonance through task enhancement and effort expenditure. *Journal of Abnormal and Social Psychology, 68,* 533-539.

Weick, K. E., & Nesset, B. (1968). Preferences among forms of equity. *Organizational Behavior and Human Performance, 3,* 400-416.

Weiss, D. J., Dawis, R. V., England, G. W., & Lofquist, L. H. (1967). *Manual for the Minnesota Satisfaction Questionnaire.* Minneapolis: University of Minnesota, Industrial Relations Center.

Zedeck, S., & Smith, P. C. (1968). A psychophysical determination of equitable payment. *Journal of Applied Psychology, 52,* 343-347.

17

High-Status Job Title as
Compensation for Underpayment

Research derived from equity theory (e.g., Adams, 1965; Walster, Berscheid, & Walster, 1973; Walster, Walster, & Berscheid, 1978) has demonstrated that performance compensated on an hourly basis often increases in response to overpayment and decreases in response to underpayment (see reviews by Campbell & Pritchard, 1976; Greenberg, 1982; Mowday, 1979). These changes in performance are interpreted by

AUTHOR'S NOTE: This chapter was originally published in the *Journal of Applied Psychology*, Vol. 68, No. 2, pp. 285-297, under the title "High Status Job Title as Compensation for Underpayment: A Test of Equity Theory," by J. Greenberg and S. Ornstein. Copyright © 1983 by the American Psychological Association. Reprinted by permission.

equity theory as behavioral attempts to adjust inputs (i.e., contributions) to match the ratio of one's outcomes (i.e., rewards) to inputs to that of some standard of comparison. Despite the proposal of equity theory that a wide variety of outcomes can affect behavior on the job, the existing studies have focused almost exclusively on one type of job outcome: pay (see Adams & Freedman, 1976; Greenberg, 1982). This bias toward studying payment outcomes in the empirical literature has left organizational researchers unaware of the possible effects of inequities created by other outcomes (Campbell & Pritchard, 1976).

One particularly interesting and prevalent job outcome is the status a worker receives by having certain duties and responsibilities, as reflected by job title (Dandridge, Mitroff, & Joyce, 1980). Having responsibilities has been recognized by Pritchard (1969), however, as potentially carrying a burden that may make it appear as an input (an added contribution) as well as an outcome (a source of pride). This ambiguity has been empirically established by Tornow (1971), who found that a feeling of duty and similar concepts could not be reliably categorized as either work outcomes or inputs. The implications of such an ambiguity are profound if one envisions the puzzlement of a manager who attempts to raise the outcomes of employees by giving them more responsible positions with higher-status titles, only to discover that the employees perceive this change as an attempt to raise their inputs!

An apparent reason for this ambiguity is that a job with a high-status title requiring added duties and responsibilities represents a potentially simultaneous increase in both inputs (expenditure of additional time and effort) and outcomes (raised status communicated by the job title). It is possible, therefore, that the added outcomes and inputs may offset each other and not disrupt the existing balance of forces constituting a worker's equity ratio. For this to result, it is essential for the title to be perceived as a positively valent outcome. On the basis of several areas of research, it was expected that a title would be more likely to be perceived as a positive outcome when it is earned on the basis of one's internally controlled behavior than when it is the unearned result of external, gratuitous factors. This assertion is supported by evidence suggesting that earned outcomes tend to be recognized as more valid and are more valued than those attributed to unexplained or external sources, such as luck (Cohen, 1982; Greenberg, 1980; Wittig, Marks, & Jones, 1981). Jones's (1964) research on ingratiation likewise suggests that potentially rewarding outcomes are not viewed as positively valent when they are believed to be bestowed ingenuinely. (When a so-called reward, such as a title bestowed for unknown reasons, is granted in conjunction with a demand for increased inputs, it is especially likely to be suspected of being a tool of manipulation and, therefore, not likely to be recognized as rewarding.) Accordingly, the two studies reported in this chapter compared the effects on work performance of granting an earned and an unearned high-status job title to establish the title's influence on the equity ratio.

EXPERIMENT 1

The first experiment was designed to examine this issue by devising a laboratory situation in which a demand for increased inputs was accompanied by either an earned or an unearned high-status job title (and no additional hourly monetary compensation). On the basis of the evidence cited above, it was expected that an earned job title would be recognized as a legitimate and valued outcome that could potentially offset the demand for additional inputs, resulting in the maintenance of an equitable state.[1] Therefore, I hypothesized that participants in the earned-title condition would report feeling equitably paid and would maintain an even level of performance that did not differ from that of participants (in the control condition) whose equity ratios were unchanged because they had been granted neither a high-status job title nor additional responsibilities. It was likewise expected that workers who earned their title would perform at a higher level than those (in the no-title condition) who expected to raise their inputs but who received no title. The possibility that an earned title may be able to compensate for additional unremunerated inputs is consistent with the findings of Burt and Sundstrom (1979) that another valued symbol of job status, the work environment, compensated for monetary rewards in the equity ratio.

In contrast to the hypothesized compensating effects of an earned job title, it was expected that an unearned title would be recognized as invalid (and possibly the result of manipulative intent) and would therefore have little efficacy as a source of reward. Accordingly, it was hypothesized that participants required to perform additional work in return for an unearned title would feel underpaid and would therefore lower their performance to reestablish equity. In fact, participants in the unearned-reward condition were expected to perform at a (low) level equal to that of participants expecting to increase their inputs but who received no title at all. Likewise, this level of performance was expected to be lower than that of participants who earned their job titles (who recognized their titles as a form of compensation and who, therefore, would not feel underpaid).

METHOD

Participants and Design

The participants were 40 male and 44 female undergraduate volunteers who agreed to participate in a study allegedly concerned with the effects of working conditions on clerical task performance. They expected to be working as proofreaders during a period ranging from 1 to 2 hours in return for $3.85 per hour. Only participants who agreed to be available for 2 hours were included in the study.

A $2 \times 4 \times 3$ mixed design was employed, with two between-participants factors—sex of participant and title-bestowal condition (earned title, un-earned title, no-title, or control)—and one within-participants factor—work period (pretitle session, posttitle session, and final session). Ten men and 11 women were randomly assigned to each of the eight conditions.

Procedure

Participants participated in mixed-sex groups of four to six members. Each participant was seated at a separate work cubicle (a study carrel) situated to deny visual access to others.

The experimenter explained and demonstrated the procedure for performing the proofreading task. This involved comparing a piece of printed copy to an original, typewritten manuscript page and circling the misprinted characters. On the average, one error was embedded in every two lines. Pilot testing revealed that college students found this work challenging, although somewhat tedious, but could perform it at a high level of accuracy. It was also determined via a pilot questionnaire that college students believed $3.85 per hour to be a fair rate of pay for this work. To familiarize participants with the task, a 2- to 3-minute practice session was given. The experimenter stressed that participants should attempt to work as rapidly and as accurately as possible. Following this, the first of three 12-minute work periods (the pretitle session) began.

At the end of the 12 minutes, the experimenter announced the end of the first session and handed each participant a questionnaire booklet. The questionnaire required participants to indicate, using 7-point scales, their liking for the experimenter, liking for the task (in both cases, 1 = *dislike very much*, 7 = *like very much*), perceived performance level (1 = *much worse than others*, 7 = *much better than others*), and the perceived fairness of payment (1 = *very overpaid*, 7 = *very underpaid*). Additional filler items concerning various aspects of the work environment were included to support the cover story that the study was allegedly concerned with working conditions. (This deception was adopted to provide a rationale for the repeated administration of the questionnaire.) To minimize the possibility of social desirability effects in responding to questionnaire items, participants were requested to not write their names on the questionnaire booklets, to place completed booklets in an envelope provided by the experimenter, and to put this envelope in a large stack of envelopes.

Following completion of the first work session and questionnaire administration, the experimenter individually escorted each participant to an adjacent office in which the title-bestowal manipulation was carried out.[2] It was announced that these brief conferences (1 to 2 minutes) would give each worker an opportunity to discuss his or her task performance. In the earned-title condition, the experimenter carefully examined the participants' work and remarked in a serious tone that it was among the best he had ever seen. With this, the experimenter said that he wanted the participants to assist him by being "senior proofreaders." (Pilot testing revealed that this title was perceived as a high-status title within this work context.) This, he said, would require the participants to stay for the second of 2 scheduled hours to help check others' work (immediately following the first hour, after the others were to be dismissed), but he would not be able to offer any additional monetary remuneration for this work. The experimenter explained that he was authorized to pay $3.85 per hour to workers only while they were actually performing the proofreading task but not while they were performing the senior proofreader duties, which they were asked to perform on an honorary basis. Accordingly, these participants were led to believe that they would be working for a total of 2 hours but that they would be paid for only 1 hour's work. In actuality, participants were not required to do any extra work, and the experimental session was terminated at the end of the first hour.

The manipulation in the unearned-title condition was carried out in an analogous manner, except that the experimenter did not examine or comment on the participants' work before bestowing the title and explaining the associated responsibilities. In other words, workers in this condition were called in and told they would be called senior proofreaders, requiring them to work for a second hour, for which they would not be paid. Hence, the title—and the additional work it brought—was granted for no apparent reason. The experimenter asked participants in the no-title condition to stay to assist in checking others' work for an additional uncompensated hour but failed to identify them as senior proofreaders.[3] Finally, a control condition was run in which no title was granted and no extra work was requested. After being called in, these participants were engaged in a nonevaluative discussion about the proofreading task.

The posttitle work session began immediately after the manipulation was carried out for each of the participants. (Because the manipulation was effected in private, it was possible for assignment to conditions to be made randomly within each session.) Following this, the questionnaire was readministered. Then the final experimental session was run, followed by the final administration of the questionnaire. The experiment was terminated at the end of approximately 1 hour, without any workers actually performing additional, unremunerated duties.[4] Before being dismissed, participants were debriefed, dehoaxed, and paid the promised rate of $3.85 for participating in the 1-hour session.

RESULTS

Preliminary Analyses

Consistent with pilot data, preliminary analyses revealed that the performance error rate was extremely low—less than 2%—and was not significantly differentiated across experimental conditions; for all sources of variance, $F < 2.00$, ns. In addition, preliminary analyses of variance for each dependent measure revealed that there were no significant main effects or interactions involving sex of participant as a factor. Accordingly, the data were collapsed across sex, and this factor was ignored in subsequent analyses.

Performance Measure

The number of lines completed in the proofreading task was analyzed with a 4 (Title) × 3 (Work Period) mixed-design analysis of variance (ANOVA) with repeated measures on the work period. This analysis revealed significant main effects of title bestowal, $F(3, 801 = 34.84, p < .0001$, and work period, $F(2, 160) = 81.13, p < .0001$, which were qualified by the significant interaction between them, $F(6, 160) = 115.43, p < .0001$. The pattern of means corresponding to this interaction is displayed in Figure 17.1.

Differences between the means were analyzed post hoc according to the Tukey HSD procedure with alpha set at .01. These comparisons enable the pointing out of several important aspects of the data. As a preliminary observation, performance in the pretitle session was not significantly different across conditions prior to the title-bestowal manipulation. Accordingly, a common base rate of performance is established against which subsequent postmanipulation changes can be interpreted.

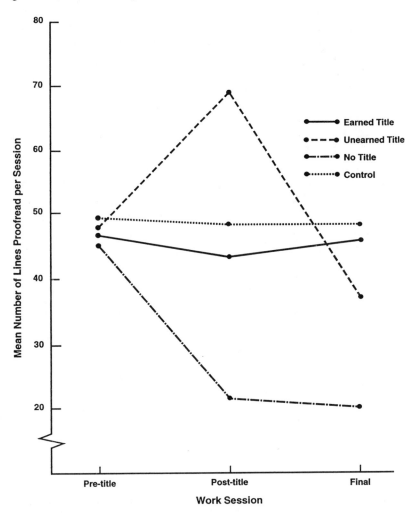

Figure 17.1. Mean Number of Lines Proofread per Work Session as a Function of Title Bestowal

The first hypothesis called for no significant change across experimental sessions for participants in the earned-title condition. Indeed, post hoc tests confirmed that there were no significant differences, as clearly revealed in Figure 17.1. Moreover, results support that participants in the earned-title condition would not perform significantly differently than control group participants who received no title and were not expecting to perform additional work. The means in both conditions were almost identical across all three work periods. The behavioral effect of underpayment inequity may be noted by comparing the significantly lower level of performance of participants in the no-title group with those in the earned-title group for the posttitle and final work sessions.

Hypotheses concerning the performance of participants in the unearned-title condition were only partially supported, although the deviation from the predictions revealed some unexpected trends. As Figure 17.1 clearly reveals, participants in the unearned-title condition showed a marked increase in performance in the posttitle session (to a mean level significantly higher than that in any other condition) but a decrease in the final session to a level significantly lower than the base rate (although significantly higher than the performance level of participants in the no-title condition). This pattern is dramatically discrepant from the hypothesized drop in performance and is consistent with the possibility of a temporary feeling of overpayment in the posttitle session before changing to underpayment in the final session. (Further support for this contention will be noted in the presentation of the results for the "fairness of payment" questionnaire item.) In contrast to this unexpected finding, it should be noted that participants in the no-title condition did, as expected, lower their performance subsequent to expecting to perform additional, uncompensated work. Although the performance of participants in the unearned-title condition did approach this level in the final work session, their performance remained higher than that of participants in the no-title condition. Also as expected, the performance of participants in the unearned-title condition was lower than that of participants in the earned-title condition but only in the final session. The direction of the difference was reversed (and much larger) during the posttitle session.

Questionnaire Responses

Participants' responses to each of the four questionnaire items were analyzed with a 4 × 3 mixed-design ANOVA with repeated measures on the work period. Tukey HSD tests (with alpha set at .05) were used to make comparisons between the means.

The use of separate univariate analyses for each questionnaire item appeared warranted in view of the low level of intercorrelation between the responses (ranging from a low of 0% to a high of only 10% common variance; absolute mean $r = .18$, ns), suggesting the absence of common method variance in questionnaire responses.

Fairness of payment. The Title Bestowal × Work Period interaction was significant for participants' ratings of the fairness of their payment, $F(6,$

156) = 14.90, $p < .0001$. Comparisons between cell means revealed that this interaction was the result of two distinct patterns. First, there was a significant tendency for participants in the no-title condition to report feeling underpaid in the posttitle and final sessions—after the expectation of doing additional uncompensated work was created ($M = 5.90$). In addition, participants in the unearned-title condition reported feeling slightly overpaid in the posttitle session ($M = 3.34$) but then reported feeling underpaid in the final session ($M = 5.27$). In all the other cells, participants reported feeling equitably paid ($M = 4.38$).

Liking for experimenter. Participants' ratings of their liking for the experimenter varied as a function of title bestowal in conjunction with work periods, $F(6, 156) = 39.64$, $p < .0001$. This effect resulted from the tendency for participants during the posttitle and final sessions to express relatively high liking for the experimenter in the earned-title condition ($M = 5.62$) and relatively high disliking in the no-title condition ($M = 2.52$). Moreover, in the unearned-title condition, participants reported liking the experimenter in the posttitle session ($M = 6.29$) but then reported disliking him in the final session ($M = 3.03$). The means in the remaining cells showed relatively neutral levels of liking ($M = 4.40$).

Liking for task. The overall Title Bestowal × Work Period interaction was significant for participants' ratings of their liking for the proofreading task, $F(6, 156) = 8.84$, $p < .0001$. This resulted from the tendency for participants in the no-title condition to report relative disliking for the task in the posttitle and final sessions ($M = 3.06$). In addition, participants in the unearned-title condition expressed relatively high liking for the task in the posttitle session ($M = 5.40$), which changed to disliking in the final session ($M = 3.53$). Relatively neutral feelings about the task were expressed in the remaining cells ($M = 4.30$).

Perceived performance level. The Title Bestowal × Work Period interaction was also significant for participants' ratings of their relative performance, $F(6, 158) = 7.84$, $p < .0001$. This was because participants in the earned-title condition tended to believe that their performance was higher in the posttitle and final work sessions ($M = 6.42$) relative to participants in any of the remaining cells ($M = 4.22$). This finding confirms the success of the title-bestowal manipulation in leading participants in the earned-title condition to believe that their bestowal of a title was the result of their superior performance.

DISCUSSION

This study provides a useful complement to the accumulated literature on equity theory in work contexts (for reviews, see Campbell & Pritchard, 1976; Greenberg, 1982; Mowday, 1979) by demonstrating that an earned high-status job title constitutes a valued job outcome that can compensate for an expected increase in work inputs. This was supported by dramatic performance differences between workers who were granted a title and added responsibilities on the basis of their superior performance and workers who were given the added responsibilities without the title. Workers who earned the title maintained their level of performance (relative to pretitle levels), whereas those not receiving any title lowered their performance after they expected to have increased responsibilities. That this behavioral response resulted from a perceived increase in outcomes among workers who earned their titles (and who therefore avoided underpayment inequity) is supported by the questionnaire responses. Most directly, after the added responsibilities were expected, workers who earned their titles reported feeling equitably paid, whereas those granted no title reported feeling underpaid. These feelings of inequity were accompanied by disliking for both the experimenter and the proofreading task; this evidence is consistent with the theorized cognitive or psychological reactions to states of inequity (Adams, 1965; Walster et al., 1973; Walster et al., 1978).

In contrast to the findings for the earned title, the bestowal of an ostensibly unearned job title had a dramatically different and unexpected effect. It was hypothesized that an unearned title would not be recognized as a legitimate outcome, therefore leading participants to lower their performance in response to the potential underpayment inequity created by requiring these workers to perform additional, uncompensated work. This hypothesis received support from the performance and questionnaire responses in the final work session. Compared with the initial, pretitle session, workers receiving an unearned title lowered their performance, reported feeling underpaid, and expressed disliking for both the experimenter and the task in the final work session. This pattern of reactions is completely opposite from that noted immediately following the bestowal of the unearned title, at which time workers dramatically raised their performance, reported feeling overpaid, and expressed high liking for both the experimenter and the task.[5]

Although an explanation for this dramatic shift in attitudes and behavior is not immediately forthcoming from this experiment itself, it is intriguing to speculate about the processes underlying its occurrence. It appears that the unearned title was at first highly rewarding; being granted a title by the experimenter may have led workers to feel honored and flattered for being singled out when there was no apparent reason for this unique treatment. Workers may have felt that the experimenter held positive personal attitudes about them—feelings that were reciprocated attitudinally and expressed behaviorally through fervently adhering to the experimenter's request to maximize productivity. In other words, the unearned title may have been particularly rewarding because it flattered workers, leading them to believe that the experimenter must have personally liked them to have shown such favoritism (Jones & Davis, 1965). These beliefs were not immediately forthcoming when the reason for the title bestowal was clear, as in the earned-title condition.

Not only did these effects not persist, but attitudes and behavior changed dramatically in the absence of any experimentally induced cues. An intriguing possibility is that the ego-enhancing self-attributions were short-lived and workers eventually came to suspect that the experimenter's motives may have been manipulative. This analysis of the situation appears plausible in light of Jones's (1964) work on ingratiation, which shows that persons who are deceitful to others to gain their favor will be liked until the deceit is suspected, at which time disliking will result. The bestowal of an unearned title (a reward of dubious origin) may well have been seen as a tool of manipulation in the present study. Because these findings in the unearned-title condition were unexpected, no attempt was made in advance to assess the types of attitudes needed to support the foregoing analyses. As a result, a second experiment was conducted to test these ideas.

EXPERIMENT 2

Because of the dramatic and unexpected effect of granting an unearned title observed in the first experiment, a second study was conducted in an attempt to replicate the results. This follow-up investigation included additional dependent measures that enabled a better understanding of the processes underlying these effects. Specifically, on the basis of the post hoc speculations regarding the attributions underlying workers' behavioral reactions, questionnaire items were included to assess participants' perceptions of the experimenter's liking for them, the degree of outcomes received and inputs contributed, as well as self-reports of mood state.

In addition to expecting to replicate the findings of the first experiment, it was hypothesized that participants would believe the experimenter liked them more immediately after they received an unearned title than before the unearned title was received. This prediction follows from the earlier argument that participants come to understand an unexplained benefit as an indication of the benefactor's liking for them (Jones & Davis, 1965). Moreover, consistent with the interpretation of Experiment 1, participants receiving an unearned reward were expected to believe the experimenter disliked them in subsequent sessions, after the immediate positive feelings about the unearned title wore off and ingratiation was suspected. In contrast, differential beliefs about the experimenter's liking were not expected either when the reason underlying the title bestowal was apparent (in the earned-title condition) or when no title was given (in the no-title condition and the control condition).

The conceptualization of the results of Experiment 1 was based, in part, on the idea that the granting of a title led participants to alter their perceptions of their outcomes and inputs. Specifically, added responsibilities given in conjunction with an earned title appeared to be perceived as primarily increasing outcomes, although the same responsibilities that were unearned appeared to be perceived as primarily increasing inputs. In Experiment 1, this was inferred on the basis of the behavioral responses, whereas Experiment 2 directly assessed the extent to which participants actually recognized differences in their outcomes (rewards) and/or inputs (contributions) in reaction to the title-bestowal manipulation. On the basis of initial theorizing (and the results supporting it), it was hypothesized that bestowal of an earned title (in conjunction with increased responsibilities) would lead to perceived increases in both outcomes and inputs relative to pretitle levels. In other words, participants were expected to recognize both the extra contributions expected of them and the rewarding nature of the title.

By contrast, bestowal of an unearned title (in conjunction with increased responsibilities) was expected to eventually (by the final work session) lead to a perception of increased inputs without increased outcomes relative to pretitle levels. Hence, participants were expected to recognize the forthcoming increase in responsibility but not to recognize the unearned title as a reward. It follows from Experiment 1, however, that immediately following the bestowal of an unearned title, participants would recognize an increase in inputs and a great increase in outcomes relative to pretitle levels. This perceived increase in outcomes would be consistent with the perceived overpayment and increase in performance noted immediately after receiving an unearned title found in Experiment 1.

On the basis of the negative intrapsychic reactions to inequitable conditions theorized by equity theory (e.g., Adams, 1965; Walster et al., 1978), self-reports of affective states were included in this study to provide a further test of the theory. It was expected that negative mood states would be experienced under conditions in which participants reported payment inequity.

METHOD

Participants and Design

Thirty-two male and 28 female undergraduate volunteers from the same population as Experiment 1 participated in this experiment.[6] The alleged purpose of the study and the terms and conditions of participation were identical to those of Experiment 1. The same independent variables that constituted Experiment 1 were used in this study, with the exception that the work periods variable was extended to four sessions (pretitle, immediately posttitle, later posttitle, and final). This resulted in a 2 (Sex of Participant) × 4 (Title-Bestowal Condition) × 4 (Work Period) mixed design. Eight men and seven women were randomly assigned to each of the four title-bestowal conditions.

Procedure

The experimental procedure was identical to that used in Experiment 1 with the exception that four 12-minute work sessions were run. The questionnaire items used in Experiment 1 were supplemented by additional items assessing perceived extent of the experimenter's liking for participants ($1 = $ dislike very much, $7 = $ like very much), perceived extent of participants' own task contributions, and overall task rewards (in both cases, $1 = $ very little, $7 = $ very great).

In addition, affective reactions were assessed after each work period using a version of the Mood Adjective Check List (MACL) used in other equity studies (see Walster et al., 1978). Participants responded to 30 adjectives describing mood states using a 4-point scale with end points labeled not at all and very much. This measure is composed of six subscales measuring elation, activation, social affection, aggression, anxiety, and depression. An overall comfort-discomfort index is derived by subtracting the sum of the ratings on the three negative mood states (aggression, anxiety, and depression) from that of three positive mood states (elation, activation, and social affection).

RESULTS

Preliminary Analyses

Consistent with the results of Experiment 1, the performance error rate was extremely low—less than 2%—and not significantly differentiated across experimental conditions; for all sources of variance, $F < 2.00$, ns.

TABLE 17.1 Mean Number of Lines Proofread per Work Session as a Function of
            Title Bestowal

| Title-Bestowal Condition | Pretitle | Work Session | | Final |
		Immediately Posttitle	Later Posttitle	
Earned	42.80$_a$	41.20$_a$	40.60$_a$	44.33$_a$
Unearned	39.33$_a$	58.60$_b$	30.20$_c$	28.00$_c$
No-title	44.60$_a$	27.00$_c$	24.60$_c$	24.33$_c$
Control	43.00$_a$	44.67$_a$	47.00$_a$	46.20$_a$

NOTE: Means not sharing a common subscript are significantly different at the .01 level or beyond according to the Tukey HSD test. In each cell, $n = 15$.

In addition, preliminary ANOVAs for each dependent measure revealed no significant main effects or interactions involving sex of participant as a factor; for all sources of variance, $F < 2.00$, *ns*. Accordingly, the data were collapsed across sex, and this factor was ignored in subsequent analyses.

Performance Measure

The number of lines completed in the proofreading task was analyzed with a 4 (Title) × 4 (Work Period) mixed-design ANOVA with repeated measures on the work period. As in Experiment 1, significant main effects were found for title bestowal, $F(3, 56) = 5.11$, $p < .005$, and work period, $F(3, 168) = 6.81$, $p < .001$, which were qualified by the significant interaction between them, $F(9, 168) = 10.13$, $p < .0001$. The means corresponding to this interaction and summaries of Tukey HSD comparisons (with alpha set at .01) are shown in Table 17.1.

Inspection of the means in Table 17.1 reveals a pattern remarkably similar to that found in Experiment 1 (compare with Figure 17.1). First, a common base rate of performance was established across conditions in the pretitle session, in which none of the means were significantly different from each other. In addition, levels of performance that were not significantly differentiated across work periods were noted in both the earned-title condition and the control condition. Also consistent with the findings of Experiment 1, these levels of performance were not significantly different from each other at any point.

It is of particular importance to note that the unexpected performance increase followed by a decrease observed in the unearned-title condition of Experiment 1 was replicated in this experiment. Specifically, as shown in the second row of Table 17.1, participants receiving an unearned title increased their performance in the posttitle session relative to the pretitle session and then significantly lowered their performance in the final two sessions. During the final two sessions, performance leveled off (i.e., no significant difference was noted between the later posttitle session and the final session) to a level not significantly higher than that noted in the no-title condition. Participants in the no-title condition showed the expected decline in performance—a decline that began with the posttitle session and continued at an equally low level through the remaining sessions.

Questionnaire Responses

As in Experiment 1, the correlations between responses to the various questionnaire measures were uniformly low (absolute mean $r = .10$, ns), thereby warranting the use of separate univariate ANOVAs. Responses to each of the seven questionnaire items, the six MACL subscales, and the overall mood index were analyzed with a 4×4 mixed-design ANOVA. Tukey HSD tests (with alpha set at .05) were used to examine the pattern of means associated with significant sources of variance.

Fairness of payment. A significant Title Bestowal × Work Period interaction was obtained for the perceived fairness of payment, $F(9, 168) = 10.27$, $p < .001$. The same pattern of means emerged as in Experiment 1. Namely, participants in the no-title condition reported feeling more underpaid after they expected to perform extra, uncompensated work (i.e., in the immediately posttitle session, $M = 5.73$; in the later posttitle session, $M = 5.68$; and in the final session, $M = 5.89$) relative to the pretitle session ($M = 4.08$). Moreover, participants in the unearned-title condition reported feelings of overpayment in the immediately posttitle session ($M = 3.08$) relative to the pretitle session ($M = 4.21$). These changed to feelings of underpayment in the later posttitle session ($M = 5.66$) and the final session ($M = 5.80$). Responses reflecting an equitable level of pay were noted in the earned-title and control conditions (for both conditions combined, $M = 4.14$).

Liking for the experimenter. Ratings of liking for the experimenter resulted in a Title Bestowal × Work Period interaction that was somewhat weaker than that obtained in Experiment 1, although still significant $F(9, 168) = 2.33$, $p < .025$. Consistent with the pattern of means obtained in Experiment 1 was the finding that after the title was bestowed, participants tended to like the experimenter in the earned-title condition (for all three posttitle sessions combined, $M = 5.75$) and dislike him in the no-title condition (for all three posttitle sessions combined, $M = 2.86$). These means were significantly different from those noted in the pretitle period for these conditions (for the earned-title condition, $M = 4.31$; for the no-title condition, $M = 4.24$). In addition, the pattern of increased liking followed by decreased liking in the unearned-title condition was replicated. These participants' pretitle levels of liking ($M = 4.63$) were significantly lower than their immediately posttitle ratings ($M = 5.89$) but higher than their rating of liking in either the later posttitle session ($M = 2.94$) or the final session ($M = 3.16$). Participants in the remaining cells expressed relatively neutral feelings toward the experimenter ($M = 4.09$).

Liking for task. Participants' ratings of their liking for the task varied as a function of title bestowal in conjunction with work periods, $F(9, 168) = 9.08$, $p < .0001$. This significant interaction resulted from a pattern of means similar to that obtained in Experiment 1. Specifically, participants in the no-title condition reported liking the task less after the extra work was assigned (for all three posttitle sessions combined, $M = 3.82$) compared with the level expressed in the pretitle session ($M = 5.03$). In the unearned-title group, liking for the task increased in the immediately posttitle session ($M = 5.26$) relative to the pretitle session ($M = 4.98$), although this difference was not statistically significant (as it was in Experiment 1). A significant decrease was noted in the later posttitle session ($M = 3.22$) that was sustained through the final session ($M = 3.30$), however, matching the pattern of Experiment 1. Participants in the earned-title and the control conditions all reported relatively neutral feelings about the task (overall M for these conditions = 4.78).

Perceived performance level. Evidence that Experiment 2 was successful in leading participants in the earned-title condition to believe that their title was granted in response to their superior performance is provided by a significant Title Bestowal × Work Period interaction, $F(9, 168) = 5.11$, $p < .005$. Relative to pretitle levels ($M = 4.62$), the level of perceived performance significantly increased for participants in the earned-title condition following bestowal of the title (for all three posttitle sessions combined, $M = 6.20$). Participants in the remaining conditions expressed relatively modest levels of perceived performance that were unaffected across work sessions (for the earned title, no-title, and control conditions combined, $M = 4.51$).

Perceived liking by the experimenter. Analyses of participants' judgments of the extent to which the experimenter liked them resulted in a significant Title Bestowal × Work Period interaction, $F(9, 168) = 5.18$, $p < .001$. This effect was because of the tendency for participants in the unearned-title condition to believe that relative to the moderate level of perceived liking in the pretitle session ($M = 5.18$), the experimenter liked them more immediately following the title bestowal ($M = 6.34$) and less in both the later posttitle session ($M = 3.42$) and the final session ($M = 3.36$). The level of perceived liking by the experimenter observed in the pretitle session in the unearned-title condition ($M = 5.18$) was not significantly different from the pretitle session responses in any of the other conditions (for the earned-title, no-title, and control conditions combined, pretitle session $M = 5.23$). Moreover, for all but the unearned-title condition, the levels of perceived liking remained at a moderate level in all three posttitle sessions ($M = 5.01$).

Perceived extent of contributions. The analysis of workers' ratings of perceived extent of contributions resulted in a significant Title Bestowal × Work Period interaction, $F(9, 168) = 2.32, p < .025$. This effect emerged from a tendency for participants who had not been given any additional responsibilities (control group $M = 4.83$) and participants who had not yet been given any added responsibilities (pretitle sessions $M = 5.02$) to feel that their contributions were significantly lower than those of participants in the remaining conditions, who expected to be performing additional work (for these cells combined, $M = 6.52$). These analyses reveal that the title-bestowal manipulation was successful in leading participants to recognize the increased demands on them.

Perceived extent of outcomes. A significant Title Bestowal × Work Period interaction was obtained for ratings of perceived outcomes, $F(9, 168) = 12.40, p < .0001$. This resulted from the tendency for participants in the earned-title condition to recognize increased rewards following title bestowal (for all three posttitle sessions combined, $M = 6.08$) relative to pretitle levels ($M = 4.77$). Moreover, these rewards were recognized by participants in the unearned-title condition only immediately after the title was bestowed ($M = 5.90$) but were deemphasized in subsequent work sessions (later posttitle session $M = 3.80$, final session $M = 3.47$). Participants who were not given a title (i.e., those in the no-title and control conditions), not surprisingly, did not perceive any change in outcomes across the work sessions (for these conditions combined, $M = 4.62$).

Affective reactions. Responses to each of the six MACL subscales, as well as the overall compositive mood index, did not differ significantly as a function of any of the experimental variables; all values of $F < 1.00$, *ns.* A supplemental analysis comparing overall mood states of participants who reported feeling overpaid, underpaid, and equitably paid also failed to yield significant results, $F < 1.00$, *ns.*

DISCUSSION

This second experiment provided an exceptionally strong replication and extension of Experiment 1. Not only was the same pattern of performance noted but also the final levels of performance noted in Experiment 1 were found to remain constant during an additional work period. Moreover, the inclusion of some additional questionnaire measures bolstered confidence in the interpretation of the behavioral data.

As in Experiment 1, workers who received an earned title in conjunction with added responsibilities maintained their performance level (relative to pretitle levels), whereas those who were given added responsibilities without being granted a title lowered their performance. Responses to several of the questionnaire measures enable the interpretation of these performance differences from an equity theory perspective. Most directly, participants receiving an earned title reported feeling equitably paid, whereas those receiving no title for expecting to perform the same work reported feeling underpaid. Converging evidence is provided by the measures of perceived rewards and contributions. Although all participants recognized the extra contributions expected of them, those who earned their title recognized that they would be rewarded more for their efforts (through the title itself) than did those who were not granted any title. Associated cognitive reactions to the inequity were observed in the form of disliking for both the experimenter and the proofreading task in the cases in which underpayment inequity was reported. No evidence was found, however, to support the negative affective reactions associated with inequity predicted by equity theory (Adams, 1965; Walster et al., 1973; Walster et al., 1978).

The unexpected effect of granting an unearned title observed in Experiment 1 was replicated in Experiment 2. To wit, participants in the unearned title condition improved their performance immediately after the title was bestowed but subsequently lowered it in the final two work periods. These changes in behavior paralleled changes in perceptions interpretable from an equity theory perspective. Specifically, the improved performance was associated with feelings of overpayment and increased outcomes relative to stable inputs. When performance dropped, however, feelings of underpayment were noted that were associated with decreased outcomes relative to stable input levels. Consistent with equity theory, negative cognitive evaluations (disliking for both the task and the experimenter) were associated with underpayment. Inconsistent with equity theory, however, liking for the task and the experimenter was reported when participants were overpaid. Although these findings may be discrepant from initial theoretical statements, they are completely in keeping with subsequent evidence suggesting that participants are actual-ly quite pleased with states of overpayment and do not find them at all objectionable (e.g., Kidder, Bellettirie, & Cohn, 1977; Rivera & Tedeschi, 1976).

In addition to replicating the first experiment and reporting additional evidence in support of the equity theory-based explanation of it, the present investigation also enabled interpretation of the findings in the context of changing perceptions about the implications of receiving an unearned title. In the discussion of Experiment 1, it was speculated that participants may have come to believe that the unearned title was granted as a result of the experimenter's liking for them. Indeed, the present study found that the immediate reaction of participants to an unearned title was to perceive its bestowal as an indication of the experimenter's liking for them. Consistent with the post hoc speculations regarding Experiment 1 is the finding that participants who believed they earned their titles had less reason to view it as an indication of the experimenter's liking for them (and they consequently showed no difference in perceived liking by the experimenter). Apparently, the unearned nature of the title led partici-pants to search for suitable causal attributions underlying their preferred treatment. Indeed, liking by the experimenter, tapped in this study, is one logical possibility. Participants for whom an earned title provided a ready-made explanation displayed less need to attribute the cause of their title to the positive personal feelings of the experimenter (cf. Jones & Davis, 1965).

Probably of most interest is the replication of the finding from Experi-ment 1 that the improved performance and positive cognitive reactions experienced by participants in the unearned-title condition declined through time. The lack of any apparent valid reason for title bestowal apparently led participants to alter their perceptions regarding the impli-cations of the unearned title: Although it was at first perceived in positive terms, it was subsequently seen (and responded to) quite negatively. Participants who once believed the experimenter liked them through time came to believe that he did not like them at all. Moreover, participants came to dislike the experimenter. The measured decline in participants' estimates of the experimenter's liking for them provides the best available evidence in support of the possibility that manipulative intent on the part of the experimenter may have been suspected.[7] Indeed, Jones's (1964) work on ingratiation supports the assertion that persons suspected of using deceit to their advantage (in this case, granting an otherwise un-earned title in the hope of getting more work done) will be disliked.

Although the nonsignificance of the affective reaction measure was somewhat disappointing, it was not totally unexpected. This is based in part on the fact that participants were not yet engaged in the inequity-creating behavior; they merely anticipated doing so. Although they were cognitively aware of the impending inequity, they were not yet experiencing any affective reaction to it (on the distinction between perceived and experienced reactions to inequity, see Greenberg, 1979). Even if different affective reactions were found, self-report measures of affective reactions are poor because of their subjectivity to social desirability (see Greenberg, 1984). Moreover, it is not unreasonable to expect that the limited involvement of participants in a laboratory experiment such as the present one would be insufficient to arouse demonstrable levels of distress. This concern need not weaken confidence in an equity-based interpretation of the present results, however, inasmuch as the role of distress in mediating reactions to inequity is highly circumspect (Greenberg, 1984).

GENERAL DISCUSSION

The studies reported here have several important implications for equity theory (Adams, 1965; Walster et al., 1973; Walster et al., 1978). Foremost is the suggestion that one type of outcome can substitute for another in determining payment equity or inequity. A similar idea is implicit in Burt and Sundstrom's (1979) finding that pleasant working conditions were able to compensate for inadequate monetary payment in determining feelings of equity. An earned high-status job title served this function in the present studies. The observations regarding the role of one outcome in compensating for another can be appreciated relative to Foa and Foa's (1974) resource exchange theory. This perspective recognizes that different classes of outcomes are frequently substituted for one another in social exchange settings. The present investigations demonstrate that for a limited time, at least, an earned high-status job title can substitute for the additional pay that would be warranted on the basis of increased responsibilities. This type of substitutability of exchange outcomes, although theoretically appreciated in interpersonal relationships (Foa & Foa, 1974), is now only beginning to be recognized in organizational settings (e.g., Nord, 1980).

A second, and equally important, implication of this research lies in demonstrating the role of attributional mediation in perceiving outcomes and inputs. Indeed, the same potential reward—a high-status job title—was responded to differently as a function of the perceived basis for its bestowal. Earned titles were recognized as valid outcomes (so much, in fact, that they compensated for inadequate payment in determining payment equity). By contrast, unearned titles were, in the long run, not recognized as desired outcomes. This allowed the responsibilities associated with that title to be recognized as greater than the status value of the title itself, thereby creating feelings of underpayment. The idea that certain job factors—such as responsibilities—may be ambiguously classified as an outcome or input is not new (see Pritchard, 1969; Tornow, 1971). The contribution of the present research lies in noting that a worker's perception of the causal basis underlying the administration of these factors may determine the extent to which it is perceived as an outcome or an input. As such, this research contributes to the growing interest in the role of attribution in the mediation of inequity (see Cohen, 1982).

In addition to the implications for equity theory, the present study provides empirical support for the suggestion that a worker's title may operate as a status symbol (Dandridge et al., 1980). Both experiments show that for a status symbol to be perceived as rewarding by the recipient, the basis for its bestowal must be recognized as legitimate. Indeed, only titles believed to be earned on the basis of one's performance helped define the status value of the symbol. Thus, whether a job title will be recognized by its holder as a symbol of status appears to depend on the holder's beliefs about the basis for the title's bestowal.

In closing, a note of caution is in order with respect to the generalizability of these findings. This caveat is based, in part, on the experiments being short-term laboratory studies that leave unanswered important questions about the potency of the demonstrated effects through time. For example, the question of how long an earned title can compensate for added responsibilities is an important one that needs to be addressed in future research. Furthermore, the generalizability of the conclusions begs to be assessed in replications conducted in other contexts.

NOTES

1. This, of course, assumes that the perceived value of the additional outcomes is equivalent to the value of the inputs—a possibility that remains untested.

2. To safeguard against order effects in bestowing a title, the order in which participants were called in by the experimenter was counterbalanced across title-bestowal conditions during the study.

3. Because participants were scheduled on the basis of their availability for a 2-hour period, the experimenter met with only minimal objections to the request to stay for an additional hour. Only two participants—both in the no-title condition, not surprisingly—expressed any objection to the experimenter's invitation to do additional work without additional pay. To assuage these participants' concerns, in both cases the experimenter immediately terminated their participation in the experimental session and debriefed them. The data collected for these participants were discarded.

4. It would have been possible at this point to ask participants (in all but the control condition) to begin their extra duties, thereby containing a behavioral measure of compliance

with the experimental request. This was avoided, however, because it could have brought undue distress and was therefore ethically dubious.

5. The tendency for workers expressing feelings of overpayment inequity (immediately after receiving an unearned title) to also report positive feelings about the experimenter and the task is discrepant from equity theory's assumption about the aversive nature of overpayment (Adams, 1965; Walster et al., 1973). These findings, however, are consistent with evidence challenging this assumption, which shows persons to actually feel quite pleased about being overpaid (Rivera & Tedeschi, 1976).

6. The participation of one additional volunteer was terminated prematurely because the volunteer objected to the performance of additional, unremunerated work. The data available from this participant were excluded from all analyses.

7. Informal postexperimental interviews confirm this suggestion, although questionnaire items more directly tapping perceived manipulative intent used in pilot studies proved too reactive to be useful.

REFERENCES

Adams, J. S. (1965). Inequity in social exchange. In L. Berkowitz (Ed.), *Advances in experimental social psychology* (Vol. 2, pp. 267-299). New York: Academic Press.

Adams, J. S., & Freedman, S. (1976). Equity theory revisited: Comments and annotated bibliography. In L. Berkowitz & E. Walster (Eds.), *Advances in experimental social psychology* (Vol. 9, pp. 43-90). New York: Academic Press.

Burt, R. E., & Sundstrom, E. (1979, September). Workspace and job satisfaction: Extending equity theory to the physical environment. In H. M. Parsons (Chair), *Physical environments at work.* Symposium presented at the meeting of the American Psychological Association, New York.

Campbell, J. P., & Pritchard, R. D. (1976). Motivation theory in industrial and organizational psychology. In M. Dunnette (Ed.), *Handbook of industrial and organizational psychology* (pp. 63-130). Chicago: Rand McNally.

Cohen, R. L. (1982). Perceiving justice: An attributional perspective. In J. Greenberg & R. L. Cohen (Eds.), *Equity and justice in social behavior* (pp. 119-160). New York: Academic Press.

Dandridge, T. C., Mitroff, I., & Joyce, W. (1980). Organizational symbolism: A topic to expand organizational analysis. *Academy of Management Review, 5,* 77-82.

Foa, U. G., & Foa, E. B. (1974). *Societal structures of the mind.* Springfield, IL: Charles C Thomas.

Greenberg, J. (1979, September). Justice perceived versus justice enacted. In J. Greenberg (Chair), *Recent developments in interpersonal justice theory and research.* Symposium presented at the meeting of the American Psychological Association, New York.

Greenberg, J. (1980). Attentional focus and locus of performance causality as determinants of equity behavior. *Journal of Personality and Social Psychology, 38,* 579-585.

Greenberg, J. (1982). Approaching equity and avoiding inequity in groups and organizations. In J. Greenberg & R. L. Cohen (Eds.), *Equity and justice in social behavior* (pp. 389-436). New York: Academic Press.

Greenberg, J. (1984). On the apocryphal nature of inequity distress. In R. Folger (Ed.), *The sense of injustice: Social psychological perspective* (pp. 167-186). New York: Plenum.

Jones, E. E. (1964). *Ingratiation.* New York: Appleton-Century-Crofts.

Jones, E. E., & Davis, K. E. (1965). From acts to dispositions: The attribution process in person perception. In L. Berkowitz (Ed.), *Advances in experimental social psychology* (Vol. 2, pp. 117-155). New York: Academic Press.

Kidder, L. H., Bellettirie, G., & Cohen, E. S. (1977). Secret ambitions and public performances. *Journal of Experimental Social Psychology, 13,* 70-80.

Mowday, R. T. (1979). Equity theory predictions of behavior in organizations. In R. M. Steers & L. W. Porter (Eds.), *Motivation and work behavior* (2nd ed., pp. 41-62). New York: McGraw-Hill.

Nord, W. R. (1980). The study of organizations through a resource-exchange paradigm. In K. J. Gergen, M. S. Greenberg, & R. H. Willis (Eds.), *Social exchange: Advances in theory and research* (pp. 119-140). New York: Plenum.

Pritchard, R. A. (1969). Equity theory: A review and critique. *Organizational Behavior and Human Performance, 4,* 176-211.

Rivera, A. N., & Tedeschi, J. T. (1976). Public versus private reactions to positive inequity. *Journal of Personality and Social Psychology, 34,* 895-900.

Tornow, W. W. (1971). The development and application of an input-outcome moderator test on the perception and reduction of inequity. *Organizational Behavior and Human Performance, 6,* 614-638.

Walster, E., Berscheid, E., & Walster, G. W. (1973). New directions in equity research. *Journal of Personality and Social Psychology, 25,* 151-176.

Walster, E., Walster, G. W., & Berscheid, E. (1978). *Equity: Theory and research.* Boston: Allyn & Bacon.

Wittig, M. A., Marks, G., & Jones, G. A. (1981). Luck versus effort attributions: Effect on reward allocation to self and other. *Personality and Social Psychology Bulletin, 7,* 71-78.

Epilogue

Lessons Learned and Work to Be Done

This is the place where I wish I could say that I had a master plan and that following it, as chronicled on these pages, led the world to some grand truth. But I cannot. Like most others who toil in the trenches of the social sciences, my research on organizational justice has followed several twists and turns. It frequently was redirected by research and funding opportunities and guidance from colleagues, coauthors, and journal editors and slowed down by failures. (My best—or worst, I suppose—tale of woe involved showing up to arrange some research details one day only to find myself, along with several hundred employees, locked out of a facility that closed unexpectedly. Talk about naturalistic manipulations!) If not completely narrow and systematic, as my teachers preached that good science should be, my work has been, at least, highly thematic—examining many facets of organizational justice and applying them to just about everything I could get my hands on. Indeed, the intensity of my interest in organizational justice and my dedication to it as a field of inquiry have grown with each subsequent project.

My experiences (both good and bad), together with some scientific reflection, have led me to recognize several lessons that can be learned from my research and to identify what more needs to be done. It is only fitting that I close this book by outlining these thoughts. I ask the reader's advance forgiveness in carrying out these tasks, however, because the exercise is fraught with professional danger. For example, I run the risk of being overly self-serving, proposing those things I know I will be doing anyway. The other risk lies in proposing things that I know I will not be doing and being faulted for not following my own advice. So, at the risk of falling into both these traps, I will outline some of the key tasks that I believe lie ahead in the field of organizational justice. There are far too many to "do justice" to them all here, so I will mention only a few.

STUDY JUSTICE IN
ORGANIZATIONAL CONTEXTS

To begin, I think it is somewhat misleading to investigate justice in a context-free manner. Whether it is performance appraisals, employee theft, the physical work environment, or anything else, it makes most sense to study justice issues as they apply to various contexts. Studies focusing on general attitudes toward fairness, to my mind, are less informative than those that examine the fairness of issues arising in specific contexts.

There are several reasons for this. First, studying justice is a valuable way of learning about specific organizational phenomena themselves. For example, despite all the work that has been done in the field of performance appraisals (e.g., Cardy & Dobbins, 1994), I think that studying what makes them fair (e.g., Chapter 6) provides important new insight into ways of effectively managing performance. Similarly, I think that my work on employee theft (e.g., Chapter 10) has implications for practitioners in that area as well. Thus, to the extent that fairness issues arise in a great number of settings, I think researchers should seize the opportunity to study them. Doing so will benefit not only those concerned about the contexts themselves but also those of us interested in the underlying justice-based theoretical issues.

This leads my second reason for advocating studying justice in specific contexts: Unique issues of justice are made salient in various settings. Consider, for example, the smokers who are forced to leave the building to smoke a cigarette because of a nonsmoking policy. They will be quick to cry "injustice," much like job candidates who are rejected because of race or gender. My point is simple, although sometimes overlooked: To understand people's feelings about fairness requires asking them questions that focus on the unique aspects of the situation in question. Focusing on the contexts will lead researchers to consider the justice-based concerns of the employees themselves—and it is these that are most salient.

With this in mind, generic survey questions, such as "How fairly are you treated?" for example, are much less insightful (and less predictive of behavior) than more focused ones, such as "When judging your job performance, to what extent does your supervisor give you a chance to explain what you have done?" In answering the first question, the respondent may be thinking of just about anything (e.g., "My supervisor is biased against me in evaluating my work"), and the investigator will never know what it is. In answering the second question, however, respondents are asked to direct their attention to a specific aspect of a situation about which they are likely to have focused attitudes. Moreover, the question is derived from a specific theoretical perspective (in this case, the role of voice in decision making; Greenberg & Folger, 1983). Generally speaking, I am not a fan of generic questions about perceptions of justice. As I see it, what makes a set of questions appropriate in one context may not make them equally appropriate in another. Questions about justice should be carefully matched to the context of interest, whether they are completely ad hoc (but theoretically based) or standardized (but tailored to fit the setting). Answers to such questions will provide the greatest insight into the phenomena of interest.

A third reason to focus on specific organizational contexts is to provide a good opportunity to assess the generalizability of the phenomena in question. Consider, for example, the question "Does interpersonal treatment moderate reactions to perceived inequities?" Not only have I found this to be the case in the context of reducing inequity-induced employee theft (Chapter 10) and fostering acceptance of a smoking ban (Chapter 12), but others have similarly found that interpersonal treatment facilitates acceptance of other negative outcomes (e.g., rejected proposals, Bies & Shapiro, 1987; layoffs from work, Brockner et al., 1994). If researchers are to converge on a thorough understanding of the role of interpersonal factors on justice judgments, it is essential for us to be able to determine the extent to which our findings are context specific.

STUDY BOTH PROCEDURAL AND DISTRIBUTIVE
JUSTICE—INCLUDING THEIR SOCIAL DETERMINANTS

As a whole, if my research reveals any one thing, it is that understanding matters of fairness in organizations requires paying careful attention to *both* distributive and procedural justice. This is worth noting in view of misunderstandings arising from the manner in which procedural justice was introduced into the study of organizations. Because procedural justice first came to researchers' attention at a time when disenchantment with equity theory was high, it is understandable that some may think that it was intended to be a substitute for distributive justice. Indeed, although some have interpreted Leventhal's (1980) answer to the question "What should be done with equity theory?" as *supplanting* it with procedural justice, it is clear that he wished only to *supplement* it with procedural justice.

This problem is compounded by the earliest studies of procedural justice in organizations (e.g., Alexander & Ruderman, 1987) that focused on reporting that procedural justice accounted for significantly more variance than distributive justice in predicting a variety of work-related attitudes. Findings such as these, showing that procedural justice is "more important," along with the broader applicability of procedural justice to organizations, led some to ignore distributive justice in their studies of organizations. As I note in Chapter 2, however, doing so is misleading; the two must be studied together as different facets of an overall assessment of fairness. In this regard, the real issue is not *which* form of justice is more important but *how* they operate together. Studies such as those reported in Chapters 6, 11, and 14 underscore this point. A particularly good case may be seen in my theft field experiment (Chapter 10). This is a straightforward test of equity theory (stealing in response to underpayment), overlaid with some procedural variables (explanations that moderated this behavior). Although scientists may be interested in either distributive or procedural factors at any given time, true understanding of justice requires consideration of both.

Adding to this, I think a strong case needs to be made for considering the role of interpersonal aspects of both procedural and distributive justice. As I described in Chapter 3 and tested in Chapters 11 and 12, some of the most powerful variables are those associated with social treatment, building on the traditional structural approaches to fairness. These aspects of procedural and distributive justice are of particular interest because they are ones that are most under the immediate control of supervisors. For example, although managers might not be able to do too much about a company's unfair pay policy, they may be quite effective in neutralizing adverse reactions by presenting information in an informative and socially sensitive manner. Accordingly, the practical implications of the social determinants of justice are considerable. This, together with the theoretical expansion provided by such a focus (see Chapter 3), lends great promise to the study of organizational justice.

DO NOT RELY ON ANY SINGLE METHOD: SEEK METHODOLOGICAL CONVERGENCE

I began my professional career as a laboratory researcher and faced criticisms from my colleagues that my research lacked external validity. Then I began doing field studies and faced criticism that my research lacked internal validity. Now, I do both lab and field studies, and the criticisms have not stopped—but at least they cancel each other out. But the value of using both approaches lies not in that it helps silence one's critics (which is likely to be only temporary, anyway) but in that it makes it possible to address a variety of different problems. Just as carpenters who use only hammers may be more limited in what they can build than those who use both hammers and saws, so too can social science researchers benefit from filling their methodological tool kits with an array of techniques.

My favorite illustration of this is the way I used a laboratory experiment on theft (Chapter 11) to follow up a field experiment on theft (Chapter 10). Although the lab study had less realism, it allowed me to control key variables that were impossible to control in the field. In the case of my studies of dealing with the physical work environment, I started with a field experiment (Chapter 15) and moved to a survey study (Chapter 16). In studying performance appraisals, I used a variety of open-ended and closed-ended questionnaires (Chapter 6) as well as a laboratory experiment (Chapter 9). My point is not to use a wide variety of techniques just for the sake of doing so but to use whatever methods make it possible to build on earlier work. This building may take the form of disentangling confoundings (e.g., Chapters 10 and 11), asking converging questions (e.g., Chapters 15 and 16), or testing specific hypotheses following from surveys (e.g., Chapters 6 and 9). Regardless, the advancements are all made possible by the use of multiple research techniques. To the extent that all scientific methods are limited in one way or another, such convergence must occur if advances are to be made. And to the extent that this can be accomplished by a single scientist, his or her confidence in the phenomena will surely be reinforced.

STRIVE FOR CONCEPTUAL CLARITY

Although it would be an overstatement to claim that "debates rage" about key conceptual issues in organizational justice, it would be accurate to say that there has been disagreement over several conceptual issues of central importance, leaving their status unclear. Two, in particular, come to mind. First, although I have found that perceptions of outcomes are highly related to the procedures that bring them about (Chapter 14), others (e.g., Tyler, 1984) claim that procedural and distributive justice operate independently. Second, although I prefer to think of the social aspects of justice as a variant of both procedural and distributive justice (Chapter 3), others have treated it as a distinct, third form of justice referred to as interactional justice (e.g., Bies & Moag, 1986). These are the very types of disagreements that could turn into debates, but this has not occurred.

Although it is tempting to speculate that this is because of the kind hearts and good nature of those who study this topic, this observation, although accurate, probably accounts for little of why more spirited arguments have not occurred. Instead, I think that the absence of an underlying conceptual approach, a strong theory, fails to direct us to an answer. And in the absence of a coherent overarching theory, we have only our independent empirical findings to guide us. Say what you want about equity theory, it was a formal statement about underlying processes and was composed of various mechanisms that generated testable hypotheses—a true theory. Subsequent writings about procedural justice (e.g., Leventhal, 1976, 1980; Thibaut & Walker, 1975), although commonly referred to as theories, are more accurately characterized as collections of loosely linked conceptual ideas. This may be a beginning, but it is not a theory. As such, not only is there no formal theory of procedural justice (especially in organizations), but there certainly is no overall theory of organizational justice. For that matter, no general theory of justice incorporates both procedural and distributive forms that may be applied to organizations. Several recent attempts to compare various conceptual models of justice processes (e.g., Sweeny & McFarlin, 1993; Tyler, 1994) are encouraging insofar as they promise to spin off into full-blown theories—useful steps, but only a beginning.

I do not think it is appropriate right now for researchers to feel bad about not having constructed such a theory—at least not yet. We are still in the formative stages of our understanding about organizational justice—what I have earlier referred to as its "intellectual adolescence" (Greenberg, 1993). The honeymoon is approaching the end, however, and the time has come for us to combine much of what we know into a unified theory that leads us into the future. If nothing else, such an approach, no matter how rudimentary, will guide our efforts in a common direction. And some guidance may be better than none at all.

EXAMINE CROSS-CULTURAL VARIABLES

One sure way to complicate any social science literature is to introduce the variable of culture. The findings we so often come to accept as law are easily challenged when subjected to tests of their generalizability across cultures. For example, in analyzing the use of different distributive norms in various European nations, a colleague and I (Miles & Greenberg, 1993) uncovered quite a mess: Different perceptions of justice and reactions to injustice existed among people in various nations, and these were not easily interpreted from a unified analytical framework (e.g., Hofstede, 1984). Such conceptual messiness, combined with the practical difficulties associated with doing cross-cultural research, leaves a void in our understanding of the cultural generalizability of organizational justice.

Nevertheless, the difficulties associated with pursuing the cross-cultural aspects of justice should not discourage research on this topic. Such efforts promise to reveal a great deal about the cultures themselves and to shed light on the universality of concerns about organizational justice. The key issues in this regard involve understanding that people from various cultures may differ with respect to both their sensitivity to different types of injustice and their willingness to react to these injustices once perceived. Little is known about these important variables, but they must be understood to have a firm understanding of organizational justice. The few studies that have examined justice issues in cross-cultural contexts thus far (e.g., Kim & Mauborgne, 1993) have yielded interesting results. So whether organizational justice researchers are motivated by the desire to understand the universality of their phenomena or the operation of a global economy, now is the time to "complicate" our studies of justice in the workplace by incorporating cross-cultural variables.

CONCLUSION

For me, studying organizational justice has been an opportunity to investigate a wide variety of important organizational variables, and in so doing, to use a variety of different research techniques. It has provided consulting opportunities that have resulted in research and research opportunities that have resulted in consulting. My ostensibly single-minded devotion to this topic has been, in reality, more broad based than it may seem on the surface. I hope that as time passes, these professional contributions, which I have found to be so professionally fulfilling, will be recognized as having enriched the study of organizations. Moreover, I hope that this book will stimulate others to join me in this work.

REFERENCES

Alexander, S., & Ruderman, M. (1987). The role of procedural and distributive justice in organizational behavior. *Social Justice Research, 1,* 177-198.

Bies, R. J., & Moag, J. S. (1986). Interactional justice: Communication criteria of fairness. In R. J. Lewicki, B. H. Sheppard, & M. H. Bazerman (Eds.), *Research on negotiation in organizations* (Vol. 1, pp. 43-55). Greenwich, CT: JAI.

Bies, R. J., & Shapiro, D. L. (1987). Interactional fairness judgments: The influence of causal accounts. *Social Justice Research, 1,* 199-218.

Brockner, J., Konovsky, M., Cooper-Schneider, R., Folger, R., Martin, C., & Bies, R. J. (1994). Interactive effects of procedural justice and outcome negativity on victims and survivors of job loss. *Academy of Management Journal, 37,* 397-409.

Cardy, R. L., & Dobbins, G. H. (1994). *Performance appraisal: Alternative perspectives.* Cincinnati, OH: South-Western.

Greenberg, J. (1993). The intellectual adolescence of organizational justice: You've come a long way, maybe. *Social Justice Research, 6,* 135-147.

Greenberg, J., & Folger, R. (1983). Procedural justice, participation, and the fair process effect in groups and organizations. In P. B. Paulus (Ed.), *Basic group processes* (pp. 235-256). New York: Springer-Verlag.

Hofstede, G. (1984). *Culture's consequences.* London: Sage.

Kim, W. C., & Mauborgne, R. A. (1993). Procedural justice, attitudes, and subsidiary top management compliance with multinationals' corporate strategic decisions. *Academy of Management Journal, 36,* 502-526.

Leventhal, G. S. (1976). Fairness in social relationships. In J. W. Thibaut, J. T. Spence, & R. C. Carson (Eds.), *Contemporary topics in social psychology* (pp. 211-239). Morristown, NJ: General Learning Press.

Leventhal, G. S. (1980). What should be done with equity theory? In K. J. Gergen, M. S. Greenberg, & R. H. Willis (Eds.), *Social exchange: Advances in theory and research* (pp. 27-55). New York: Plenum.

Miles, J. A., & Greenberg, J. (1993). Cross-national differences in preferences for distributive justice norms: The challenge of establishing fair resource allocations in the European Community. In J. B. Shaw, P. S. Kirkbride, & K. M. Rowland (Eds.), *Research in personnel and human resources management* (Suppl. 3, pp. 133-156). Greenwich, CT: JAI.

Sweeny, P. D., & McFarlin, D. B. (1993). Workers' evaluations of the "ends" and the "means": An examination of four models of distributive and procedural justice. *Organizational Behavior and Human Decision Processes, 55,* 23-40.

Thibaut, J., & Walker, L. (1975). *Procedural justice: A psychological analysis.* Hillsdale, NJ: Lawrence Erlbaum.

Tyler, T. R. (1984). The role of perceived injustice in defendants' evaluations of their courtroom experience. *Law and Society Review, 18,* 386-401.

Tyler, T. R. (1994). Psychological models of the justice motive: Antecedents of distributive and procedural justice. *Journal of Personality and Social Psychology, 67,* 850-863.

Author Index

Subject Index

About the Author

Jerald Greenberg, Ph.D., is Abramowitz Professor of Business Ethics and Professor of Organizational Behavior at the Ohio State University (OSU). He is a Fellow of both the American Psychological Association (Division 14, Society for Industrial/Organizational Psychology) and the American Psychological Society. He also was elected to membership in the honorary group, the Society for Organizational Behavior. Among the professional honors he has received are a Fulbright Senior Research Fellowship (1980), the New Concept Award from the Organizational Behavior Division of the Academy of Management (1986), and the Pace Setter's Research Award from OSU's College of Business (1989). He received his doctorate in Industrial/Organizational Psychology from Wayne State University in 1975.

He has been an active member of several professional committees, most notably, the Academy of Management's Ethics Task Force and the

Executive Committee of the Organizational Behavior Division. He has served as a member of several professional editorial review boards, including the *Journal of Applied Psychology* and *Organizational Behavior and Human Decision Processes.*

Dr. Greenberg has authored more than 110 publications, specializing in the topic of organizational ethics and justice. He has lectured extensively on this topic, with more than 80 national and international professional presentations to his credit. Among his publications are seven books published or in press, including *Behavior in Organizations* (5th ed.; with Robert Baron), *Organizational Behavior: The State of the Science, Controversial Issues in Social Research Methods* (with Robert Folger), *Justice in Social Relations* (with Hans Werner Bierhoff and Ronald Cohen), *Equity and Justice in Social Behavior* (with Ronald Cohen), and *Managing Behavior in Organizations.*

He has been a consultant with many organizations, focusing on ethical behavior, such as ethical practices in rightsizing, reducing employee theft, and conducting fair and effective performance appraisals. He has been on the faculties of Case Western Reserve University and Tulane University and was a visiting professor at the University of California at Berkeley.